The Negro in American History

I. BLACK AMERICANS 1928-1968

II. A TASTE OF FREEDOM 1854-1927

III. SLAVES AND MASTERS 1567-1854

Mortimer J. Adler *General Editor*

Charles Van Doren *Editor*

George Ducas *Executive Editor*

The Negro in American History

III. SLAVES AND MASTERS 1567-1854

With an Introduction by Charles H. Wesley

ENCYCLOPAEDIA BRITANNICA EDUCATIONAL CORPORATION

William Benton *Publisher*

The editors wish to express their gratitude for
permission to reprint material from the
following sources:

Ray Allen Billington for the selection on
pp. 3-6, from *Journal of Charlotte L. Forten*,
ed. by Ray Allen Billington, New York:
The Dryden Press, copyright 1953 by Ray
Allen Billington. Collier Books, Inc., New
York, 1961. Second printing, 1967. The
Arthur H. Clark Company for the selection
by J. J. Flournoy on pp. 189-190, from
*A Documentary History of American
Industrial Society*, ed. by John R. Commons
et al. Louisiana State University Press for
the selection on pp. 210-218, from *William
Johnson's Natchez: The Ante-Bellum Diary
of a Free Negro*, ed. by William Hogan and
Edwin Adams Davis, Source Studies in
Southern History, ed. by Edwin Adams Davis,
No. I.

Contents

4. A Firebell in the Night 1820-1831

5. The New Nation 1777-1819

6. Traffic of Mens-body 1567-1758

Introduction

It is not the purpose of this essay to present a history of the Negro people in America in the years before the Civil War, but rather to give an introduction to the documentary history that follows. The importance of documents was stressed by Langlois and Seignobos in their study of history in the brief statement: "No documents, no history." Documents are necessary in history, but their interpretation is also needed for realistic conclusions, each document speaking for itself to the intelligent and inquiring mind. Moreover, we may assume that readers know only a part of the origins of the black problems that now present themselves on the American scene. They will appreciate the fact that present problems can be solved best by an understanding of the historical background of black Americans, who have constituted an important part of the American population across the years.

Because school, college, and university courses and books have presented almost no historical information on this subject, typical white Americans have had no background knowledge of black Americans. They see no solution, so long as the black man is what they conceive him to be on the basis of their meager knowledge of him, for they remain unaware of what he was in history. But how can this knowledge be obtained when it is not now presented in courses and books, while vast amounts of information are presented relating to the history of white people? To fill this gap in knowledge concerning black people in American history, and to give an introduction to the historical material that follows – these are the purposes of this introduction.

Students of history, looking into America's past, conclude that not only has there been a "European background" to our history, there has also been an "Asiatic background" and an "African background." None of these should be omitted or neglected in the interest of historical truth. Increased interest in Asiatic studies has fulfilled one of the needs. But the neglect of African studies serves to create an assumption of an inferior history in addition to a difference of culture. For historical accounts have failed to call attention to indigenous African history and civilization, while giving large place to the European background.

African influences on Egyptian civilization were ignored, while Greece and Rome were treated as if their civilizations were self-originating. In fact, Egypt was made almost an island standing alone in Africa, the impression being given that the rest of Africa was uncivilized. On the contrary, civilizing influences moved from South to North in Africa and across Africa to southern Europe. This neglect in the field of cultural history has caused some students to conclude that the African peoples, except in certain restricted areas, lived and still live in a land without a civilization or a history, at the same time that even the tribal history of Europe – its Goths, Visigoths, Angles, Saxons, Franks, Huns, Vandals – is acknowledged.

Europe's civilization was not an indigenous Northern European product. It was a blending and a borrowing from the peoples of the Tigris-Euphrates area, Babylonia, Assyria, Israel, Phoenicia, Greece, Rome, Arabia, China, and also Africa. The defense of the great contributions by white Europeans and the blatant attacks on and criticisms of the contributions of "Dark Africa" are totally clumsy and essentially false. Western European civilization was a mixture. Even now historians and teachers refer to the "Barbarian Invasion of Rome," from the North.

However, civilizations of black and brown peoples flourished in West, East, South, and Central Africa, from which a majority of the

American slaves came. In the west, Benin, Yoruba, Nupe, Melle (Mali), Songhai, Mossi, and other kingdoms had flourishing civilizations. From these sections of West Africa, Africans set out on voyages to the West, reaching the Americas and the islands of the Caribbean.

In the period when European tribal life was primitive over large areas, Africa had organized kingdoms that spread over the west and central parts of the continent, from which black slaves were drawn. These civilizations declined after the Muslim conquests and the rise of the slave trade. Some few smaller kingdoms were stimulated to greater temporary activity by the Muslim influences, but the slave trade proved to be a blight upon civilizing developments. Whole villages were depopulated, and kings turned to the easier ways of living provided by the trade in men rather than to the slower processes of permanent state building. Africa will be seen historically as peopled by civilizations prior to the rise of the slave trade.

An author or a teacher usually presents the following subjects: the introduction of Negroes into Virginia in 1619, the slave trade, slavery as a labor system, the opposition to it, implied defenses of it, and unsatisfactory references to the ability of Negroes to do arduous labor far better than Indians who revolted or died. Slavery is treated as a desirable, humane, and benevolent labor system for Negroes. But historical researches and scholarly writings have produced a body of fact and interpretation concerning the Negro-American that cannot be ignored any longer. With the facts that the members of the Association for the Study of Negro Life and History have published and made widely known, is it any wonder that now some textbook writers and publishers are engaged in revisions of their view of slavery?

Negroes were with the Spanish explorers in the sixteenth century. They were active with explorers in pre-Columbian America. One of their number was Estevanico, who discovered the territory now included in Arizona and New Mexico. The evidence that a Negro was a pilot in the fleet of Columbus is entirely too unhistoric. Professor Leo Wiener of Harvard suggests in his three-volume *Africa and the Discovery of America* that Negroes may have come prior to the Spanish discoverers as well as with them. Additional evidence leads to the conclusion that Negroes were with the Spanish explorer,

De Ayllon, when he made a settlement within the present limits of the United States in Virginia in 1526, and that they began the first Negro revolt within the present United States in this settlement. In 1619 twenty blacks were brought into the Jamestown colony and in 1624 William Tucker was born, the first Negro child in the Jamestown colony.

Slavery as a labor system has been receiving new interpretations from the economic and social points of view. Revisions have had to be made in many traditional views: the relation to the labor force of indentured servants—the first Negroes brought to the American shores were servants for terms of years and not slaves *durante vita*; the evidence that some slaves became free Negroes and had sued in the courts and voted as citizens prior to 1789; the doctrine of racial inferiority as a justification for slavery; the study of plantation traditions in letters of overseers and plantation records; Negro biographies; the insurrectionary and revolutionary attitudes of Negroes as contrasted with the general view of their contentment with slavery, for resistance to slavery was extensive in the South; the presence of intelligent slaves as well as unintelligent ones, and the similar variation in the character of the planter class; the support of the slave trade by Northerners and the existence of virtual slavery in Northern areas; the legal fictions concerning the Negro as a human being and not as property; and the individual and organized efforts of Negroes in search of freedom. The first organized protest against slavery was made by the Germantown Society of Friends in 1688. Such protests continued and led to the rise of free black persons.

From the early periods of indenture servitude, there were free Negroes. We learn of Anthony Johnson, who was listed among the first black immigrants, and who became a free man in 1625. He was a landowner, a slaveholder, and prosecuted a suit in the courts to determine his right to a slave, John Castor, with an expired term of seven years. From this beginning in the English colonies there was a continuous increase in this free group of black Americans. There were numerous slave revolts in the colonies as a result of which efforts were made to control them. In 1712 a revolt occurred in New York; twenty-one slaves were executed, with six committing suicide. During the following years there were repeated revolts, but none succeeded. Slaves made petitions and pleas for freedom. Eight petitions were received by the Massachusetts legislature between 1773 and 1779.

A Hessian officer wrote during the War for American Independence: "No regiment is seen in which there are not Negroes in abundance and among them are able-bodied, strong fellows. Here, too, there are many families of free Negroes who live in good homes, have property and live like the rest of the inhabitants." Over 5,000 free Negroes served in the Revolution as American soldiers. Others were in the British Army, and are numbered among the American Tories, as were American whites. The first martyr of the Revolution was Crispus Attucks, a Negro. He and three white Americans were the first martyrs to freedom; they were integrated in life as in death and were buried together. A monument with their names is on Boston Common.

It can be said with a sense of reality that Thomas Jefferson, thinking on this scene, dipped his pen in the blood of these martyrs, one of them a Negro, and wrote the immortal words of the Declaration of Independence – all men are created equal. (In the original draft, which was not adopted, there was a section denouncing the slave trade.) Negroes fought in integrated armies in the American Revolution for the freedom of their country. From Lexington and Concord to Yorktown, they were there.

By the first census of 1790 there were 59,000 free Negroes in the United States. Many of them were property owners, voters, and regarded as citizens. It has been said by some historians that the use of the phrase in the Declaration of Independence – "all men are created equal" – did not include slaves and free Negroes, for some of the men who supported the Declaration were owners of slaves, notably George Washington and Thomas Jefferson. But free men of color could justifiably claim the natural rights of free men, for most of them were substantial citizens. For them as for others the Declaration of Independence was a prophecy of equality on the American scene then being born for the first time. They and the later antislavery societies in their statements frequently referred to the Declaration.

These free men of color during this period organized churches, a Baptist Church at Silver Bluffs, South Carolina, a Free African Society in Philadelphia, deposited money in a Philadelphia bank, established schools and a Masonic lodge. In 1790, Jean Baptiste du Sable, of African descent, was the first settler in the Chicago area. They continued to protest their condition as free men. They protested school conditions in Massachusetts in 1787 and in South Carolina they asked that the laws be made more equitable. Richard Allen and Absolom Jones had founded the Free African Society in Philadelphia in 1787, and each of them established a church in 1794, Allen the Bethel African Methodist Episcopal Church and Jones the First African Church of St. Thomas. Two years later in New York City the Zion Methodist Church, which became the African Methodist Episcopal Zion Church, was organized.

Anti-slavery petitions were adopted by black Americans protesting against their continued enslavement as the new century opened. The first petition to Congress on this subject by Negroes was presented on January 30, 1797. The Gabriel insurrection was organized in 1800 by Gabriel Prosser, a Negro, with several thousand others, but the revolt was betrayed and Prosser with 35 of his followers were hanged.

Negotiations had led to the cession of the Louisiana area by France to Spain and then by Spain to France. This caused fear in the Jefferson administration. Congress appropriated money for the purchase of the territory and negotiators were sent to Paris. Napoleon's army had been in Haiti endeavoring to suppress the revolt under Toussaint L'Ouverture and Dessalines, who had set up an independent nation. Napoleon's effort to suppress this revolt failed. Toussaint L'Ouverture was seized under a flag of truce and carried to prison in France, where he died. Napoleon then agreed to dispose of Louisiana to the United States and by a convention of April 30, 1803, the United States agreed to pay France sixty million francs. A black leader of black men was mainly responsible for this acquisition of territory by the United States.

The U.S. Constitution had forbidden any interference with the international slave trade for 20 years after ratification—*i.e.*, until 1808. In his annual message to Congress of December 2, 1806, President Jefferson reminded the legislators of "the approach of that period at which you may interpose your authority constitutionally to withdraw the citizens of the United States from all further participation in those violations so long continued on the unoffending inhabitants of Africa." An act to prohibit the importation of slaves was passed on March 21, 1807, effective January 1, 1808. The law laid down severe penalties for participants in the slave trade after that date, but it was badly enforced, and illegal smuggling of slaves into the United States continued for many years, at rates in excess of 15,000 slaves a year. The law did not, of course, prohibit the domestic slave trade, which was not ended until the Civil War.

Negroes were active in the War of 1812. Fifty were with Commodore Perry in the Battle of Lake Erie, and 500 were with General Andrew Jackson at the Battle of New Orleans.

Jackson had declared to them as free men in a Proclamation:

> As sons of freedom, you are now called upon to defend our most inestimable blessing. As Americans your country looks with confidence to her adopted children for a valorous support, as a faithful return for the advantages engaged under her mild and equitable government. As fathers and brothers, you are summoned to rally around the standard of the Eagle, to defend all that which is dear in existence.

They responded to this and he praised them when the battle was won. They also formed local guards in several cities threatened by British attacks.

The African Methodist Episcopal Church, the first of the independent churches to be organized on a national platform, was established at Philadelphia in 1816. Richard Allen was elected its first bishop. His slogan was "God our Father, Christ our Redeemer and Man our Brother." In the same year the American Colonization Society was organized for the purpose of planning the transportation of Negroes to Africa.

The nation faced continuously the fear of black insurrection. Revolts occurred in 1816, at Camden, South Carolina, and in North Carolina in the years following. At Augusta, Georgia, a revolt was quelled with the execution of its leader in 1819. Charleston, South Carolina, had to face in 1822 a better planned effort by Denmark Vesey, an educated Negro who had come from San Domingo. Vesey stimulated others to action by inducing them to read debates on the Missouri Compromise and other pamphlets brought into the state by the promoters of freedom. Here again, however, the history of Negro insurrections repeated itself. A slave, hearing about it, told his master; but the uprising had been so well planned that the first investigation did not yield any damaging evidence. A second inquiry uncovered the project, and the leaders were tried and convicted. Denmark Vesey and thirty-five of his followers were hanged; forty-three were banished.

As a precaution against further uprisings, South Carolina enacted certain laws known as "Seamen Acts," which, to prevent the escape of slaves and the spread of abolition sentiment among them, required all Negroes on vessels to go to jail on arrival and to remain there until the ships departed. This measure proved so drastic that it had to be amended with regard to Negro citizens of foreign countries.

The next effort of the Negroes toward insurrection was the famous Appeal of David Walker, a Boston Negro, in 1829. In this address he urged slaves to rise against their masters. He referred to their state as "our wretchedness on consequence of slavery, our wretchedness on consequence of ignorance, our wretchedness in consequence of the preachers of the religion of Jesus Christ, and our wretchedness in consequence of the colonization plan." Walker wrote: "For although the destruction of the oppressors God may not effect by the oppressed, yet the Lord our God will bring other destruction upon them, for not unfrequently will he cause them to rise up one against the other, to be split, divided, and to oppress each other and sometimes to open hostilities with sword in hand."

In most cases the Negroes did not carry out their plans. In Southampton, Virginia, in 1831, however, Nat Turner actually embarked upon the slaughter of the masters to free the slaves. Turner was born in 1800; he early learned to read and made progress in the study of the Bible and religious literature while mastering also the art of making paper, gunpowder, and pottery. He developed into a man of steady habits, and he spent much time fasting and praying and "communing with the spirit." Voices, he believed, spoke to him. He laid careful plans for an uprising.

An eclipse of the sun was interpreted by Nat Turner as the sign for him to begin the insurrection. He gathered a band which killed the slave-owners in his vicinity. He and his followers succeeded in carrying out their designs for the first night, but most of them frustrated their own plans by the noise they made as a result of over-drinking. Turner himself, however, never indulged in strong drink; and he gave his men instructions against committing outrages. During the next three days they rapidly weakened until they lost all the ground they had gained. With some provisions, Turner hid under a nearby fence from which he emerged only at night. Here for six weeks he evaded his pursuers, although state and Federal troops were scouring the country to find him.

The Negroes put to death about sixty whites. In suppressing the uprising, the authorities killed 120 Negroes. After the excitement subsided fifty-three other Negroes were tried for insurrection: seventeen were convicted and executed, twelve convicted and transported, and ten acquitted. Three of the four free Negroes subsequently tried were executed and one discharged. The Virginia authorities tried to connect David Walker and William Lloyd Garrison with this insurrection, but no evidence could be found for legal extradition of these men.

The excitement and dismay evoked by this incident were not confined to Virginia. In North Carolina, to make slavery secure, the authorities determined that the one thing most needed was to close up the avenues of information to the Negroes by outlawing their schools and depriving them of contact with intelligent people. Many states enacted stringent measures to regulate the travel of slaves and free Negroes in order to make them ineffective for insurrectionary purposes or for information obtained through contact. It was made unlawful for more than a certain number of Negroes, usually five, to assemble without the permission of their masters, even for worship, unless the services were conducted by a recognized white minister or observed by "certain discreet and reputable persons."

The strongest influence against slavery that had hitherto developed was that of the Quakers. After exterminating the institution among themselves they had done effective work in Virginia and North Carolina, and when they could not operate there as they desired they sent their slaves and others to the Northwest Territory where they had the opportunity to become citizens. This transplantation began about 1815 and reached its highest point about 1835. It is significant, too, that about that time a proposal in the General Assembly of Virginia to abolish slavery failed only by the casting of the deciding vote by the Speaker. The institution was fearlessly attacked in the Virginia Convention of 1829-30 and in the state legislature the following year.

The once extensive antislavery sentiment in the South, however, was declining, although there was a frank discussion of the institution in connection with the Missouri Compromise from 1819 to 1821. It was evident that the South was preparing to defend slavery, whereas the North, in the interest of free labor, had unconsciously become opposed to the extension of the system. In its militant defense of the institution, the South alarmed the whole country. Thomas Jefferson, an uplander, thinking of this as an apple of discord from the tree of evil, said: "I tremble for my country when I reflect that God is just."

Lack of concern for the Negro was not restricted to the South. In the proportion that free Negroes, finding it uncomfortable to live in the slave states, sought refuge on free soil, race prejudice increased and often culminated in riots. Negro students were forced away from the academy thrown open to them at Canaan, New Hampshire, in 1834. New Haven citizens publicly protested against establishing in that city a manual labor school for the education of Negroes. At Canterbury, Connecticut, Prudence Crandall was imprisoned for admitting Negro girls to her seminary. The people were stirred up to do these things for fear that too many Negroes might invade the Northern communities, with the possibility that they would compete with white labor, Africanize certain centers, or become public charges.

Racial conflicts of a serious nature were common in the free states during these years. In 1829 a mob undertook to drive the Negroes out of Cincinnati. In 1836 another mob not only attacked Negroes there but also broke up the Abolitionist press, which was charged with encouraging the influx of Negroes.

The first of the annual Negro conventions met in Philadelphia in 1830, and was followed by other annual meetings. Southern writers, of whom Thomas R. Dew was typical, continued their arguments for slavery, while John Greenleaf Whittier and Lydia M. Child wrote against it. The American Anti-Slavery Society was a product of these individual voices, and its Declaration, prepared by white and black Abolitionists, raised the issue of freedom in an organized way.

The first of this society's lecturers was Charles Lenox Remond, a Negro, who issued his protest against segregation in travel in 1839.

Two essentially peaceful and nonviolent attacks on slavery were waged during the first half of the nineteenth century. On the one hand, many writers and speakers endeavored to argue with pro-slavery advocates to abandon slavery; on the other hand, Abolitionists sought to influence Congress to take action against slavery under the Constitution. However, the higher prices of cotton and the increasing cost of slaves served to develop the hold of slavery on the South. Then, too, its advocates felt that their way of life brought satisfaction to the slaves and that the efforts of Northern abolitionists contributed to insurrection by slaves.

Southerners were enraged by Abolitionist literature sent through the mails. Their excitement grew as antislavery petitions were presented in Congress in 1836, and the demand that these resolutions be tabled became known as the Gag Rule. Ironically, this gave strength to the Abolitionist cause, and although its supporters were resented by the slavery representatives in Congress, John Quincy Adams of Massachusetts continued his presentation of petitions. These petitions preceded the statements of James G. Birney and Stephen Foster on "Slavery and the Churches," along with Wendell Phillips' "Impossibility of Union with Slaveholders," and the implications that slavery and its defenders were sinful and despotic in a Christian democracy.

It was in the midst of these depressing conditions that the slaves broke into song. They did not hang their harps upon the willows but expressed themselves in singing as they worked, worshipped, and played. While en route northward on the Underground Railroad, they sang for their brothers and sisters still in slavery, "Go down Moses, Way down in Egypt's land, tell old Pharaoh, to let my people go." They sang "Steal away to Jesus" because they were forbidden to worship unless a white observer was present, and they would "Follow the Drinking Gourd," which pointed the way northward and to freedom.

Others, of whom Frederick Douglass was an example, not only protested against slavery but also showed its relation to the politics of international affairs. Douglass in his *North Star* in 1848 wrote of Mexico as "a doomed victim to Anglo-Saxon stupidity and love of dominion," and urged "the instant recall of our forces from Mexico." The war was regarded by many in the North as an act of aggression motivated by those interested in the extension of slavery. The Wilmot Proviso, although it was not approved, was their negative answer to the opening to slavery of any territory acquired by the war. Sojourner Truth, Harriet Tubman, and others participated in women's antislavery societies and women's rights organizations, and their voices were heard.

With threat of disunion in the air over slavery, the reopening of the slave trade, the opening of schools to black children in the Roberts case in Massachusetts, the debates on slavery in the territories, and the question of a new fugitive slave law, sectional differences became acute by 1850. Division was postponed by compromise legislation despite talk of secession. The Underground Railroad continued its activities as the Fugitive Slave Law was enforced. William Still's *The Underground Railroad* illustrates this development.

Slavery was a hard institution, though there were some benevolent masters. There were many cruel masters who were of the belief that slaves had to be forced to work, whipped for punishment and bad conduct and sold further southward. Harriet Beecher Stowe's *Uncle Tom's Cabin* (1852) dramatized in book form the life of a slave and received an extensive circulation with translation into several languages. Southerners reported that the book was untrue and exaggerated, and they resented this presentation of slaveholders and overseers. Many Northerners were impressed by it and wanted to do something about it. In addition, William Wells Brown published *Clotelle, or the President's Daughter*, the first published novel by a Negro-American author.

Education became a question of much importance to free Negroes in the fifties. The public schools were for the education of the poor, but when the charitable stigma was removed and Negroes were taxed for their benefits, plans for separate schools were developed in Pennsylvania, New Jersey, New York, Rhode Island, Connecticut, Massachusetts, in many New England towns, and in Ohio, Indiana, and other states in the West and North.

Opposition often arose to these schools and their teachers. Richard Baker's "The Crime of Mrs. Douglass in Teaching Colored Children to Read" is an example of this opposition. In spite of the difficulties, schools for Negroes were undertaken in Baltimore, Philadelphia, New York, Boston, Pittsburgh, Cincinnati, Columbus, Cleveland, and Chicago. Free blacks who were able sent their children to Northern centers to be educated in the private schools.

Oral education and religious instruction were carried on in parts of the South. In a number of homes, the planter would decide to have his Negroes taught, and his wife or children would engage in religious teaching. At the same time slaves were taught for special business purposes on the plantations, and their education continued to the extent of learning to read, write, and cipher.

While free Negroes were not considered citizens in the South and the U.S. Supreme Court remained passive on the status of slavery, Dred Scott initiated his suit for freedom in the U.S. Circuit Court at St. Louis in 1846. The nation remained divided in its views, with the Supreme Court hesitating to enter the conflict with an opinion. Frederick Law Olmsted, who traveled extensively, had observed this division as it related to the South in his *King Cotton and His Subjects* and George Fitzhugh saw it in his *The Failure of a Free Society*. The impending crisis was apparent to the nation in the early fifties, with some leaders in the South advocating withdrawal from the Union. Many in the North would have settled at this time for some limitation on slavery extension. Nevertheless, there were those who thought that a few years of peace and talk would end the sectional strife and unify the country once and for all.

Charles H. Wesley
Washington, 1968

1. The Great Compromise

1850-1854

CHARLOTTE L. FORTEN
The Difficulty of Being a Negro Christian

Charlotte Forten was the child of a distinguished Negro family that had long worked toward the abolition of slavery. Her father, a wealthy Philadelphia merchant, sent Charlotte to school in Salem, Massachusetts, where she lived with a Negro Abolitionist family. It was there that she witnessed the capture of the fugitive slave Anthony Burns. She became a teacher and after the Civil War participated in the federal government's Sea Island program designed to instruct 10,000 former slaves in the rudiments of citizenship. The following selection from Miss Forten's journal, which was first published in 1953, is a vivid account of her daily struggle to live by Christian principles of love and tolerance in the face of overwhelming prejudice exhibited by whites toward her race. [Source: Journal of Charlotte L. Forten. Ray A. Billington, ed., New York, 1953.]

May 26, 1854. Had a conversation with Miss Shepard [grammar school principal in Salem] about slavery; she is, as I thought, thoroughly opposed to it, but does not agree with me in thinking that the churches and ministers are generally supporters of the infamous system; I believe it firmly.

Mr. Barnes, one of the most prominent of the Philadelphia clergy, who does not profess to be an Abolitionist, has declared his belief that "the American church is a bulwark of slavery."

Words cannot express all that I feel; all that is felt by the friends of freedom, when thinking of this great obstacle to the removal of slavery from our land. Alas! that it should be so.

June 2. Our worst fears are realized. The decision was against poor Burns [Anthony Burns, arrested in Boston under the Fugitive Slave Act], and he has been sent back to a bondage worse, a thousand times worse, than death.

With what scorn must that government be regarded which cowardly assembles thousands of soldiers to satisfy the demands of slaveholders; to deprive of his freedom a man, created in God's own image, whose sole offense is the color of his skin! And if resistance is offered to this outrage, these soldiers are to shoot down American citizens without mercy; and this by the express orders of a government which proudly boasts of being the freest in the world; this on the very soil where the Revolution of 1776 began.

I can write no more. A cloud seems hanging over me, over all our persecuted race, which nothing can dispel.

June 4. Tomorrow school commences, and although the pleasure I shall feel in again seeing my beloved teacher, and in resuming my studies, will be much saddened by recent events, yet they shall be a fresh incentive to more earnest study, to aid me in fitting myself for laboring in a holy cause, for enabling me to do much toward changing the condition of my oppressed and suffering people.

Would that those with whom I shall recite tomorrow could sympathize with me in this; would that they could look upon all God's creatures without respect to color, feeling that it is character alone which makes the true man or woman!

June 5. Miss Church [a student from Nova Scotia] and I counted the merits of the first and second classes for Miss Shepard; after school, had an hour's conversation with her about slavery and prejudice.

I fully appreciate her kindness and sympathy with me; she wishes me to cultivate a Christian spirit in thinking of my enemies; I know it is right, and will endeavor to do so, but it does seem very difficult. . . .

June 25. This afternoon went to an anti-slavery meeting in Danvers, from which I have just returned. Mr. Foss spoke eloquently, and with that warmth and sincerity which evidently comes from the heart.

He said he was rejoiced that the people at the North were beginning to feel that slavery is no longer confined to the black man alone but that they too must wear the yoke; and they are becoming roused on the subject at last.

He spoke of the objections made by many to the Abolitionists, on the plea of their using too violent language; they say that the slaveholders are driven by it to worse measures; what they need is mild entreaty, etc. But the petition against the Nebraska Bill, couched in the very mildest terms by the clergymen of the North, was received even less favorably by the South than the hardest sayings of the

Abolitionists; and they were abused and denounced more severely than the latter have ever been.

July 17. I have seen today a picture of a dear old English church. Oh, England, my heart yearns toward thee as to a loved and loving friend! I long to behold thee, to dwell in one of thy quiet homes, far from the scenes of my early childhood; far from the land, my native land, where I am hated and oppressed because God has given me a dark skin. How did this cruel, this absurd prejudice ever exist? How can it exist?

August 11. I have been thinking lately very much about death, that strange, mysterious, awful reality that is constantly around and among us, that power which takes away from us so many of those whom we love and honor, or those who have persecuted and oppressed us, our bitter enemies whom we vainly endeavor not to hate.

Oh! I long to be good, to be able to meet death calmly and fearlessly, strong in faith and holiness. But this I know can only be through One who died for us, through the pure and perfect love of Him who was all holiness and love.

But how can I hope to be worthy of His love while I still cherish this feeling toward my enemies, this unforgiving spirit? This is a question which I ask myself very often. Other things in comparison with this seem easy to overcome. But hatred of oppression seems to me so blended with hatred of the oppressor I cannot separate them. I feel that no other injury could be so hard to bear, so very hard to forgive, as that inflicted by cruel prejudice. How can I be a Christian when so many in common with myself, for no crime, suffer so cruelly, so unjustly?

September 5. I have suffered much today. My friends Mrs. Putnam [Negro wife of a Salem grocer] and her daughters were refused admission to the Museum, after having tickets given them, solely on account of their complexion. Insulting language was used to them. Of course they felt and exhibited deep, bitter indignation; but of what avail was it? None but to excite the ridicule of those contemptible creatures, miserable doughfaces who do not deserve the name of men. I will not attempt to write more. No words can express my feelings. But these cruel wrongs cannot be much longer endured. A day of retribution must come. God grant that it may come very soon!

5

September 12. I wonder that every colored person is not a misanthrope. Surely we have everything to make us hate mankind. I have met girls in the schoolroom — they have been thoroughly kind and cordial to me; perhaps the next day met them in the street — they feared to recognize me; these I can but regard now with scorn and contempt; once I liked them, believing them incapable of such meanness. Others gave the most distant recognition possible. I, of course, acknowledge no such recognitions, and they soon cease entirely.

These are but trifles, certainly, to the great public wrongs which we as a people are obliged to endure. But to those who experience them, these apparent trifles are most wearing and discouraging: even to the child's mind they reveal volumes of deceit and heartlessness, and early teach a lesson of suspicion and distrust.

O! it is hard to go through life meeting contempt with contempt, hatred with hatred, fearing, with too good reason, to love and trust hardly anyone whose skin is white, however lovable, attractive, and congenial in seeming.

In the bitter, passionate feelings of my soul, again and again there rises the questions—"When, oh! when shall this cease?" "Is there no help?" "How long, oh! How long must we continue to suffer, to endure?" Conscience answers it is wrong, it is ignoble to despair; let us labor earnestly and faithfully to acquire knowledge, to break down the barriers of prejudice and oppression. Let us take courage; never ceasing to work, hoping and believing that if not for us, for another generation there is a better, brighter day in store, when slavery and prejudice shall vanish before the glorious light of liberty and truth; when the rights of every colored man shall everywhere be acknowledged and respected, and he shall be treated as a *man* and a *brother!*

RALPH WALDO EMERSON
On the Fugitive Slave Law

*Emerson remained aloof from the Abolition movement through the 1830s and
1840s; as a descendant of nine generations of ministers he had "other slaves
to free than those Negroes, to wit, imprisoned spirits, imprisoned thoughts."
However, events ultimately drew him into the controversy, especially the
enactment of the stronger fugitive slave law that was part of the Compromise
of 1850. "This filthy enactment," he wrote in his journal, "was made in the
nineteenth century, by people who could read and write. I will not obey it, by
God!" He summarized his opposition to the law and to the slave system in
an address delivered in New York on March 4, 1854, and reprinted here
in part.* [*Source:* Miscellanies, *Boston, 1886, pp. 205-230.*]

I have lived all my life without suffering any known inconvenience
from American slavery. I never saw it; I never heard the whip; I
never felt the check on my free speech and action until the other
day, when Mr. Webster, by his personal influence, brought the
Fugitive Slave Law on the country. I say Mr. Webster, for though the
bill was not his, it is yet notorious that he was the life and soul of it,
that he gave it all he had. It cost him his life, and under the shadow
of his great name inferior men sheltered themselves, threw their
ballots for it and made the law. I say inferior men. There were all
sorts of what are called brilliant men, accomplished men, men of
high station, a President of the United States, senators, men of
eloquent speech, but men without self-respect, without character;
and it was strange to see that office, age, fame, talent, even a repute
for honesty all count for nothing.

They had no opinions, they had no memory for what they had
been saying like the Lord's Prayer all their lifetime: they were only
looking to what their great Captain did. If he jumped, they jumped;
if he stood on his head, they did. In ordinary, the supposed sense of
their district and state is their guide, and that holds them to the part
of liberty and justice. But it is always a little difficult to decipher
what this public sense is; and when a great man comes who knots
up into himself the opinions and wishes of the people, it is so much
easier to follow him as an exponent of this. He too is responsible;

7

they will not be. It will always suffice to say, "I followed him." . . .

I said I had never in my life up to this time suffered from the slave institution. Slavery in Virginia or Carolina was like slavery in Africa or the Fijis for me. There was an old Fugitive Law, but it had become, or was fast becoming, a dead letter, and, by the genius and laws of Massachusetts, inoperative. The new bill made it operative, required me to hunt slaves, and it found citizens in Massachusetts willing to act as judges and captors. Moreover, it discloses the secret of the new times, that slavery was no longer mendicant but was become aggressive and dangerous.

The way in which the country was dragged to consent to this, and the disastrous defection (on the miserable cry of Union) of the men of letters, of the colleges, of educated men, nay, of some preachers of religion, was the darkest passage in the history. It showed that our prosperity had hurt us and that we could not be shocked by crime. It showed that the old religion and the sense of the right had faded and gone out; that while we reckoned ourselves a highly cultivated nation, our bellies had run away with our brains, and the principles of culture and progress did not exist.

For I suppose that liberty is an accurate index, in men and nations, of general progress. The theory of personal liberty must always appeal to the most refined communities and to the men of the rarest perception and of delicate moral sense. For there are rights which rest on the finest sense of justice, and, with every degree of civility, it will be more truly felt and defined. A barbarous tribe of good stock will, by means of their best heads, secure substantial liberty. But where there is any weakness in a race, and it becomes in a degree matter of concession and protection from their stronger neighbors, the incompatibility and offensiveness of the wrong will of course be most evident to the most cultivated. For it is—is it not?—the essence of courtesy, of politeness, of religion, of love, to prefer another, to postpone oneself, to protect another from oneself. That is the distinction of the gentleman, to defend the weak and redress the injured, as it is of the savage and the brutal to usurp and use others. . . .

Now, gentlemen, I think we have in this hour instruction again in the simplest lesson. Events roll, millions of men are engaged, and the result is the enforcing of some of those first commandments

8

which we heard in the nursery. We never get beyond our first lesson, for, really, the world exists, as I understand it, to teach the science of liberty, which begins with liberty from fear.

The events of this month are teaching one thing plain and clear, the worthlessness of good tools to bad workmen; that official papers are of no use; resolutions of public meetings, platforms of conventions, no, nor laws, nor constitutions, anymore. These are all declaratory of the will of the moment, and are passed with more levity and on grounds far less honorable than ordinary business transactions of the street.

You relied on the Constitution. It has not the word "slave" in it; and very good argument has shown that it would not warrant the crimes that are done under it; that, with provisions so vague for an object not named, and which could not be availed of to claim a barrel of sugar or a barrel of corn, the robbing of a man and of all his posterity is effected. You relied on the Supreme Court. The law was right, excellent law for the lambs. But what if unhappily the judges were chosen from the wolves, and give to all the law a wolfish interpretation? You relied on the Missouri Compromise. That is ridden over. You relied on state sovereignty in the free states to protect their citizens. They are driven with contempt out of the courts and out of the territory of the slave states—if they are so happy as to get out with their lives—and now you relied on these dismal guarantees infamously made in 1850; and, before the body of Webster is yet crumbled, it is found that they have crumbled. This eternal monument of his fame and of the Union is rotten in four years. They are no guarantee to the free states. They are a guarantee to the slave states that, as they have hitherto met with no repulse, they shall meet with none.

I fear there is no reliance to be put on any kind or form of covenant, no, not on sacred forms, none on churches, none on Bibles. For one would have said that a Christian would not keep slaves; but the Christians keep slaves. Of course they will not dare to read the Bible. Won't they? They quote the Bible, quote Paul, quote Christ to justify slavery. If slavery is good, then is lying, theft, arson, homicide, each and all good, and to be maintained by Union societies.

These things show that no forms, neither constitutions, nor laws, nor covenants, nor churches, nor Bibles, are of any use in them-

9

selves. The devil nestles comfortably into them all. There is no help but in the head and heart and hamstrings of a man. Covenants are of no use without honest men to keep them; laws of none but with loyal citizens to obey them. To interpret Christ it needs Christ in the heart. The teachings of the Spirit can be apprehended only by the same spirit that gave them forth. To make good the cause of freedom, you must draw off from all foolish trust in others. You must be citadels and warriors yourselves, declarations of independence, the charter, the battle, and the victory. Cromwell said, "We can only resist the superior training of the king's soldiers by enlisting godly men." And no man has a right to hope that the laws of New York will defend him from the contamination of slaves another day until he has made up his mind that he will not owe his protection to the laws of New York, but to his own sense and spirit. Then he protects New York.

He only who is able to stand alone is qualified for society. And that I understand to be the end for which a soul exists in this world — to be himself the counterbalance of all falsehood and all wrong. "The army of unright is encamped from pole to pole, but the road of victory is known to the just." Everything may be taken away; he may be poor, he may be houseless, yet he will know out of his arms to make a pillow, and out of his breast a bolster. Why have the minority no influence? Because they have not a real minority of one. . . .

No excess of good nature or of tenderness in individuals has been able to give a new character to the system, to tear down the whipping house. The plea in the mouth of a slaveholder that the Negro is an inferior race sounds very oddly in my ear. "The masters of slaves seem generally anxious to prove that they are not of a race superior in any noble quality to the meanest of their bondmen." And, indeed, when the Southerner points to the anatomy of the Negro and talks of chimpanzee, I recall Montesquieu's remark, "It will not do to say that Negroes are men, lest it should turn out that whites are not."

Slavery is disheartening; but nature is not so helpless but it can rid itself at last of every wrong. But the spasms of nature are centuries and ages, and will tax the faith of short-lived men. Slowly, slowly the Avenger comes, but comes surely. The proverbs of the nations affirm these delays, but affirm the arrival. They say, "God

10

may consent, but not forever." The delay of the divine justice — this was the meaning and soul of the Greek tragedy; this the soul of their religion. "There has come, too, one to whom lurking warfare is dear, Retribution, with a soul full of wiles; a violator of hospitality; guileful without the guilt of guile; limping, late in her arrival." They said of the happiness of the unjust that "at its close it begets itself an offspring and does not die childless, and instead of good fortune, there sprouts forth for posterity ever-ravening calamity"

> For evil word shall evil word be said,
> For murder-stroke a murder-stroke be paid.
> Who smites must smart.

These delays, you see them now in the temper of the times. The national spirit in this country is so drowsy, preoccupied with interest, deaf to principle. The Anglo-Saxon race is proud and strong and selfish. They believe only in Anglo-Saxons. In 1825 Greece found America deaf, Poland found America deaf, Italy and Hungary found her deaf. England maintains trade, not liberty; stands against Greece; against Hungary; against Schleswig-Holstein, against the French Republic while it was a republic.

To faint hearts the times offer no invitation, and torpor exists here throughout the active classes on the subject of domestic slavery and its appalling aggressions. Yes, that is the stern edict of Providence, that liberty shall be no hasty fruit, but that event on event, population on population, age on age, shall cast itself into the opposite scale; and not until liberty has slowly accumulated weight enough to countervail and preponderate against all this can the sufficient recoil come. . . .

While the inconsistency of slavery with the principles on which the world is built guarantees its downfall, I own that the patience it requires is almost too sublime for mortals and seems to demand of us more than mere hoping. And when one sees how fast the rot spreads — it is growing serious — I think we demand of superior men that they be superior in this, that the mind and the virtue shall give their verdict in their day, and accelerate so far the progress of civilization. Possession is sure to throw its stupid strength for existing power, and appetite and ambition will go for that. Let the aid of virtue, intelligence, and education be cast where they rightfully

11

belong. They are organically ours. Let them be loyal to their own. I wish to see the instructed class here know their own flag and not fire on their comrades. We should not forgive the clergy for taking on every issue the immoral side; nor the bench, if it put itself on the side of the culprit; nor the government, if it sustain the mob against the laws.

It is a potent support and ally to a brave man standing single, or with a few, for the right, and outvoted and ostracized, to know that better men in other parts of the country appreciate the service and will rightly report him to his own and the next age. Without this assurance, he will sooner sink. He may well say, "If my countrymen do not care to be defended, I too will decline the controversy, from which I only reap invectives and hatred."

Yet the lovers of liberty may with reason tax the coldness and indifferentism of scholars and literary men. They are lovers of liberty in Greece and Rome and in the English Commonwealth, but they are lukewarm lovers of the liberty of America in 1854. The universities are not, as in Hobbes's time, "the core of rebellion," no, but the seat of inertness. They have forgotten their allegiance to the Muse, and grown worldly and political. . . .

Now at last we are disenchanted and shall have no more false hopes. I respect the Anti-Slavery Society. It is the Cassandra that has foretold all that has befallen, fact for fact, years ago; foretold all, and no man laid it to heart. It seemed, as the Turks say, "Fate makes that a man should not believe his own eyes." But the Fugitive Law did much to unglue the eyes of men, and now the Nebraska Bill leaves us staring. The Anti-Slavery Society will add many members this year. The Whig Party will join it; the Democrats will join it. The population of the free states will join it. I doubt not, at last, the slave states will join it. But be that sooner or later, and whoever comes or stays away, I hope we have reached the end of our unbelief, have come to a belief that there is a divine Providence in the world which will not save us but through our own cooperation.

WILLIAM J. GRAYSON

The Hireling and the Slave

The enormous success of Uncle Tom's Cabin, *as both a novel and a play,*
infuriated Southerners, who condemned the work as unrealistic, exaggerated,
and oversentimental. In 1854 William Grayson, South Carolina lawyer and
politician, attempted to counter the effectiveness of Mrs. Stowe's story in his
long, didactic poem, The Hireling and the Slave. *Like George Fitzhugh, he*
attacked the economic system of the industrial North as producing
wage-slaves who, he contended, were much worse off than the average
Negro slave in the South. A portion of Grayson's poem is reprinted below.
[*Source:* The Hireling and the Slave, Chicora, and Other Poems, *Charleston,*
S.C., 1856.]

> Fallen from primeval innocence and ease,
> When thornless fields employed him but to please,
> The laborer toils; and from his dripping brow
> Moistens the length'ning furrows of the plow;
> In vain he scorns or spurns his altered state,
> Tries each poor shift, and strives to cheat his fate;
> In vain new shapes his name to shun the ill —
> Slave, hireling, help — the curse pursues him still;
> Changeless the doom remains, the mincing phrase
> May mock high heaven, but not reverse its ways.
> How small the choice, from cradle to the grave,
> Between the lot of hireling, help, or slave!
> To each alike applies the stern decree,
> That man shall labor; whether bond or free,
> For all that toil, the recompense we claim —
> Food, fire, a home, and clothing — is the same.
> The manumitted serfs of Europe find
> Unchanged this sad estate of all mankind;
> What blessing to the churl has freedom proved,
> What want supplied, what task or toil removed?
> Hard work and scanty wages still their lot,
> In youth o'erlabored, and in age forgot,
> The mocking boon of freedom they deplore,
> In wants, and labors never known before.

13

Free but in name — the slaves of endless toil,
In Britain still they turn the stubborn soil,
Spread on each sea her sails for every mart,
Ply in her cities every useful art;
But vainly may the peasant toil and groan
To speed the plow in furrows not his own;
In vain the art is plied, the sail is spread,
The day's work offered for the daily bread;
With hopeless eye, the pauper hireling sees
The homeward sail swell proudly to the breeze,
Rich fabrics wrought by his unequaled hand,
Borne by each breeze to every distant land;
For him, no boon successful commerce yields,
For him, no harvest crowns the joyous fields;
The streams of wealth that foster pomp and pride,
No food nor shelter for his wants provide;
He fails to win, by toil intensely hard,
The bare subsistence — labor's least reward.

In squalid hut — a kennel for the poor,
Or noisome cellar, stretched upon the floor,
His clothing rags, of filthy straw his bed,
With offal from the gutter daily fed,
Thrust out from nature's board, the hireling lies —
No place for him that common board supplies,
No neighbor helps, no charity attends,
No philanthropic sympathy befriends;
None heed the needy wretch's dying groan,
He starves unsuccored, perishes unknown.

These are the miseries, such the wants, the cares,
The bliss that freedom for the serf prepares;
Vain is his skill in each familiar task,
Capricious fashion shifts her Protean mask,
His ancient craft gives work and bread no more,
And want and death sit scowling at his door.

· · · · ·

Hesperian lands, beyond the Atlantic wave,
Home of the poor and refuge of the brave,
Who, vainly striving with oppression, fly
To find new homes beneath a happier sky;

The Hireling and the Slave

Hither, to quiet vale or mountainside,
Where peace and nature undisturbed abide,
In humble scenes unwonted lore to learn,
Patriot and prince their banished footsteps turn.

. . . . .

Here, with determined will and patient toil,
From wood and swamp he wins the fertile soil;
To every hardship stern endurance brings,
And builds a fortune undisturbed by kings;
Fair fields of wealth and ease his children find,
Nor heed the homes their fathers left behind.

Companions of his toil, the axe to wield,
To guide the plow and reap the teeming field,
A sable multitude unceasing pour
From Niger's banks and Congo's deadly shore;
No willing travelers they, that widely roam,
Allured by hope to seek a happier home,
But victims to the trader's thirst for gold,
Kidnapped by brothers, and by fathers sold,
The bondsman born, by native masters reared,
The captive band in recent battle spared;
For English merchants bought; across the main,
In British ships, they go for Britain's gain;
Forced on her subjects in dependent lands,
By cruel hearts and avaricious hands,
New tasks they learn, new masters they obey,
And how submissive to the white man's sway.
    But Providence, by his o'erruling will,
Transmutes to lasting good the transient ill,
Makes crime itself the means of mercy prove,
And avarice minister to works of love.
In this new home, whate'er the Negro's fate—
More bless'd his life than in his native state!

. . . . .

    And now, with sturdy hand and cheerful heart,
He learns to master every useful art,
To forge the axe, to mold the rugged share,
The ship's brave keel for angry waves prepare:

The rising wall obeys his plastic will,
And the loom's fabric owns his ready skill.

. . . . .

In broader limits, by the loftier maize,
The silklike cotton all its wealth displays:
Through forked leaves, in endless rows unfold
Gay blossoms tinged with purple dyes and gold;
To suns autumnal bursting pods disclose
Their fleeces, spotless as descending snows;
These, a rich freight, a thousand ships receive,
A thousand looms with fairy fingers weave;
And hireling multitudes in other lands
Are blessed with raiment from the Negro's hands.

. . . . .

New life he gives to Europe's busy marts,
To all the world new comforts and new arts;
Loom, spinner, merchant, from his hands derive
Their wealth, and myriads by his labor thrive;
While slothful millions, hopeless of relief,
The slaves of pagan priest and brutal chief,
Harassed by wars upon their native shore,
Still lead the savage life they led before.
Instructed thus, and in the only school
Barbarians ever know—a master's rule,
The Negro learns each civilizing art
That softens and subdues the savage heart,
Assumes the tone of those with whom he lives,
Acquires the habit that refinement gives,
And slowly learns, but surely, while a slave,
The lessons that his country never gave.

. . . . .

Hence is the Negro come, by God's command,
For wiser teaching to a foreign land;
If they who brought him were by Mammon driven,
Still have they served, blind instruments of Heaven;
And though the way be rough, the agent stern,
No better mode can human wits discern,
No happier system wealth or virtue find,
To tame and elevate the Negro mind:

16

Thus mortal purposes, whate'er their mood,
Are only means with Heaven for working good;
And wisest they who labor to fulfill,
With zeal and hope, the all-directing will,
And in each change that marks the fleeting year,
Submissive see God's guiding hand appear.

. . . . .

But if, though wise and good the purposed end,
Reproach and scorn the instrument attend;
If, when the final blessing is confessed,
Still the vile slaver all the world detest.

. . . . .

But modern slavers, more sagacious grown,
In all the wrong, can see no part their own;
They drag the Negro from his native shore,
Make him a slave, and then his fate deplore;
Sell him in distant countries, and when sold,
Revile the buyers, but retain the gold.

. . . . .

Such now the maxims of the purer school
Of ethic lore, where sons of slavers rule;
No more allowed the Negro to enslave,
They damn the master and for freedom rave,
Strange modes of morals and of faith unfold,
Make newer gospels supersede the old,
Prove that ungodly Paul connived at sin,
And holier rites, like Mormon's priest, begin;
There, chief and teacher, Gerrit Smith appears,
There Tappan mourns, like Niobe, all tears,
Carnage and fire, mad Garrison invokes,
And Hale, with better temper, smirks and jokes.

. . . . .

There supple Sumner, with the Negro cause,
Plays the sly game for office and applause;
What boots it if the Negro sink or swim?
He wins the Senate—'tis enough for him.

. . . . .

There Greeley, grieving at a brother's woe,
Spits with impartial spite on friend and foe;

17

His Negro griefs and sympathies produce
No nobler fruits than malice and abuse;
To each fanatical delusion prone,
He damns all creeds and parties but his own.

. . . . .

There Seward smiles the sweet perennial smile,
Skilled in the tricks of subtlety and guile;
The sliest schemer that the world e'er saw;
Peddler of sentiment and patent law;
Ready for fee or faction to display
His skill in either, if the practice pay,
But void of all that makes the frank and brave,
And smooth, and soft, and crafty like the slave.

. . . . .

There Stowe, with prostituted pen, assails
One-half her country in malignant tales;
Careless, like Trollope, whether truth she tells,
And anxious only how the libel sells,
To slander's mart she furnishes supplies,
And feeds its morbid appetite for lies
On fictions fashioned with malicious art,
The venal pencil and malignant heart,
With fact distorted, inference unsound,
Creatures in fancy, not in nature found.

. . . . .

These use the Negro, a convenient tool,
That yields substantial gain or party rule,
Gives what without it they could never know,
To Chase, distinction, courtly friends to Stowe,
To Parker, themes for miracles of rant,
And Beecher blesses with new gifts of cant.
The master's task has been the black to train,
To form his mind, his passions to restrain;
With anxious care and patience to impart
The knowledge that subdues the savage heart,
To give the Gospel lessons that control
The rudest breast and renovate the soul—
Who does, or gives as much, of all who raise
Their sland'rous cry for foreign pence or praise,

The Hireling and the Slave

Of all the knaves who clamor and declaim
For party power or philanthropic fame,
Or use the Negro's fancied wrongs and woes
As pretty themes for maudlin verse or prose?
    Taught by the master's efforts, by his care,
Fed, clothed, protected many a patient year,
From trivial numbers now to millions grown,
With all the white man's useful arts their own,
Industrious, docile, skilled in wood and field,
To guide the plow, the sturdy axe to wield,
The Negroes schooled by slavery embrace
The highest portion of the Negro race;
And none the savage native will compare,
Of barbarous Guinea, with its offspring here.
    If bound to daily labor while he lives,
His is the daily bread that labor gives;
Guarded from want, from beggary secure,
He never feels what hireling crowds endure,
Nor knows, like them, in hopeless want to crave,
For wife and child, the comforts of the slave,
Or the sad thought that, when about to die,
He leaves them to the cold world's charity,
And sees them slowly seek the poorhouse door—
The last, vile, hated refuge of the poor.

          . . . . .

No mobs of factious workmen gather here,
No strikes we dread, no lawless riots fear;
Nuns, from their convent driven, at midnight fly,
Churches, in flames, ask vengeance from the sky,
Seditious schemes in bloody tumults end,
Parsons incite, and senators defend,
But not where slaves their easy labors ply,
Safe from the snare, beneath a master's eye;
In useful tasks engaged, employed their time,
Untempted by the demagogue to crime,
Secure they toil, uncursed their peaceful life,
With labor's hungry broils and wasteful strife.
No want to goad, no faction to deplore,
The slave escapes the perils of the poor.

19

Why peril, then, the Negro's humble joys,
Why make him free, if freedom but destroys?
Why take him from that lot that now bestows
More than the Negro elsewhere ever knows—
Home, clothing, food, light labor, and content,
Childhood in play, and age in quiet spent,
To vex his life with factious strife and broil,
To crush his nature with unwonted toil,
To see him, like the Indian tribes, a prey
To war or peace, destruction or decay?

. . . . .

Let, then, the master still his course pursue,
"With heart and hope" perform his mission too;
Heaven's ruling power confessed, with patient care
The end subserve, the fitting means prepare,
In faith unshaken guide, restrain, command,
With strong and steady, yet indulgent hand,
Justly, "as in the great Taskmaster's eye,"
His task perform—the Negro's wants supply,
The Negro's hand to useful arts incline,
His mind enlarge, his moral sense refine,
With Gospel truth his simple heart engage,
To his dull eyes unseal its sacred page,
By gradual steps his feebler nature raise,
Deserve, if not receive, the good man's praise;
The factious knave defy, and meddling fool,
The pulpit brawler and his lawless tool,
Scorn the grave cant, the supercilious sneer,
The mawkish sentiment and maudlin tear,
Assured that God all human power bestows,
Controls its uses, and its purpose knows,
And that each lot on earth to mortals given,
Its duties duly done, is blessed of Heaven.

GEORGE FITZHUGH
The Failure of Free Society

George Fitzhugh, Southern sociologist, lawyer, and apologist for the slave system, differed from most Southerners in his approach to the slavery issue. Whereas most Southerners were continually on the defensive against Abolitionist attacks on their "peculiar institution," Fitzhugh took the offensive and attacked the Northern economic system as a failure. In his view, the Southern patriarchal system was not only morally superior but was also certain eventually to dominate all of the United States. His first major work was Sociology for the South, *published in 1854, from which the following selections are printed.* [Source: Sociology for the South, or the Failure of Free Society, *Richmond, Va., 1854, pp. iii, 7-12, 34-48, 83-95, 161-163, 177-186.*]

To the People of the South:

We dedicate this little work to you, because it is a zealous and honest effort to promote your peculiar interests. Society has been so quiet and contented in the South—it has suffered so little from crime or extreme poverty, that its attention has not been awakened to the revolutionary tumults, uproar, mendicity and crime of free society. Few are aware of the blessings they enjoy, or of the evils from which they are exempt.

From some peculiarity of taste, we have for many years been watching closely the perturbed workings of free society. Its crimes, its revolutions, its sufferings and its beggary, have led us to investigate its past history, as well as to speculate on its future destiny. This pamphlet has been hastily written, but is the result of long observation, some research, and much reflection. Should it contain suggestions that will enlist abler pens to show that free society is a failure and its philosophy false, our highest ambition will be gratified. Believing our positions on these subjects to be true, we feel sanguine they are destined to final vindication and triumph. . . .

On all subjects of social science, Southern men, from their position, possess peculiar advantages when they undertake discussion. History . . . informs them of all the phenomena of other forms of society, and they see every day around them the peculiarities and characteristics of slave society, of which little is to be learned from books. . . . The South can lose nothing, and may gain, by the discussion. She has, up to this time, been condemned without a hearing.

FREE TRADE

Political economy is the science of free society. Its theory and its history alike establish this position. Its fundamental maxims, *laissez faire* and *pas trop gouverner* [minimum government], are at war with all kinds of slavery, for they in fact assert that individuals and peoples prosper most when governed least. It is not, therefore, wonderful that such a science should not have been believed or inculcated while slavery was universal. . . .

Until now, industry had been controlled and directed by a few minds. Monopoly in its every form had been rife. Men were suddenly called on to walk alone, to act and work for themselves without guide, advice, or control from superior authority. In the past, nothing like it had occurred; hence no assistance could be derived from books. The prophets themselves had overlooked or omitted to tell of the advent of this golden era and were no better guides than the historians and philosophers.

A philosophy that should guide and direct industry was equally needed with a philosophy of morals. The occasion found and made the man. For writing a one-sided philosophy, no man was better fitted than Adam Smith. He possessed extraordinary powers of abstraction, analysis, and generalization. He was absent, secluded, and unobservant. He saw only that prosperous and progressive portion of society whom liberty or free competition benefited and mistook its effects on them for its effects on the world. He had probably never heard the old English adage, "Every man for himself, and devil take the hindmost." This saying comprehends the whole philosophy, moral and economical, of the *Wealth of Nations*. But he and the political economists who have succeeded him seem never to have dreamed that there would have been any "hindmost."

There can never be a wise moral philosopher, or a sound philosophy, till someone arises who sees and comprehends all the "things in heaven and earth." Philosophers are the most abstracted, secluded, and least observant of men. Their premises are always false, because they see but few facts; and hence their conclusions must

22

also be false. Plato and Aristotle have today as many believers as Smith, Paley, or Locke, and between their times a hundred systems have arisen, flourished for a time, and been rejected. There is not a true moral philosophy, and from the nature of things there never can be. Such a philosophy has to discover first causes and ultimate effects, to grasp infinitude, to deal with eternity at both ends. Human presumption will often attempt this, but human intellect can never achieve it. We shall build up no system, attempt to account for nothing, but simply point out what is natural and universal and humbly try to justify the ways of God to man.

Adam Smith's philosophy is simple and comprehensive (*teres et rotundus* [elegant and polished]). Its leading and almost its only doctrine is that individual well-being and social and national wealth and prosperity will be best promoted by each man eagerly pursuing his own selfish welfare unfettered and unrestricted by legal regulations, or governmental prohibitions, farther than such regulations may be necessary to prevent positive crime. That some qualifications of this doctrine will not be found in his book we shall not deny; but this is his system. It is obvious enough that such a governmental policy as this doctrine would result in would stimulate energy, excite invention and industry, and bring into livelier action, genius, skill, and talent. It had done so before Smith wrote, and it was no doubt the observation of those effects that suggested the theory. His friends and acquaintances were of that class who, in the war of the wits to which free competition invited, were sure to come off victors. His country, too, England and Scotland, in the arts of trade and in manufacturing skill, was an overmatch for the rest of the world. International free trade would benefit his country as much as social free trade would benefit his friends. This was his world, and had it been the only world his philosophy would have been true. . . .

FAILURE OF FREE SOCIETY AND RISE OF SOCIALISM
The advocates of universal liberty concede that the laboring class enjoy more material comfort, are better fed, clothed, and housed as slaves than as freemen. The statistics of crime demonstrate that the moral superiority of the slave over the free laborer is still greater than his superiority in animal well-being. There never can be among slaves a class so degraded as is found about the wharves and

23

suburbs of cities. The master requires and enforces ordinary morality and industry. We very much fear, if it were possible to indite a faithful comparison of the conduct and comfort of our free Negroes with that of the runaway Anglo-Saxon serfs, that it would be found that the Negroes have fared better and committed much less crime than the whites. . . .

How slavery could degrade men lower than universal liberty has done, it is hard to conceive; how it did and would again preserve them from such degradation is well explained by those who are loudest in its abuse. A consciousness of security, a full comprehension of his position, and a confidence in that position, and the absence of all corroding cares and anxieties, make the slave easy and self-assured in his address, cheerful, happy, and contented, free from jealousy, malignity, and envy, and at peace with all around him. His attachment to his master begets the sentiment of loyalty than which none more purifies and elevates human nature. . . .

The free laborer rarely has a house and home of his own; he is insecure of employment; sickness may overtake him at any time and deprive him of the means of support; old age is certain to overtake him, if he lives, and generally finds him without the means of subsistence; his family is probably increasing in numbers and is helpless and burdensome to him. In all this there is little to incite to virtue, much to tempt to crime, nothing to afford happiness, but quite enough to inflict misery. Man must be more than human to acquire a pure and a high morality under such circumstances.

In free society the sentiments, principles, feelings and affections of high and low, rich and poor, are equally blunted and debased by the continual war of competition. It begets rivalries, jealousies, and hatred on all hands. The poor can neither love nor respect the rich, who, instead of aiding and protecting them, are endeavoring to cheapen their labor and take away their means of subsistence. The rich can hardly respect themselves, when they reflect that wealth is the result of avarice, caution, circumspection, and hard dealing. These are the virtues which free society in its regular operation brings forth. Its moral influence is therefore no better on the rich than on the poor. The number of laborers being excessive in all old countries, they are continually struggling with, scandalizing, and underbidding each other to get places and employment.

24

Every circumstance in the poor man's situation in free society is one of harassing care, of grievous temptation, and of excitement to anger, envy, jealousy, and malignity. That so many of the poor should nevertheless be good and pure, kind, happy, and high-minded is proof enough that the poor class is not the worst class in society. But the rich have their temptations, too. Capital gives them the power to oppress, selfishness offers the inducement, and political economy, the moral guide of the day, would justify the oppression. Yet there are thousands of noble and generous and disinterested men in free society who employ their wealth to relieve and not to oppress the poor. Still, these are exceptions to the general rule. The effect of such society is to encourage the oppression of the poor. . . .

Liberty places those classes in positions of antagonism and war. Slavery identifies the interests of rich and poor, master and slave, and begets domestic affection on the one side and loyalty and respect on the other. Young England sees clearly enough the character of the disease but is not bold enough to propose an adequate remedy.

The poor themselves are all practical Socialists and in some degree pro-slavery men. They unite in strikes and trade unions and thus exchange a part of their liberties in order to secure high and uniform wages. The exchange is a prudent and sensible one; but they who have bartered off liberty are fast verging toward slavery. Slavery to an association is not always better than slavery to a single master. The professed object is to avoid ruinous underbidding and competition with one another; but this competition can never cease while liberty lasts. Those who wish to be free must take liberty with this inseparable burden.

Odd Fellows' societies, temperance societies, and all other societies that provide for sick and unfortunate members are instances of socialism. The muse in England for many years has been busy in composing dissonant laborer songs, bewailing the hardships, penury, and sufferings of the poor, and indignantly rebuking the cruelty and injustice of their hardhearted and closefisted employers. . . .

A well-conducted farm in the South is a model of associated labor that Fourier might envy. One old woman nurses all the children while the mothers are at work; another waits on the sick, in a house set aside for them; another washes and cooks; and a fourth makes and mends the clothing. It is a great economy of labor and is a good idea of the Socialists.

Slavery protects the infants, the aged, and the sick; nay, takes far better care of them than of the healthy, the middle-aged, and the strong. They are part of the family, and self-interest and domestic affection combine to shelter, shield, and foster them. A man loves not only his horses and his cattle, which are useful to him, but he loves his dog, which is of no use. He loves them because they are his. What a wise and beneficent provision of Heaven that makes the selfishness of man's nature a protecting aegis to shield and defend wife and children, slaves, and even dumb animals. The Socialists propose to reach this result too, but they never can if they refuse to march in the only road Providence has pointed out. Who will check, govern, and control their superintending authority? Who prevent his abuse of power? Who can make him kind, tender, and affectionate to the poor, aged, helpless, sick, and unfortunate? *Qui custodiat [ipsos] custodes?* [Who is to guard the guards?]

Nature establishes the only safe and reliable checks and balances in government. . . .

Socialism proposes to do away with free competition; to afford protection and support at all times to the laboring class; to bring about, at least, a qualified community of property and to associate labor. All these purposes slavery fully and perfectly attains. . . .

NEGRO SLAVERY
It is clear the Athenian Democracy would not suit a Negro nation, nor will the government of mere law suffice for the individual Negro. He is but a grown-up child, and must be governed as a child, not as a lunatic or criminal. The master occupies towards him the place of parent or guardian. We shall not dwell on this view, for no one will differ with us who thinks as we do of the Negro's capacity, and we might argue till doomsday, in vain, with those who have a high opinion of the Negro's moral and intellectual capacity.

Second, the Negro is improvident; will not lay up in summer for the wants of winter; will not accumulate in youth for the exigencies of age. He would become an insufferable burden to society. Society

26

has the right to prevent this, and can only do so by subjecting him to domestic slavery.

In the last place, the Negro race is inferior to the white race, and living in their midst, they would be far outstripped or outwitted in the chase of free competition. Gradual but certain extermination would be their fate. We presume the maddest abolitionist does not think the Negro's providence of habits and moneymaking capacity at all to compare to those of the whites. This defect of character would alone justify enslaving him, if he is to remain here. In Africa or the West Indies, he would become idolatrous, savage and cannibal, or be devoured by savages and cannibals. At the North he would freeze or starve.

We would remind those who deprecate and sympathize with Negro slavery, that his slavery here relieves him from a far more cruel slavery in Africa, or from idolatry and cannibalism, and every brutal vice and crime that can disgrace humanity; and that it Christianizes, protects, supports, and civilizes him; that it governs him far better than free laborers at the North are governed. There, wife-murder has become a mere holiday pastime; and where so many wives are murdered, almost all must be brutally treated. Nay, more, men who kill their wives or treat them brutally must be ready for all kinds of crime, and the calendar of crime at the North proves the inference to be correct. Negroes never kill their wives. If it be objected that legally they have no wives, then we reply that in an experience of more than forty years, we have never yet heard of a Negro man killing a Negro woman. Our Negroes are not only better off as to physical comfort than free laborers, but their moral condition is better. . . .

Negro slavery would be changed immediately to some form of peonage, serfdom, or villeinage, if the Negroes were sufficiently intelligent and provident to manage a farm. No one would have the labor and trouble of management, if his Negroes would pay in hires and rents one-half what free tenants pay in rent in Europe. Every Negro in the South would be soon liberated, if he would take liberty on the terms that white tenants hold it. The fact that he cannot enjoy liberty on such terms seems conclusive that he is only fit to be a slave.

But for the assaults of the abolitionists, much would have been done ere this to regulate and improve Southern slavery. Our Negro mechanics do not work so hard, have many more privileges and holidays, and are better fed and clothed than field hands, and are yet more valuable to their masters. The slaves of the South are cheated of their rights by the purchase of Northern manufactures which they could produce. Besides, if we would employ our slaves in the coarser processes of the mechanic arts and manufactures, such as brick making, getting and hewing timber for ships and houses, iron mining and smelting, coal mining, grading railroads and plank roads, in the manufacture of cotton, tobacco, etc., we would find a vent in new employments for their increase, more humane and more profitable than the vent afforded by new states and territories. The nice and finishing processes of manufactures and mechanics should be reserved for the whites, who only are fitted for them, and thus, by diversifying pursuits and cutting off dependence on the North, we might benefit and advance the interests of our whole population. Exclusive agriculture has depressed and impoverished the South. We will not here dilate on this topic, because we intend to make it the subject of a separate essay. Free trade doctrines, not slavery, have made the South agricultural and dependent, given her a sparse and ignorant population, ruined her cities, and expelled her people.

Would the abolitionists approve of a system of society that set white children free, and remitted them at the age of fourteen, males and females, to all the rights, both as to person and property, which belong to adults? Would it be criminal or praiseworthy to do so? Criminal, of course. Now, are the average of Negroes equal in information, in native intelligence, in prudence or providence, to well-informed white children of fourteen? We who have lived with them for forty years think not. The competition of the world would be too much for the children. They would be cheated out of their property and debased in their morals. Yet they would meet everywhere with sympathizing friends of their own color, ready to aid, advise, and assist them. The Negro would be exposed to the same competition and greater temptations, with no greater ability to contend with them, with these additional difficulties. He would be welcome nowhere; meet with thousands of enemies and no friends.

28

If he went North, the white laborers would kick him and cuff him, and drive him out of employment; if he went to Africa, the savages would cook him and eat him. If he went to the West Indies, they would not let him in, or if they did, they would soon make of him a savage and idolator.

We have a further question to ask. If it be right and incumbent to subject children to the authority of parents and guardians, and idiots and lunatics to committees, would it not be equally right and incumbent to give the free Negroes masters, until at least they arrive at years of discretion, which very few ever did or will attain? What is the difference between the authority of a parent and of a master? Neither pay wages, and each is entitled to the services of those subject to him. The father may not sell his child forever, but may hire him out till he is twenty-one. The free Negro's master may also be restrained from selling. Let him stand in *loco parentis*, and call him papa instead of master. Look closely into slavery, and you will see nothing so hideous in it, or if you do, you will find plenty of it at home in its most hideous form. . . .

But far the worst feature of modern civilization, which is the civilization of free society, remains to be exposed. While labor-saving processes have probably lessened by one half, in the last century, the amount of work needed for comfortable support, the free laborer is compelled by capital and competition to work more than he ever did before, and is less comfortable. The organization of society cheats him of his earnings and those earnings go to swell the vulgar pomp and pageantry of the ignorant millionaires, who are the only great of the present day. These reflections might seem, at first view, to have little connection with Negro slavery; but it is well for us of the South not to be deceived by the tinsel glare and glitter of free society, and to employ ourselves in doing our duty at home, and studying the past, rather than in insidious rivalry of the expensive pleasures and pursuits of men whose sentiments and whose aims are low, sensual, and groveling.

Human progress consisting in moral and intellectual improvement, and there being no agreed and conventional standard weights or measures of moral and intellectual qualities and quantities, the question of progress can never be accurately decided. We maintain that man has not improved, because in all save the mechanic arts

29

he reverts to the distant past for models to imitate, and he never imitates what he can excel. . . .

We abhor the doctrine of the *Types of Mankind;* first, because it is at war with Scripture, which teaches us that the whole human race is descended from a common parentage; and, second, because it encourages and incites brutal masters to treat Negroes, not as weak, ignorant, and dependent brethren, but as wicked beasts, without the pale of humanity. The Southerner is the Negro's friend, his only friend. Let no intermeddling Abolitionist, no refined philosophy, dissolve this friendship.

THE ASSOCIATION OF LABOR

If the Socialists had done no other good, they would be entitled to the gratitude of mankind for displaying in a strong light the advantages of the association of labor. Adam Smith, in his elaborate treatise on the "Division of Labor," nearly stumbled on the same truth. But the division of labor is a curse to the laborer, without the association of labor. Division makes labor ten times more efficient, but, by confining each workman to some simple, monotonous employment, it makes him a mere automaton and an easy prey to the capitalist. The association of labor, like all association, requires a head or ruler, and that head or ruler will become a cheat and a tyrant unless his interests are identified with the interests of the laborer. In a large factory, in free society, there is division of labor, and association too, but association and division for the benefit of the employer and to the detriment of the laborer.

On a large farm whatever advances the health, happiness, and morals of the Negroes renders them more prolific and valuable to their master. It is his interest to pay them high wages in way of support, and he can afford to do so, because association renders the labor of each slave five times as productive and efficient as it would be, were the slaves working separately. One man could not enclose an acre of land, cultivate it, send his crops to market, do his own cooking, washing, and mending. One man may live as a prowling beast of prey but not as a civilized being. One hundred human beings, men, women, and children, associated, will cultivate ten acres of land each, enclose it, and carry on every other operation of civilized life. Labor becomes at least twenty times as productive when a hundred associate as when one acts alone. The same is as true in other pursuits as in farming. But in free society the employer robs the laborer, and he is no better off than the prowling savage, although he might live in splendor if he got a fair proportion of the proceeds of his own labor.

We have endeavored to show, heretofore, that the Negro slave, considering his indolence and unskillfulness, often gets his fair share, and sometimes more than his share of the profits of the farm and is exempted, besides, from the harassing cares and anxieties of the free laborer. Grant, however, that the Negro does not receive adequate wages from his master, yet all admit that in the aggregate the Negroes get better wages than free laborers; therefore, it follows that, with all its imperfections, slave society is the best form of society yet devised for the masses. When Socialists and Abolitionists, by full and fair experiments, exhibit a better, it will be time to agitate the subject of abolition.

The industrial products of black slave labor have been far greater and more useful to mankind than those of the same amount of any other labor. In a very short period the South and Southwest have been settled, cleared, fenced in, and put in cultivation by what were, a century ago, a handful of masters and slaves. This region now feeds and clothes a great part of mankind; but free trade cheats them of the profits of their labor. In the vast amount of our industrial products, we see the advantages of association; in our comparative poverty, the evils of free trade.

DECLARATION OF INDEPENDENCE AND VIRGINIA BILL OF RIGHTS

It is, we believe, conceded on all hands that men are not born physically, morally, or intellectually equal; some are males, some females, some from birth, large, strong, and healthy, others weak, small, and sickly; some are naturally amiable, others prone to all kinds of wickedness; some brave, others timid. Their natural inequalities beget inequalities of rights. The weak in mind or body require guidance, support, and protection; they must obey and work for those who protect and guide them; they have a natural right to guardians, committees, teachers, or masters. Nature has made them slaves; all that law and government can do is to regulate, modify, and mitigate their slavery. In the absence of legally insti-

31

tuted slavery, their condition would be worse under that natural slavery of the weak to the strong, the foolish to the wise and cunning.

The wise and virtuous, the brave, the strong in mind and body, are by nature born to command and protect, and law but follows nature in making them rulers, legislators, judges, captains, husbands, guardians, committees, and masters. The naturally depraved class, those born prone to crime, are our brethren too; they are entitled to education, to religious instruction, to all the means and appliances proper to correct their evil propensities, and all their failings; they have a right to be sent to the penitentiary, for there, if they do not reform, they cannot at least disturb society. Our feelings and our consciences teach us that nothing but necessity can justify taking human life.

We are but stringing together truisms which everybody knows as well as ourselves, and yet, if men are created unequal in all these respects, what truth or what meaning is there in the passage under consideration? Men are not created or born equal, and circumstances and education and association tend to increase and aggravate inequalities among them from generation to generation. Generally, the rich associate and intermarry with each other, the poor do the same; the ignorant rarely associate with or intermarry with the learned; and all society shuns contact with the criminal, even to the third and fourth generations.

Men are not "born entitled to equal rights!" It would be far nearer the truth to say that "some were born with saddles on their backs, and others booted and spurred to ride them"—and the riding does them good. They need the reins, the bit, and the spur. No two men by nature are exactly equal or exactly alike. No institutions can prevent the few from acquiring rule and ascendancy over the many. Liberty and free competition invite and encourage the attempt of the strong to master the weak and insure their success. . . .

Property is not a natural and divine but conventional right; it is the mere creature of society and law. In this all lawyers and publicists agree. In this country the history of property is of such recent date that the simplest and most ignorant man must know that it commenced in wrong, injustice, and violence a few generations ago and derives its only title now from the will of society through the

32

sanction of law. Society has no right, because it is not expedient, to resume any one man's property because he abuses its possession and does not so employ it as to redound to public advantage; but if all private property, or if private property generally were so used as to injure, instead of promote public good, then society might and ought to destroy the whole institution.

From these premises it follows that government, in taxing private property, should only be limited by the public good. If the tax be so heavy as to deter the owner from improving the property, then, in general, will the whole public be injured.

False notions of the right of property and of the duties and liabilities of property-holders, destroy all public spirit and patriotism, cripple and injure, and prevent the growth and development of the South.

FREDERICK LAW OLMSTED
King Cotton and His Subjects

Landscape artist and city planner Frederick Law Olmsted was first encouraged to tour the slave states by a conversation with William Lloyd Garrison. In 1852 he began what was to be the first of three journeys through the South. His letters were printed serially in the New-York Daily Times, whose editor, Henry J. Raymond, had commissioned the trip. The reports of the three tours, later condensed and published as The Cotton Kingdom (1861), have been acclaimed as the most accurate and unprejudiced account of the region before the Civil War. The following article of January 12, 1854, was one of the last written by Olmsted during his first trip. It was titled "Slavery in its Effects on Character, and the Social Relations of the Master Class," and was not included in his book.

The wealthy and educated, and especially the fashionable people of all civilized countries, are now so nearly alike in their ordinary manners and customs that the observations of a passing traveler upon them must commonly be of much too superficial a character to

33

warrant him in deducing from them, with confidence, any important conclusions. I have spent an evening at the plantation residence of a gentleman in Louisiana, in which there was very little in the conversation or customs and manners of the family to distinguish them from others whom I have visited in Massachusetts, England, and Germany. I shall, therefore, undertake with diffidence to describe certain apparently general and fundamental peculiarities of character in the people, which it is a part of my duty to notice, from their importance with reference to the condition and prospects of the slave states and their institution.

Slavery exerts an immense quiet influence upon the character of the master, and the condition of the slave is greatly affected by the modifications of character thus effected. I do not believe there are any other people in the world with whom the Negro would be as contented and, if contentment is happiness, so happy as with those who are now his masters. The hopeless perpetuation of such an intolerable nuisance as this labor system, it is, however, also apparent, depends mainly upon the careless, temporizing, shiftless disposition to which the Negro is indebted for this mitigation of the natural wretchedness of slavery.

The calculating, indefatigable New Englander, the go-ahead Western man, the exact and stern Englishman, the active Frenchman, the studious, observing, economical German would all and each lose patience with the frequent disobedience and the constant indolence, forgetfulness, and carelessness, and the blundering, awkward, brutelike manner of work of the plantation slave.

The Southerner, if he sees anything of it, generally disregards it and neglects to punish it. Although he is naturally excitable and passionate, he is less subject to impatience and passionate anger with the slave than is, I believe, generally supposed, because he is habituated to regard him so completely as his inferior dependent and subject. For the same reason, his anger, when aroused, is usually easily and quickly appeased, and he forgives him readily and entirely, as we do a child or a dog who has annoyed us. And, in general, the relation of master and slave on small farms, and the relations of the family and its household servants everywhere, may be considered a happy one, developing, at the expense of decision, energy, self-reliance, and self-control, some of the most beautiful

34

traits of human nature. But it is a great error—although one nearly universal with Southerners themselves—to judge of slavery by the light alone of the master's fireside.

The direct influence of slavery is, I think, to make the Southerner indifferent to small things; in some relations, we should say rightly, superior to small things; prodigal, improvident, and ostentatiously generous. His ordinarily uncontrolled authority (and from infancy the Southerner is more free from control, in all respects, I should judge, than any other person in the world) leads him to be habitually impulsive, impetuous, and enthusiastic; gives him self-respect and dignity of character; and makes him bold, confident, and true. Yet it has not appeared to me that the Southerner was frank as he is, I believe, commonly thought to be. He seems to me to be very secretive, or at least reserved, on topics which most nearly concern himself. He minds his own business and lets alone that of others, not in the English way but in a way peculiarly his own; resulting partly, perhaps, from want of curiosity, in part from habits formed by such constant intercourse as he has with his inferiors (Negroes), and partly from the caution in conversation which the "rules of honor" are calculated to give.

Not, I said, in the English way, because he meets a stranger easily and without timidity or thought of how he is himself appearing, and is ready and usually accomplished in conversation. He is much given to vague and careless generalization, and greatly disinclined to exact and careful reasoning. He follows his natural impulses nobly, has nothing to be ashamed of, and is, therefore, habitually truthful; but his carelessness, impulsiveness, vagueness, and want of exactness in everything make him speak from his mouth that which is in point of fact untrue, rather more often than anyone else.

From early intimacy with the Negro (an association fruitful in other respects of evil) he has acquired much of his ready, artless, and superficial benevolence, good nature, and geniality. The comparatively solitary nature and somewhat monotonous duties of plantation life make guests usually exceedingly welcome, while the abundance of servants at command and other circumstances make the ordinary duties of hospitality very light. The Southerner, however, is greatly wanting in hospitality of mind, closing his doors to

35

all opinions and schemes to which he has been bred a stranger, with a contempt and bigotry which sometimes seem incompatible with his character as a gentleman. He has a large but unexpansive mind.

The Southerner has no pleasure in labor except with reference to a result. He enjoys life itself. He is content with being. Here is the grand distinction between him and the Northerner; for the Northerner enjoys progress in itself. He finds his happiness in doing. Rest, in itself, is irksome and offensive to him, and however graceful or beatific that rest may be, he values it only with reference to the power of future progress it will bring him. Heaven itself will be dull and stupid to him if there is no work to be done in it—nothing to struggle for—if he reaches perfection at a jump and has no chance to make an improvement.

The Southerner cares for the end only; he is impatient of the means. He is passionate and labors passionately, fitfully, with the energy and strength of anger rather than of resolute will. He fights rather than works to carry his purpose. He has the intensity of character which belongs to Americans in general, and therefore enjoys excitement and is fond of novelty. But he has much less curiosity than the Northerner; less originating genius, less inventive talent, less patient and persevering energy. And I think this all comes from his want of aptitude for close observation and his dislike for application to small details. And this, I think, may be reasonably supposed to be mainly the result of habitually leaving all matters not either of grand and exciting importance, or of immediate consequence to his comfort, to his slaves, and of being accustomed to see them slighted or neglected as much as he will, in his indolence, allow them to be by them.

Of course, I have been speaking of the general tendencies only of character in the North and the South. There are individuals in both communities in whom these extreme characteristics are reversed, as there are graceful Englishmen and awkward Frenchmen. There are, also, in each, those in whom they are more or less harmoniously blended. Those in whom they are the most enviably so—the happiest and the most useful in the social sphere—are equally common, so far as I know, in both; and the grand distinction remains in the mass—manifesting itself, by strikingly contrasting symptoms, in our religion, politics, and social life.

36

In no way more than this: The South endeavors to close its eyes to every evil the removal of which will require self-denial, labor, and skill. If, however, an evil is too glaring to be passed by unnoticed, it is immediately declared to be constitutional, or providential, and its removal is declared to be either treasonable or impious—usually both; and, what is worse, it is improper, impolite, ungentlemanly, unmanlike. And so it is ended at the South. But at the North this sort of opposition only serves to develop the reform by ridding it of useless weight and drapery.

Northern social life usually leaves a rather melancholy and disagreeable feeling upon the minds of our Southern friends, as many have confessed to me. I think the different tendency of life at the North from that of existence at the South, which I have asserted, will give a key to this unfavorable impression which the Southerner obtains of our social character.

The people of the North are generally well aware of their social deficiencies, and of the unfitness of many of the customs and mannerisms, required by conventional politeness, to their character and duties. A man comes to our house, and custom requires that our countenance should brighten and that we should say we are glad to see him. This custom makes it unkind in us toward him not to do so. We have no unkindness in our hearts to the man, but entirely the contrary; yet it happens that we are not glad to see him, and such is our constitution that we have no impulsive and natural brightening up under hardly any circumstances. Now we have to choose between a forced, artificial, formal, and false expression of a true kindness and truth and simplicity. Amiable people take sides with kindness; the silent and reliable sort, with truth. Each are constantly aware, to a greater or less degree, of the difficulty they are engaged with. Some attach an absurd importance to the value of expression and become "affected"; others rebel against the falseness of the conventional forms of expression and become supercilious or sour and forbidding. Both classes are constantly led to make awkward attempts to compromise their quarrel with themselves.

The Southerner can understand nothing of all this. He naturally accepts the institutions, manners, and customs in which he is educated as necessities imposed upon him by Providence. He is loyal to "society," and it is opposed to his fundamental idea of a

37

gentleman to essentially deduct from them or add to them. This "clothes philosophy" of the North he does not in the least comprehend, or, if he does, he sees nothing in it but impudent and vulgar quackery. And yet I think there is, perhaps, good to come out of it. We believe not, in our day, in good William of Wickham's maxim. This new democratic man is not "made of manners"; it may be best he should make manners to suit himself. Between this slavish conformity and anarchical nonconformity, it is to be hoped that the good sense of our society is drifting toward both a nobler and a happier social life.

But, at the present, the social intercourse of the wealthy people of the South is certainly more agreeable, rational, and to be respected than that of the nearest corresponding class at the North. I should be sorry to think this the highest compliment it deserved.

The wealthy class is the commanding class in most districts of the South and gives character to all the slaveholding class. Wealth is less distributed and is more retained in families at the South than the North. With the slaveholding class there is a pride of birth and social position, much more than in any class at the North. This affects the character and conduct of individuals, and reacts on their associates and on the whole community—in some respects perniciously, but in many respects favorably.

The "high-toned gentleman" (a Southern expression) of the South is rare at the North. He is not an article of city manufacture, as the most cultivated people of the North are. He has a peculiar character and peculiar habits—more like those of the "old English gentleman" than any class to be found now, perhaps, even in England itself. He rides much, and hunts, and is given to field sports, and never knows the want of oxygen; for, even in winter, his windows and doors are always forgotten to be closed. Accordingly, though his diet is detestable, he is generally well physically developed—lighter and more delicate of frame than the English squires, but tall and sinewy. His face would commonly be handsome but that his mouth is made gross, lifeless, and inexpressive by his habit of using tobacco excessively. He has a peculiar pride and romance, and, though he often appears laughably quixotic, he is, in the best sense of the word, also chivalrous. He is brave and magnanimous, courteous and polite to all white people.

If he often values his comfort, or the success of his designs, or the gratification of his passions more than he does a strict adherence to the received rules of Christian morality, he never values life or aught else more than he does his honor. This "honor" — though if you analyze it, it comes to be little else than a conventional standard of feelings and actions, which must be habitual to entitle a man to consider himself a gentleman — is often really far nobler, and makes a nobler man than what often passes for religion at the North, at least in this world.

There is, however, a quality, or perhaps it is a faculty of the soul, which is distinct, though seldom separate, from love to the person of God and love to man, or in our time from the Christian faith, which is most nearly defined by the term "an enlightened conscience" — a spontaneous requisite perception and loyal love of the fundamental laws of right — the laws that God himself is subject to. This quality or faculty is the noblest endowment of man and is essential to the noblest character. I think it is strongly developed in more individuals at the North than at the South, and I think there are obvious causes for its absence at the South. The habitual reference of the Southerner in his judgment of conduct, whether of himself or another, whether past or contemplated, to the conventional standard of honor prevents the ascendancy of a higher standard. This habitual contemplation of a relation so essentially wrong as that of slavery, as a permanent and necessary one not reformable, not in progress of removal and abolition, destroys or prevents the development of his sense of any standard of right and wrong above a mere code of laws or conventional rules.

But to the Southern gentleman (by distinction), as I have often met him, I wish to pay great respect. The honest and unstudied dignity of character, the generosity and the real nobleness of habitual impulses, and the well-bred, manly courtesy which distinguish him in all the relations and occupations of life, equally in his business, in his family, and in general society, are sadly rare at the North — much more rare at the North than at the South. I acknowledge it freely but with deep regret and melancholy. There are qualities of character (not of deportment, merely) which are common among the planters of many parts of the South, as they are among the aristocratic classes of Europe, which are incompatible with the possession of nothing else that a man should glory in, which the mass of the people of the North have nearly lost or have failed to gain.

This has been often observed by intelligent travelers visiting us, and is sometimes thought sufficient to condemn our democratic form of government and our approximately democratic state of society. This is the judgment of many Southerners (for the government and society of the South is the most essentially aristocratic in the world), and I have reason to believe that there are many whose confidence in the democracy of the North is so small that they anticipate, and are acting politically with reference to, a division of the present Union and the formation of another great Southern republic—that is, a republic of white capitalists, in which the slavery of the working classes shall be provided for and every means taken to make it complete and permanent.

But acknowledging the rarity of the thoroughbred gentleman at the North: Is an inference to be drawn from it unfavorable to democratic institutions? I think not. Without regard to the future and to what we may yet become under democracy, the condition and character of our people as a whole, to the best of my judgment, is better, more gentlemanly even, far more entitled to respect than that of the people, including all classes, of any other nation. Very much more so than of those of the South. I do not say more happy. The people of the Northern states, as a whole, probably enjoy life less than any other civilized people. Perhaps it would be equally true to add—or than any uncivilized people. Those who consider that, if so, the uncivilized people (perchance slaves) are to be envied will do right to condemn democracy.

But the only conclusion which the fact seems to me to suggest, with regard to our democratic government, is perhaps this: that simple protection to capital and letting alone to native genius and talent is not the whole duty of government; possibly that patent laws and the common schools, with their common teachers and common instruction (not education) such as our institutions as yet give to the people, are not enough. That the esthetic faculties need to be educated—drawn out; that taste and refinement need to be encouraged as well as the useful arts. That there need to be places and time for reunions, which shall be so attractive to the nature of

all but the most depraved men, that the rich and the poor, the cultivated and well-bred, and the sturdy and self-made people shall be
attached together and encouraged to assimilate.

I think there is no sufficient reason why the aid of the state
should not be given to assist corporations and voluntary associations for such purposes, on the same principle and with the same
restrictions that it is in New York to schools, to colleges, and to
agricultural societies. Thus, I think, with a necessity for scarcely
any additional governmental offices, or increase of the friction of
governmental machinery, might be encouraged and sustained, at
points so frequent and convenient that they would exert an elevating influence upon all the people, public parks and gardens,
galleries of art and instruction in art, music, athletic sports, and
healthful recreations, and other means of cultivating taste and
lessening the excessive materialism of purpose in which we are, as
a people, so cursedly absorbed that even the natural capacity for
domestic happiness and, more obviously, for the enjoyment of
simple and sensible social life in our community seems likely to be
entirely destroyed. The enemies of democracy could bring no charge
more severe against it than that such is its tendency, and that it has
no means of counteracting it.

Slavery is claimed at the South to be the remedy for this evil. In
some respects it is a remedy. But (disregarding the slaves and the
poor whites) where there is one true gentleman, and to be respected,
at the South, there are two whose whole life seems to be absorbed in
sensualism and sickly excitements. Everywhere you meet them,
well dressed and spending money freely, constantly drinking, smoking, and chewing; cardplaying and betting; and unable to converse
upon anything that is not either grossly sensual or exciting, such as
street rencounters, filibustering schemes, or projects of disunion or
war. These persons are, however, gentlemen in the sense that they
are familiar with the forms and usages of the best society, that they
are deferential to women, and that (except in money matters) their
word is to be implicitly relied upon. They far exceed in numbers any
class of at all similar habits that we yet have at the North.

They are invariably politicians, and they generally rule in all
political conventions and caucuses. They are brave in the sense that
they are reckless of life, and they are exceedingly fond of the excite-

ment of the hazard of life. They are as careless of the life of others as of themselves. They are especially ambitious of military renown, and in the Mexican War they volunteered almost to a man, many of those who went as privates taking with them several Negro servants. If they were not dependent on the price of cotton for the means of their idleness, they would keep the country incessantly at war. Being so, however, they are as conservative in the policy they favor toward any powerful nation as the cotton lords of England or the landlords of Austria. They hate and despise the democrats of Europe as much as Francis Joseph himself. They glorify Napoleon, and they boast of the contempt with which they were able to treat the humbug Kossuth.

They call themselves Democrats, and sometimes Democratic Whigs. Call them what you will, they are a mischievous class – the dangerous class at present of the United States. They are not the legitimate offspring of democracy, thanks to God, but of slavery under a democracy.

RICHARD BAKER

The Crime of Mrs. Douglass in Teaching Colored Children to Read

Except for the most elementary religious instruction, all education in the Southern states was forbidden to slaves. In Virginia it was also unlawful for any white person to assemble even free Negroes for educational purposes. In 1853 Mrs. Margaret Douglass was arrested for teaching free Negro children to read and write in Norfolk. She was tried and convicted of the offense before the Circuit Court of Norfolk in November 1853. Although the jury fixed a nominal fine of one dollar, this was overruled by Judge Richard Baker on January 10,1854. Mrs. Douglass spent one month in prison. [Source: American State Trials, John D. Lawson, ed., Vol. VII, St. Louis, 1917, pp. 56-60.]

42

Upon an indictment found against you for assembling with Negroes to instruct them to read and write, and for associating with them in an unlawful assembly, you were found guilty, and a mere nominal fine imposed, on the last day of this court held in the month of November.

At the time the jury came in and rendered their verdict, you were not in court, and the court, being about to adjourn for the purpose of attending to other official duties in a distant part of the state, it was necessary and proper, under the law, to award a *capias* against you, returnable to the present adjourned term, so that the judgment and sentence of the law may be fulfilled. The court is not called on to vindicate the policy of the law in question, for so long as it remains upon the statute book, and unrepealed, public and private justice and morality require that it should be respected and sustained.

There are persons, I believe, in our community opposed to the policy of the law in question. They profess to believe that universal intellectual culture is necessary to religious instruction and education, and that such culture is suitable to a state of slavery, and there can be no misapprehension as to your opinions on this subject, judging from the indiscreet freedom with which you spoke of your regard for the colored race in general. Such opinions in the present state of our society I regard as manifestly mischievous.

It is not true that our slaves cannot be taught religious and moral duty without being able to read the Bible and use the pen. Intellectual and religious instruction often go hand in hand, but the latter may well exist without the former; and the truth of this is abundantly vindicated by the well-known fact that in many parts of our own commonwealth, as in other parts of the country in which among the whites one-fourth or more are entirely without a knowledge of letters, respect for the law, and for moral and religious conduct and behavior, are justly and properly appreciated and practised.

A valuable report, or document, recently published in the city of New York by the Southern Aid Society sets forth many valuable and important truths upon the condition of the Southern slaves, and the utility of moral and religious instruction, apart from a knowledge of books. I recommend the careful perusal of it to all whose opinions concur with your own. It shows that a system of catechetical instruction, with a clear and simple exposition of Scripture, has been employed with gratifying success; that the slave population of the South are peculiarly susceptible of good religious influences. Their mere residence among a Christian people has wrought a great and happy change in their condition: they have been raised from the night of heathenism to the light of Christianity, and thousands of them have been brought to a saving knowledge of the Gospel.

Of the 100 million of the Negro race, there cannot be found another so large a body as the 3 million slaves in the United States, at once so intelligent, so inclined to the Gospel, and so blessed by the elevating influence of civilization and Christianity. Occasional instances of cruelty and oppression, it is true, may sometimes occur, and probably will ever continue to take place under any system of laws; but this is not confined to wrongs committed upon the Negro. Wrongs are committed and cruelly practised in a like degree by the lawless white man upon his own color; and while the Negroes of our town and state are known to be surrounded by most of the substantial comforts of life, and invited both by precept and example to participate in proper moral and religious duties, it argues, it seems to me, a sickly sensibility toward them to say their persons, and feelings, and interests are not sufficiently respected by our laws, which, in effect, tend to nullify the act of our legislature passed for the security and protection of their masters.

The law under which you have been tried and found guilty is not to be found among the original enactments of our legislature. The first legislative provision upon this subject was introduced in the year 1831, immediately succeeding the bloody scenes of the memorable Southampton insurrection; and that law, being found not sufficiently penal to check the wrongs complained of, was reenacted with additional penalties in the year 1848, which last mentioned act, after several years' trial and experience, has been reaffirmed by adoption and incorporated into our present code.

After these several and repeated recognitions of the wisdom and propriety of the said act, it may well be said that bold and open opposition to it is a matter not to be slightly regarded, especially as we have reason to believe that every Southern slave state in our country, as a measure of self-preservation and protection, has

44

deemed it wise and just to adopt laws with similar provisions. There might have been no occasion for such enactments in Virginia, or elsewhere, on the subject of Negro education but as a matter of self-defense against the schemes of Northern incendiaries and the outcry against holding our slaves in bondage.

Many now living well remember how and when and why the antislavery fury began, and by what means its manifestations were made public. Our mails were clogged with Abolition pamphlets and inflammatory documents, to be distributed among our Southern Negroes to induce them to cut our throats. Sometimes, it may be, these libelous documents were distributed by Northern citizens professing Southern feelings, and at other times by Southern people professing Northern feelings. These, however, were not the only means resorted to by the Northern fanatics to stir up insubordination among our slaves. They scattered, far and near, pocket handkerchiefs and other similar articles, with frightful engravings and printed over with antislavery nonsense, with the view to work upon the feeling and ignorance of our Negroes, who otherwise would have remained comfortable and happy. Under such circumstances there was but one measure of protection for the South, and that was adopted.

Teaching the Negroes to read and write is made penal by the laws of our state. The act imposes a fine not exceeding $100, to be ascertained by the jury, and imprisonment not exceeding six months, to be fixed and ascertained by the court. And, now, since the jury in your case has in my opinion properly settled the question of guilt, it devolves on me, under the law, to ascertain and decide upon the quantum of imprisonment under the circumstances of your trial; and I exceedingly regret that, in being called on for the first time to act under the law in question, it becomes my duty to impose the required punishment upon a female, apparently of fair and respectable standing in the community. The only mitigating circumstances in your case, if in truth there be any, according to my best reason and understanding of it, is that to which I have just referred, namely, you being a female.

Under the circumstances of this case, if you were of a different sex, I should regard the full punishment of six months' imprisonment as eminently just and proper. Had you taken the advice of

45

your friends and of the court and had employed counsel to defend you, your case, no doubt, would have been presented in a far more favorable light, both to the court and to the jury. The opinions you advanced, and the pertinacity and zeal you manifested in behalf of the Negroes, while they indicated perfect candor and sincerity on your part, satisfied the court, and must have satisfied all who heard you, that the act complained of was the settled and deliberate purpose of your mind, regardless of consequences, however dangerous to your peace.

In conformity with these views, I am impelled by a feeling of common honesty to say that this is not a case in which a mere formal judgment should be announced as the opinion of the court. Something more substantial under the circumstances of this case, I think, is demanded and required. The discretionary power to imprison for the term of six months or less, in good sense and sound morality, does not authorize a mere minimum punishment, such as imprisonment for a day or week, in a case in which the question of guilt is free from doubt, and there are many facts and circumstances of aggravation. A judgment of that sort, therefore, in this case, would doubtless be regarded by all true advocates of justice and law as mere mockery. It would be no terror to those who acknowledge no rule of action but their own evil will and pleasure, but would rather invite to still bolder incendiary movements.

For these reasons, as an example to all others in like cases disposed to offend, and in vindication of the policy and justness of our laws, which every individual should be taught to respect, the judgment of the court is, in addition to the proper fine and costs, that you be imprisoned for the period of one month in the jail of this city.

Plan for a Negro School

While Abolitionists were agitating for the freedom of slaves in the South, the free Negroes of the North were fighting another battle against civil and economic inequities. Several national Negro conventions were held prior to the Civil War. At a convention in Rochester, New York, July 6-8, 1853, a National Council of Colored People was formed as a permanent body to pursue equal rights for Negroes. The following report, emphasizing the Negro's need for training in manual labor, was submitted on July 8.
[Source: Proceedings of the National Colored Convention held in Rochester, July 6th, 7th and 8th, 1853, Rochester, 1853, pp. 30-33.]

The aim and the end of a right culture is primarily to develop power and to turn that power into a proper channel. Educational institutions ought therefore to be so modeled and so conducted as to draw out thought, incite useful inquiry, and give such aid and strength to the individual as will enable him to be something in the world, in addition to the mere scholar. Every person is here not merely to enjoy but to work; and schools are only valuable in their teachings as they assist in making both thinker and worker. They may saturate men with the learning of every age, yet, except they strive to make them something more than literary flowers, they sin greatly against the individual and humanity also. The hungry world asks for grain and those growths that give nutriment. Not by floral beauty is the physical being built up. Not by mere word study do the races grow intellectually strong. Not by eloquent, abstract preaching do the nations prove Christianity. The elements of truth, the principles of industrial advancement, of national greatness, that lie in questionable shapes amid the knowledge of the schools must be separated from the useless materials that surround them, and made as chyle to the human body, the givers of nutriment, the restorers of expended energy.

And as in the human body the richness of the digested food goes to make up bone, and muscle, and flesh, and the various tissues of vessels of the system, in like manner schools ought so to be fashioned as to deposit here and there, on the surface of society, artisan and merchant, mechanic and farmer, linguist and mathematician: mental power in every phase and practical science in as many as may be. The truth of this view is virtually acknowledged in part already. Where men know beforehand what kind of knowledge their duties in life will require, they avail themselves of institutions whose course of study is specific and well-digested. Hence exist our law schools, and military academies, and medical colleges. And these are necessary, even amid a class of people whose position enables them to make the most of a *general* course of study, by the application of some of the specialties of such course, to any avocation that in afterlife they may choose to pursue.

When *we* are called upon to consider the subject of education with reference to ourselves, and to ask what kind of an institution would best befit *us*, the answer comes in the light of the announced doctrine, namely, one that would develop *power;* and that kind of power most essential to our elevation. If after submitting to a general system of instruction, according to the provisions of the colleges of the land, *we* can add the store of knowledge gained to any pursuit in life *we* please, as so much starting capital, then we might not need to ask the establishing of institutions different from those already erected. But this is not the case. We have, indeed, a few literary colleges accessible to those of us who can pay; two manual labor colleges with the system partially carried out; besides an academy of the same kind established in southern Ohio.

Between these two varieties of schools, there need be no hesitation in deciding as to which is best adapted to our special wants. Under any circumstance, manual labor establishments commend themselves to the patronage of all classes. The long-entertained beliefs that mental effort may be made and continued without any reference to physical exercise are rapidly passing away. And with them, also, those more injurious and unfriendly views of true gentility and scholarship that hitherto have held labor in contempt. Literature has too long kept itself aloof from the furrowed field, and from the dust and bustle of the workshop. The pale, sickly brow and emaciated form have been falsely shown to the world as the ripeness of mental discipline; and sunburnt and brawny muscular arms have been among the majority of students synonymous with dullness of parts and ignorant vulgarity. Thanks, however, to true views of the dignity of human nature and an appreciation of the correct laws of physical development, labor has received the anointing of the highest refinement, and healthy frames are proven to be the best accompaniment to high intellectual power.

Moreover, with regard to ourselves, a consideration of our position in this country teaches us that our inheritance is one that can only be ameliorated by the combination of practical art with literary preparation. Hitherto our educated youth have found no corresponding channel to their academic equipment, and so they have failed to make their mark on society and the age. The workshops, as a general thing, are closed to them, while at the same time they are reproached for lack of inventive or industrial talent. We know that we cannot form an equally useful part of any people without the ability to contribute our full share to the wealth, activity, social comforts, and progress of such people. If, then, the necessary education to fit us to share in these responsibilities cannot be generally had, by reason of the prejudices of the country, where best they can be taught, namely in the workshops and countinghouses, and the other varied establishments of the land that have to do with the machinery of activities carried on around us; we must needs consider the importance of making our literary institutions contribute by a change of form to filling up this want in our midst.

The agricultural life, standing preeminent and looming in importance above all others, would demand a prominent place among the internal arrangements of such a school. Farming, as a scientific system, ought to be a part of the course of every scholar, and especially of that class of students whose highest interests would be benefited by leaving the cities for the freer and no less noble life in the country. No professorship in any college can claim more on the score of usefulness than that of agriculture. In none of the institutions thus far open to us has labor in this department been at all regulated on scientific principles.

Literary preparation has absorbed most of the attention of students because of the order and beauty infused into that phase of college life. The department of labor has ever remained crude and unseemly — subordinate in position and outline to the other, and therefore unable to provide that extensive field for industry as to warrant the title assumed by them of manual labor institutions. We make no complaint against the incompleteness of any of the existing schools in order to detract from their usefulness in other ways.

49

We only believe it desirable that a more thorough plan be established that will combine the literary course of the schools, scientific agricultural knowledge, theoretic mechanics and engineering, and, what is a feature we hope to see engrafted on the plan, a series of workshops under systematic and skillful instruction; not simply as a means of furnishing poor students with the facilities of continuing under instruction but to remedy also as far as may be the disadvantages under which we labor in acquiring a knowledge of the mechanical arts.

To this end we advise the maturing of a plan by some other suitable committee for erecting in some locality, central as to population, a school of a high intellectual grade, having incorporated an agricultural professorship, or an equivalent thereto, a professorship to superintend the practical application of mathematics and natural philosophy to surveying, mechanics, and engineering, the following branches of industry: general smithing, turning, wheelwrighting, and cabinetmaking; and a general workshop in which may be combined such application of skill in wood, iron, and other material as to produce a variety of salable articles, with suitable buildings and machinery for producing the same. These superintended by competent workmen, under pay precisely as other teachers, would give students a foundation for after self-support in life, and break down the distinctions that never ought to exist between the study and the workshop.

The above industrial pursuits are named, not because others more desirable, perhaps, or more difficult to secure, might not have had a place given them in this imperfect report but because it seemed wise to choose some which are primary to most others in general usefulness and, at the same time, such as whose products have an extensive marketable demand. In establishing workshops, it must be remembered that the introducing of any large part of the very useful or lucrative branches is an utter impossibility. All that can be aimed at in the beginning is to elevate labor to its own true standard—vindicate the laws of physical health, and, at the same time, as a repaying benefit, make the work done as intrinsic and *profitable*, a part of education as a proficiency in Latin, mathematics, or medicine.

As to the *means* by which such an institution may be erected and carried on, we advise the issuing of joint stock under proper directors, to the amount of $50,000 in shares of $10 each, or a less number of larger amount, if considered advisable. The committee are of opinion that $50,000 used in the purchase of land and the erecting and fitting up of buildings will be fully enough to warrant the beginning of a thorough manual labor school on the plan suggested.

The sale of scholarships at judicious rates and the contributions of the liberal and the philanthropic ought to give an additional $100,000 as an endowment, which sum properly invested would be a guarantee that the liabilities and expense of the institution would be faithfully met.

The department of industry for females, the committee cannot, in the short time given them, intelligently settle upon, except in outline. We are of opinion that looms could be erected for the weaving of carriage and other trimmings; for bindings of various kinds; that the straw hat business in some of its branches, paper box making, and similar occupations, might from time to time be connected.

The shareholders, if such a plan be approved, would compose the college association; and would have a right to appoint the trustees of the school, said trustees being citizens of the state wherein such institution shall be located.

Such is the rough outline of a plan which we think would be, in judicious hands, and so modified as to conform to the proper school laws, feasible and fraught with unbounded good.

In the past, the misfortune has been that our knowledge has been much distributed. We have had educated *heads* in one large division among us and educated *hands* in another. We do not concede in this remark that the mind worker is not a benefactor and a creator. The inventing, the directing intellect produces the demand for mechanical labor; but we believe that the instances of the marriage, so to speak, of thoroughly educated mind with manual labor are lamentably rare among us. All over the land, our earnest youth have gone asking to be cared for by the workshops of the country, but no acknowledgment has been made of their human relationships; their mental and bodily fitness have had the same contumely heaped upon them as is received by those unfortunate beings who in social life bear upon their persons the brand of illegitimacy.

As a consequence, we have grown up to too large an extent — mere scholars on one side and muscular giants on the other. We would equalize those discrepancies. We would produce a harmonious development of character. In the sweat of their brows, we would have our scholars grow powerful, and their sympathies run out for humanity everywhere. On the altar of labor, we would have every mother dedicate her child to the cause of freedom; and then, in the breeze wafted over the newly plowed field, there will come encouragement and hope; and the ringing blows of the anvil and the axe, and the keen cutting edge of the chisel and the plane will symbolize, on the one hand, human excellence is rough hewn by self-exertion, and, on the other, fashioned into models of beauty by reflection and discipline.

Let us educate our youth in suchwise as shall give them means of success adapted to their struggling condition; and ere long, following the enterprise of the age, we may hope to see them filling everywhere positions of responsibility and trust, and, gliding on the triple tide of wealth, intelligence, and virtue, reach eventually to a sure resting place of distinction and happiness.

Songs of Slaves and Their Masters

While the future and the moral status of slavery were debated by statesmen, little was heard from the slaves themselves. However, an indication of their attitude may be seen in the songs they sang as they worked the fields and carried out their domestic tasks. "Blue Tail Fly," also known as "Jimmy Crack Corn," probably originated with the blackface minstrels, but it was taken up by slaves and became widely popular among them. It tells of the delight, only half hidden, with which a slave might view the untimely death of his master. "All the Pretty Little Horses" is an authentic slave lullaby; it reveals the bitter feelings of Negro mothers who had to watch over their white charges while neglecting their own children. [*Source:* Minstrel Songs, Old and New, *Boston, 1882, p. 211.*]

Blue Tail Fly

When I was young I use to wait
On Master and give him his plate,
And pass the bottle when he got dry,
And brush away the blue tail fly.

Chorus:
Jimmy crack corn and I don't care,
Jimmy crack corn and I don't care,
Jimmy crack corn and I don't care,
   My master's gone away.

When he ride in the afternoon,
I follow him with a hickory broom;
The pony being rather shy
When bitten by a blue tail fly.

One day he ride around the farm,
The flies so numerous they did swarm;
One chanced to bite him on the thigh—
The devil take the blue tail fly.

The pony run, he jump, he pitch;
He tumble Master in the ditch.
He died and the jury wondered why—
The verdict was the blue tail fly.

They laid him under a 'simmon tree;
His epitaph is there to see:
"Beneath this stone I'm forced to lie,
A victim of the blue tail fly."

Old Master's gone, now let him rest,
They say all things are for the best;
I'll never forget, till the day I die,
Old Master and that blue tail fly.

All the Pretty Little Horses

Hushaby, don't you cry,
Go to sleepy, little baby.
When you wake, you shall have cake,
And all the pretty little horses.
Blacks and bays, dapples and grays,
Coach and six-a little horses.

Way down yonder in the meadow,
There's a poor little lambie;
The bees and the butterflies pickin' out his eyes,
The poor little thing cries, "Mammy."

Hushaby, don't you cry,
Go to sleepy, little baby.

HARRIET BEECHER STOWE

Uncle Tom Defies Simon Legree

Few attacks upon slavery were as effective as Harriet Beecher Stowe's Uncle Tom's Cabin. *First written as a serial for the Abolitionist journal,* National Era, *beginning in 1851, it appeared in book form in 1852. It was an immediate and enduring success, selling 300,000 copies during the first year and nearly 3,000,000 since. The portrayal of Uncle Tom, the first Negro fictional hero created by an American author, elicited much sympathy for the plight of the slave. Southerners, challenging the book's authenticity, wrote seething denunciations; it was a "criminal prostitution," according to a critic in the* Southern Literary Messenger, *"of the high functions of the imagination." Mrs. Stowe attempted to silence this criticism with a sequel,* A Key to Uncle Tom's Cabin *(1853), documenting the characters and events. [Source:* Uncle Tom's Cabin, *Boston, 1883, pp. 419-423.]*

Long after dusk, the whole weary train, with their baskets on their heads, defiled up to the building appropriated to the storing and weighing the cotton. Legree was there, busily conversing with the two drivers.

"Dat ar Tom's gwine to make a powerful deal o' trouble; kept a puttin' into Lucy's basket. One o' these yer dat will get all der niggers to feelin' 'bused if Mas'r don't watch him!" said Sambo.

"Hey-dey! The black cuss!" said Legree. "He'll have to get a breakin' in, won't he, boys?"

Both Negroes grinned a horrid grin at this intimation.

"Ay, ay! let Mas'r Legree alone, for breakin' in! De debil heself couldn't beat Mas'r at dat!" said Quimbo.

"Wal, boys, the best way is to give him the flogging to do, till he gets over his notions. Break him in!"

"Lord, Mas'r'll have hard work to get dat out o' him!"

"It'll have to come out of him, though!" said Legree, as he rolled his tobacco in his mouth.

"Now, dar's Lucy—de aggravatinest, ugliest wench on de place!" pursued Sambo.

"Take care, Sam; I shall begin to think what's the reason for your spite agin Lucy."

"Well, Mas'r knows she sot herself up agin Mas'r, and wouldn't have me, when he told her to."

"I'd a flogged her into 't," said Legree, spitting, "only there's such a press o' work, it don't seem wuth a while to upset her jist now. She's slender; but these yer slender gals will bear half killin' to get their own way!"

"Wal, Lucy was real aggravatin' and lazy, sulkin' round; wouldn't do nothin'—and Tom he tuck up for her."

"He did, eh! Wal, then, Tom shall have the pleasure of flogging her. It'll be a good practice for him, and he won't put it on to the gal like you devils, neither."

"Ho, ho! haw! haw! haw!" laughed both the sooty wretches; and the diabolical sounds seemed, in truth, a not unapt expression of the fiendish character which Legree gave them.

"Wal, but, Mas'r, Tom and Misse Cassy, and dey among 'em, filled Lucy's basket. I ruther guess der weight's in it, Mas'r!"

"*I do the weighing!*" said Legree, emphatically.

Both the drivers laughed again their diabolical laugh.

"So!" he added, "Misse Cassy did her day's work."

"She picks like de debil and all his angels!"

"She's got 'em all in her, I believe!" said Legree; and growling a brutal oath, he proceeded to the weighing room. . . .

Slowly, the weary, dispirited creatures wound their way into the room, and, with crouching reluctance, presented their baskets to be weighed.

Legree noted on a slate, on the side of which was pasted a list of names, the amount.

Tom's basket was weighed and approved; and he looked, with an anxious glance, for the success of the woman he had befriended.

Tottering with weakness, she came forward and delivered her basket. It was of full weight, as Legree well perceived; but, affecting anger, he said,

"What, you lazy beast! Short again! Stand aside, you'll catch it, pretty soon!"

The woman gave a groan of utter despair and sat down on a board.

The person who had been called Misse Cassy now came forward and, with a haughty, negligent air, delivered her basket. As she delivered it, Legree looked in her eyes with a sneering yet inquiring glance.

She fixed her black eyes steadily on him, her lips moved slightly, and she said something in French. What it was, no one knew, but Legree's face became perfectly demoniacal in its expression as she spoke; he half raised his hand as if to strike—a gesture which she regarded with fierce disdain as she turned and walked away.

"And now," said Legree, "come here, you Tom. You see I told ye I didn't buy ye jest for the common work; I mean to promote ye and make a driver of ye; and tonight ye may jest as well begin to get yer hand in. Now, ye jest take this yer gal and flog her; ye've seen enough on't to know how."

"I beg Mas'r's pardon," said Tom, "hopes Mas'r won't set me at that. It's what I an't used to—never did—and can't do, no way possible."

"Ye'll larn a pretty smart chance of things ye never did know before I've done with ye!" said Legree, taking up a cowhide and striking Tom a heavy blow across the cheek, and following up the infliction by a shower of blows.

56

"There!" he said, as he stopped to rest, "now will ye tell me ye can't do it?"

"Yes, Mas'r," said Tom, putting up his hand to wipe the blood that trickled down his face. "I'm willin' to work night and day, and work while there's life and breath in me; but this yer thing I can't feel it right to do; and, Mas'r, I *never* shall do it—*never!*"

Tom had a remarkably smooth, soft voice, and a habitually respectful manner that had given Legree an idea that he would be cowardly and easily subdued. When he spoke these last words, a thrill of amazement went through everyone; the poor woman clasped her hands and said, "O Lord!" and everyone involuntarily looked at each other and drew in their breath, as if to prepare for the storm that was about to burst.

Legree looked stupefied and confounded; but at last burst forth—

"What! ye blasted black beast! tell *me* ye don't think it *right* to do what I tell ye! What have any of you cussed cattle to do with thinking what's right? I'll put a stop to it! Why, what do ye think ye are? May be ye think ye're a gentleman, master Tom, to be a telling your master what's right and what an't! So you pretend it's wrong to flog the gal!"

"I think so, Mas'r," said Tom, "the poor crittur's sick and feeble; 't would be downright cruel, and it's what I never will do, not begin to. Mas'r, if you mean to kill me, kill me; but as to my raising my hand agin anyone here, I never shall—I'll die first!"

Tom spoke in a mild voice but with a decision that could not be mistaken. Legree shook with anger; his greenish eyes glared fiercely and his very whiskers seemed to curl with passion; but, like some ferocious beast that plays with its victim before he devours it, he kept back his strong impulse to proceed to immediate violence and broke out into bitter raillery.

"Well, here's a pious dog, at last, let down among us sinners!—a saint, a gentleman, and no less, to talk to us sinners about our sins! Powerful, holy crittur, he must be! Here, you rascal, you make believe to be so pious—didn't you never hear out of yer Bible, 'Servants, obey yer masters'? An't I yer master? Didn't I pay down $1,200 cash for all there is inside yer old cussed black shell? An't yer mine, now, body and soul?" he said, giving Tom a violent kick with his heavy boot. "Tell me!"

In the very depth of physical suffering, bowed by brutal oppression, this question shot a gleam of joy and triumph through Tom's soul. He suddenly stretched himself up, and, looking earnestly to heaven, while the tears and blood that flowed down his face mingled, he exclaimed—

"No! no! no! my soul an't yours, Mas'r! You haven't bought it—ye can't buy it! It's been bought and paid for by one that is able to keep it—no matter, no matter, you can't harm me!"

"I can't!" said Legree, with a sneer, "we'll see—we'll see! Here, Sambo, Quimbo, give this dog such a breakin' in as he won't get over this month!"

The two gigantic Negroes that now laid hold of Tom, with fiendish exultation in their faces, might have formed no unapt personification of the powers of darkness. The poor woman screamed with apprehension and all rose as by a general impulse while they dragged him unresisting from the place.

LEVI COFFIN
The Underground Railroad

The "underground railroad" was a vast interstate network established by Abolitionists to aid slaves in escaping to freedom. Focal points of the "road" were in such places as southern Indiana and Ohio, free states, yet close to slave states. The number of Negroes who actually gained their freedom by this means is uncertain, but Southern outrage over the system far exceeded its actual effectiveness. One of the leaders of the underground railroad was Levi Coffin, who worked both in Indiana and in Ohio to help slaves escape. The following selection from his Reminiscences *describes the operation of the road around 1850. [Source:* Reminiscences, *2nd edition, Cincinnati, 1880, pp. 298-311.]*

I was personally acquainted with all the active and reliable workers on the Underground Railroad in the city, both colored and white.

There were a few wise and careful managers among the colored people, but it was not safe to trust all of them with the affairs of our work. Most of them were too careless, and a few were unworthy — they could be bribed by the slave hunters to betray the hiding places of the fugitives. We soon found it to be the best policy to confine our affairs to a few persons and to let the whereabouts of the slaves be known to as few people as possible.

When slave hunters were prowling around the city we found it necessary to use every precaution. We were soon fully initiated into the management of Underground Railroad matters in Cincinnati, and did not lack for work. Our willingness to aid the slaves was soon known, and hardly a fugitive came to the city without applying to us for assistance. There seemed to be a continual increase of runaways, and such was the vigilance of the pursuers that I was obliged to devote a large share of time from my business to making arrangements for their concealment and safe conveyance of the fugitives.

They sometimes came to our door frightened and panting and in a destitute condition, having fled in such haste and fear that they had no time to bring any clothing except what they had on, and that was often very scant. The expense of providing suitable clothing for them when it was necessary for them to go on immediately, or of feeding them when they were obliged to be concealed for days or weeks, was very heavy.

Added to this was the cost of hiring teams when a party of fugitives had to be conveyed out of the city by night to some Underground Railroad depot, from twenty to thirty miles distant. The price for a two-horse team on such occasions was generally ten dollars, and sometimes two or three teams were required. We generally hired these teams from a certain German livery stable, sending some irresponsible though honest colored man to procure them, and always sending the money to pay for them in advance. The people of the livery stable seemed to understand what the teams were wanted for, and asked no questions.

It was necessary to use every precaution, and I thought it wise to act, as the monkey did, take the cat's paw to draw the chestnut from the fire, and not burn my own fingers. I generally gave the money to a second person to hand to the colored man. We had several trusty colored men who owned no property and who could lose nothing in a prosecution, who understood Underground Railroad matters; and we generally got them to act as drivers, but in some instances white men volunteered to drive—generally young and able-bodied. Sometimes the depot to which the fugitives were consigned was not reached until several hours after daylight, and it required a person of pluck and nerve to conduct them to their stopping place. If the party of fugitives were large they were soon scattered among the Abolitionists in the neighborhood, and remained in safe concealment until the next night. . . .

Our house was large and well adapted for secreting fugitives. Very often slaves would lie concealed in upper chambers for weeks without the boarders or frequent visitors at the house knowing anything about it. My wife had a quiet unconcerned way of going about her work as if nothing unusual was on hand, which was calculated to lull every suspicion of those who might be watching, and who would have been at once aroused by any sign of secrecy or mystery. Even the intimate friends of the family did not know when there were slaves hidden in the house, unless they were directly informed. . . .

The fugitives generally arrived in the night and were secreted among the friendly colored people or hidden in the upper room of our house. They came alone or in companies, and in a few instances had a white guide to direct them.

One company of twenty-eight that crossed the Ohio River at Lawrenceburg, Indiana—twenty miles below Cincinnati—had for conductor a white man whom they had employed to assist them. The character of this man was full of contradictions. He was a Virginian by birth and spent much of his time in the South, yet he hated slavery. He was devoid of moral principle, but was a true friend to the poor slave.

Sometimes slaves would manage to accumulate a little money by working at making baskets at night or on the Sabbath, and when they had saved a few dollars they were very willing to give it all to some white man in whom they had confidence, if he would help them across the river and direct them how to reach the Underground Railroad. Thus I have always contended that this road was a

Southern institution, being conducted however on a different principle from what it was on this side Mason and Dixon's line.

The company of twenty-eight slaves referred to, all lived in the same neighborhood in Kentucky, and had been planning for some time how they could make their escape from slavery. This white man—John Fairfield—had been in the neighborhood for some weeks buying poultry, etc., for market, and though among the whites he assumed to be very pro-slavery, the Negroes soon found that he was their friend. He was engaged by the slaves to help them across the Ohio River and conduct them to Cincinnati. They paid him some money which they had managed to accumulate. The amount was small considering the risk the conductor assumed, but it was all they had.

Several of the men had their wives with them, and one woman a little child with her, a few months old. John Fairfield conducted the party to the Ohio River opposite the mouth of the Big Miami, where he knew there were several skiffs tied to the bank, near a woodyard. When I asked him afterward if he did not feel compunctions of conscience for breaking these skiffs loose and using them, he replied: "No; slaves are stolen property, and it is no harm to steal boats or anything else that will help them gain their liberty."

The entire party crowded into three large skiffs or yawls and made their way slowly across the river. The boats were overloaded and sank so deep that the passage was made in much peril. The boat John Fairfield was in was leaky and began to sink when a few rods from the Ohio bank, and he sprang out on the sandbar, where the water was two or three feet deep, and tried to drag the boat to the shore. He sank to his waist in mud and quicksands and had to be pulled out by some of the Negroes.

The entire party waded out through mud and water and reached the shore safely, though all were wet and several lost their shoes. They hastened along the bank toward Cincinnati, but it was now late in the night and daylight appeared before they reached the city. Their plight was a most pitiable one. They were cold, hungry and exhausted; those who had lost their shoes in the mud suffered from bruised and lacerated feet, while to add to their discomfort a drizzling rain fell during the latter part of the night. They could not

61

enter the city for their appearance would at once proclaim them to be fugitives.

When they reached the outskirts of the city, below Mill Creek, John Fairfield hid them as well as he could in ravines that had been washed in the sides of the steep hills, and told them not to move until he returned. He then went directly to John Hatfield, a worthy colored man, a deacon in the Zion Baptist Church, and told his story. He had applied to Hatfield before and knew him to be a great friend to the fugitives—one who had often sheltered them under his roof and aided them in every way he could.

John Fairfield also knew me and knew that I was a friend to the slave. I had met him several times and was acquainted with the plan of his operations in the South, but I was opposed to the principles on which he worked. . . .

When he arrived, wet and muddy, at John Hatfield's house, he was scarcely recognized. He soon made himself and his errand known, and Hatfield at once sent a messenger to me, requesting me to come to his house without delay, as there were fugitives in danger. I went at once and met several prominent colored men who had also been summoned. While dry clothes and a warm breakfast were furnished to John Fairfield, we anxiously discussed the situation of the twenty-eight fugitives who were lying hungry and shivering in the hills in sight of the city.

Several plans were suggested, but none seemed practicable. At last I suggested that someone should go immediately to a certain German livery stable in the city and hire two coaches, and that several colored men should go out in buggies and take the women and children from their hiding places, then that the coaches and buggies should form a procession as if going to a funeral, and march solemnly along the road leading to Cumminsville, on the west side of Mill Creek.

In the western part of Cumminsville was the Methodist Episcopal burying ground, where a certain lot of ground had been set apart for the use of the colored people. They should pass this and continue on the Colerain pike till they reached a right-hand road leading to College Hill. At the latter place they would find a few colored families living in the outskirts of the village, and could take refuge among them. Jonathan Cable, a Presbyterian minister, who lived

62

near Farmer's College, on the west side of the village, was a prominent Abolitionist, and I knew that he would give prompt assistance to the fugitives.

I advised that one of the buggies should leave the procession at Cumminsville, after passing the burying ground, and hasten to College Hill to apprise friend Cable of the coming of the fugitives that he might make arrangements for their reception in suitable places. My suggestions and advice were agreed to and acted upon as quickly as possible, John Hatfield agreeing to apprise friend Cable of the coming of the fugitives. We knew that we must act quickly and with discretion, for the fugitives were in a very unsafe position, and in great danger of being discovered and captured by the police, who were always on the alert for runaway slaves.

While the carriages and buggies were being procured, John Hatfield's wife and daughter, and other colored women of the neighborhood, busied themselves in preparing provisions to be sent to the fugitives. A large stone jug was filled with hot coffee, and this, together with a supply of bread and other provisions, was placed in a buggy and sent on ahead of the carriages that the hungry fugitives might receive some nourishment before starting. The conductor of the party, accompanied by John Hatfield, went in the buggy, in order to apprise the fugitives of the arrangements that had been made, and have them in readiness to approach the road as soon as the carriages arrived.

Several blankets were provided to wrap around the women and children, whom we knew must be chilled by their exposure to the rain and cold. The fugitives were very glad to get the supply of food, the hot coffee especially being a great treat to them, and felt much revived. About the time they finished their breakfast the carriages and buggies drove up and halted in the road, and the fugitives were quickly conducted to them and placed inside. The women in the tight carriages wrapped themselves in the blankets, and the woman who had a young babe muffled it closely to keep it warm, and to prevent its cries from being heard. The little thing seemed to be suffering much pain, having been exposed so long to the rain and cold.

All the arrangements were carried out, and the party reached College Hill in safety, and were kindly received and cared for. But,

63

sad to relate, it was a funeral procession not only in appearance but in reality, for when they arrived at College Hill, and the mother unwrapped her sick child, she found to her surprise and grief that its stillness, which she supposed to be that of sleep, was that of death. All necessary preparations were made by the kind people of the village, and the child was decently and quietly interred the next day in the burying ground on the hill.

When it was known by some of the prominent ladies of the village that a large company of fugitives were in the neighborhood, they met together to prepare some clothing for them. Jonathan Cable ascertained the number and size of the shoes needed, and the clothes required to fit the fugitives for traveling, and came down in his carriage to my house, knowing that the Antislavery Sewing Society had their depository there. I went with him to purchase the shoes that were needed, and my wife selected all the clothing we had that was suitable for the occasion; the rest was furnished by the noble women of College Hill.

I requested friend Cable to keep the fugitives as secluded as possible until a way could be provided for safely forwarding them on their way to Canada. Friend Cable was a stockholder in the Underground Railroad, and we consulted together about the best route, finally deciding on the line by way of Hamilton, West Elkton, Eaton, Paris and Newport, Indiana. West Elkton, twenty-five or thirty miles from College Hill, was the first Underground Railroad depot. That line always had plenty of locomotives and cars in readiness.

I agreed to send information to that point, and accordingly wrote to one of my particular friends at West Elkton, informing him that I had some valuable stock on hand which I wished to forward to Newport, and requested him to send three two-horse wagons— covered—to College Hill, where the stock was resting, in charge of Jonathan Cable. I said: "Please put straw in the wagons so that they may rest easy on the journey, for many of them have sore feet, having traveled hastily over rough ground. I wish you to get to College Hill tomorrow evening; come without fail."

The three wagons arrived promptly at the time mentioned, and a little after dark took in the party, together with another fugitive, who had arrived the night before, and whom we added to the company. They went through to West Elkton safely that night, and the

64

next night reached Newport, Indiana. With little delay they were forwarded on from station to station through Indiana and Michigan to Detroit, having fresh teams and conductors each night and resting during the day. I had letters from different stations, as they progressed, giving accounts of the arrival and departure of the train, and I also heard of their safe arrival on the Canada shore.

HORACE MANN

Slavery in the Territories

While the greatest debate in congressional history raged in the Senate over Henry Clay's compromise resolutions of January 29, 1850, the House of Representatives was also giving its attention to the problem of the expansion of slavery into the territories. Among those who spoke on the issue was Horace Mann, who had resigned his post as secretary to the Massachusetts Board of Education to take the seat of John Quincy Adams. Mann conceded his close relations with the Free-Soil Party, which had arisen in 1848 in opposition to the extension of slavery into any newly acquired territory, and he also admitted to being an Abolitionist. In his speech, given on February 15, he formulated many of the positions later developed by Lincoln in his debates with Stephen A. Douglas. Portions of the speech appear here. [Source: Slavery: Letters and Speeches, Boston, 1851, pp. 180-225.]

Ever since the organization of this House, before its organization, and even in a preliminary caucus that preceded the commencement of the session, Southern gentlemen have pressed the cause, not only of human slavery but of slavery extension, upon us. From motives of forbearance, and not from any question as to our rights, we of the North have maintained an unbroken silence. The time has surely come when the voice of freedom should find an utterance. Would to God that on the present occasion it might find an abler defender than myself, although if my ability to defend it were equal to the love I bear it, it could ask no stronger champion.

I wish to premise a few words respecting the propriety and true significance of some of the epithets by which the parties to this discussion are characterized. The term "Free Soiler" is perpetually used upon this floor as a term of ignominy and reproach; yet I maintain that in its original and legitimate sense, as denoting an advocate of the doctrine that all our territorial possessions should be consecrated to freedom, there is no language that can supply a more honorable appellation. . . .

For myself, I will engage in any honorable measure most likely to secure freedom to the new territories. I will resist any and every measure that proposes to abandon them to slavery. The epithet "Free Soiler," therefore, when rightly understood and correctly applied, implies both political and moral worth; and I covet the honor of its application to myself. But what does its opposite mean? What does the term "Slave Soiler" signify? It signifies one who desires and designs that all soil should be made to bear slaves. . . .

And again; those of us at the North who resist slavery extension, who mean to withstand its spread beyond the limits where it now exists, are denounced as Abolitionists. This epithet is applied to us as a term of reproach and obloquy; as a brand and stigma upon our characters and principles. No distinction is made between those few individuals among us who desire to abolish the Constitution of the United States and that great body of the people who, while their allegiance to this Constitution is unshaken, mean also to maintain their allegiance to truth and to duty in withstanding the hitherto onward march of slavery.

Among the latter class, Mr. Collamer, the postmaster general, is called an Abolitionist. Mr. John Quincy Adams was denounced as an arch-Abolitionist. Every man who advocates the Jefferson proviso against the spread of slavery is so called; and if an unspeakable abhorrence of this institution, and the belief that it is the second greatest enormity which the oppressor, in his power, ever committed against the oppressed, in his weakness—being inferior only to that ecclesiastical domination which has trampled upon the religious freedom of man—I say, if this abhorrence of slavery and this belief in its criminality entitle a man to be denominated an Abolitionist, then I rejoice in my unquestionable right to the name. . . .

If we are Abolitionists, then, we are abolitionists of human bondage; while those who oppose us are abolitionists of human

66

liberty. We would prevent the extension of one of the greatest wrongs that man ever suffered upon earth; they would carry bodily chains and mental chains—chains in a literal and chains in a figurative sense—into realms where even the half-civilized descendants of the Spaniard and the Indian have silenced their clanking. We would avert the impending night of ignorance and superstition; they would abolish the glorious liberty wherewith God makes His children free. In using this word, therefore, to calumniate us, they put darkness for light and light for darkness; good for evil and evil for good.

The constitutional right of Congress to legislate for the territories is still debated. Having presented my views on this subject before, I shall now treat it with brevity. In a speech by General Cass, which has lately been published, that distinguished senator, in order to prove that Congress has no power to legislate on the subject of slavery in the territories, has attempted to prove that it has no right to legislate for the territories at all. I refer to the senator from Michigan because he now stands before the country in the twofold character of being the head of the Democratic Party, which goes for the "largest liberty," and also of the extreme pro-slavery party, which goes for the *largest bondage*. He would sever all diplomatic relations between this country and Austria, because she has robbed the Hungarians of a part of their liberties, while he is drawing closer the political ties which bind him to the South, which has despoiled 3 million of the African race of all their liberties, and is now intent on propagating other millions for new despoliations. . . .

General Cass, in a speech that fills more than nineteen columns in the *Washington Union*, has reviewed the decisions of all the judges of the Supreme Court who have ever expressed any opinion on the subject of congressional power over territorial legislation; he has commented upon the views of all the jurists who have written upon it and of most of the speakers in both houses of Congress who have discussed it; he has surveyed the course of administration of all the presidents we have ever had; and has come to the clear conclusion that all of them—judges, jurists, legislators, and presidents—have systematically violated the Constitution of the United States, or commended its violation, on every practicable occasion for the last sixty years.

Omitting the hundred ways in which the absurdity of this conclusion can be exposed, let me subject it to one practical test. We have acquired territory from Mexico. General Cass voted to ratify the treaty of cession. Measures have been instituted for the formation of three separate governments in this territory—those of California, Deseret [the Colorado River Basin and the Great Basin], and New Mexico. The boundaries marked out by California and Deseret overlay each other to the amount of thousands of square miles. If they have the exclusive right of self-government, as General Cass declares, and Congress none, then they must settle this question of boundary themselves. They may declare war against each other, make alliances with foreign powers, equip armies, build fleets; while Congress can do nothing within their limits but sell land.

But what renders the argument of General Cass still more extraordinary is the fact that, according to his own doctrine, he has spent the greater part of his political life in violating the Constitution, while constantly repeating his oath to support it. As marshal of Ohio, as governor of Michigan, as Indian agent, he has appointed officers and magistrates, and executed laws, when, according to his own showing, he was a mere interloper and usurper; he has met territorial legislatures which had no more right to assemble than a mob; he has doubtless imprisoned, if not executed, many alleged offenders who had as good a legal right to execute or to imprison him; and he has received salaries for more than twenty years, to which the khan of Tartary was as much entitled as he. Now, if he will refund the salaries he has unconstitutionally received; make reparation for the penalties or forfeitures he has wrongfully extorted; show some signs of contrition for the men whom he has unlawfully imprisoned or hung, it will remove the suspicions of many minds in regard to the sincerity, if not the soundness, of his argument.

I mention these facts from no personal feelings in regard to the senator from Michigan; but only to show to what desperate extremities men are driven in order to defend the right of spreading slavery from the Atlantic to the Pacific Ocean; and because this is the last reading of the Constitution which has been invented for the purpose.

Since the last session of Congress, the condition of a part of this territory has greatly changed. The unexampled velocity with which a living stream of men has poured into it within the last twelve months has reversed its condition and decided its destiny. In other countries, individuals seek their fortunes by changing their residence. Under the vehement action of our enterprise, cities migrate. The new residents of California have framed a constitution, have applied for admission into this Union, and their application is now pending before us. Of their own accord, they have excluded slavery from their borders by their fundamental law. Until the discovery of gold in that country, and until all incredulity in regard to that remarkable fact had been overcome, it was confidently anticipated at the South, and intensely feared at the North, that the whole region would be overrun with slaveholders and with slaves.

As far back as 1842, Mr. Wise, of Virginia, the administration leader in the House of Representatives, boldly declared that "slavery should pour itself abroad without restraint, and find no limit but the Southern Ocean." The war with Mexico was waged for the twofold purpose of robbing that republic of its territory, and then robbing that territory of its freedom. Congressional orators and the Southern press avowed that the object of acquiring territory was to extend the "divine institution." I could quote pages in proof of this assertion. The North had no hope, the South had no fear, if the territories were left without control, but that they would first be filled with slaveholders and would then incorporate slavery into their organic law.

While these prospects continued, the South insisted that the territories should be left untrammeled. Distinguished men in this House, Mr. Calhoun and other senators, the government organ, which was supposed to express the views of President Polk and his cabinet, all proclaimed that the territories should be left free to institute such government as they might choose. But since California has formed a *free* constitution, what a sudden change has taken place in the convictions of men! Within the present week we have had three most elaborate speeches in this House in which the admission of California, with her free constitution, is vehemently opposed on constitutional grounds. Yes, sir, did you know it? The Constitution of the United States has just been altered; or, what is intended to produce the same effect, without the trouble of an alteration in the manner prescribed by itself, its interpretation has been altered.

While California promised to be a slave state, all interference was unconstitutional. Now, as she desires to be a free state, it has become constitutional to interfere and repel her. Not only so, but, according to the gentleman from Alabama (Mr. Inge), in swearing to support the Constitution we have sworn to perpetuate, and not only to perpetuate but to extend slavery. "To those," he says, "who are disposed to resist my views, I commend a more attentive reading of that instrument. They will find that it not only guarantees slavery but provides for its extension." Or, as he says in another place, it makes provision "to extend the institution indefinitely." And, therefore, when a territory asks to be admitted as a free state, it is to be repulsed and virtually told, "If you will incorporate slavery into your constitution, you shall be admitted; if not, not." Had the man who first uttered the adage that "circumstances alter cases" foreseen our times, he would have said, "circumstances alter *principles*." . . .

It is further objected to the admission of California that its dimensions are too large for a single state. The force of this objection is somewhat abated when we reflect that it comes from men who were most strenuous for the admission of Texas. However, I shall not object very earnestly to the reduction of its limits. I will say in frankness, that the southern portion of California is understood to be even more attached to freedom than the northern. The result may, therefore, be, if this objection is persisted in and a division made, that we shall soon have two free states instead of one. It was said by the last administration that Mexico was to be dismembered in order "to extend the area of freedom." The most just retribution for that diabolical irony is to carry out the declaration literally.

But I now come to a more substantial part of this great question. The South rests its claims to the new territory upon the great doctrine of equality. There are fifteen slave states; there are only fifteen free states. The South contributed men and money for the conquest, not less than the North; hence, equal ownership and equal rights of enjoyment. This is the argument. In a long and most elaborate speech delivered in the Senate this week by one of the most eminent jurists in the Southern states (Judge Berrien), he founds the whole claim of the South on this doctrine of equality.

70

Now, I admit this principle in its fullest extent, and without hesitation. That country is equally free to all the people of the United States. The government can sell the lands not already covered by valid titles; and any citizen who will comply with its terms can buy them. The people of each of the United States can go there and establish their domicile. The laws of Congress make no discrimination between them. The Constitution makes no such discrimination. The law of nature and of nations makes none. The North has no privilege over the South, and the South has none over the North. If the North has any greater right there than the South, the equality is destroyed. If the South has any greater right there than the North, the equality is equally destroyed.

And now, practically, what right has the North, or what right is claimed by the North, which the South has not to an equal extent? What article of property can a citizen of Massachusetts carry there which a citizen of Georgia *cannot* carry there? Can we carry any of our local laws there, even though all the inhabitants of the state should remove thither in a body? Certainly not. When we leave our state, we leave our local laws behind us. A citizen of Boston has a right to educate his children at school, at the public expense. In the Boston public schools, he can prepare his son to enter any college in this country, even though he is too poor to pay a cent for taxes and never has paid a cent for taxes. Has he any such right on arriving at San Francisco? If the city of Boston debars him of this right of educating his son at the public charge, he can institute a suit against it and recover full damages. Can he do the same thing at San Francisco or San Jose? Certainly not. He has left the laws and institutions of Massachusetts behind him. But, it is said, we can carry our property there, and you cannot carry your property there. I think those who use this argument, like the old Roman augurs, must smile at each other askance for the credulity or simplicity of those they beguile by it. Will not every man, even of the feeblest discernment, see the fallacy which is here covered up under the word "property"?

What is meant by this deceptive term "property"? If you mean silver, or gold, or seeds, or grains, or sheep, or horses, cannot you carry these there as freely as we can? But you have special laws—local and peculiar laws—laws contrary to the great principles of the common law by which you call men and women property. And then, forsooth, because we can carry property there, when property means grain and cattle, you can carry property there when it means human beings, perhaps your own brothers, or sisters, or children. Because we can carry our property there, when property means inanimate substances, you have only to call a human being property; you have only to call a creature, formed in the image of God, property, and then he can be smuggled in under the new name.

Why, sir, there is not a respectable village in the country where, if a juggler or mountebank were to attempt to palm off upon his audience so flimsy a trick as this, he would not be hissed from the stage. There are certain kinds of property and rights which we can carry with us to the territories, and other kinds which we cannot. We can carry movable property, but not immovable; a diamond or a library, but not a cotton factory nor a cotton field. . . .

The reason is that the law of slavery is a *local* law. Like lotteries, or polygamy, or infanticide, it can legally exist in no land where the principles of the common law prevail, until it is legalized and sanctioned by a special law. Then it is permitted on the simple ground that so much of the common law as secures liberty and property, the right of habeas corpus and freedom of speech to each individual, has been cut out and cast away. The Constitution proceeds upon this doctrine when it provides for the recapture of fugitive slaves. Why did it not provide for the capture of a fugitive horse or ox? Why did it not provide that, if a horse or an ox should escape from a slave state into a free state, it should be delivered up or be recoverable by legal process? Because horses and oxen are property by the common consent of mankind. It needed no law to make them property. They are property by the law of nations, by the English common law, by the law of every state in this Union, while men and women are not. An escaped slave could not be recovered before the adoption of the Constitution. The power to seize upon escaping slaves was one of the motives for adopting it.

These considerations demonstrate that slaves are not property, within the meaning of this word, when it is affirmed that if the North can carry its property into the territories, so can the South. As the Constitution, in terms, adopts the common law, it leaves slavery nothing to stand upon but the local laws of the states where it is established. Freedom is the rule, slavery is the exception. Judge Berrien's favorite doctrine of equality would, therefore, be destroyed if the exception should prevail over the rule. For, if slavery can be carried into any of our territories by force of the Constitution, it can into all of them; and if carried into all of them, the exception becomes the rule and the rule perishes. Ay, the rule ceases to be even so much as an exception to that which was its own exception. It is wholly swallowed up and lost.

I know it is said that the *fact* of slavery always precedes the *law* of slavery; that law does not go before the institution and create it, but comes afterward to sanction and regulate it. But this is no more true of slavery than of every other institution or practice among mankind, whether right or wrong. Homicide existed before law; the law came in subsequently and declared that he who took an innocent man's life without law should lose his own by law. The law came in to regulate homicide; to authorize the taking of human life for crime, just as we authorize involuntary servitude for crime; and it may just as well be argued that murder is a natural right because it existed before law as that slavery is a natural right because it existed before law. This argument appeals to the crime which the law was enacted to prevent, in order to establish the supremacy of the crime over the law that forbids it.

There is another fallacy in the arguments which Southern gentlemen use on this subject, which, though not as transparent as the preceding, is quite as unsound. They speak of the *rights* of the slaveholder in the new territories. They speak as though the collective ownership of the territories by the government were the ownership of the people in severalty; as though each citizen could go there and draw a line round a "placer," and say *this is mine;* and, then, because it is his, introduce his slaves upon it. But nothing is more clear than that there is no such individual right. The right of the government is first, a right of sovereignty and jurisdiction; and second, the right of ownership of all lands, navigable waters, etc., which have not been conveyed away by the preexisting government. Individuals retain their citizenship on going there, as they do on going to Great Britain or France; but a slave has just as much right to a portion of the public lands in California when he gets there as his master.

Again, if the master carries into California the legal right to hold slaves which he possessed at home, does not the slave also retain his legal rights when he is transferred there? The laws which govern slaves are as various as the states where they exist. In some states manumission is comparatively unobstructed. In Delaware, it is a penal offense even to sell a slave to a notorious slave dealer. In Georgia, the law forbids, or lately forbade, the importation of slaves for sale. Now, how can a Georgian import slaves into California from Georgia when the very laws of his own state, under which he claims to hold slaves and under which laws he claims to carry slaves with him, forbid their importation?

And, further, political franchises or privileges are just as much a part of a man's rights as any tangible commodity. In South Carolina, the ownership of ten slaves constitutes a property qualification for being a member of the legislature. On removing to California, will the citizen of South Carolina who owns ten slaves carry an eligibility to the legislature of California with him? Nay, this political privilege in South Carolina goes further. It is a right in every owner of ten slaves that no man who does not own ten slaves (or some legal equivalent) shall be a member of the legislature. The aspirant for office has a legal right in the limitation of the number of his competitors as much as in anything else. Can he carry this to California with him? The inference is inevitable that if the inhabitants of the fifteen slave states can carry slaves into California by virtue of the laws of their respective states, then they must also carry all the incidents of slavery known to their respective codes. For, how can the incident be separated from the principal? You might, therefore, have, in a neighborhood of fifteen families, fifteen slave codes in operation at the same time: a manifest absurdity.

The conclusion, then, is irresistible: that when you come to the boundary line between a slave state and a free state, you come to the boundary line of slavery itself. On one side of the line, down to the nadir and up to the zenith, the blackness of the slave code pervades all things; but, on the other side, as high above and as deep below, is the purity of freedom. Virginia cannot extend her laws one hairbreadth over the line into Pennsylvania or into Ohio, because their soil is beyond her jurisdiction. So neither Virginia, nor all the fifteen slave states combined, can extend their slave laws one hairbreadth into the new territories; and for the same reason: the territories are beyond their jurisdiction.

As to the argument that the Constitution of the United States recognizes slavery, and that, upon the cession of new territories, the Constitution, by some magical and incomprehensible elasticity, extends itself over them and carries slavery into them, I think I speak with all due respect when I say it does not come up to the dignity of a sophism. Where do strict constructionists, or even latitudinarian constructionists, find any clause, or phrase, or word which shows that the Constitution is anything but a compact between states? Where do they find anything that shows it to be a compact between territories, or between territories and states conjoined? On its very face, the Constitution meets this pretension with a denial.

The Preamble declares, "We the people of the United States," — not the people of the territories, nor the people of the states and territories — "in order to form a more perfect Union . . . do ordain and establish this Constitution for the United States of America." If the Constitution is a compact between the United States and the territories, then the people of the territories have all the rights under it which the people of the states have: the right to choose electors for President and Vice-President, etc., and to be represented in Congress by a member who can vote as well as speak. The only way in which the Constitution ever was extended, or ever can be extended over any part of the earth's surface outside of the "original thirteen," is this. The Constitution in express terms authorizes the admission of new states, and, therefore, when a new state is admitted, it becomes one of these "United States of America." The Constitution does not extend over the territories, but Congress, being the creature of the Constitution, is, when legislating for the territories, not only invested with constitutional powers but is limited by constitutional restrictions. . . .

But there is another consideration, one which appertains to the party supposed to be insulted rather than the party charged with the insult. In his *Theory of Moral Sentiments,* Adam Smith maintains that it is the judgment of men — the opinion of the bystanders — that gives us the pleasure of being approved, or the pain of being disapproved, on account of our conduct. Now, in this contest between the North and the South on the subject of extending slavery, who are the bystanders? They are the civilized nations of the earth. We, the North and the South, are contending in the arena. All civilized men stand around us. They are a ring of lookers-on. It is an august spectacle. It is a larger assemblage than ever witnessed any other struggle in the history of mankind; and their shouts of approbation or hisses of scorn are worthy of our heed.

And what do these spectators say, in the alternations of the combat? Do they urge on the South to mightier efforts, to the wider spread of slavery and the multiplication of its victims? Do they shout when she triumphs? When new chains are forged and riveted, when new realms are subdued by haughty taskmasters and overrun by imbruted slaves, do their plaudits greet your ears and rouse you to more vehement efforts? All the reverse; totally the reverse.

They are now looking on with disgust and abhorrence. They groan, they mock, they hiss. The brightest pages of their literature portray you as covered with badges of dishonor; their orators hold up your purposes as objects for the execration of mankind; their wits hurl the lightnings of satire at your leaders; their statute books abound in laws in which institutions like yours are branded as crimes; their moralists, from their high and serene seats of justice, arraign and condemn you; their theologians find your doom of retribution in the oracles of God.

England has abolished slavery. France, in one fervid moment of liberty, struck the chains from off all her slaves, as the bonds of Paul and Silas were loosed in the inner prison by the mighty power of God. Sweden has abolished it. More than twenty years ago, impotent, half-civilized Mexico did the same. Tunis, a Barbary state, and, I might add, a barbarous state, has abolished slavery. Mohammedanism precedes Christianity, and sets it an example of virtue. Liberia, a republic of emancipated slaves, the very brothers and sisters of those whom you now hold in bondage, has been acknowledged as an independent sovereignty and welcomed into the family of nations by two of the most powerful governments on the globe.

By this act, freedom secures a new domain on the Eastern continent, while you are striving to give a new domain to bondage on the Western. A monarchy hails the advent of a free nation in Africa,

76

where slavery existed before; a republic is seeking to create 10,000 absolute despotisms in America, where freedom existed before.

Now, these are the bystanders and lookers-on in this grand and awful contestation. They are all agreed, as one man, in their opinions about it. They are unitedly visiting your course with execration and anathema. There is not a nation on the globe that has a printing press and a people that can read from which you can extort one token of approval. I would agree to submit the question now at issue between the North and the South to the arbitrament of any people on the face of the earth not absolutely savage, and to abide its decision. Nay, the wild tribes of the Caucasus and of Upper India, who have defended themselves so nobly against aggression, would spurn your claim and deride its pretexts. And yet you say you are insulted, dishonored, disgraced in the eyes of mankind if you are not permitted to bring down upon our heads, also, the curses they are pouring upon yours. So far is this from truth that if you would promptly and cheerfully consecrate the new territories to freedom, every nation in the world would send their plaudits of your conduct to the skies.

But gentlemen of the South not only argue the question of right and of honor; they go further, and they tell us what they will proceed to do if we do not yield to their demands. A large majority of the Southern legislatures have solemnly "resolved" that if Congress prohibits slavery in the new territories, they will resist the law "at any and at every hazard." And yet they say they do not mean to threaten us. They desire to abstain from all language of menace, for threats and menaces are beneath the character of gentlemen. Sir, what is the meaning of the terms "threats" and "menaces"? Mr. Troup, formerly governor of Georgia, speaking of us who are upon this floor, and of others who resist the extension of slavery, calls each of us a "fanatic." He says that it is only the dread of death that will stay our hands or stop our machinations; and then adds, "That dread you must present to him in a visible palpable form." "If," he says in another place, "the Abolitionists resolve to force emancipation, or to force dishonor upon the Southern states by any act of Congress, then it is my decided opinion that, with the military preparation here indicated, conjoined to a good volunteer instead of a militia system, the state should march upon Washington and dissolve the government."

The gentleman from North Carolina [Mr. Clingman] forewarns us that if certain measures—and they are legal and constitutional measures which he indicates—are taken in order to carry on the business of legislation in this House, the House itself shall be the "Lexington" of a new revolution, and that "such a struggle would not leave a quorum to do business." I could occupy my hour in citing passages of a similar character from the Southern press and from Southern men. Now, if these are not threats—threats most gross, flagrant, and offensive—I know not the meaning of the word. Perhaps those who utter such sentiments are only practising an inversion of language equal to their inversion of ideas on this subject and would call them "enticements"; like the sailor who said he was enticed to join a mutiny, and being asked what arts had been used to entice him, said that the ringleader sprang at him with a handspike and swore if he did not join it he would knock out his brains.

And do those gentlemen who make these threats soberly consider how deeply they are pledging themselves and their constituents by them? Threats of dissolution, if executed, become rebellion and treason. The machinery of this government is now moving onward in its majestic course. Custom-houses, post offices, land offices, Army, Navy are fulfilling their prescribed circle of duties. They will continue to fulfill them until arrested by violence. Should the hand of violence be laid upon them, then will come that exigency expressly provided for in the Constitution and in the President's inaugural oath, "to take care that the laws be faithfully executed." Mr. Chairman, such collision would be *war*. Such forcible opposition to the government would be *treason*. Its agents and abettors would be *traitors*. Wherever this rebellion rears its crest, martial law will be proclaimed; and those found with hostile arms in their hands must prepare for the felon's doom.

Sir, I cannot contemplate this spectacle without a thrill of horror. If the two sections of this country ever marshal themselves against each other and their squadrons rush to the conflict, it will be a war carried on by such powers of intellect, animated by such vehemence of passion, and sustained by such an abundance of resources as the world has never before witnessed. "Ten foreign wars," it has been

The Abolitionist Era

Congress called a halt to the international slave trade in 1808 (although slaves were imported illegally as late as 1859 and the states north of Maryland had abolished slavery by 1804). The slave-owning states of the South soon became the targets of the growing anti-slavery forces. Black men and women played a crucial role in the Abolitionist movement. In 1817 black freemen gathered in Philadelphia and Richmond and resolved to combat both slavery and the back-to-Africa movement and to press for full citizenship. In 1829 a Boston Negro, David Walker, published a fiery "Appeal to the Coloured Citizens of the World" that threatened armed revolt if slavery did not end; the pamphlet so frightened slave owners that several Southern states immediately passed laws forbidding the circulation of all Abolitionist writings within their borders. Escaped slaves described their experiences in print and from the speaker's platform. Freemen gave heavily of their time and money to the cause. The most eloquent and influential black abolitionist was Frederick Douglass, above, a runaway slave whose autobiography and platform oratory aroused anti-slavery feeling at home and abroad.

To be an active advocate of Abolition was to
risk one's life and livelihood. The Constitution
had left the question of slavery up to the
individual states and so, to many Americans,
the Abolitionists' uncompromising demand
for an end to slavery throughout the nation
seemed somehow anti-American and
subversive. While many whites were
convinced that slavery was wrong,
comparatively few were willing to support
any movement that might widen the growing
split between those states that allowed slavery
and those that had banned it. Pro-slavery
mobs often harassed Abolitionists, breaking
up their meetings and burning the homes,
meeting halls, and churches in which they
met. Many prominent Abolitionists, including
Frederick Douglass and such white leaders as
Theodore Weld and William Lloyd Garrison,
were beaten by angry crowds. Douglass twice
was forced to flee the country to escape
prosecution. Abolitionist newspapers were
also the victims of mobs. The presses of
Reverend Elijah P. Lovejoy, who edited an
anti-slavery newspaper called The Observer,
were destroyed by mobs three times before he
was murdered during a riot in Alton, Illinois,
in 1837.

Harriet Tubman, herself an escaped slave, made nineteen perilous journeys back into the South to bring more than 300 slaves north to freedom. During the Civil War she served the Union as a spy behind Confederate lines.

The fierce determination of black people to be free was seen in the ingenuity with which so many of them fled their masters. Perhaps the most ingenious of all was Henry "Box" Brown, right, who in 1850 had himself shipped northward in a packing crate.

The "Underground Railroad" was a chain of churches and homes that offered havens to runaway slaves during their long journey northward. The owners of these "railway stations" were liable to prosecution for their kindness. This house, the home of a Quaker family in Christian County, Illinois, provided refuge for many runaways.

Despite their zeal, Abolitionists were discouraged by a series of laws and court decisions that seemed to block all progress toward their goal. The Fugitive Slave Law of 1850, attacked in the Abolitionist cartoon shown above, provided severe penalties for anyone who failed to turn in runaway slaves.

The Kansas-Nebraska Act of 1854 allowed settlers in those territories to decide whether they would enter the Union as slave or free states. Slave-owners and their sympathizers from nearby Missouri, below, crossed into Kansas and packed the ballot boxes to bring Kansas into the Union as a slave state.

In 1857, the U.S. Supreme Court handed down a decision that seemed to make open warfare between North and South inevitable. Dred Scott, above, a Virginia-born slave, sued for his freedom after living for four years in free states. The court ruled against him, ordered him returned to his master, and stated that Negroes had "no rights which the white man was bound to respect." This decision seemed to imply that all anti-slavery laws were unconstitutional and that black people could never become full citizens. Protest meetings were held throughout the North; slave owners and their allies were jubilant.

While black and white Abolitionists pressed for an end to slavery through
political means, some anti-slavery stalwarts wanted to destroy the system
through force of arms. John Brown, above, an uncompromising foe of slavery
and a veteran of bloody conflicts in Kansas and Nebraska, led a small band of
black and white followers in a raid on the Federal armory at Harpers Ferry,
Virginia, in 1859. He hoped to seize the armory and then arm the slaves who
lived in the surrounding countryside. With a growing following of armed slaves,
he then hoped to lead a rebellion that would spread throughout the South. The
Virginia militia trapped Brown and his men in the armory and, after a minor
skirmish, Brown and the surviving members of his band were forced to surrender.
Brown himself was hanged, but his desperate gamble and the eloquence with
which he defended his actions at his trial did much to arouse anti-slavery
sentiment throughout the North.

well said, "are a luxury compared with one civil war." But I turn from this scene with a shudder. If, in the retributive Providence of God, the volcano of civil war should ever burst upon us, it will be amid thunderings above and earthquakes below and darkness around; and when that darkness is lifted up, we shall see this once glorious Union—this oneness of government under which we have been prospered and blessed as Heaven never prospered and blessed any other people—rifted in twain from east to west, with a gulf between us wide and profound, save that this gulf will be filled and heaped high with the slaughtered bodies of our countrymen; and when we reawaken to consciousness, we shall behold the garments and the hands of the survivors red with fratricidal blood. . . .

In conclusion, I have only to add that such is my solemn and abiding conviction of the character of slavery that under a full sense of my responsibility to my country and my God, I deliberately say, better disunion—better a civil or a servile war—better anything that God in His Providence shall send, than an extension of the bounds of slavery.

JOHN C. CALHOUN
Either Slavery or Disunion

As the great debate continued in the Senate over Henry Clay's compromise resolutions, it was inevitable that the senior senator from South Carolina, the "grand old man of the South," should have his say. Calhoun worked for a month on his speech, but when the time came to deliver it he was too sick to stand—he died on March 31—and it was read by a colleague, Senator James A. Mason of Virginia. For twenty years Calhoun had been the South's ablest spokesman and had fought to retain the delicate balance between slave and free states that was now threatened by the proposed admission of California as a free state. The speech enumerated the South's grievances and stated the demands that made the compromise resolutions unacceptable. It was read by Mason on March 4, 1850. [Source: Congressional Globe, *31 Cong., 1 Sess., pp. 451-455.]*

I have, senators, believed from the first that the agitation of the subject of slavery would, if not prevented by some timely and effective measure, end in disunion. Entertaining this opinion, I have, on all proper occasions, endeavored to call the attention of each of the two great parties which divide the country to adopt some measure to prevent so great a disaster, but without success. The agitation has been permitted to proceed, with almost no attempt to resist it, until it has reached a period when it can no longer be disguised or denied that the Union is in danger. You have thus had forced upon you the greatest and the gravest question that can ever come under your consideration: How can the Union be preserved?

To give a satisfactory answer to this mighty question, it is indispensable to have an accurate and thorough knowledge of the nature and the character of the cause by which the Union is endangered. Without such knowledge, it is impossible to pronounce, with any certainty, by what measure it can be saved. . . .

The first question, then . . . is: What is it that has endangered the Union? . . .

One of the causes is, undoubtedly, to be traced to the long continued agitation of the slave question on the part of the North and the many aggressions which they have made on the rights of the South during the time. . . .

There is another lying back of it, with which this is intimately connected, that may be regarded as the great and primary cause. That is to be found in the fact that the equilibrium between the two sections in the government, as it stood when the Constitution was ratified and the government put into action, has been destroyed. At that time there was nearly a perfect equilibrium between the two which afforded ample means to each to protect itself against the aggression of the other; but, as it now stands, one section has the exclusive power of controlling the government, which leaves the other without any adequate means of protecting itself against its encroachment and oppression. . . .

The result of the whole is to give the Northern section a predominance in every part of the government and thereby concentrate in it the two elements which constitute the federal government—a majority of states and a majority of their population, estimated in federal numbers. Whatever section concentrates the two in itself possesses the control of the entire government.

But we are just at the close of the sixth decade and the commencement of the seventh. The census is to be taken this year, which must add greatly to the decided preponderance of the North in the House of Representatives and in the electoral college. The prospect is also that a great increase will be added to its present preponderance in the Senate during the period of the decade by the addition of new states. Two territories, Oregon and Minnesota, are already in progress, and strenuous efforts are being made to bring in three additional states from the territory recently conquered from Mexico; which, if successful, will add three other states in a short time to the Northern section, making five states and increasing the present number of its states from fifteen to twenty, and of its senators from thirty to forty. On the contrary, there is not a single territory in progress in the Southern section and no certainty that any additional state will be added to it during the decade.

The prospect, then, is that the two sections in the Senate, should the efforts now made to exclude the South from the newly acquired territories succeed, will stand before the end of the decade twenty Northern states to twelve Southern (considering Delaware as neutral), and forty Northern senators to twenty-eight Southern. This great increase of senators, added to the great increase of members of the House of Representatives and electoral college on the part of the North, which must take place over the next decade, will effectually and irretrievably destroy the equilibrium which existed when the government commenced.

Had this destruction been the operation of time, without the interference of government, the South would have had no reason to complain; but such was not the fact. It was caused by the legislation of this government, which was appointed as the common agent of all and charged with the protection of the interests and security of all.

The legislation by which it has been effected may be classed under three heads. The first is that series of acts by which the South has been excluded from the common territory belonging to all of the states as the members of the federal Union, and which had the effect of extending vastly the portion allotted to the Northern section, and restricting within narrow limits the portion left the South. And the next consists in adopting a system of revenue and disbursements by which an undue proportion of the burden of taxation has been imposed upon the South and an undue proportion of its proceeds appropriated to the North. And the last is a system of political measures by which the original character of the government has been radically changed.

I propose to bestow upon each of these . . . a few remarks with the view of showing that it is owing to the action of this government that the equilibrium between the two sections has been destroyed and the whole powers of the system centered in a sectional majority.

The first of the series of acts by which the South was deprived of its due share of the territories originated with the Confederacy which preceded the existence of this government. It is to be found in the provision of the Ordinance of 1787. Its effect was to exclude the South entirely from that vast and fertile region which lies between the Ohio and the Mississippi rivers now embracing five states and one territory. The next of the series is the Missouri Compromise, which excluded the South from that large portion of Louisiana which lies north of 36°30', excepting what is included in the state of Missouri.

The last of the series excluded the South from the whole of the Oregon Territory. All these, in the slang of the day, were what are called slave territories and not free soil; that is, territories belonging to slaveholding powers and open to the emigration of masters with their slaves. By these several acts, the South was excluded from 1,238,025 square miles, an extent of country considerably exceeding the entire valley of the Mississippi.

To the South was left the portion of the territory of Louisiana lying south of 36°30', and the portion north of it included in the state of Missouri; the portion lying south of 36°30' including the states of Louisiana and Arkansas, and the territory lying west of the latter and south of 36°30', called the Indian Country. These, with the territory of Florida, now the state, make, in the whole, 283,503 square miles. To this must be added the territory acquired with Texas. If the whole should be added to the Southern section, it would make an increase of 325,520, which would make the whole left to the South, 609,023. But a large part of Texas is still in contest between the two sections, which leaves it uncertain what will be the real extent of the portion of her territory that may be left to the South.

I have not included the territory recently acquired by the treaty with Mexico. The North is making the most strenuous efforts to appropriate the whole to herself by excluding the South from every foot of it. If she should succeed, it will add to that from which the South has already been excluded 526,078 square miles, and would increase the whole which the North has appropriated to herself to 1,764,023, not including the portion that she may succeed in excluding us from in Texas.

To sum up the whole, the United States, since they declared their independence, have acquired 2,373,046 square miles of territory, from which the North will have excluded the South if she should succeed in monopolizing the newly acquired territories, from about three-fourths of the whole, leaving to the South but about one-fourth.

Such is the first and great cause that has destroyed the equilibrium between the two sections in the government.

The next is the system of revenue and disbursements which has been adopted by the government. It is well known that the government has derived its revenue mainly from duties on imports. I shall not undertake to show that such duties must necessarily fall mainly on the exporting states, and that the South, as the great exporting portion of the Union, has in reality paid vastly more than her due proportion of the revenue because . . . the subject has on so many occasions been fully discussed. Nor shall I, for the same reason, undertake to show that a far greater portion of the revenue has been disbursed at the North than its due share, and that the joint effect of these causes has been to transfer a vast amount from South to North, which, under an equal system of revenue and disbursement, would not have been lost to her.

If to this be added that many of the duties were imposed, not for revenue but for protection; that is, intended to put money, not in the Treasury but directly into the pocket of the manufacturers, some conception may be formed of the immense amount which, in the long course of sixty years, has been transferred from South to

North. There are no data by which it can be estimated with any certainty, but it is safe to say that it amounts to hundreds of millions of dollars. Under the most moderate estimate, it would be sufficient to add greatly to the wealth of the North, and thus greatly increase her population by attracting emigration from all quarters to that section. . . .

That the government claims, and practically maintains, the right to decide in the last resort as to the extent of its powers will scarcely be denied by anyone conversant with the political history of the country. That it also claims the right to resort to force to maintain whatever power she claims, against all opposition, is equally certain. Indeed, it is apparent, from what we daily hear, that this has become the prevailing and fixed opinion of a great majority of the community. Now, I ask, what limitation can possibly be placed upon the powers of a government claiming and exercising such rights? And, if none can be, how can the separate governments of the states maintain and protect the powers reserved to them by the Constitution, or the people of the several states maintain those which are reserved to them, and among others the sovereign powers by which they ordained and established, not only their separate state constitutions and governments but also the Constitution and government of the United States?

But, if they have no constitutional means of maintaining them against the right claimed by this government, it necessarily follows that they hold them at its pleasure and discretion, and that all the powers of the system are in reality concentrated in it. It also follows that the character of the government has been changed, in consequence, from a federal republic, as it originally came from the hands of its framers, and that it has been changed into a great national, consolidated democracy. It has, indeed, at present, all the characteristics of the latter and not one of the former, although it still retains its outward form.

The result of the whole of these causes combined is that the North has acquired a decided ascendancy over every department of this government, and through it a control over all the powers of the system. A single section, governed by the will of the numerical majority, has now in fact the control of the government and the entire powers of the system. What was once a constitutional federal republic is now converted, in reality, into one as absolute as that of the Autocrat of Russia, and as despotic in its tendency as any absolute government that ever existed.

As, then, the North has the absolute control over the government, it is manifest that on all questions between it and the South, where there is a diversity of interests, the interests of the latter will be sacrificed to the former, however oppressive the effects may be, as the South possesses no means by which it can resist through the action of the government. But if there was no question of vital importance to the South, in reference to which there was a diversity of views between the two sections, this state of things might be endured without the hazard of destruction to the South. There is a question of vital importance to the Southern section, in reference to which the views and feelings of the two sections are as opposite and hostile as they can possibly be.

I refer to the relation between the two races in the Southern section, which constitutes a vital portion of her social organization. Every portion of the North entertains views and feelings more or less hostile to it. Those most opposed and hostile regard it as a sin, and consider themselves under the most sacred obligation to use every effort to destroy it. Indeed, to the extent that they conceive they have power, they regard themselves as implicated in the sin and responsible for suppressing it by the use of all and every means. Those less opposed and hostile regard it as a crime—an offense against humanity, as they call it—and, although not so fanatical, feel themselves bound to use all efforts to effect the same object; while those who are least opposed and hostile regard it as a blot and a stain on the character of what they call the nation, and feel themselves accordingly bound to give it no countenance or support. On the contrary, the Southern section regards the relation as one which cannot be destroyed without subjecting the two races to the greatest calamity and the section to poverty, desolation, and wretchedness; and accordingly they feel bound by every consideration of interest and safety to defend it.

This hostile feeling on the part of the North toward the social organization of the South long lay dormant, but it only required some cause to act on those who felt most intensely that they were responsible for its continuance to call it into action. The increasing power of this government and of the control of the Northern section over all its departments furnished the cause. It was this which made an impression on the minds of many that there was little or no restraint to prevent the government from doing whatever it might choose to do. This was sufficient of itself to put the most fanatical portion of the North in action for the purpose of destroying the existing relation between the two races in the South.

The first organized movement toward it commenced in 1835. Then, for the first time, societies were organized, presses established, lecturers sent forth to excite the people of the North, and incendiary publications scattered over the whole South through the mail. The South was thoroughly aroused. Meetings were held everywhere and resolutions adopted calling upon the North to apply a remedy to arrest the threatened evil, and pledging themselves to adopt measures for their own protection if it was not arrested. At the meeting of Congress, petitions poured in from the North calling upon Congress to abolish slavery in the District of Columbia and to prohibit what they called the internal slave trade between the states, announcing at the same time that their ultimate object was to abolish slavery, not only in the District but in the states and throughout the whole Union.

At this period, the number engaged in the agitation was small and possessed little or no personal influence. Neither party in Congress had, at that time, any sympathy with them or their cause. The members of each party presented their petitions with great reluctance. Nevertheless, as small and as contemptible as the party then was, both of the great parties of the North dreaded them. They felt that, though small, they were organized in reference to a subject which had a great and commanding influence over the Northern mind. Each party, on that account, feared to oppose their petitions lest the opposite party should take advantage of the one who might do so by favoring their petitions. The effect was that both united in insisting that the petitions should be received and that Congress should take jurisdiction over the subject for which they prayed. To justify their course they took the extraordinary ground that Congress was bound to receive petitions on every subject, however objectionable it might be, and whether they had or had not jurisdiction over the subject.

94

These views prevailed in the House of Representatives, and partially in the Senate; and thus the party succeeded, in their first movements, in gaining what they proposed—a position in Congress from which agitation could be extended over the whole Union. This was the commencement of the agitation, which has ever since continued, and which, as is now acknowledged, has endangered the Union itself.

As for myself, I believed, at that early period, if the party who got up the petitions should succeed in getting Congress to take jurisdiction, that agitation would follow and that it would, in the end, if not arrested, destroy the Union. I then so expressed myself in debate and called upon both parties to take grounds against assuming jurisdiction; but in vain. Had my voice been heeded and had Congress refused to take jurisdiction, by the united votes of all parties the agitation which followed would have been prevented, and the fanatical zeal that gives impulse to the agitation, and which has brought us to our present perilous condition, would have become extinguished from the want of something to feed the flame. *That* was the time for the North to have shown her devotion to the Union; but, unfortunately, both of the great parties of that section were so intent on obtaining or retaining party ascendancy that all other considerations were overlooked or forgotten.

What has since followed are but the natural consequences. With the success of their first movement, this small, fanatical party began to acquire strength; and, with that, to become an object of courtship to both the great parties. The necessary consequence was a further increase of power and a gradual tainting of the opinions of both of the other parties with their doctrines, until the infection has extended over both, and the great mass of the population of the North who, whatever may be their opinion of the original Abolition Party which still preserves its distinctive organization, hardly ever fail, when it comes to acting, to cooperate in carrying out their measures. . . .

Unless something decisive is done, I again ask what is to stop this agitation before the great and final object at which it aims— the abolition of slavery in the South—is consummated? Is it, then, not certain that if something decisive is not now done to arrest it, the South will be forced to choose between abolition and secession? Indeed, as events are now moving, it will not require the South to secede to dissolve the Union. Agitation will of itself effect it. . . .

It is a great mistake to suppose that disunion can be effected by a single blow. The cords which bind these states together in one common Union are far too numerous and powerful for that. Disunion must be the work of time. It is only through a long process, and successively, that the cords can be snapped, until the whole fabric falls asunder. Already the agitation of the slavery question has snapped some of the most important and has greatly weakened all the others. . . .

If the agitation goes on, the same force, acting with increased intensity . . . will snap every cord, when nothing will be left to hold the states together except force. But surely that can, with no propriety of language, be called a union, when the only means by which the weaker is held connected with the stronger portion is *force*. It may, indeed, keep them connected; but the connection will partake much more of the character of subjugation on the part of the weaker to the stronger than the union of free, independent, and sovereign states in one confederation, as they stood in the early stages of the government, and which only is worthy of the sacred name of Union.

Having now, senators, explained what it is that endangers the Union, and traced it to its cause, and explained its nature and character, the question again recurs: How can the Union be saved? To this I answer there is but one way by which it can be; and that is by adopting such measures as will satisfy the states belonging to the Southern section that they can remain in the Union consistently with their honor and their safety. . . .

The plan of the administration cannot save the Union, because it can have no effect whatever toward satisfying the states composing the Southern section of the Union that they can, consistently with safety and honor, remain in the Union. It is, in fact, but a modification of the Wilmot Proviso. It proposes to effect the same object: to exclude the South from all territory acquired by the Mexican treaty. It is well known that the South is united against the Wilmot Proviso and has committed itself, by solemn resolutions, to resist should it be adopted. Its opposition *is not to the name* but that which it *proposes to effect;* that the Southern states hold to be unconstitutional, unjust, inconsistent with their equality as members of the common Union and calculated to destroy irretrievably the equilibrium between the two sections.

These objections equally apply to what, for brevity, I will call the Executive Proviso. There is no difference between it and the Wilmot, except in the mode of effecting the object; and, in that respect, I must say that the latter is much the least objectionable. It goes to its object openly, boldly, and distinctly. It claims for Congress unlimited power over the territories, and proposes to assert it over the territories acquired from Mexico, by a positive prohibition of slavery. Not so the Executive Proviso. It takes an indirect course, and in order to elude the Wilmot Proviso, and thereby avoid encountering the united and determined resistance of the South, it denies, by implication, the authority of Congress to legislate for the territories, and claims the right as belonging exclusively to the inhabitants of the territories.

But to effect the object of excluding the South, it takes care, in the meantime, to let in emigrants freely from the Northern states and all other quarters except from the South, which it takes special care to exclude by holding up to them the danger of having their slaves liberated under the Mexican laws. The necessary consequence is to exclude the South from the territory just as effectually as would the Wilmot Proviso. The only difference in this respect is that what one proposes to effect directly and openly, the other proposes to effect indirectly and covertly.

But the Executive Proviso is more objectionable than the Wilmot in another and more important particular. The latter, to effect its object, inflicts a dangerous wound upon the Constitution by depriving the Southern states, as joint partners and owners of the territories, of their rights in them; but it inflicts no greater wound than is absolutely necessary to effect its object. The former, on the contrary, while it inflicts the same wound, inflicts others equally great and, if possible, greater. . . .

In claiming the right for the inhabitant, instead of Congress, to legislate over the territories, in the Executive Proviso it assumes that the sovereignty over the territories is vested in the former; or to express it in the language used in a resolution offered by one of the senators from Texas (General Houston, now absent), they have "the same inherent right of self-government as the people in the states." The assumption is utterly unfounded, unconstitutional, without example, and contrary to the entire practice of the government from its commencement to the present time. . . .

The recent movements of individuals in California to form a constitution and a state government, and to appoint senators and representatives, is the first fruit of this monstrous assumption. If the individuals who made this movement had gone into California as adventurers, and if, as such, they had conquered the territory and established their independence, the sovereignty of the country would have been vested in them as a separate and independent community. In that case they would have had the right to form a constitution and to establish a government for themselves; and if, afterward, they thought proper to apply to Congress for admission into the Union as a sovereign and independent state, all this would have been regular and according to established principles. But such is not the case. It was the United States who conquered California and finally acquired it by treaty. The sovereignty, of course, is vested in them and not in the individuals who have attempted to form a constitution and a state without their consent. All this is clear beyond controversy, unless it can be shown that they have since lost or been divested of their sovereignty.

Nor is it less clear that the power of legislating over the acquired territory is vested in Congress and not, as is assumed, in the inhabitants of the territories. None can deny that the government of the United States has the power to acquire territories, either by war or by treaty; but if the power to acquire exists, it belongs to Congress to carry it into execution. On this point there can be no doubt, for the Constitution expressly provides that Congress shall have power "to make all laws which shall be necessary and proper to carry into execution the foregoing powers" (those vested in Congress) "and all other powers vested by this Constitution in the *government* of the United States or in *any department* or *officer* thereof."

It matters not, then, where the power is vested; for, if vested at all in the government of the United States, or any of its departments or officers, the power of carrying it into execution is clearly vested in Congress. But this important provision, while it gives to Congress the power of legislating over territories, imposes important restrictions on its exercise by restricting Congress to passing laws necessary and proper for carrying the power into execution. The prohibition extends not only to all laws not suitable or appropriate to the object of the power but also to all that are unjust, unequal, or unfair; for all such laws would be unnecessary and improper and therefore unconstitutional.

Having now established beyond controversy that the sovereignty over the territories is vested in the United States—that is, in the several states composing the Union—and that the power of legislating over them is expressly vested in Congress, it follows that the individuals in California who have undertaken to form a constitution and a state, and to exercise the power of legislating without the consent of Congress, have usurped the sovereignty of the state and the authority of Congress, and have acted in open defiance of them both. In other words, what they have done is revolutionary and rebellious in its character, anarchical in its tendency, and calculated to lead to the most dangerous consequences. Had they acted from premeditation and design, it would have been in fact actual rebellion; but such is not the case. The blame lies much less upon them than upon those who have induced them to take a course so unconstitutional and dangerous. They have been led into it by language held here and the course pursued by the executive branch of the government. . . .

Having now shown what cannot save the Union, I return to the question with which I commenced: How can the Union be saved? There is but one way by which it can with any certainty, and that is by a full and final settlement on the principle of justice of all the questions at issue between the two sections. The South asks for justice, simple justice, and less she ought not to take. She has no compromise to offer but the Constitution, and no concession or surrender to make. She has already surrendered so much that she has little left to surrender. Such a settlement would go to the root of the evil and remove all cause of discontent by satisfying the South that she could remain honorably and safely in the Union; and thereby restore the harmony and fraternal feelings between the sections which existed anterior to the Missouri agitation. Nothing else can, with any certainty, finally and forever settle the questions at issue, terminate agitation, and save the Union.

But can this be done? Yes, easily; not by the weaker party, for it can of itself do nothing—not even protect itself—but by the stronger. The North has only to will it to accomplish it; to do justice by conceding to the South an equal right in the acquired territory, and to do her duty by causing the stipulations relative to fugitive slaves to be faithfully fulfilled; to cease the agitation of the slave question; and to provide for the insertion of a provision in the Constitution, by an amendment, which will restore to the South in substance the power she possessed of protecting herself before the equilibrium between the sections was destroyed by the action of this government. There will be no difficulty in devising such a provision —one that will protect the South and which, at the same time, will improve and strengthen the government instead of impairing and weakening it.

But will the North agree to do this? It is for her to answer this question. But I will say she cannot refuse if she has half the love of the Union which she professes to have, or without justly exposing herself to the charge that her love of power and aggrandizement is far greater than her love of the Union. At all events, the responsibility of saving the Union rests on the North and not the South. The South cannot save it by any act of hers, and the North may save it without any sacrifice whatever, unless to do justice and to perform her duties under the Constitution should be regarded by her as a sacrifice.

2. Slavery As It Is

1839-1849

CHARLES SUMNER

Segregation and the Common School

The "separate but equal" doctrine justifying Negro segregation in education and in public accommodations originated not in the South but in the North in the period before the Civil War. The doctrine was only prevalent in a section of the country where Negroes were theoretically free, but in fact forced to live as second-class citizens; until the end of Reconstruction, this was true only of the North. The first authoritative judicial statement of the doctrine occurred in the decision of Justice Lemuel Shaw in the Massachusetts case of Sarah C. Roberts v. The City of Boston (1849). Sarah Roberts was a five-year-old Negro girl who had been denied admission to an all-white public school and had thereby been forced to walk a half mile to an all-Negro school. Charles Sumner argued her case before the Massachusetts Supreme Court on December 4. His plea gave American jurisprudence a new concept: "equality before the law." But, though his argument was praised by the court, the decision went in favor of the city's policy of discrimination. Portions of Sumner's plea are reprinted here. [Source: Complete Works, Statesman Edition, Boston, 1900, Vol. III: "Equality Before the Law."]

Can any discrimination on account of race or color be made among children entitled to the benefit of our common schools under the constitution and laws of Massachusetts? This is the question which the Court is now to hear, to consider, and to decide.

Or, stating the question with more detail, and with more particular application to the facts of the present case, is the Committee having superintendence of the common schools of Boston entrusted with *power*, under the constitution and laws of Massachusetts, to exclude colored children from the schools and compel them to find education at separate schools, set apart for colored children only, at distances from their homes less convenient than schools open to white children?

This important question arises in an action by a colored child only five years old who, *by her next friend*, sues the city of Boston for damages on account of a refusal to receive her into one of the common schools.

It would be difficult to imagine any case appealing more strongly to your best judgment, whether you regard the parties or the subject. On the one side is the City of Boston, strong in wealth, influence, character; on the other side is a little child, of degraded color, of humble parents, and still within the period of natural infancy, but strong from her very weakness and from the irrepressible sympathies of good men which, by a divine compensation, come to succor the weak.

This little child asks at your hands her *personal rights*. So doing, she calls upon you to decide a question which concerns the personal rights of other colored children; which concerns the constitution and laws of the Commonwealth; which concerns that peculiar institution of New England, the common schools; which concerns the fundamental principles of human rights; which concerns the Christian character of this community. Such parties and such interests justly challenge your earnest attention.

Though this discussion is now for the first time brought before a judicial tribunal, it is no stranger to the public. In the School Committee of Boston for five years it has been the occasion of discord. No less than four different reports, two majority and two minority forming pamphlets, of solid dimensions, devoted to this question, have been made to this Committee, and afterward published. The opinions of learned counsel have been enlisted. The controversy, leaving these regular channels, overflowed the newspaper press, and numerous articles appeared, espousing opposite sides. At last it has reached this tribunal. It is in your power to make it subside forever. . . .

In opening this argument, I begin naturally with the fundamental proposition which, when once established, renders the conclusion irresistible. According to the constitution of Massachusetts, *all men, without distinction of race or color, are equal before the law.* In the statement of this proposition I use language which, though new in our country, has the advantage of precision. . . .

The Declaration of Independence, which followed the French Encyclopedia and the political writings of Rousseau, announces among self-evident truths, *"that all men are created equal;* that they are endowed by their Creator with certain unalienable rights; that among these are life, liberty, and the pursuit of happiness." The constitution of Massachusetts repeats the same truth in a different form, saying, in its first article: *"All men are born free and equal* and have certain natural, essential, and unalienable rights, among which may be reckoned the right of enjoying and defending their lives and liberties."

Another article explains what is meant by equality, saying: "No man, nor corporation or association of men, have any other title to obtain advantages, or particular and exclusive privileges, distinct from those of the community, than what arises from the consideration of services rendered to the public; and this title being in nature neither hereditary, nor transmissible to children, or descendants, or relations by blood, the idea of a man being born a magistrate, lawgiver, or judge is absurd and unnatural." This language, in its natural signification, condemns every form of inequality in civil and political institutions.

These declarations, though in point of time before the ampler declarations of France, may be construed in the light of the latter. Evidently, they seek to declare the same principle. They are declarations of *rights;* and the language employed, though general in character, is obviously limited to those matters within the design of a declaration of *rights.* And permit me to say, it is a childish sophism to adduce any physical or mental inequality in argument against equality of rights.

Obviously, men are not born equal in physical strength or in mental capacity, in beauty of form or health of body. Diversity or inequality in these respects is the law of creation. From this difference springs divine harmony; but this inequality is, in no particular, inconsistent with complete civil and political equality.

The equality declared by our fathers in 1776, and made the fundamental law of Massachusetts in 1780, was *equality before the law.* Its object was to efface all political or civil distinctions and to abolish all institutions founded upon *birth.* "All men are *created* equal," says the Declaration of Independence. "All men are *born* free and equal," says the Massachusetts Bill of Rights. These are not vain words. Within the sphere of their influence, no person can be *created,* no person can be *born,* with civil or political privileges not enjoyed equally by all his fellow citizens; nor can any institution be established, recognizing distinction of birth.

Here is the Great Charter of every human being drawing vital

105

breath upon this soil, whatever may be his condition, and whoever may be his parents. He may be poor, weak, humble, or black; he may be of Caucasian, Jewish, Indian, or Ethiopian race; he may be of French, German, English, or Irish extraction; but before the constitution of Massachusetts all these distinctions disappear. He is not poor, weak, humble, or black; nor is he Caucasian, Jew, Indian, or Ethiopian; nor is he French, German, English, or Irish; he is a MAN, the equal of all his fellowmen. He is one of the children of the state, which, like an impartial parent, regards all its offspring with an equal care. To some it may justly allot higher duties, according to higher capacities; but it welcomes all to its equal hospitable board. The state, imitating the divine justice, is no respecter of persons. . . .

The legislature of Massachusetts, in entire harmony with the constitution, has made no discrimination of race or color in the establishment of common schools. Any such discrimination by the laws would be unconstitutional and void. But the legislature has been too just and generous, too mindful of the Bill of Rights, to establish any such privilege of birth. The language of the statutes is general and applies equally to all children, of whatever race or color.

The provisions of the law are entitled, *Of the Public Schools,* meaning our common schools. To these we must look to ascertain what constitutes a public school. Only those established in conformity with the law can be legally such. They may, in fact, be more or less public; yet, if they do not come within the terms of the law, they do not form part of the beautiful system of our public schools. They are not public schools or, as I prefer to call them, common schools.

The two terms are used as identical; but the latter is that by which they were earliest known, while it is most suggestive of their comprehensive character. A "common" in law is defined to be "*open ground equally used* by many persons"; and the same word, when used as an adjective, is defined by lexicographers as "belonging equally to many or to the public," thus asserting equality.

If we examine the text of this statute, we shall find nothing to sustain the rule of exclusion which has been set up. The first section provides, that "in every town, containing fifty families or householders, there shall be kept in each year, at the charge of the town, by a teacher or teachers of competent ability and good morals, one school for the instruction of children in orthography, reading, writing, English grammar, geography, arithmetic, and good behavior, for the term of six months, or two or more such schools, for terms of time that shall together be equivalent to six months."

The second, third, and fourth sections provide for the number of such schools in towns having respectively 100, 150, and 500 families or householders. There is no language recognizing any discrimination of race or color. Thus, in every town, the schools, whether one or more, are "for the instruction of children" generally, not children of any particular class or race or color, but children — meaning the children of the town where the schools are.

The fifth and sixth sections provide a school, in certain cases, where additional studies are to be pursued, which "shall be kept for the benefit of all the inhabitants of the town." The language here recognizes no discrimination among the children but seems directly to exclude it.

In conformity with these sections is the peculiar phraseology of the memorable colonial law of 1647, founding common schools, "to the end that learning may not be buried in the graves of our forefathers." This law obliged townships having fifty householders to "forthwith appoint one within their towns to teach *all such children as shall resort to him* to write and read." Here again there is no discrimination among the children. *All* are to be taught.

On this legislation the common schools of Massachusetts have been reared. The section of the Revised Statutes and the statute of 1838, appropriating small sums, in the nature of a contribution, from the school fund, for the support of common schools among the Indians, do not interfere with this system. These have the anomalous character of all the legislation concerning the Indians. It does not appear, however, that separate schools are established by law among the Indians, nor that the Indians are in any way excluded from the common schools in their neighborhood.

I conclude, on this head, that there is but one public school in Massachusetts. This is the common school, equally free to all the inhabitants. There is nothing establishing an exclusive or separate school for any particular class, rich or poor, Catholic or Protestant, white or black. In the eye of the law there is but *one class*, where all interests, opinions, conditions, and colors commingle in harmony – excluding none, therefore comprehending all.

The courts of Massachusetts, in harmony with the constitution and the laws, have never recognized any discrimination founded on race or color, in the administration of the common schools, but have constantly declared the equal rights of all the inhabitants. . . . It is easy to see that the exclusion of colored children from the public schools is a constant inconvenience to them and their parents, which white children and white parents are not obliged to bear. Here the facts are plain and unanswerable, showing a palpable violation of equality. *The black and white are not equal before the law.* I am at a loss to understand how anybody can assert that they are.

Among the regulations of the Primary School Committee is one to this effect. "Scholars to go to the school nearest their residences. Applicants for admission to our schools (with the exception and provision referred to in the preceding rule) are especially entitled to enter the schools nearest to their places of residence." The exception here is "of those for whom special provision has been made" in separate schools, that is, colored children.

In this rule, without the unfortunate exception, is part of the beauty so conspicuous in our common schools. It is the boast of England that, through the multitude of courts, justice is brought to every man's door. It may also be the boast of our common schools that, through the multitude of schools, education in Boston is brought to every *white* man's door. But it is not brought to every *black* man's door. He is obliged to go for it, to travel for it, to walk for it, often a great distance.

The facts in the present case are not so strong as those of other cases within my knowledge. But here the little child, only five years old, is compelled, if attending the nearest African school, to go a distance of 2,100 feet from her home, while the nearest primary school is only 900 feet, and, in doing this, she passes by no less than five different primary schools, forming part of our common schools and open to white children, all of which are closed to her. Surely this is not equality before the law. . . .

Looking beyond the facts of this case, it is apparent that the inconvenience from the exclusion of colored children is such as to affect seriously the comfort and condition of the African race in Boston. The two primary schools open to them are in Belknap Street and Sun Court. I need not add that the whole city is dotted with schools open to white children. Colored parents, anxious for the education of their children, are compelled to live in the neighborhood of the schools, to gather about them, as in Eastern countries people gather near a fountain or a well. The liberty which belongs to the white man, of choosing his home, is not theirs. Inclination or business or economy may call them to another part of the city; but they are restrained for their children's sake. There is no such restraint upon the white man; for he knows, that, wherever in the city inclination or business or economy may call him, there will be a school open to his children near his door. Surely this is not equality before the law.

If a colored person, yielding to the necessities of position, removes to a distant part of the city, his children may be compelled daily, at an inconvenience which will not be called trivial, to walk a long distance for the advantages of the school. In our severe winters this cannot be disregarded, in the case of children so tender in years as those of the primary schools.

There is a peculiar instance of hardship which has come to my knowledge. A respectable colored parent became some time since a resident of East Boston, separated from the mainland by water. Of course there are common schools at East Boston, but none open to colored children. This parent was obliged to send his children, three in number, daily across the ferry to the distant African school. The tolls amounted to a sum which formed a severe tax upon a poor man, while the long way to travel was a daily tax upon the time and strength of his children. Every toll paid by this parent, as every step taken by the children, testifies to that inequality which I now arraign.

This is the conduct of a colored parent. He is well deserving of honor for his generous efforts to secure the education of his children. As they grow in knowledge they will rise and call him blessed; but at the same time they will brand as accursed that arbitrary discrimination of color in the common schools of Boston which rendered it necessary for their father, out of small means, to make such sacrifices for their education.

Here is a grievance which, independent of any stigma from color, calls for redress. It is an inequality which the constitution and the laws of Massachusetts repudiate. But it is not on the ground of inconvenience only that it is odious. And this brings me to the next head.

The separation of children in the schools, on account of race or color, is in the nature of *caste* and, on this account, a violation of equality. The case shows expressly that the child was excluded from the school nearest to her dwelling – the number in the school at the time warranting her admission – "on the sole ground of color." The first Majority Report presented to the School Committee . . . presents the grounds of this discrimination with more fullness, saying, "It is one of *races*, not of *colors* merely. The distinction is one which the Allwise Creator has seen fit to establish; and it is founded deep in the physical, mental, and moral natures of the two races. No legislation, no social customs can efface this distinction." Words cannot be chosen more apt than these to describe the heathenish relation of caste. . . .

Boston is set on a hill, and her schools have long been the subject of observation, even in this respect. As far back as the last century, the French Consul here made a report on our "separate" school; and De Tocqueville, in his masterly work, testifies, with evident pain, that the same schools do not receive the children of the African and European. . . . Strange that here, under a state constitution declaring the equality of all men, we should follow the worst precedents and establish among us a caste. Seeing the discrimination in this light, we learn to appreciate its true character.

In India, Brahmins and Sudras, from generation to generation, were kept apart. If a Sudra presumed to sit upon a Brahmin's carpet, his punishment was banishment. With similar inhumanity here, the black child who goes to sit on the same benches with the white is banished, not indeed from the country but from the school. In both cases it is the triumph of caste. But the offense is greater with us, because, unlike the Hindus, we acknowledge that men are born equal. . . .

We abjure nobility of all kinds; but here is a nobility of the skin. We abjure all hereditary distinctions; but here is an hereditary distinction, founded not on the merit of the ancestor but on his color.

We abjure all privileges of birth; but here is a privilege which depends solely on the accident whether an ancestor is black or white. We abjure all inequality before the law; but here is an inequality which touches not an individual, but a race. We revolt at the relation of caste; but here is a caste which is established under a constitution declaring that all men are born equal. . . .

The Committee charged with the superintendence of the common schools of Boston have no power to make any discrimination on account of race or color. It has been seen already that this power is inconsistent with the Declaration of Independence, with the constitution and laws of Massachusetts, and with adjudications of the Supreme Court. The stream cannot rise higher than the fountainhead; and if there be nothing in these elevated sources from which this power can spring, it must be considered a nullity. Having seen that there is nothing, I might here stop; but I wish to show the shallow origin of this pretension.

Its advocates, unable to find it among express powers conferred upon the School Committee and forgetful of the constitution, where "either it must live or bear no life," place it among implied or incidental powers. The Revised Statutes provide for a School Committee "who shall have *the general charge and superintendence* of all the public schools" in their respective towns. Another section provides that "the School Committee shall determine the number and qualifications of the scholars to be admitted into the school kept for the use of the whole town." These are all the clauses conferring powers on the Committee.

From them no person will imply a power to defeat a cardinal principle of the constitution. It is absurd to suppose that the Committee in general charge and superintendence of schools, and in determining the number and qualifications of scholars may engraft upon the schools a principle of inequality, not only unknown to the constitution and laws but in defiance of their letter and spirit. In the exercise of these powers they cannot put colored children to personal inconvenience greater than that of white children. Still further, they cannot brand a whole race with the stigma of inferiority and degradation, constituting them a caste. They cannot in any way violate that fundamental right of all citizens, equality before the law. To suppose that they can do this would place the Committee

111

above the constitution. It would enable them, in the exercise of a brief and local authority, to draw a fatal circle, within which the constitution cannot enter, nay, where the very Bill of Rights becomes a dead letter. . . .

It is clear that the Committee may classify scholars according to age and sex, for the obvious reasons that these distinctions are inoffensive, and that they are especially recognized as legal in the law relating to schools. They may also classify scholars according to moral and intellectual qualifications, because such a power is necessary to the government of schools. But the Committee cannot assume, a priori and without individual examination, that all of an entire race are so deficient in proper moral and intellectual qualifications as to justify their universal degradation to a class by themselves. Such an exercise of discretion must be unreasonable and, therefore, illegal.

But it is said that the School Committee, in thus classifying the children, have not violated any principle of equality, inasmuch as they provide a school with competent instructors for colored children, where they have advantages equal to those provided for white children. It is argued, that, in excluding colored children from common schools open to white children, the Committee furnish an equivalent.

Here there are several answers. I shall touch them briefly, as they are included in what has been already said.

1. The separate school for colored children is not one of the schools established by the law relating to public schools. It is not a common school. As such it has no legal existence and, therefore, cannot be a *legal equivalent*. In addition to what has been already said, bearing on this head, I call attention to one other aspect. It has been decided that a town can execute its power to form school districts only by geographical divisions of its territory, that there cannot be what I would call a personal limitation of a district, and that certain individuals cannot be selected and set off by themselves into a district.

The admitted effect of this decision is to render a separate school for colored children illegal and impossible in towns divided into districts. They are so regarded in Salem, Nantucket, New Bedford, and in other towns of this Commonwealth. The careful opinion of a learned member of this Court, who is not sitting in this case, given while at the bar and extensively published, is considered as practically settling this point.

But there cannot be one law for the country and another for Boston. It is true that Boston is not divided strictly into geographical districts. In this respect its position is anomalous. But if separate colored schools are illegal and impossible in the country, they must be illegal and impossible in Boston. It is absurd to suppose that this city, failing to establish school districts and treating all its territory as a single district, should be able to legalize a caste school, which otherwise it could not do. Boston cannot do indirectly what other towns cannot do directly. This is the first answer to the allegation of equivalents.

2. The second is that in point of fact the separate school is not an equivalent. We have already seen that it is the occasion of inconvenience to colored children, which would not arise, if they had access to the nearest common school, besides compelling parents to pay an additional tax and inflicting upon child and parent the stigma of caste. Still further—and this consideration cannot be neglected—the matters taught in the two schools may be precisely the same, but a school exclusively devoted to one class must differ essentially in spirit and character from that common school known to the law, where all classes meet together in equality. It is a mockery to call it an equivalent.

3. But there is yet another answer. Admitting that it is an equivalent, still the colored children cannot be compelled to take it. Their rights are found in equality before the law; nor can they be called to renounce one jot of this. They have an equal right with white children to the common schools. . . .

In determining that the School Committee has no power to make this discrimination we are strengthened by another consideration. If the power exists in the present case, it cannot be restricted to this. The Committee may distribute all the children into classes, according to mere discretion. They may establish a separate school for Irish or Germans, where each may nurse an exclusive nationality alien to our institutions. They may separate Catholics from Protestants or, pursuing their discretion still further, may separate different sects of Protestants and establish one school for Unitarians, another for Presbyterians, another for Baptists, and another for Methodists.

They may establish a separate school for the rich, that the delicate taste of this favored class may not be offended by the humble garments of the poor. They may exclude the children of mechanics, and send them to separate schools. All this, and much more, can be done in the exercise of that high-handed power which makes a discrimination on account of race or color. The grand fabric of our common schools, the pride of Massachusetts; where, at the feet of the teacher, innocent childhood should come, unconscious of all distinctions of birth; where the equality of the constitution and of Christianity should be inculcated by constant precept and example, will be converted into a heathen system of proscription and caste.

We shall then have many different schools, representatives of as many different classes, opinions, and prejudices; but we shall look in vain for the true common school of Massachusetts. Let it not be said that there is little danger that any Committee will exercise a discretion to this extent. They must not be entrusted with the power. Here is the only safety worthy of a free people. . . .

In extenuation of the Boston system, it is sometimes said that the separation of white and black children was originally made at the request of colored parents. This is substantially true. It appears from the interesting letter of Dr. Belknap, in reply to Judge Tucker's queries respecting slavery in Massachusetts, at the close of the last century, that no discrimination on account of color existed then in the common schools of Boston. "The same provision," he says, "is made by the public for the education of the children of the blacks as for those of the whites. In this town the Committee who superintend the free schools have given in charge to the schoolmasters to receive and instruct black children as well as white." Dr. Belknap had "not heard of more than three or four who had taken advantage of this privilege, though the number of blacks in Boston probably exceeded 1,000."

Much I fear that the inhuman bigotry of caste — sad relic of the servitude from which they had just escaped — was at this time too strong to allow colored children kindly welcome in the free schools, and that, from timidity and ignorance, they hesitated to take a place on the same benches with the white children. Perhaps the prejudice was so inveterate that they could not venture to assert their rights. In 1800 a petition from sixty-six colored persons was presented to the School Committee, requesting the establishment of a school for their benefit. Some time later, private munificence came to the aid of this work, and the present system of separate schools was brought into being.

These are interesting incidents belonging to the history of the Boston schools, but they cannot in any way affect the rights of colored people or the powers of the School Committee. These rights and these powers stand on the constitution and laws. Without adopting the suggestion of Jefferson, that one generation cannot by legislation bind its successors, all must agree that the assent of a few to an unconstitutional and illegal course nearly half a century ago, when their rights were imperfectly understood, cannot alter the constitution and the laws so as to bind their descendants forever in the thrall of caste. . . .

But it is said that these separate schools are for the benefit of both colors and of the public schools. In similar spirit slavery is sometimes said to be for the benefit of master and slave, and of the country where it exists. There is a mistake in the one case as great as in the other. This is clear. Nothing unjust, nothing ungenerous, can be for the benefit of any person or any thing. From some seeming selfish superiority, or from the gratified vanity of class, short-sighted mortals may hope to draw permanent good; but even-handed justice rebukes these efforts and redresses the wrong. The whites themselves are injured by the separation. Who can doubt this?

With the law as their monitor, they are taught to regard a portion of the human family, children of God, created in His image, co-equals in His love, as a separate and degraded class; they are taught practically to deny that grand revelation of Christianity, the brotherhood of man. Hearts, while yet tender with childhood, are hardened and ever afterward testify to this legalized uncharitableness. Nursed in the sentiments of caste, receiving it with the earliest food of knowledge, they are unable to eradicate it from their natures, and then weakly and impiously charge upon our Heavenly Father the prejudice derived from an unchristian school. Their characters are debased, and they become less fit for the duties of citizenship . . . .

115

The whole system of common schools suffers also. It is a narrow perception of their high aim which teaches that they are merely to furnish an equal amount of knowledge to all, and therefore, provided all be taught, it is of little consequence where and in what company. The law contemplates not only that all shall be taught, but that *all* shall be taught *together*. They are not only to receive equal quantities of knowledge, but all are to receive it in the same way. All are to approach the same common fountain together; nor can there be any exclusive source for individual or class.

The school is the little world where the child is trained for the larger world of life. It is the microcosm preparatory to the macrocosm, and therefore it must cherish and develop the virtues and the sympathies needed in the larger world. And since, according to our institutions, all classes, without distinction of color, meet in the performance of civil duties, so should they all, without distinction of color, meet in the school, beginning there those relations of equality which the constitution and laws promise to all.

As the state derives strength from the unity and solidarity of its citizens without distinction of class, so the school derives strength from the unity and solidarity of all classes beneath its roof. In this way the poor, the humble, and the neglected not only share the companionship of the more favored but enjoy also the protection of their presence, which draws toward the school a more watchful superintendence. A degraded or neglected class, if left to themselves, will become more degraded or neglected. . . .

Happily, our educational system, by the blending of all classes, draws upon the whole school that attention which is too generally accorded only to the favored few, and thus secures to the poor their portion of the fruitful sunshine. But the colored children, placed apart in separate schools, are deprived of this peculiar advantage. Nothing is more clear than that the welfare of classes, as well as of individuals, is promoted by mutual acquaintance.

Prejudice is the child of ignorance. It is sure to prevail, where people do not know each other. Society and intercourse are means established by Providence for human improvement. They remove antipathies, promote mutual adaptation and conciliation, and establish relations of reciprocal regard. Whoso sets up barriers to these thwarts the ways of Providence, crosses the tendencies of

116

human nature, and directly interferes with the laws of God.

May it please Your Honors: Such are some of the things which I feel it my duty to say in this important cause. I have occupied much time, but the topics are not yet exhausted. Still, which way soever we turn, we are brought back to one single proposition, *the equality of men before the law.* This stands as the mighty guardian of the colored children in this case. It is the constant, ever-present, tutelary genius of this Commonwealth, frowning upon every privilege of birth, every distinction of race, every institution of caste. You cannot slight it or avoid it. You cannot restrain it. God grant that you may welcome it!

Do this, and your words will be a "charter and freehold of rejoicing" to a race which by much suffering has earned a title to much regard. Your judgment will become a sacred landmark, not in jurisprudence only but in the history of freedom, giving precious encouragement to the weary and heavy-laden wayfarers in this great cause. Massachusetts, through you, will have fresh title to respect and be once more, as in times past, an example to the whole land. . . .

This is not all. The vaunted superiority of the white race imposes corresponding duties. The faculties with which they are endowed, and the advantages they possess, must be exercised for the good of all. If the colored people are ignorant, degraded, and unhappy, then should they be especial objects of care. From the abundance of our possessions must we seek to remedy their lot. And this Court, which is parent to all the unfortunate children of the Commonwealth, will show itself most truly parental, when it reaches down, and, with the strong arm of law, elevates, encourages, and protects our colored fellow citizens.

CHARLES LYELL

The Relative Merits of Negro and White Labor

The great English geologist Sir Charles Lyell visited the United States in 1841 and again in 1845-1846 in order to observe firsthand the geology of the North American continent. He estimated the rate of recession of Niagara Falls, calculated the average annual accumulation of alluvial matter in the Mississippi Delta, and studied the Great Dismal Swamp of Virginia; the last investigations led to several papers on the formation of beds of coal. He also wrote two books in which he commented on America from other than a geological point of view. The second of these books contained some comments about slavery in Louisiana. [Source: A Second Visit to the United States of North America, *London, 1849, pp. 160-163.]*

I . . . remarked that the growth of New Orleans seemed to show that a large city may increase and flourish in a slave state; but Dr. Carpenter and Mr. Wilde both observed, that the white race has been superseding the Negroes. Ten years ago, say they, all the draymen of New Orleans, a numerous class, and the cabmen, were colored. Now, they are nearly all white. The servants at the great hotels were formerly of the African, now they are of the European race. Nowhere is the jealousy felt by the Irish towards the Negroes more apparent. According to some estimates, in a permanently resident population not much exceeding 80,000, there are only 22,000 colored persons, and a large proportion of these are free.

Over a door in the principal street of New Orleans we read the inscription, "Negroes on sale here." It is natural that Southerners should not be aware how much a foreigner is shocked at this public mode of treating a large part of the population as mere chattels. . . .

In a St. Louis paper, I read, in the narrative of a steamboat collision, the following passage: "We learn that the passengers, with few exceptions, lost all their effects; one gentleman in particular lost nine Negroes (who were on deck) and fourteen horses."

Among the laws recently enacted in Louisiana, I was glad to see one to prevent persons of color exiled from other states, or trans-

118

ported for some offense, from becoming citizens. In spite of such statutes the Negro-exporting portions of the Union will always make the newer states play in some degree the part of penal settlements.

Free blacks are allowed to be witnesses in the courts here, in cases where white men are concerned, a privilege they do not enjoy in some free states, as in Indiana; but they do not allow free blacks to come and settle here and say they have been compelled to adopt this precaution by the Abolitionists.

An intelligent Louisianian said to me, "Were we to emancipate our Negroes as suddenly as your government did the West Indians, they would be a doomed race; but there can be no doubt that white labor is more profitable even in this climate." "Then, why do you not encourage it?" I asked. "It must be the work of time," he replied; "The prejudices of owners have to be overcome, and the sugar and cotton crop is easily lost, if not taken in at once when ripe — the canes being damaged by a slight frost, and the cotton requiring to be picked dry as soon as mature, and being ruined by rain. Very lately a planter, five miles below New Orleans, having resolved to dispense with slave labor, hired one hundred Irish and German emigrants at very high wages. In the middle of the harvest they all struck for double pay. No others were to be had, and it was impossible to purchase slaves in a few days. In that short time he lost produce to the value of $10,000."

The Mexican War

The treaty that terminated the Mexican War was signed at Guadalupe Hidalgo on February 2, 1848. With minor modifications it was approved by the U.S. Senate on March 10 and by the Mexican congress on May 25, and it was ratified by both parties on May 30. The treaty was opposed in America both by those who wanted more territory from Mexico than the treaty secured and by those who wanted no territory at all. Frederick Douglass, an escaped slave who in 1847 had begun the Abolitionist newspaper the North Star *(Rochester,*

N.Y.), belonged to the latter group. He had started the paper against the advice of his white Abolitionist friends and despite the danger to his own life. An editorial that originally appeared in his newspaper on March 17, 1848, is reprinted below.

PEACE! PEACE! PEACE!

The shout is on every lip, and emblazoned on every paper. The joyful news is told in every quarter with enthusiastic delight. We are such an exception to the great mass of our fellow countrymen in respect to everything else, and have been so accustomed to hear them rejoice over the most barbarous outrages committed upon an unoffending people, that we find it difficult to unite with them in their general exultation at this time; and, for this reason, we believe that by *peace* they mean *plunder*.

In our judgment, those who have all along been loudly in favor of a vigorous prosecution of the war, and heralding its bloody triumphs with apparent rapture, and glorifying the atrocious deeds of barbarous heroism on the part of wicked men engaged in it, have no sincere love of peace, and are not now rejoicing over *peace* but *plunder*. They have succeeded in robbing Mexico of her territory, and are rejoicing over their success under the hypocritical pretense of a regard for peace. Had they not succeeded in robbing Mexico of the most important and most valuable part of her territory, many of those now loudest in their professions of favor for peace would be loudest and wildest for war—war to the knife.

Our soul is sick of such hypocrisy. We presume the churches of Rochester will return thanks to God for peace they did nothing to bring about, and boast it as a triumph of Christianity! That an end is put to the wholesale murder in Mexico is truly just cause for rejoicing; but we are not the people to rejoice; we ought rather blush and hang our heads for shame, and, in the spirit of profound humility, crave pardon for our crimes at the hands of a God whose mercy endureth forever.

120

Songs of the Underground Railroad

Estimates of the effectiveness of the Underground Railroad in helping slaves escape to freedom in the North vary widely, ranging between forty and one hundred thousand persons between 1830 and 1860. But there is no disputing the emotions created by the Railroad in the South — among slaves, for whom it was the only hope for freedom, and among slaveholders, for whom it was at best organized thievery. The two famous spirituals reprinted here, both of which have been traced to the mid-1840s, are expressive of both points of view. Each reveals the intensity of the Negro's desire to be free — which combined in his mind with the Christian idea of salvation — and each also reveals the necessity for secrecy in any and all discussions of the Railroad's activities. One of the most celebrated of the "conductors" of the Railroad was an escaped slave named Harriet Tubman (c. 1821-1913), who was known as "Moses." "Go Down, Moses" is supposed to have been about her. "Steal Away" is supposed to have been sung at many a Negro meeting as a signal for one or more slaves to begin the long dangerous journey northward. And "Follow the Drinking Gourd" was a kind of musical map for the slaves who were already on their way. The "Drinking Gourd" is another name for the Big Dipper, which pointed north and to freedom. [Source: The Story of the Jubilee Singers with Their Songs, J. B. T. Marsh, ed., Boston, 1880.]

Go Down Moses

When Israel was in Egypt's land,
    Let my people go;
Oppressed so hard they could not stand,
    Let my people go.

Chorus:
Go down, Moses, way down in Egypt's land;
Tell old Pharaoh, to let my people go.

Thus saith the Lord, bold Moses said,
    Let my people go;
If not I'll smite your first born dead,
    Let my people go.

No more shall they in bondage toil,
   Let my people go;
Let them come out with Egypt's spoil,
   Let my people go.

O 'twas a dark and dismal night,
   Let my people go;
When Moses led the Israelites,
   Let my people go.

The Lord told Moses what to do,
   Let my people go;
To lead the children of Israel through,
   Let my people go.

O come along, Moses, you won't get lost,
   Let my people go;
Stretch out your rod and come across,
   Let my people go.

As Israel stood by the water side,
   Let my people go;
At the command of God it did divide,
   Let my people go.

And when they reached the other side,
   Let my people go;
They sang a song of triumph o'er,
   Let my people go.

You won't get lost in the wilderness,
   Let my people go;
With a lighted candle in your breast,
   Let my people go.

O let us all from bondage flee,
   Let my people go;
And let us all in Christ be free,
   Let my people go.

We need not always weep and moan,
   Let my people go;
And wear these slavery chains forlorn,
   Let my people go.

What a beautiful morning that will be,
   Let my people go;
When time breaks up in eternity,
   Let my people go.

Steal Away

Steal away, steal away,
Steal away to Jesus.
Steal away, steal away home,
I ain't got long to stay here.

My Lord calls me
He calls me by the thunder;
The trumpet sounds it in my soul:
I ain't got long to stay here.

My Lord calls me,
He calls me by the lightning;
The trumpet sounds it in my soul:
I ain't got long to stay here.

Follow the Drinking Gourd

Follow the drinking gourd,
Follow the drinking gourd,
For the old man is a-waiting
For to carry you to freedom,
Follow the drinking gourd.

WENDELL PHILLIPS

Concerning the Impossibility of Union with Slaveholders

As early as 1841, the Abolitionist leader William Lloyd Garrison maintained that since slavery could not be abolished under the existing Constitution, the North must in justice secede from the Union. In January 1843 the Massachusetts Anti-Slavery Society adopted his idea, and later in the same year the national society endorsed disunion by a vote of 59 to 21. In 1845 the society published a pamphlet, Can Abolitionists Vote or Take Office Under the United States Constitution?, *supporting its decision. The Introduction to the pamphlet was written by Wendell Phillips and is reproduced below.* [Source: Anti-Slavery Examiner, No. 13, New York, 1845.]

The American Anti-Slavery Society, at its annual meeting in May 1844, adopted the following resolution:

> *Resolved*, that secession from the present United States government is the duty of every Abolitionist; since no one can take office or throw a vote for another to hold office, under the United States Constitution, without violating his anti-slavery principles and rendering himself an abettor of the slaveholder in his sin.

The passage of this resolution has caused two charges to be brought against the Society: First, that it is a *no-government* body, and that the whole doctrine of nonresistance is endorsed by this vote; and second, that the Society transcended its proper sphere and constitutional powers by taking such a step.

The logic which infers that because a man thinks the federal government bad he must necessarily think *all* government so, has, at least, the merit and the charm of novelty. There is a spice of arrogance just perceptible in the conclusion that the Constitution of these United States is so perfect that one who dislikes it could never be satisfied with any form of government whatever!

Were O'Connell and his fellow Catholics nonresistants because, for 200 years, they submitted to exclusion from the House of Lords and the House of Commons rather than qualify themselves for a seat by an oath abjuring the pope? Were the *nonjuring* bishops of England nonresistants when they went down to the grave without taking their seats in the House of Lords rather than take an oath denying the Stuarts and to support the House of Hanover? Both might have purchased power at the price of one annual falsehood.

There are some in this country who do not seem to think that price at all unreasonable. It were a rare compliment indeed to the nonresistants if every exhibition of rigid principle on the part of an individual is to make the world suspect him of leaning toward their faith.

The Society is not opposed to government but only to *this* government, based upon and acting for slavery.

With regard to the second charge, of exceeding its proper limits and trespassing on the rights of the minority, it is enough to say that the object of the American Anti-Slavery Society is the "entire abolition of slavery in the United States." Of course it is its duty to find out all the sources of pro-slavery influence in the land. It is its right, it is its duty to try every institution in the land, no matter how venerable or sacred, by the touchstone of anti-slavery principle; and if it finds anyone false, to proclaim that fact to the world, with more or less of energy according to its importance in society. It has tried the Constitution and pronounced it unsound.

No member's conscience need be injured; the qualification for membership remains the same—"the belief that slaveholding is a heinous crime." No new test has been set up; but the majority of the Society, for the time being, faithful to its duty of trying every institution by the light of the present day, of uttering its opinion on every passing event that touches the slave's welfare, has seen it to be duty to sound forth its warning—No UNION WITH SLAVEHOLDERS!

No one who did not vote for the resolution is responsible for it. No one is asked to quit our platform. We, the majority, only ask him to extend to our opinions the same toleration that we extend to him, and, agreeing to differ on this point, work together where we can. We proscribe no man for difference of opinion.

It is said that, having refused in 1840 to say that a man *ought to vote* on the ground that such a resolution would be tyrannical and intolerant, the Society is manifestly inconsistent now in taking upon itself to say that no Abolitionist *can* consistently vote. But the inconsistency is only apparent and not real.

There may be a thousand reasons why a particular individual ought not to do an act, though the act be innocent in itself. It would be tyranny, therefore, in a society which can properly take notice of but one subject, slavery, to promulgate the doctrine that all its members ought to do any particular act, as, for instance, to vote, to give money, to lecture, to petition, or the like. The particular circumstances and opinions of each one must regulate his actions. All we have a right to ask is that he do for the slave's cause as much as he does for any other of equal importance.

But when an act is wrong, it is no intolerance to say to the whole world that it ought *not to be done*. After the Abolitionist has granted that slavery is wrong, we have the right to judge him by his own principles and arraign him for inconsistency that, so believing, he helps the slaveholder by his oath. . . .

I am aware that we nonvoters are rather singular. But history, from the earliest Christians downward, is full of instances of men who refused all connection with government and all the influence which office could bestow rather than deny their principles or aid in doing wrong. Yet I never heard them called either idiots or overscrupulous. Sir Thomas More need never have mounted the scaffold had he only consented to take the oath of supremacy. He had only to tell a lie with solemnity, as we are asked to do, and he might not only have saved his life but, as the trimmers of his day would have told him, doubled his influence. Pitt resigned his place as prime minister of England rather than break faith with the Catholics of Ireland. Should I not resign a petty ballot rather than break faith with the slave?

But I was specially glad to find a distinct recognition of the principle upon which we have acted applied to a different point, in the life of that patriarch of the anti-slavery enterprise, Granville Sharpe. It is in a late number of the *Edinburgh Review*. While an underclerk in the War Office, he sympathized with our fathers in their struggle for independence. "Orders reached his office to ship munitions of war to the revolted colonies. If his hand had entered the account of such a cargo, it would have contracted in his eyes the stain of innocent blood. To avoid this pollution, he resigned his place and his means of subsistence at a period of life when he could no longer hope to find any other lucrative employment." As the thoughtful clerk of the War Office takes his hat down from the peg where it has used to hang for twenty years, methinks I hear one of our opponents cry out, "Friend Sharpe, you are absurdly scrupulous." "You may innocently aid government in doing wrong," adds another. While Liberty Party yelps at his heels, "My dear sir, you are quite losing your influence!" And indeed it is melancholy to reflect how, from that moment, the mighty underclerk of the War Office (!) dwindled into the mere Granville Sharpe of history! The man of whom Mansfield and Hargrave were content to learn law, and Wilberforce, philanthropy.

One friend proposes to vote for men who shall be pledged not to take office unless the oath of the Constitution is dispensed with, and who shall then go on to perform in their offices only such duties as we, their constituents, approve. He cites, in support of his view, the election of O'Connell to the House of Commons, in 1828, I believe, just one year before the "oath of supremacy," which was the objectionable one to the Catholics, was dispensed with. Now, if we stood in the same circumstances as the Catholics did in 1828, the example would be in point. When the public mind is thoroughly revolutionized and ready for the change, when the billow has reached its height and begins to crest into foam, then such a measure may bring matters to a crisis. But let us first go through, in patience, as O'Connell did, our twenty years of agitation.

Waiving all other objections, this plan seems to me mere playing at politics and an entire waste of effort. It loses our high position as moral reformers; it subjects us to all that malignant opposition and suspicion of motives which attend the array of parties; and while thus closing up our access to the national conscience, it wastes in fruitless caucusing and party tactics the time and the effort which should have been directed to efficient agitation.

The history of our Union is lesson enough, for every candid mind, of the fatal effects of every, the least, compromise with evil. The experience of the fifty years passed under it shows us the slaves trebling in numbers, slaveholders monopolizing the offices and dictating the policy of the government, prostituting the strength and influence of the nation to the support of slavery here and elsewhere,

127

trampling on the rights of the free states and making the courts of the country their tools. To continue this disastrous alliance longer is madness. The trial of fifty years only proves that it is impossible for free and slave states to unite on any terms without all becoming partners in the guilt and responsible for the sin of slavery. Why prolong the experiment? Let every honest man join in the outcry of the American Anti-Slavery Society.

NO UNION WITH SLAVEHOLDERS!

JOSHUA GIDDINGS

Texas and Slavery

A treaty providing for the annexation of Texas by the United States was presented to the Senate for ratification on April 22, 1844, and was rejected by the Senate on June 8. President Tyler had tried to make annexation a wholly national issue but, with the publication in April of a communique from the secretary of state, John C. Calhoun, to the British envoy in Washington stating that the annexation of Texas was necessary to protect the institution of slavery in the United States, the issue assumed sectional overtones. Representative Joshua Giddings of Ohio combined both Whig and Abolitionist sentiments in an address to the House on May 21, 1844, opposing annexation. A portion of his speech is reprinted below. [Source: Appendix to the Congressional Globe, 28 Cong., 1 Sess., pp. 704-708.]

It is well known, Mr. Chairman, that since the formation of this confederacy there has long been a supposed conflict between the interests of free labor and of slave labor, between the Southern and Northern states. I do not say that the conflict is real; I only say that in the minds of the people, both North and South, and in this hall, such conflict exists. This supposed conflict has given rise to difference of policy in our national councils. I refer to the tariff, in particular, as being a favorite measure of the North, while free trade is advocated by the South. I refer also to our harbor improvements and the improvement of our river navigation, as another measure in which the Northwest and West have felt great interest and much anxiety and to which the South [has] been constantly opposed.

But so equally balanced has been the political power between these opposing interests that for five years past our lake commerce has been entirely abandoned; and such were the deficits of the tariff that for many years our revenues were unequal to the support of government. Time eventually gave the friends of Northern interests power to amend the tariff, and, by the fixed order of nature's law, our population at the north has increased so much faster than it has in the slave states that, under the late census, the North and West now hold the balance of political power; and at the present session we have passed a bill for the protection of our lake and river commerce, which now awaits the action of the Senate and will soon become a law.

But let us admit Texas, and we shall place the balance of power in the hands of the Texans themselves. They, with the Southern states, will control the policy and the destiny of this nation; our tariff will then be held at the will of the Texan advocates of free trade. Are our friends of the North prepared to deliver over this great national policy to the people of Texas? Are the liberty-loving Democrats of Pennsylvania ready to give up our tariff? — to strike off all protection from the articles of iron and coal, and other productions of that state in order to purchase a slave market for their neighbors, who, in the words of Thomas Jefferson Randolph, "breed men for the market like oxen for the shambles?"

Negro Resolutions on Segregated Schools

Laws discriminating against Negroes in Massachusetts had been largely done away with by the 1840s, through the efforts of the antislavery forces operating there, but the public school system remained segregated until 1855. In spite of opposition, the School Committee of Boston turned down several petitions to desegregate the schools. One such petition was rejected in 1844. A mass meeting of Negroes in the city on June 24 protested this denial and issued the following resolutions urging the School Committee to reconsider its action. [Source: Liberator, June 28, 1844.]

Resolved, that, impelled by a deep sense of gratitude, we tender to Dr. D. H. Storer our unfeigned thanks for his successful efforts in instituting the late investigation of affairs connected with the Smith School, and for his unremitting attention to the same from the commencement to the close.

Resolved, that we present our most grateful acknowledgements to the Hon. John C. Park, for the late voluntary and disinterested devotion of his time and eminent talents in the cause of the wronged and neglected colored children of this city.

Whereas, we, the colored citizens of the city of Boston, have recently sent a petition to the School Committee respectfully praying for the abolition of the separate schools for colored children, and asking for the rights and privileges extended to other citizens in respect to the common-school system, viz., the right to send our children to the schools established in the respective districts in which we reside; and

Whereas, the School Committee, at their last meeting, passed a vote stating, in substance, that the prayer of our petition would not be granted, and that the separate schools for colored children would be continued; and

Whereas, we believe, and have the opinion of eminent counsel, that the institution and support of separate schools, at the public charge, for any one class of the inhabitants in exclusion of any other class is contrary to the laws of this Commonwealth; therefore,

Resolved, that we consider the late action of the School Committee, in regard to our petition asking for the entire abolition of separate schools for colored children, as erroneous and unsatisfactory.

Resolved, that while we would not turn aside from our main object, the abolition of the separate colored schools, we cannot allow this occasion to pass without an expression of our surprise and regret at the recent acquittal by the School Committee of Abner Forbes, principal of the Smith School, and of our deep conviction that he is totally unworthy of his present responsible station; and that the colored parents of this city are recommended to withdraw their children from the exclusive school established in contravention of that equality of privileges which is the vital principle of the school system of Massachusetts.

Resolved, that a copy of the above preamble and resolutions be sent to the chairman of the School Committee, with a request that the petition heretofore presented may be reconsidered, and that we be allowed a hearing on said petition before them.

Resolved, that the heartfelt thanks of the colored citizens of Boston are due to Messrs. George S. Hillard and John T. Sargent for the humane and independent stand recently taken by them in the School Committee in behalf of the rights and welfare of the colored children.

Resolved, that the expression of the sense of this meeting be transmitted to the several gentlemen named in the foregoing resolutions, and be also published in the city papers.

Pro-Slavery Churches

Both of the following selections attacking pro-slavery churches were written by staunch Abolitionists. The first is taken from a pamphlet entitled The American Churches, the Bulwarks of American Slavery, *by Southerner James G. Birney. It was originally published in England in 1840 on the occasion of the London World Anti-Slavery Conference, which Birney attended, and was addressed to the English reader. It was issued in the United States in 1842 and reissued in an enlarged edition in 1885. The second selection is from a letter in Stephen S. Foster's book,* The Brotherhood of Thieves; or A True Picture of the American Church and Clergy. *The letter was written in July 1843 to Nathaniel Barney, who had requested that Foster justify the strong anticlerical language employed at an antislavery convention in Massachusetts. [Source: Birney,* The American Churches, *1885, pp. 7-11, 48. Foster,* The Brotherhood of Thieves, *1843, pp. 5-14.]*

JAMES G. BIRNEY
The Guilt of the Churches Supporting Slavery

The extent to which most of the churches in America are involved in the guilt of supporting the slave system is known to but few in this country [England]. So far from being even suspected by the great mass of the religious community here, it would not be believed but on the most indisputable evidence. Evidence of this character it is proposed now to present – applying to the Methodist Episcopal, the Baptist, the Presbyterian, and the Protestant Episcopal churches. It is done with a single view to make the British Christian public acquainted with the real state of the case, in order that it may in the most intelligent and effective manner exert the influence it possesses with the American churches to persuade them to purify themselves from a sin that has greatly debased them and that threatens in the end wholly to destroy them.

The following memoranda will assist English readers in more readily apprehending the force and scope of the evidence.

1. Of the twenty-six American states, thirteen are slave states. Of the latter, Maryland, Virginia, Kentucky, Missouri, and Tennessee (in part), are slave-*selling* states; the states south of them are slave-*buying* and slave-*consuming* states.

2. Between the slave-selling and slave-buying states the slave trade is carried on extensively and systematically. The slave trader, on completing his purchases for a single adventure, brings the gang together at a convenient point; confines the men in double rows to a large chain running between the rows, by means of smaller lateral chains tightly riveted around the wrists of the slaves and connected with the principal chain. They are in this way driven along the highways (the small boys, the women, and girls following), without any release from their chains till they arrive at the ultimate place of sale. Here they occupy barracoons [temporary barracks] till they are disposed of, one by one or in lots, to those who will give most for them.

3. Ministers and office-bearers and members of churches are slaveholders – buying and selling slaves (not as the regular slave trader but as their convenience or interest may from time to time require). As a general rule, the itinerant preachers in the Methodist Church are not permitted to hold slaves, but there are frequent exceptions to the rule, especially of late.

4. There are in the United States, about 2,487,113 slaves and 386,069 *free people of color*. Of the slaves, 80,000 are members of the Methodist Church; 80,000 of the Baptist; and about 40,000 of the other churches. These church members have no exemption from

being sold by their owners as other slaves are. Instances are not rare of slaveholding members of churches selling slaves who are members of the same church with themselves. And members of churches have followed the business of slave auctioneers.

5. In most of the slave states, the master is not permitted formally to emancipate, unless the emancipated person be removed from the state (which makes the formal act unnecessary), or, unless by a special act of the legislature. If, however, he disregards the law and permits the slave to go at liberty and "do" for himself, the law — on the theory that every slave ought to have a master to *see to him* — directs him to be sold for the benefit of the state. Instances of this, however, must be very rare. The people are better than their laws, for the writer, during a residence of more than thirty years in the slave states, never knew an instance of such a sale nor has he ever heard of one that was fully proved to have taken place.

6. There is no law in any of the slave states forbidding the slaveholder to remove his slaves to a free state; nor against his giving the slaves themselves a "pass" for that purpose. The laws of some of the *free* states present obstructions to the settlement of colored persons within their limits — but these obstructions are not insurmountable, and if the validity of the laws should be tried in the tribunals, it would be found they are unconstitutional.

7. In the slave states a slave cannot be a witness in any case, civil or criminal, in which a white is a party; neither can a free colored person, except in Louisiana. Ohio, Indiana, and Illinois (free states) make colored persons incompetent as witnesses in any case in which a white is a party. In Ohio, a white person can prove his own ("book") account, not exceeding a certain sum, by his own oath or affirmation; a colored person cannot, as against a white. In Ohio, the laws regard all who are mulattoes or above the grade of mulattoes, as *white*.

8. There is no law in the slave states forbidding the several church authorities making slaveholding an offense, for which those guilty of it might be excluded from membership.

The Society of Friends exists in the slave states — it excludes slaveholders.

The United Brethren exist as a church in Maryland and Virginia, slave states. Their annual conference for those two states (in

which are thirty preachers) met in February [1840]. The following is
an extract from its minutes: —

> No charge is preferred against any (preachers) except
> Franklin Echard and Moses Michael.
> It appeared in evidence that Moses Michael was the owner
> of a female slave, which is contrary to the discipline of our
> church. Conference therefore resolved that unless brother
> Michael manumit or set free such slave in six months, he no
> longer be considered a member of our church.

9. When ecclesiastical councils excuse themselves from acting
for the removal of slavery from their respective communions by
saying they cannot *legislate* for the abolition of slavery; that slavery
is a *civil* or *political* institution; that it "belongs to Caesar" and not
to the church to put an end to it, they shun the point at issue. To the
church member who is a debauchee, a drunkard, a seducer, a murderer, they find no difficulty in saying, "We cannot indeed proceed
against your person, or your property—*this* belongs to Caesar, to the
tribunals of the country, to the *legislature;* but we can suspend or
wholly cut you off from the communion of the church, with a view
to your repentance and its purification." If a white member should
by force or intimidation, day after day, deprive another white member of his property, the authorities of the churches would expel him
from their body should he refuse to make restitution or reparation,
although it could not be *enforced* except through the tribunals, over
which they have no control. There is, then, nothing to prevent these
authorities from saying to the slaveholder, "Cease being a slaveholder and remain in the church, or continue a slaveholder and go
out of it. You have your choice."

10. The slave states make it penal to teach the slaves to read. So
also some of them to teach the *free colored people* to read. Thus a
free colored parent may suffer the penalty for teaching his own
children to read even the Scriptures. None of the slaveholding
churches or religious bodies, so far as is known, have, at any time,
remonstrated with the legislatures against this iniquitous legislation or petitioned for its repeal or modification. Nor have they re-
proved or questioned such of their members, as, being also members

of the legislatures, sanctioned such legislation by their votes.

11. There is no systematic instruction of the slave members of churches, either orally or in any other way.

12. Uniting with a church makes no change in the condition of slaves *at home*. They are thrown back just as before, among their old associates, and subjected to their corrupting influences.

13. But little pains are taken to secure their attendance at public worship on Sundays.

14. The "house servants" are rarely present at family worship; the "field hands," never.

15. It is only one here and there who seems to have any intelligent views of the nature of Christianity or of a future life.

16. In the Methodist, Baptist, Presbyterian, and Episcopal churches, the colored people, during service, sit in a particular part of the house, now generally known as the "Negro pew." They are not permitted to sit in any other, nor to hire or purchase pews as other people, nor would they be permitted to sit, even if invited, in the pews of white persons. This applies to all colored persons, whether *members* or not, and even to *licensed ministers* of their respective connections. The "Negro pew" is almost as rigidly kept up in the free states as in the slave.

17. In some of the older slave states, as Virginia and South Carolina, churches, in their *corporate* character, hold slaves, who are generally hired out of the support of the minister. The following is taken from the *Charleston Courier* of February 12, 1835.

FIELD NEGROES
by Thomas Gadsden

On Tuesday, the 17th instant, will be sold, at the north of the exchange, at ten o'clock, a prime gang of ten Negroes, accustomed to the culture of cotton and provisions, belonging to the Independent Church, in *Christ's Church Parish.* . . .

18. Nor are instances wanting in which Negroes are *bequeathed* for the benefit of the Indians, as the following Chancery notice, taken from a Savannah (Ga.) paper, will show.

BRYAN SUPERIOR COURT
Between John J. Maxwell and others, executors of Ann Pray,

complainants, and Mary Sleigh and others, devisees and legatees, under the will of Ann Pray, defendants, IN EQUITY.

A bill having been filed for the distribution of the estate of the Testatrix, Ann Pray, and it appearing that among other legacies in her will, is the following, viz., a legacy of one-fourth of certain Negro slaves to the American Board of Commissioners for domestic [foreign it probably should have been] missions, for the purpose of sending the gospel to the heathen, and particularly to the Indians of this continent. It is on motion of the solicitors of the complainants ordered, that all persons claiming the said legacy, do appear and answer the bill of the complainants, within four months from this day. And it is ordered that this order be published in a public gazette of the city of Savannah and in one of the gazettes of Philadelphia, once a month for four months.

Extract from the minutes, Dec. 2, 1832. . . . The bequest was not accepted. . . .

We would have the reader bear in mind that the foregoing presents but one side of the antislavery cause in the several churches whose proceedings have been considered; and that in them all, there are Abolitionists earnestly laboring to purify them from the defilements of slavery; and that they have strong encouragement to proceed, not only in view of what they have already effected toward that end, but in the steady increase of their numbers, and in other omens of success.

We wish him also to bear in mind that the churches which have been brought before him are not the only American churches which are guilty in giving their countenance and support to slavery. Of others we have said nothing, simply because, to examine their cases, would be to make this work too long for the object we have in view — and because enough has been said to show substantially the state of the slavery question in America, so far as the *church* in that country is connected with it.

Last, we take pleasure in assuring him that there are considerable portions of the Methodist, Baptist, and Presbyterian churches, as well as the entire of some of the smaller religious bodies in America, that maintain a commendable testimony against slavery and its abominations.

136

STEPHEN S. FOSTER
A Brotherhood of Thieves

The remarks which I made at your convention were of a most grave and startling character. They strike at the very foundation of all our popular ecclesiastical institutions and exhibit them to the world as the apologists and supporters of the most atrocious system of oppression and wrong beneath which humanity has ever groaned. They reflect on the church the deepest possible odium, by disclosing to public view the chains and handcuffs, the whips and branding irons, the rifles and bloodhounds, with which her ministers and deacons bind the limbs, and lacerate the flesh of innocent men and defenseless women. They cast upon the clergy the same dark shade which Jesus threw over the ministers of his day, when he tore away the veil beneath which they had successfully concealed their diabolical schemes of personal aggrandizement and power, and denounced them before all the people, as a "den of thieves," as "fools and blind," "whited sepulchers," "blind guides, which strain at a gnat and swallow a camel," "hypocrites, who devour widow's houses, and for a pretense make long prayers," "liars," "adulterers," "serpents," "a generation of vipers" who could not "escape the damnation of hell."

But appalling and ominous as they were, I am not aware that I gave the parties accused, or their mobocratic friends, any just cause of complaint. They were all spoken in public, in a free meeting, where all who dissented from me were not only invited but warmly urged to reply. I was an entire stranger among you, with nothing but the naked truth and a few sympathizing friends to sustain me, while the whole weight of popular sentiment was in their favor. Was the controversy unequal, on their part? Were they afraid to meet me with the same honorable weapons which I had chosen? Conscious innocence seldom consents to tarnish its character by a dishonorable defense.

Had my charges been unfounded, a refutation of them, under the circumstances, would have been most easy and triumphant. My opponents, had they been innocent, could have acquitted themselves honorably, and overwhelmed their accuser in deep disgrace, without the necessity of resorting to those arguments which appeal

137

only to one's fears of personal harm and which are certain to react upon their authors when the threatened danger subsides.

But if all that I have alleged against them be true, it was, obviously, my right, nay, my imperative duty, to make the disclosures which I did, even though it might be, as you well know it was, at the peril of my life and the lives of my associates.

In exposing the deep and fathomless abominations of those *pious* thieves who gain their livelihood by preaching sermons and stealing babies, I am not at liberty to yield to any intimidations, however imposing the source from which they come. The right of speech — the liberty to utter our own convictions *freely*, at all times, and in all places, at discretion, unawed by fear, unembarrassed by force — is the gift of God to every member of the family of man and should be preserved inviolate. And for one, I can consent to surrender it to no power on earth, but with the loss of life itself. Let not the petty tyrants of our land, in church or state, think to escape the censures which their crimes deserve by hedging themselves about with the frightful penalties of human law or the more frightful violence of a drunken and murderous mob.

There live the men who are not afraid to die, even though called to meet their fate within the gloomy walls of a dismal prison, with no kind hand to wipe the cold deathsweat from their sinking brow; and they scorn a fetter on limb or spirit. They know their rights and know how to defend them or to obtain more than an equivalent for their loss, in the rewards of a martyr to the right. While life remains, they will speak, and speak *freely*, though it be in "A voice from the jail." Nor will they treat the crimes and vices of slave-breeding priests and their *consecrated* abettors of the North with less severity than they do the crimes and vices of other *marauders* on their neighbor's property and rights. Nor should the friends of freedom be alarmed at the consequences of this faithful dealing with "spiritual wickedness in high places." The *mobs* which it creates are but the violent contortions of the patient, as the deep gashes of the operator's knife severs the infected limb from his sickly and emaciated body.

The fact that my charges against the religious sects of our country were met with violence and outrage, instead of sound arguments and invalidating testimony, is strong presumptive evidence of their

138

truth. The innocent never find occasion to resort to this disgraceful mode of defense. If our clergy and church were the ministers and church of Christ, would their reputation be defended by drunken and murderous mobs? Are brickbats and rotten eggs the weapons of truth and Christianity? Did Jesus say to his disciples, "Blessed are ye when the *mob* shall speak well of you and shall defend you"?

The church, slavery, and the mob are a queer trinity! And yet that they are a trinity — that they all "agree in one" — cannot be denied. Every assault which we have made upon the bloody slave system . . . has been promptly met and repelled by the church, which is herself the claimant of several hundred thousand slaves; and whenever we have attempted to expose the guilt and hypocrisy of the church, the *mob* has uniformly been first and foremost in her defense. But I rest not on presumptive evidence, however strong and conclusive, to sustain my allegations against the American church and clergy. The proof of their identity with slavery and of their consequent deep and unparalleled criminality is positive and overwhelming; and is fully adequate to sustain the gravest charges and to justify the most denunciatory language that have ever fallen from the lips of their most inveterate opponents.

I said at your meeting, among other things, that the American church and clergy, as a body, were thieves, adulterers, manstealers, pirates, and murderers — that the Methodist Episcopal Church was more corrupt and profligate than any house of ill fame in the city of New York — that the Southern ministers of that body were desirous of perpetuating slavery for the purpose of supplying themselves with concubines from among its hapless victims — and that many of our clergymen were guilty of enormities that would disgrace an Algerine pirate!! These sentiments called forth a burst of holy indignation from the *pious* and *dutiful* advocates of the church and clergy, which overwhelmed the meeting with repeated showers of stones and rotten eggs and eventually compelled me to leave your island, to prevent the shedding of human blood.

But whence this violence and personal abuse, not only of the author of the obnoxious sentiments but also of your own unoffending wives and daughters whose faces and dresses, you will recollect, were covered with the most loathsome filth? It is reported of the ancient Pharisees and their adherents that they stoned Stephen to

139

death for preaching doctrines at war with the popular religion of their times, and charging them with the murder of the Son of God; but their successors of the modern church, it would seem, have discovered some new principle in theology, by which it is made their duty not only to stone the heretic himself but all those also who may at any time be found listening to his discourse without a *permit* from their *priest*. Truly, the church is becoming "Terrible as an army with banners."

This violence and outrage on the part of the church were, no doubt, committed to the glory of God and the honor of religion, although the connection between rotten eggs and holiness of heart is not very obvious. It is, I suppose, one of the mysteries of religion which laymen cannot understand without the aid of the clergy; and I therefore suggest that the pulpit make it a subject of Sunday discourse. But are not the charges here alleged against the clergy strictly and literally true? I maintain that they are true to the letter—that the clergy and their adherents are literally, and beyond all controversy, a "brotherhood of thieves"—and in support of this opinion I submit the following considerations.

You will agree with me, I think, that slaveholding involves the commission of all the crimes specified in my first charge, viz., theft, adultery, manstealing, piracy, and murder. But should you have any doubts on this subject, they will be easily removed by analyzing this atrocious outrage on the laws of God and the rights and happiness of man and examining separately the elements of which it is composed. Wesley, the celebrated founder of the Methodists, once denounced it as the "sum of all villainies." Whether it be the sum of *all* villainies or not, I will not here express an opinion, but that it is the sum of at least *five*, and those by no means the least atrocious in the catalog of human aberrations, will require but a small tax on your patience to prove.

1. *Theft*. To steal is to take that which belongs to another without his consent. Theft and robbery are, *morally*, the same act, differing only in form. Both are included under the command, "Thou shalt not steal"—that is, thou shalt not take thy neighbor's property. Whoever, therefore, either secretly or by force, possesses himself of the property of another is a thief. Now, no proposition is plainer than that every man owns his own industry. He who tills the soil has a

right to its products and cannot be deprived of them but by an act of felony. This principle furnishes the only solid basis for the right of private or individual property, and he who denies it, either in theory or practice, denies that right also. But every slaveholder takes the entire industry of his slaves from infancy to gray hairs. They dig the soil, but he receives its products. No matter how kind or humane the master may be, he lives by plunder. He is emphatically a freebooter, and, as such, he is as much more despicable a character than the common horse thief, as his depredations are more extensive.

2. *Adultery*. This crime is disregard for the requisitions of marriage. The conjugal relation has its foundation deeply laid in man's nature, and its observance is essential to his happiness. Hence, Jesus Christ has thrown around it the sacred sanction of his written law and expressly declared that the man who violates it, even by a lustful eye, is an adulterer. But does the slaveholder respect this sacred relation? Is he cautious never to tread upon forbidden ground? No! His very position makes him the minister of unbridled lust. By converting woman into a commodity, to be bought and sold and used by her claimant as his avarice or lust may dictate, he totally annihilates the marriage institution; and transforms the wife into what he very significantly terms a *"breeder,"* and her children into *"stock."*

This change in woman's condition from a free moral agent to a chattel places her domestic relations entirely beyond her own control and makes her a mere instrument for the gratification of another's desires. The master claims her body as his property and of course employs it for such purposes as best suit his inclinations, demanding free access to her bed; nor can she resist his demands, but at the peril of her life. Thus is her chastity left entirely unprotected, and she is made the lawful prey of every pale-faced libertine who may choose to prostitute her!! To place woman in this situation, or to retain her in it, when placed there by another, is the highest insult that one could possibly offer to the dignity and purity of her nature; and the wretch who is guilty of it deserves an epithet, compared with which adultery is spotless innocence. *Rape* is his crime! — death his desert, if death be ever due to criminals!

Am I too severe? Let the offense be done to a sister or a daughter of yours; nay, let the Rev. Dr. Witherspoon, or some other *ordained* miscreant from the South, lay his vile hands on your own bosom companion and do to her what he has done to the companion of another and what Prof. Stuart and Dr. Fisk say he may do, "without violating the Christian faith," and I fear not your reply. None but a moral monster ever consented to the enslavement of his own daughter, and none but fiends incarnate ever enslaved the daughter of another. Indeed, I think the demons in hell would be ashamed to do to their fellow demons what many of our clergy do to their own church members.

3. *Manstealing*. What is it to steal a man? Is it not to claim him as your property? To call him yours? God has given to every man an inalienable right to himself—a right of which no conceivable circumstance of birth or forms of law can divest him; and he who interferes with the free and unrestricted exercise of that right; who, not content with the proprietorship of his own body, claims the body of his neighbor is a manstealer. This truth is self-evident. Every man, idiots and the insane only excepted, knows that he has no possible right to another's body; and he who persists, for a moment, in claiming it incurs the guilt of manstealing. The plea of the slave claimant, that he has bought or inherited his slaves, is of no avail. What right had he, I ask, to purchase or to inherit his neighbors? The purchase, or the inheritance of them as a legacy, was itself a crime of no less enormity than the original act of kidnapping. But every slaveholder, whatever his profession or standing in society may be, lays his felonious hands on the body and soul of his equal brother, robs him of himself, converts him into an article of merchandise, and leaves him a mere chattel personal in the hands of his claimant. Hence, he is a kidnapper or man-thief.

4. *Piracy*. The American people, by an act of solemn legislation, have declared the enslaving of human beings, on the coast of Africa, to be piracy and have affixed to this crime the penalty of death. And can the same act be piracy in Africa and not be piracy in America? Does crime change its character by changing longitude? Is killing with malice aforethought no murder where there is no human enactment against it? Or can it be less piratical and heaven-daring to enslave our own native countrymen than to enslave the heathen sons of a foreign and barbarous realm? If there be any difference in the two crimes, the odds [are] in favor of the foreign

142

enslaver. Slaveholding loses none of its enormity by a voyage across the Atlantic nor by baptism into the Christian name. It is piracy in Africa—it is piracy in America—it is piracy the wide world over.

And the American slaveholder, though he possess all the sanctity of the ancient Pharisees, and make prayers as numerous and long, is a *pirate* still, a base, profligate adulterer, and wicked contemner of the holy institution of marriage, identical in moral character with the African slave trader, and guilty of a crime which, if committed on a foreign coast, he must expiate on the gallows.

5. *Murder*. Murder is an act of the mind and not of the hand. "Whosoever hateth his brother is a murderer." A man may kill—that is, his hand may inflict a mortal blow—without committing murder. On the other hand, he may commit murder without actually taking life. The intention constitutes the crime. He who, with a pistol at my breast, demands my pocketbook or my life is a murderer, whichever I may choose to part with. And is not he a murderer who, with the same deadly weapon, demands the surrender of what to me is of infinitely more value than my pocketbook, nay, than life itself—my liberty—myself—my wife and children—all that I possess on earth or can hope for in heaven?

But this is the crime of which every slaveholder is guilty. He maintains his ascendancy over his victims, extorting their unrequited labor and sundering the dearest ties of kindred, only by the threat of extermination. With the slave, as every intelligent person knows, there is no alternative. It is submission or death, or, more frequently, protracted torture more horrible than death. Indeed, the South never sleeps, but on dirks and pistols and bowie knives, with a troop of bloodhounds standing sentry at every door!

What, I ask, means this splendid enginery of death, which gilds the palace of the tyrant master? It tells the story of his guilt. The burnished steel which waits beneath his slumbering pillow, to drink the blood of outraged innocence, brands him as a murderer. It proves, beyond dispute, that the submission of his victims is the only reason why he has not already shed their blood.

By this brief analysis of slavery, we stamp upon the forehead of the slaveholder with a brand deeper than that which marks the victim of his wrongs, the infamy of theft, adultery, manstealing, piracy, and murder. We demonstrate beyond the possibility of doubt that he who enslaves another, that is, robs him of his right to himself, to his own hands and head and feet, and transforms him from a free moral agent into a mere *brute,* to obey, not the commands of God but his claimant, is guilty of every one of these atrocious crimes. And in doing this, we have only demonstrated what, to every reflecting mind, is self-evident. Every man, if he would but make the case of the slave his own, would feel in his inmost soul the truth and justice of this charge.

But these are the crimes which I have alleged against the American church and clergy. Hence, to sustain my charge against them, it only remains for me to show that they are slaveholders. That they are slaveholders—party to a conspiracy against the liberty of more than 2 million of our countrymen, and, as such, are guilty of the crimes of which they stand accused—I affirm, and will now proceed to prove.

It may be necessary for me first, however, to show what constitutes slaveholding, as there seems to be no little confusion in the minds of many on this point. And here let me say, the word itself, if analyzed, will give an accurate description of the act. It is to *hold* one in slavery—to keep him in the condition of a chattel. But slaveholding, in all cases, is necessarily a social crime. A man may commit theft or murder alone, but no *solitary* individual can ever *enslave* another. It is only when several persons associate together and combine their influence against the liberty of an individual, that he can be deprived of his freedom and reduced to slavery. Hence, connection with an association, any part of whose object is to hold men in slavery, constitutes one a slaveholder.

Nor is the nature or criminality of his offense altered or affected by the number of persons connected with him in such an association. If a million of people conspire together to enslave a solitary individual, each of them is a slaveholder, and no less guilty than if he were alone in the crime. It is no palliation of his offense to say that he is opposed to slavery. The better feelings of every slaveholder are opposed to slavery. But if he be opposed to it, why, I ask, is he concerned in it? Why does he countenance, aid, or abet the infernal system? The fact of his opposition to it, in feeling instead of mitigating his guilt only enhances it, since it proves, conclusively, that

144

he is not unconscious of the wrong he is doing.

It is a common but mistaken opinion that to constitute one a slaveholder he must be the claimant of slaves. That title belongs alike to the slave claimant and all those who, by their countenance or otherwise, lend their influence to support the slave system. If I aid or countenance another in stealing, I am a thief, though he receive all the booty. The Knapps, it will be recollected, were hung as the murderers of Mr. White, though Crowninshield gave the fatal blow, and that, too, while they were at a distance from the bloody scene. It matters little who does the mastery and puts on the drag chain and handcuffs, whether it be James B. Gray, or the Boston Police, Judge Story, or some distinguished doctor of divinity of the South; the guilt of the transaction consists in authorizing or allowing it to be done. Hence, all who, through their political or ecclesiastical connections, aid or countenance the master in his work of death, are slaveholders, and as such, are stained with all the moral turpitude which attaches to the man, who, by their sanction, wields the bloody lash over the heads of his trembling victims and buries it deep in their quivering flesh. Nay, the human hounds which guard the plantation, ever eager to bark on the track of the flying fugitive, are objects of deeper indignation and abhorrence than even its lordly proprietor.

How stands this matter, then, in regard to the American church and clergy? Is it true of them, that they are either claimants of slaves, or *watchdogs* of the plantation? Such, I regret to say, is the shameful and humiliating fact. It is undeniably true that, with comparatively few exceptions, they occupy one of these two positions in relation to the "peculiar institution." Thousands of the ministers and tens of thousands of the members of the different sects are actual claimants of slaves. They buy and sell, mortgage and lease their own "brethren in the Lord," not infrequently breaking up families and scattering their bleeding fragments over all the land, never to be gathered again, till the archangel's trumpet shall wake their slumbering ashes into life.

145

CHARLES LENOX REMOND

A Negro Protest Against Segregation in Travel

In 1840 the American Anti-Slavery Society sent the distinguished Negro, Charles Remond, to the London World Anti-Slavery Conference. Remond remained abroad for nearly two years, lecturing in England and Ireland and enjoying the absence of Negro prejudice there. Immediately after he returned to Massachusetts he was compelled to take a seat in a special railroad car for Negroes, and his friends prevailed on him to testify about the situation at the hearings then being conducted by a committee of the Massachusetts House of Representatives. Remond addressed the committee in late February 1842; portions of his remarks are reprinted below. In April 1848 the Massachusetts railroads were desegregated. [Source: Liberator, February 25, 1842.]

Mr. Chairman, and Gentlemen of the Committee:

In rising at this time and on this occasion, being the first person of color who has ever addressed either of the bodies assembling in this building, I should, perhaps, in the first place, observe that, in consequence of the many misconstructions of the principles and measures of which I am the humble advocate, I may in like manner be subject to similar misconceptions from the moment I open my lips in behalf of the prayer of the petitioners for whom I appear, and therefore feel I have the right at least to ask, at the hands of this intelligent Committee, an impartial hearing; and that whatever prejudices they may have imbibed be eradicated from their minds, if such exist. I have, however, too much confidence in their intelligence and too much faith in their determination to do their duty as the representatives of this Commonwealth to presume they can be actuated by partial motives.

Trusting, as I do, that the day is not distant when, on all questions touching the rights of the citizens of this state, men shall be considered *great* only as they are *good*, and not that it shall be told and painfully experienced, that, in this country, this state, aye, this city, the Athens of America, the rights, privileges, and immunities of its citizens are measured by complexion, or any other physical peculiarity or conformation, especially such as over which no man has any control. Complexion can in no sense be construed into crime, much less be rightfully made the criterion of rights. Should the people of color, through a revolution of Providence, become a majority, to the last I would oppose it upon the same principle; for, in either case, it would be equally reprehensible and unjustifiable—alike to be condemned and repudiated. It is JUSTICE I stand here to claim and not FAVOR for either complexion. . . .

Our right to citizenship in this state has been acknowledged and secured by the allowance of the elective franchise and consequent taxation; and I know of no good reason, if admitted in this instance, why it should be denied in any other.

With reference to the wrongs inflicted and injuries received on railroads by persons of color, I need not say they do not end with the termination of the route, but, in effect, tend to discourage, disparage, and depress this class of citizens. All hope of reward for upright conduct is cut off. Vice in them becomes a virtue. No distinction is made by the community in which we live. The most vicious is treated as well as the most respectable, both in public and private.

But it is said we all look alike. If this is true, it is not true that we all behave alike. There is a marked difference; and we claim a recognition of this difference.

In the present state of things, they find God's provisions interfered with in such a way, by these and kindred regulations, that virtue may not claim her divinely appointed rewards. Color is made to obscure the brightest endowments, to degrade the fairest character, and to check the highest and most praiseworthy aspirations. If the colored man is vicious, it makes but little difference; if besotted, it matters not; if vulgar, it is quite as well; and he finds himself as well treated and received as readily into society as those of an opposite character. . . .

Nay, the higher our aspirations, the loftier our purposes and pursuits, does this iniquitous principle of prejudice fasten upon us; and especial pains are taken to irritate, obstruct, and injure. No reward of merit, no remuneration for services, no equivalent is rendered the deserving.

And I submit whether this unkind and unchristian policy is not well calculated to make every man disregardful of his conduct, and

147

every woman unmindful of her reputation.

The grievances of which we complain, be assured, sir, are not imaginary but real; not local but universal; not occasional but continual, every-day, matter-of-fact things, and have become, to the disgrace of our common country, matter of history.

Mr. Chairman, the treatment to which colored Americans are exposed in their own country finds a counterpart in no other; and I am free to declare that, in the course of nineteen months' traveling in England, Ireland, and Scotland, I was received, treated, and recognized in public and private society without any regard to my complexion. . . . In no instance was I insulted or treated in any way distinct or dissimilar from other passengers or travelers, either in coaches, railroads, steampackets, or hotels; and if the feeling was entertained, in no case did I discover its existence. . . .

There is a marked difference between social and civil rights. It has been well and justly remarked by my friend Mr. Phillips that we all claim the privilege of selecting our society and associations; but, in civil rights, one man has not the prerogative to define rights for another. For instance, sir, in public conveyances, for the rich man to usurp the privileges to himself, to the injury of the poor man, would be submitted to in no well-regulated society. And such is the position suffered by persons of color.

On my arrival home from England, I went to the railway station to go to Salem, being anxious to see my parents and sisters as soon as possible; asked for a ticket; paid 50 cents for it; and was pointed to the American designation car. Having previously received information of the regulations, I took my seat peaceably, believing it better to suffer wrong than do wrong. I felt then, as I felt on many occasions prior to leaving home, unwilling to descend so low as to bandy words with the superintendents or contest my rights with conductors, or any others in the capacity of servants of any stage or steamboat company or railroad corporation; although I never, by any means, gave evidence that, by my submission, I intended to sanction usages which would derogate from uncivilized, much less long and loud professing and high pretending America.

Bear with me while I relate an additional occurrence. On the morning after my return home, I was obliged to go to Boston again, and, on going to the Salem station, I met two friends, who inquired

148

if I had any objection to their taking seats with me. I answered I should be most happy. They took their seats accordingly, and soon afterward one of them remarked to me; "Charles, I don't know if they will allow us to ride with you." It was some time before I could understand what they meant, and, on doing so, I laughed, feeling it to be a climax to every absurdity I had heard attributed to Americans. To say nothing of the wrong done those friends, and the insult and indignity offered me by the appearance of the conductor, who ordered the friends from the car in a somewhat harsh manner, they immediately left the carriage.

On returning to Salem some few evenings afterward, Mr. Chase, the superintendent on this road, made himself known to me by recalling bygone days and scenes; and then inquired if I was not glad to get home after so long an absence in Europe. I told him I was glad to see my parents and family again, and this was the only object I could have, unless he thought I should be glad to take a hermit's life in the great pasture, inasmuch as I never felt to loathe my American name so much as since my arrival. He wished to know my reasons for the remark. I immediately gave them and wished to know of him if, in the event of his having a brother with red hair, he should find himself separated while traveling because of this difference he should deem it just. He could make no reply. I then wished to know if the principle was not the same; and if so, there was an insult implied by his question.

In conclusion, I challenged him as the instrument inflicting the manifold injuries upon all not colored like himself to the presentation of an instance in any other Christian or unchristian country, tolerating usages at once so disgraceful, unjust, and inhuman. What if some few of the West or East India planters and merchants should visit our liberty-loving country with their colored wives; how would he manage? Or, if R. M. Johnson, the gentleman who has been elevated to the second office in the gift of the people, should be traveling from Boston to Salem, if he was prepared to separate him from his wife or daughters. [*Involuntary burst of applause, instantly restrained.*]

Sir, it happens to be my lot to have a sister a few shades lighter than myself; and who knows, if this state of things is encouraged, whether I may not on some future occasion be mobbed in Washing-

ton Street on the supposition of walking with a white young lady!
[*Suppressed indications of sympathy and applause.*]

Gentlemen of the Committee, these distinctions react in all their
wickedness, to say nothing of their concocted and systematized
odiousness and absurdity, upon those who instituted them; and
particularly so upon those who are illiberal and mean enough to
practise them.

Mr. Chairman, if colored people have abused any rights granted
them, or failed to exhibit due appreciation of favors bestowed, or
shrunk from dangers or responsibility, let it be made to appear. Or if
our country contains a population to compare with them in loyalty
and patriotism, circumstances duly considered, I have it yet to
learn. The history of our country must ever testify in their behalf. In
view of these and many additional considerations, I unhesitatingly
assert their claim, on the naked principle of merit, to every advantage set forth in the constitution of this Commonwealth.

Finally, Mr. Chairman, there is in this and other states a large
and growing colored population, whose residence in your midst has
not been from choice (let this be understood and reflected upon), but
by the force of circumstances over which they never had control.
Upon the heads of their oppressors and calumniators be the censure and responsibility. If to ask at your hands redress for injuries,
and protection in our rights and immunities, as citizens is reasonable, and dictated alike by justice, humanity, and religion, you will
not reject, I trust, the prayer of your petitioners.

THEODORE WELD

Slavery As It Is

*Theodore Weld was the most influential Abolitionist of his time, far more
effective than William Lloyd Garrison. Both at Lane Theological Seminary in
Cincinnati and at New York in the 1830s, he consolidated the antislavery
movement in the North, converting many important persons. The following
was the most widely read (100,000 copies were sold) of the many*

pamphlets he published. It served as the source for Uncle Tom's Cabin *and was compiled from thousands of Southern newspapers with the help of the Grimke sisters, noted Abolitionists from Charleston, one of whom Weld married. He afterwards (1841-1843) organized the antislavery bloc in Congress, led by John Quincy Adams. [Source:* American Slavery As It Is: Testimony of a Thousand Witnesses, *New York, 1839, pp. 7-9, 164-167.]*

Reader, you are impaneled as a juror to try a plain case and bring in an honest verdict. The question at issue is not one of law but of fact—What is the actual condition of the slaves in the United States? A plainer case never went to a jury. Look at it. TWENTY-SEVEN HUNDRED THOUSAND PERSONS in this country, men, women, and children, are in SLAVERY. Is slavery, as a condition for human beings, good, bad, or indifferent? We submit the question without argument. You have common sense, and conscience, and a human heart—pronounce upon it. You have a wife, or a husband, a child, a father, a mother, a brother, or a sister—make the case your own, make it theirs, and bring in your verdict.

The case of Human Rights against Slavery has been adjudicated in the court of conscience times innumerable. The same verdict has always been rendered—"Guilty"; the same sentence has always been pronounced, "Let it be accursed"; and human nature, with her million echoes, has rung it round the world in every language under heaven, "Let it be accursed. Let it be accursed." His heart is false to human nature who will not say "Amen." There is not a man on earth who does not believe that slavery is a curse. Human beings may be inconsistent, but human *nature* is true to herself. She has uttered her testimony against slavery with a shriek ever since the monster was begotten; and till it perishes amidst the execrations of the universe, she will traverse the world on its track, dealing her bolts upon its head, and dashing against it her condemning brand.

We repeat it, every man knows that slavery is a curse. Whoever denies this, his lips libel his heart. Try him; clank the chains in his ears and tell him they are for *him*. Give him an hour to prepare his wife and children for a life of slavery. Bid him make haste and get ready their necks for the yoke, and their wrists for the coffle chains, then look at his pale lips and trembling knees, and you have *nature's* testimony against slavery.

151

Two million seven hundred thousand persons in these states are in this condition. They were made slaves and are held such by force, and by being put in fear, and this for no crime! Reader, what have you to say of such treatment? Is it right, just, benevolent? Suppose I should seize you, rob you of your liberty, drive you into the field, and make you work without pay as long as you live—would that be justice and kindness, or monstrous injustice and cruelty?

Now, everybody knows that the slaveholders do these things to the slaves every day, and yet it is stoutly affirmed that they treat them well and kindly, and that their tender regard for their slaves restrains the masters from inflicting cruelties upon them. We shall go into no metaphysics to show the absurdity of this pretense. The man who *robs* you every day is, forsooth, quite too tenderhearted ever to cuff or kick you!

True, he can snatch your money, but he does it gently lest he should hurt you. He can empty your pockets without qualms, but if your *stomach* is empty, it cuts him to the quick. He can make you work a lifetime without pay, but loves you too well to let you go hungry. He fleeces you of your *rights* with a relish, but is shocked if you work bareheaded in summer or in winter without warm stockings. He can make you go without your *liberty*, but never without a shirt. He can crush, in you, all hope of bettering your condition by vowing that you shall die his slave, but, though he can coolly torture your feelings, he is too compassionate to lacerate your back; he can break your heart, but he is very tender of your skin. He can strip you of all protection and thus expose you to all outrages, but if you are exposed to the *weather*, half-clad and half-sheltered, how yearn his tender bowels!

What! Slaveholders talk of treating men well, and yet not only rob them of all they get, and as fast as they get it, but rob them of *themselves*, also; their very hands and feet, and all their muscles, and limbs, and senses, their bodies and minds, their time and liberty and earnings, their free speech and rights of conscience, their right to acquire knowledge and property and reputation; and yet they who plunder them of all these would fain make us believe that their soft hearts ooze out so lovingly toward their slaves that they always keep them well-housed and well-clad, never push them too hard in the field, never make their dear backs smart, nor let their dear stomachs get empty.

152

But there is no end to these absurdities. Are slaveholders dunces, or do they take all the rest of the world to be, that they think to bandage our eyes with such thin gauzes? Protesting their kind regard for those whom they hourly plunder of all they have and all they get! What! When they have seized their victims and annihilated all their *rights*, still claim to be the special guardians of their *happiness!* Plunderers of their liberty, yet the careful suppliers of their wants? Robbers of their earnings, yet watchful sentinels round their interests, and kind providers of their comforts? Filching all their time, yet granting generous donations for rest and sleep? Stealing the use of their muscles, yet thoughtful of their ease? Putting them under drivers, yet careful that they are not hard-pushed? Too humane, forsooth, to stint the stomachs of their slaves, yet force their *minds* to starve, and brandish over them pains and penalties if they dare to reach forth for the smallest crumb of knowledge, even a letter of the alphabet!

It is no marvel that slaveholders are always talking of their *kind treatment* of their slaves. The only marvel is that men of sense can be gulled by such professions. Despots always insist that they are merciful. The greatest tyrants that ever dripped with blood have assumed the titles of "most gracious," "most clement," "most merciful," etc., and have ordered their crouching vassals to accost them thus. When did not vice lay claim to those virtues which are the opposites of its habitual crimes? The guilty, according to their own showing, are always innocent, and cowards brave, and drunkards sober, and harlots chaste, and pickpockets honest to a fault. . . .

As slaveholders and their apologists are volunteer witnesses in their own cause and are flooding the world with testimony that their slaves are kindly treated; that they are well-fed, well-clothed, well-housed, well-lodged, moderately worked, and bountifully provided with all things needful for their comfort, we propose, first, to disprove their assertions by the testimony of a multitude of impartial witnesses, and then to put slaveholders themselves through a course of cross-questioning which shall draw their condemnation out of their own mouths.

We will prove that the slaves in the United States are treated with barbarous inhumanity; that they are overworked, underfed, wretchedly clad and lodged, and have insufficient sleep; that they are often made to wear round their necks iron collars armed with prongs, to drag heavy chains and weights at their feet while working in the field, and to wear yokes, and bells, and iron horns; that they are often kept confined in the stocks day and night for weeks together, made to wear gags in their mouths for hours or days, have some of their front teeth torn out or broken off that they may be easily detected when they run away; that they are frequently flogged with terrible severity, have red pepper rubbed into their lacerated flesh, and hot brine, spirits of turpentine, etc., poured over the gashes to increase the torture; that they are often stripped naked, their backs and limbs cut with knives, bruised and mangled by scores and hundreds of blows with the paddle, and terribly torn by the claws of cats, drawn over them by their tormentors; that they are often hunted with bloodhounds and shot down like beasts, or torn in pieces by dogs; that they are often suspended by the arms and whipped and beaten till they faint, and, when revived by restoratives, beaten again till they faint, and sometimes till they die; that their ears are often cut off, their eyes knocked out, their bones broken, their flesh branded with red hot irons; that they are maimed, mutilated, and burned to death over slow fires. All these things, and more, and worse, we shall *prove*. Reader, we know whereof we affirm, we have weighed it well; *more and worse* WE WILL PROVE.

Mark these words, and read on; we will establish all these facts by the testimony of scores and hundreds of eyewitnesses, by the testimony of *slaveholders* in all parts of the slave states, by slaveholding members of Congress and of state legislatures, by ambassadors to foreign courts, by judges, by doctors of divinity, and clergymen of all denominations, by merchants, mechanics, lawyers, and physicians, by presidents and professors in colleges and professional seminaries, by planters, overseers, and drivers. We shall show, not merely that such deeds are committed but that they are frequent; not done in corners but before the sun; not in one of the slave states but in all of them; not perpetrated by brutal overseers and drivers merely but by magistrates, by legislators, by professors of religion, by preachers of the gospel, by governors of states, by "gentlemen of property and standing," and by delicate females moving

154

in the "highest circles of society."

We know, full well, the outcry that will be made by multitudes, at these declarations; the multiform cavils, the flat denials, the charges of "exaggeration" and "falsehood" so often bandied, the sneers of affected contempt at the credulity that can believe such things, and the rage and imprecations against those who give them currency. We know, too, the threadbare sophistries by which slaveholders and their apologists seek to evade such testimony. If they admit that such deeds are committed, they tell us that they are exceedingly rare, and therefore furnish no grounds for judging of the general treatment of slaves; that occasionally a brutal wretch in the *free* states barbarously butchers his wife, but that no one thinks of inferring from that the general treatment of wives at the North and West.

They tell us, also, that the slaveholders of the South are proverbially hospitable, kind, and generous, and it is incredible that they can perpetrate such enormities upon human beings; further, that it is absurd to suppose that they would thus injure their own property, that self-interest would prompt them to treat their slaves with kindness, as none but fools and madmen wantonly destroy their own property; further, that Northern visitors at the South come back testifying to the kind treatment of the slaves, and that the slaves themselves corroborate such representations. All these pleas, and scores of others, are bruited in every corner of the free states; and who that has eyes to see has not sickened at the blindness that saw not, at the palsy of heart that felt not, or at the cowardice and sycophancy that dared not expose such shallow fallacies. We are not to be turned from our purpose by such vapid babblings. . . .

The foregoing declarations touching the inflictions upon slaves are not haphazard assertions, nor the exaggerations of fiction conjured up to carry a point; nor are they the rhapsodies of enthusiasm, nor crude conclusions jumped at by hasty and imperfect investigation, nor the aimless outpourings either of sympathy or poetry; but they are proclamations of deliberate, well-weighed convictions, produced by accumulations of proof, by affirmations and affidavits, by written testimonies and statements of a cloud of witnesses who speak what they know and testify what they have seen; and all these impregnably fortified by proofs innumerable in the relation of the slaveholder to his slave, the nature of arbitrary power, and the nature and history of man. . . .

The barbarous indifference with which slaveholders regard the forcible sundering of husbands and wives, parents and children, brothers and sisters, and the unfeeling brutality indicated by the language in which they describe the efforts made by the slaves, in their yearnings after those from whom they have been torn away, reveals a "public opinion" toward them as dead to their agony as if they were cattle. It is well-nigh impossible to open a Southern paper without finding evidence of this. Though the truth of this assertion can hardly be called in question, we subjoin a few illustrations, and could easily give hundreds. . . .

From the *Southern Argus*, Oct. 31, 1837.

"Runaway—my negro man, Frederick, about 20 years of age. He is no doubt near the plantation of G. W. Corprew, Esq. of Noxubbee county, Mississippi, as *his wife belongs to that gentleman, and he followed her from my residence*. The above reward will be paid to any one who will confine him in jail and inform me of it at Athens, Ala.

"Athens, Alabama.

KERKMAN LEWIS."

From the *Savannah* (Ga.) *Republican*, May 24, 1838.

"$40 Reward.—Ran away from the subscriber in Savannah, his negro girl Patsey. She was purchased among the gang of negroes, known as the Hargreave's estate. She is no doubt lurking about Liberty county, at which place *she has relatives*.

EDWARD HOUSTOUN, of Florida."

From the *Charleston* (S.C.) *Courier*, June 29, 1837.

"$20 Reward will be paid for the apprehension and delivery, at the work-house in Charleston, of a mulatto woman, named Ida. It is probable she may have made her way into Georgia, where she has *connections*.

MATTHEW MUGGRIDGE."

From the *Norfolk* (Va.) *Beacon*, March 31, 1838.

"The subscriber will give $20 for the apprehension of his negro woman, Maria, who ran away about twelve months since. She is known to be lurking in or about Chuckatuch, in the county of Nansemond, where *she has a husband*, and *formerly belonged.*

PETER ONEILL."

From the *Macon* (Ga.) *Messenger*, Jan. 16, 1839.
"Ranaway from the subscriber, two negroes, Davis, a man about 45 years old; also Peggy, his wife, near the same age. Said negroes will probably make their way to Columbia county, as *they have children* living in that county. I will liberally reward any person who may deliver them to me.

NEHEMIAH KING."

From the *Petersburg* (Va.) *Constellation*, June 27, 1837.
"Ranaway, a negro man, named Peter. *He has a wife* at the plantation of Mr. C. Haws, near Suffolk, where it is supposed he is still lurking.

JOHN L. DUNN."

From the *Richmond* (Va.) *Whig*, Dec. 7, 1839.
"Ranaway from the subscriber, a negro man, named John Lewis. It is supposed that he is lurking about in New Kent county, where he professes to have *a wife.*

HILL JONES,
Agent for R. F. & P. Railroad Co."

From the *Richmond* (Va.) *Enquirer*, Feb. 20, 1838.
"$10 Reward for a negro woman, named Sally, 40 years old. We have just reason to believe the said negro to be now lurking on the James River Canal, or in the Green Spring neighborhood, where, we are informed, *her husband resides.* The above reward will be given to any person *securing* her.

POLLY C. SHIELDS.
Mount Elba, Feb. 19, 1838."

"$50 Reward.—Ran away from the subscriber, his negro man Pauladore, commonly called Paul. I understand GEN. R. Y. HAYNE *has purchased his wife and children* from H. L. PINCKNEY, ESQ. and has them now on his plantation at Goosecreek, where, no doubt, the fellow is frequently *lurking.*

T. DAVIS."

157

"$25 Reward.—Ran away from the subscriber, a negro woman, named Matilda. It is thought she may be somewhere up James River, as she was claimed as *a wife* by some boatman in Goochland.

J. ALVIS."

"Stop the Runaway!!!—$25 Reward. Ranaway from the Eagle Tavern, a negro fellow, named Nat. He is no doubt attempting to *follow his wife, who was lately sold to a speculator* named Redmond. The above reward will be paid by Mrs. Lucy M. Downman, of Sussex county, Va."

Multitudes of advertisements like the above appear annually in the Southern papers. Reader, look at the preceding list—mark the unfeeling barbarity with which their masters and *mistresses* describe the struggles and perils of sundered husbands and wives, parents and children, in their weary midnight travels through forests and rivers, with torn limbs and breaking hearts, seeking the embraces of each other's love. In one instance, a mother, torn from all her children and taken to a remote part of another state, presses her way back through the wilderness, hundreds of miles, to clasp once more her children to her heart; but, when she has arrived within a few miles of them, in the same county, is discovered, seized, dragged to jail, and her purchaser told, through an advertisement, that she awaits his order. But we need not trace out the harrowing details already before the reader.

3. The Abolitionists
1832-1839

FRANCES ANNE KEMBLE

Life on a Georgia Plantation

The Abolitionist movement in England had a long history prior to its formation in the United States. Thus when Frances Anne Kemble, an English actress, came to the United States in 1832, she was already enlisted among slavery's foes. In 1834 she married a wealthy Philadelphian, Pierce Mease Butler, and two years after their marriage he inherited a plantation in Georgia. Fanny Kemble Butler thereby became the mistress of more than 700 slaves. The estate comprised two islands, one specializing in cotton and the other in rice, and the Butlers spent two months there in the winter of 1838-1839. Because her husband did not share her scruples about benefiting from the labor of slaves, Fanny confided her observations on plantation life to a diary. The Butlers were later divorced and Fanny returned to England. She published her diary in 1863 to discourage the British from supporting the Confederacy in the American Civil War and to promote sympathy for the North. [Source: Journal of a Residence on a Georgian Plantation in 1838-1839, New York, 1863, pp. 16 37.]

Dear E – – –,

Minuteness of detail and fidelity in the account of my daily doings will hardly, I fear, render my letters very interesting to you now; but, cut off as I am here from all the usual resources and amusements of civilized existence, I shall find but little to communicate to you that is not furnished by my observations on the novel appearance of external nature, and the moral and physical condition of Mr. – – –'s people. . . .

I shall furnish you with no details but those which come under my own immediate observation.

The rice mill . . . is worked by a steam engine of 30 horsepower, and, besides threshing a great part of our own rice, is kept constantly employed by the neighboring planters, who send their grain to it in preference to the more distant mill at Savannah, paying, of course, the same percentage, which makes it a very profitable addition to the estate. Immediately opposite to this building is a small shed, which they call the cook's shop, and where the daily allowance of rice and corn grits of the people is boiled and distributed to them by an old woman, whose special business this is.

There are four settlements or villages (or, as the Negroes call them, camps) on the island, consisting of from ten to twenty houses, and to each settlement is annexed a cook's shop with capacious caldrons, and the oldest wife of the settlement for officiating priestess. . . .

I must inform you of a curious conversation which took place between my little girl and the woman who performs for us the offices of chambermaid here—of course, one of Mr. — — —'s slaves. What suggested it to the child, or whence indeed she gathered her information, I know not; but children are made of eyes and ears, and nothing, however minute, escapes their microscopic observation. She suddenly began addressing this woman.

"Mary, some persons are free and some are not (the woman made no reply). I am a free person (of a little more than three years old). I say, I am a free person, Mary—do you know that?"

"Yes, missis."

"Some persons are free and some are not—do you know that, Mary?"

"Yes, missis, *here*," was the reply; "I know it is so here, in this world."

Here my child's white nurse, my dear Margery, who had hitherto been silent, interfered, saying: "Oh, then you think it will not always be so?"

"Me hope not, missis."

I am afraid, E— — —, this woman actually imagines that there will be no slaves in heaven; isn't that preposterous, now, when, by the account of most of the Southerners, slavery itself must be heaven, or something uncommonly like it? Oh, if you could imagine how this title "Missis," addressed to me and to my children, shocks all my feelings! Several times I have exclaimed: "For God's sake do not call me that!" and only been awakened by the stupid amazement of the poor creatures I was addressing to the perfect uselessness of my thus expostulating with them; once or twice, indeed, I have done more—I have explained to them, and they appeared to comprehend me well, that I had no ownership over them, for that I held such ownership sinful, and that, though I was the wife of the man who pretends to own them, I was, in truth, no more their mistress than they were mine. Some of them, I know, understood me, more of them did not.

Our servants—those who have been selected to wait upon us in the house—consist of a man, who is quite a tolerable cook (I believe this is a natural gift with them, as with Frenchmen); a dairywoman, who churns for us; a laundrywoman; her daughter, our housemaid, the aforesaid Mary; and two young lads of from fifteen to twenty, who wait upon us in the capacity of footmen. As, however, the latter are perfectly filthy in their persons and clothes—their faces, hands, and naked feet being literally encrusted with dirt—their attendance at our meals is not, as you may suppose, particularly agreeable to me, and I dispense with it as often as possible. Mary, too, is so intolerably offensive in her person that it is impossible to endure her proximity, and the consequence is that, among Mr. — — —'s slaves, I wait upon myself more than I have ever done in my life before. About this same personal offensiveness, the Southerners, you know, insist that it is inherent with the race, and it is one of their most cogent reasons for keeping them as slaves.

But, as this very disagreeable peculiarity does not prevent Southern women from hanging their infants at the breasts of Negresses, nor almost every planter's wife and daughter from having one or more little pet blacks sleeping like puppy dogs in their very bedchamber, nor almost every planter from admitting one or several of his female slaves to the still closer intimacy of his bed, it seems to me that this objection to doing them right is not very valid. I cannot imagine that they would smell much worse if they were free, or come in much closer contact with the delicate organs of their white fellow countrymen; indeed, inasmuch as good deeds are spoken of as having a sweet savor before God, it might be supposed that the freeing of the blacks might prove rather an odoriferous process than the contrary.

However this may be, I must tell you that this potent reason for enslaving a whole race of people is no more potent with me than most of the others adduced to support the system, inasmuch as, from observation and some experience, I am strongly inclined to believe that peculiar ignorance of the laws of health and the habits of decent cleanliness are the real and only causes of this disagreeable characteristic of the race, thorough ablutions and change of linen, when tried, have been perfectly successful in removing all such objections; and if ever you have come into anything like neighborly proximity with a low Irishman or woman, I think you will allow that the same causes produce very nearly the same effects. The stench in an Irish, Scotch, Italian, or French hovel is quite as intolerable as any I ever found in our Negro houses, and the filth and vermin which abound about the clothes and persons of the lower peasantry of any of those countries as abominable as the same conditions in the black population of the United States. A total absence of self-respect begets these hateful physical results, and in proportion as moral influences are remote, physical evils will abound. Well-being, freedom, and industry induce self-respect, self-respect induces cleanliness and personal attention, so that slavery is answerable for all the evils that exhibit themselves where it exists—from lying, thieving, and adultery to dirty houses, ragged clothes, and foul smells.

But to return to our Ganymedes. One of them—the eldest son of our laundrywoman and Mary's brother, a boy of the name of Aleck (Alexander)—is uncommonly bright and intelligent; he performs all the offices of a well-instructed waiter with great efficiency, and anywhere out of slaveland would be able to earn $14 or $15 a month for himself; he is remarkably good tempered and well disposed. The other poor boy is so stupid that he appears sullen from absolute darkness of intellect; instead of being a little lower than the angels, he is scarcely a little higher than the brutes, and to this condition are reduced the majority of his kind by the institutions under which they live. I should tell you that Aleck's parents and kindred have always been about the house of the overseer, and in daily habits of intercourse with him and his wife; and wherever this is the case the effect of involuntary education is evident in the improved intelligence of the degraded race. . . .

Now, E— — —, I have no intention of telling you a one-sided story, or concealing from you what are cited as the advantages which these poor people possess; you, who know that no indulgence is worth simple justice, either to him who gives or him who receives, will not thence conclude that their situation thus mitigated is, therefore, what it should be. On this matter of the $60 earned by Mr. — — —'s two men much stress was laid by him and his overseer. I look at it thus: if these men were industrious enough, out of their scanty leisure, to earn $60, how much more of remuneration, of comfort, of improvement might they not have achieved were the price of their daily labor duly paid them instead of being unjustly withheld to support an idle young man and his idle family, *i.e.*, myself and my children.

And here it may be well to inform you that the slaves on this plantation are divided into field hands and mechanics or artisans. The former, the great majority, are the more stupid and brutish of the tribe; the others, who are regularly taught their trades, are not only exceedingly expert at them but exhibit a greater general activity of intellect, which must necessarily result from even a partial degree of cultivation. There are here a gang (for that is the honorable term) of coopers, of blacksmiths, of bricklayers, of carpenters, all well acquainted with their peculiar trades. The latter constructed the wash-hand stands, clothespresses, sofas, tables, etc., with which our house is furnished, and they are very neat pieces of workmanship—neither veneered or polished indeed, nor of very costly materials, but of the white pinewood planed as smooth as marble—a species of furniture not very luxurious perhaps, but all the better adapted, therefore, to the house itself, which is certainly rather more devoid of the conveniences and adornments of modern existence than anything I ever took up my abode in before.

It consists of three small rooms, and three still smaller, which would be more appropriately designated as closets, a wooden recess by way of pantry, and a kitchen detached from the dwelling—a mere wooden outhouse with no floor but the bare earth, and for furniture a congregation of filthy Negroes who lounge in and out of it like hungry hounds at all hours of the day and night, picking up such scraps of food as they can find about, which they discuss squatting down upon their hams, in which interesting position and occupation I generally find a number of them whenever I have sufficient hardihood to venture within those precincts, the sight of which and its tenants is enough to slacken the appetite of the hungriest hunter that ever lost all nice regards in the mere animal desire for food. Of our three apartments, one is our sitting, eating, and *living* room, and is sixteen feet by fifteen. The walls are plastered indeed, but neither painted nor papered. It is divided from our bedroom (a similarly elegant and comfortable chamber) by a dingy wooden partition covered all over with hooks, pegs, and nails, to which hats, caps, keys, etc., etc., are suspended in graceful irregularity. The doors open by wooden latches, raised by means of small bits of pack-thread—I imagine, the same primitive order of fastening celebrated in the touching chronicle of Red Riding Hood; how they shut I will not attempt to describe, as the shutting of a door is a process of extremely rare occurrence throughout the whole Southern country. The third room, a chamber with sloping ceiling, immediately over our sitting room and under the roof, is appropriated to the nurse and my two babies.

Of the closets, one is Mr. — — —, the overseer's, bedroom, the other his office or place of business; and the third, adjoining our bedroom and opening immediately out-of-doors, is Mr. — — —'s dressing room and *cabinet d'affaires*, where he gives audiences to the Negroes, redresses grievances, distributes red woolen caps (a singular grati-fication to a slave), shaves himself, and performs the other offices of his toilet. Such being our abode, I think you will allow there is little danger of my being dazzled by the luxurious splendors of a South-ern slave residence. Our sole mode of summoning our attendants is by a packthread bell rope suspended in the sitting room. From the bedrooms we have to raise the windows and our voices, and bring them by power of lungs, or help ourselves—which, I thank God, was never yet a hardship to me. . . .

In the part of Georgia where this estate is situated, the custom of task labor is universal, and it prevails, I believe, throughout Geor-gia, South Carolina, and parts of North Carolina; in other parts of the latter state, however—as I was informed by our overseer who is a native of that state—the estates are small, rather deserving the name of farms, and the laborers are much upon the same footing as the laboring men at the North, working from sunrise to sunset in the fields with the farmer and his sons, and coming in with them to their meals, which they take immediately after the rest of the fami-ly.

In Louisiana and the new Southwestern slave states, I believe, task labor does not prevail; but it is in those that the condition of the poor human cattle is most deplorable. As you know, it was there that the humane calculation was not only made but openly and unhesi-tatingly avowed that the planters found it, upon the whole, their most profitable plan to work off (kill with labor) their whole number of slaves about once in seven years, and renew the whole stock. By-the-by, the Jewish institution of slavery is much insisted upon by the Southern upholders of the system; perhaps this is their notion of the Jewish jubilee, when the slaves were by Moses' strict enactment to be all set free.

Well, this task system is pursued on this estate; and thus it is that the two carpenters were enabled to make the boat they sold for $60. These tasks, of course, profess to be graduated according to the sex, age, and strength of the laborer; but in many instances this is not the case, as I think you will agree when I tell you that on Mr. – – –'s first visit to his estates he found that the men and the women who labored in the fields had the same task to perform. This was a noble admission of female equality, was it not? And thus it had been on the estate for many years past. Mr. – – –, of course, altered the distribution of the work, diminishing the quantity done by the women.

I had a most ludicrous visit this morning from the midwife of the estate – rather an important personage both to master and slave, as to her unassisted skill and science the ushering of all the young Negroes into their existence of bondage is entrusted. . . . Mr. – – – opened my room door, ushering in a dirty, fat, good-humored-looking old Negress, saying: "The midwife, Rose, wants to make your acquaintance."

"Oh massa!" shrieked out the old creature, in a paroxysm of admiration, "where you get this lilly alabaster baby?"

For a moment I looked round to see if she was speaking of my baby; but no, my dear, this superlative apostrophe was elicited by the fairness of *my skin*: so much for degrees of comparison. Now, I suppose that if I chose to walk arm in arm with the dingiest mulatto through the streets of Philadelphia nobody could possibly tell by my complexion that I was not his sister, so that the mere quality of mistress must have had a most miraculous effect upon my skin in the eyes of poor Rose. But this species of outrageous flattery is as usual with these people as with the low Irish, and arises from the ignorant desire, common to both the races, of propitiating at all costs the fellow creature who is to them as a Providence – or rather, I should say, a fate – for it is a heathen and no Christian relationship.

167

Soon after this visit, I was summoned into the wooden porch, or piazza, of the house to see a poor woman who desired to speak to me. This was none other than the tall, emaciated-looking Negress who, on the day of our arrival, had embraced me and my nurse with such irresistible zeal. She appeared very ill today, and presently unfolded to me a most distressing history of bodily afflictions. She was the mother of a very large family, and complained to me that, what with childbearing and hard field labor, her back was almost broken in two.

With an almost savage vehemence of gesticulation, she suddenly tore up her scanty clothing and exhibited a spectacle with which I was inconceivably shocked and sickened. The facts, without any of her corroborating statements, bore tolerable witness to the hardships of her existence. I promised to attend to her ailments and give her proper remedies; but these are natural results, inevitable and irremediable ones, of improper treatment of the female frame; and, though there may be alleviation, there cannot be any cure when once the beautiful and wonderful structure has been thus made the victim of ignorance, folly, and wickedness.

After the departure of this poor woman, I walked down the settlement toward the infirmary, or hospital, calling in at one or two of the houses along the row. These cabins consist of one room, about twelve feet by fifteen, with a couple of closets, smaller and closer than the staterooms of a ship, divided off from the main room and each other by rough wooden partitions, in which the inhabitants sleep. They have almost all of them a rude bedstead, with the gray moss of the forests for mattress, and filthy, pestilential-looking blankets for covering.

Two families (sometimes eight and ten in number) reside in one of these huts, which are mere wooden frames pinned, as it were, to the earth by a brick chimney outside, whose enormous aperture within pours down a flood of air, but little counteracted by the miserable spark of fire which hardly sends an attenuated thread of lingering smoke up its huge throat. A wide ditch runs immediately at the back of these dwellings, which is filled and emptied daily by the tide. Attached to each hovel is a small scrap of ground for a garden, which, however, is for the most part untended and uncultivated.

168

Such of these dwellings as I visited today were filthy and wretched in the extreme, and exhibited that most deplorable consequence of ignorance and an abject condition, the inability of the inhabitants to secure and improve even such pitiful comfort as might yet be achieved by them. Instead of the order, neatness, and ingenuity which might convert even these miserable hovels into tolerable residences, there was the careless, reckless, filthy indolence which even the brutes do not exhibit in their lairs and nests, and which seemed incapable of applying to the uses of existence the few miserable means of comfort yet within their reach. . . .

In the midst of the floor, or squatting round the cold hearth, would be four or five little children from four to ten years old, the latter all with babies in their arms, the care of the infants being taken from the mothers (who are driven afield as soon as they recover from child labor) and devolved upon these poor little nurses, as they are called, whose business it is to watch the infant, and carry it to its mother whenever it may require nourishment. To these hardly human little beings I addressed my remonstrances about the filth, cold, and unnecessary wretchedness of their room, bidding the older boys and girls kindle up the fire, sweep the floor, and expel the poultry.

For a long time my very words seemed unintelligible to them, till, when I began to sweep and make up the fire, etc., they first fell to laughing and then imitating me. The incrustations of dirt on their hands, feet, and faces were my next object of attack, and the stupid Negro practice (by-the-by, but a short time since nearly universal in enlightened Europe) of keeping the babies with their feet bare, and their heads, already well capped by nature with their wooly hair, wrapped in half a dozen hot, filthy coverings.

Thus I traveled down the "street," in every dwelling endeavoring to awaken a new perception, that of cleanliness, sighing, as I went, over the futility of my own exertions, for how can slaves be improved? Nevertheless, thought I, let what can be done; for it may be that, the two being incompatible, improvement may yet expel slavery; and so it might, and surely would, if, instead of beginning at the end, I could but begin at the beginning of my task. If the mind and soul were awakened instead of mere physical good attempted, the physical good would result and the great curse vanish away; but

169

my hands are tied fast, and this corner of the work is all that I may do. Yet it cannot be but, from my words and actions, some revelations should reach these poor people; and going in and out among them perpetually, I shall teach and they learn involuntarily a thousand things of deepest import. They must learn, and who can tell the fruit of that knowledge alone, that there are beings in the world, even with skins of a different color from their own, who have sympathy for their misfortunes, love for their virtues, and respect for their common nature—but oh! my heart is full almost to bursting as I walk among these most poor creatures.

The infirmary is a large two-story building, terminating the broad orange-planted space between the two rows of houses which form the first settlement; it is built of whitewashed wood, and contains four large-sized rooms. But how shall I describe to you the spectacle which was presented to me on entering the first of these? But half the casements, of which there were six, were glazed, and these were obscured with dirt, almost as much as the other windowless ones were darkened by the dingy shutters, which the shivering inmates had fastened to in order to protect themselves from the cold.

In the enormous chimney glimmered the powerless embers of a few sticks of wood, round which, however, as many of the sick women as could approach were cowering, some on wooden settles, most of them on the ground, excluding those who were too ill to rise; and these last poor wretches lay prostrate on the floor, without bed, mattress, or pillow, buried in tattered and filthy blankets, which, huddled round them as they lay strewn about, left hardly space to move upon the floor. And here, in their hour of sickness and suffering, lay those whose health and strength are spent in unrequited labor for us; those who, perhaps even yesterday, were being urged on to their unpaid task; those whose husbands, fathers, brothers, and sons were even at that hour sweating over the earth; whose produce was to buy for us all the luxuries which health can revel in, all the comforts which can alleviate sickness.

I stood in the midst of them, perfectly unable to speak, the tears pouring from my eyes at this sad spectacle of their misery, myself and my emotion alike strange and incomprehensible to them. Here lay women expecting every hour the terrors and agonies of childbirth; others who had just brought their doomed offspring into the world; others who were groaning over the anguish and bitter disappointment of miscarriages. Here lay some burning with fever; others chilled with cold and aching with rheumatism, upon the hard cold ground, the drafts and dampness of the atmosphere increasing their sufferings, and dirt, noise, and stench, and every aggravation of which sickness is capable, combined in their condition. Here they lay like brute beasts, absorbed in physical suffering; unvisited by any of those Divine influences which may ennoble the dispensations of pain and illness, forsaken, as it seemed to me, of all good; and yet, O God, Thou surely hadst not forsaken them! Now pray take notice that this is the hospital of an estate where the owners are supposed to be humane, the overseer efficient and kind, and the Negroes remarkably well-cared for and comfortable.

As soon as I recovered from my dismay, I addressed old Rose, the midwife, who had charge of this room, bidding her open the shutters of such windows as were glazed and let in the light. I next proceeded to make up the fire; but, upon my lifting a log for that purpose, there was one universal outcry of horror, and old Rose, attempting to snatch it from me, exclaimed: "Let alone, missis — let be; what for you lift wood? You have nigger enough, missis, to do it!" I hereupon had to explain to them my view of the purposes for which hands and arms were appended to our bodies, and forthwith began making Rose tidy up the miserable apartment, removing all the filth and rubbish from the floor that could be removed, folding up in piles the blankets of the patients who were not using them, and placing, in rather more sheltered and comfortable positions, those who were unable to rise. It was all that I could do, and having enforced upon them all my earnest desire that they should keep their room swept and as tidy as possible, I passed on to the other room on the ground floor, and to the two above, one of which is appropriated to the use of the men who are ill.

They were all in the same deplorable condition, the upper rooms being rather the more miserable inasmuch as none of the windows were glazed at all, and they had, therefore, only the alternative of utter darkness, or killing drafts of air from the unsheltered casements. In all, filth, disorder, and misery abounded; the floor was the only bed, and scanty begrimed rags of blankets the only covering. I

171

left this refuge for Mr. – – –'s sick dependents with my clothes covered with dust and full of vermin, and with a heart heavy enough, as you will well believe.

My morning's work had fatigued me not a little, and I was glad to return to the house, where I gave vent to my indignation and regret at the scene I had just witnessed to Mr. – – – and his overseer, who, here, is a member of our family. The latter told me that the condition of the hospital had appeared to him, from his first entering upon his situation (only within the last year), to require a reform, and that he had proposed it to the former manager Mr. K– – –, and Mr. – – –'s brother, who is part proprietor of the estate, but, receiving no encouragement from them, had supposed that it was a matter of indifference to the owners, and had left it in the condition in which he had found it, in which condition it has been for the last nineteen years and upward.

This new overseer of ours has lived fourteen years with an old Scotch gentleman, who owns an estate adjoining Mr. – – –'s, on the island of St. Simons, upon which estate, from everything I can gather and from what I know of the proprietor's character, the slaves are probably treated with as much humanity as is consistent with slavery at all, and where the management and comfort of the hospital, in particular, had been most carefully and judiciously attended to. With regard to the indifference of our former manager upon the subject of the accommodation for the sick, he was an excellent overseer, *videlicet* the estate returned a full income under his management, and such men have nothing to do with sick slaves: they are tools, to be mended only if they can be made available again; if not, to be flung by as useless, without further expense of money, time, or trouble. . . .

I forgot to tell you that in the hospital were several sick babies whose mothers were permitted to suspend their field labor in order to nurse them. Upon addressing some remonstrances to one of these, who, besides having a sick child was ill herself, about the horribly dirty condition of her baby, she assured me that it was impossible for them to keep their children clean; that they went out to work at daybreak and did not get their tasks done till evening, and that then they were too tired and worn out to do anything but throw themselves down and sleep. This statement of hers I mentioned on my return from the hospital, and the overseer appeared extremely annoyed by it, and assured me repeatedly that it was not true.

In the evening, Mr. – – –, who had been over to Darien, mentioned that one of the storekeepers there had told him that, in the course of a few years, he had paid the Negroes of this estate several thousand dollars for moss, which is a very profitable article of traffic with them. They collect it from the trees, dry and pick it, and then sell it to the people in Darien for mattresses, sofas, and all sorts of stuffing purposes, which, in my opinion, it answers better than any other material whatever that I am acquainted with. . . .

There is a preliminary to my repose, however, in this agreeable residence, which I rather dread, namely, the hunting for, or discovering without hunting, in fine relief upon the whitewashed walls of my bedroom, a most hideous and detestable species of reptile called centipedes, which come out of the cracks and crevices of the walls, and fill my very heart with dismay. They are from an inch to two inches long, and appear to have not a hundred but a thousand legs. I cannot ascertain very certainly from the Negroes whether they sting or not, but they look exceedingly as if they might, and I visit my babies every night in fear and trembling lest I should find one or more of these hateful creatures mounting guard over them. Good night; you are well to be free from centipedes – better to be free from slaves.

Appeal of Forty Thousand Negroes, Threatened with Disfranchisement

The original constitutions of most of the states were silent on the question of Negro franchise. But, beginning in the 1820s, the Negro's voting rights were abrogated or severely curtailed, even in the Northern states, and most notably in New York, Ohio, New Jersey, and Pennsylvania. The action of the Pennsylvania Reform Convention of 1837 restricting the suffrage to white men was based on a decision by the state's Supreme Court (Fogg v. Hobbs, 1837) that Negroes were not freemen and therefore could not vote. Neither the many petitions against the change nor a mass protest meeting held in Philadelphia on March 14, 1838 (which produced the pamphlet reprinted in part below), could prevent disfranchisement. [Source: Appeal of Forty Thousand Citizens, Threatened with Disfranchisement to the People of Pennsylvania, Philadelphia, 1838.]

We appeal to you from the decision of the "Reform Convention," which has stripped us of a right peaceably enjoyed during forty-seven years under the constitution of this commonwealth. We honor Pennsylvania and her noble institutions too much to part with our birthright, as her free citizens, without a struggle. To all her citizens the right of suffrage is valuable in proportion as she is free; but surely there are none who can so ill afford to spare it as ourselves.

Was it the intention of the people of this commonwealth that the convention to which the constitution was committed for revision and amendment should tear up and cast away its first principles? Was it made the business of the convention to deny "that all men are born equally free," by making political rights depend upon the skin in which a man is born or to divide what our fathers bled to unite, to wit, TAXATION and REPRESENTATION?

We will not allow ourselves for one moment to suppose that the majority of the people of Pennsylvania are not too respectful of the rights and too liberal toward the feelings of others, as well as too much enlightened to their own interests, to deprive of the right of suffrage a single individual who may safely be trusted with it. And we cannot believe that you have found among those who bear the burdens of taxation any who have proved, by their abuse of the right, that it is not safe in their hands. This is a question, fellow citizens, in which we plead *your* cause as well as our own. It is the safeguard of the strongest that he lives under a government which is obliged to respect the voice of the weakest.

When you have taken from an individual his right to vote, you have made the government, in regard to him, a mere despotism; and you have taken a step toward making it a despotism to all. To your women and children, their inability to vote at the polls may be no evil, because they are united by consanguinity and affection with those who can do it. To foreigners and paupers, the want of the right may be tolerable, because a little time or labor will make it theirs. They are candidates for the privilege, and hence substantially enjoy its benefits.

But when a distinct class of the community, already sufficiently the objects of prejudice, are wholly and forever disfranchised and excluded, to the remotest posterity, from the possibility of a voice in regard to the laws under which they are to live, it is the same thing as if their abode were transferred to the dominions of the Russian autocrat or of the Grand Turk. They have lost their check upon oppression, their wherewith to buy friends, their panoply of manhood; in short, they are thrown upon the mercy of a despotic majority. Like every other despot, this despot majority will believe in the mildness of its own sway; but who will the more willingly submit to it for that?

To us, our right under the constitution has been more precious and our deprivation of it will be the more grievous, because our expatriation has come to be a darling project with many of our fellow citizens. Our abhorrence of a scheme which comes to us in the guise of Christian benevolence, and asks us to suffer ourselves to be transplanted to a distant and barbarous land, *because we are a "nuisance" in this*, is not more deep and thorough than it is reasonable. We love our native country, much as it has wronged us; and in the peaceable exercise of our inalienable rights, we will cling to it.

The immortal Franklin and his fellow laborers in the cause of humanity have bound us to our homes here with chains of gratitude. We are PENNSYLVANIANS, and we hope to see the day when Pennsylvania will have reason to be proud of us, as we believe she has now none to be ashamed! Will you starve our patriotism? Will you cast our hearts out of the treasury of the commonwealth? Do you count our enmity better than our friendship?

Fellow citizens, we entreat you, in the name of fair dealing, to look again at the just and noble charter of Pennsylvania freedom, which you are asked to narrow down to the lines of caste and color. The constitution reads as follows:

> Article 3, paragraph 1. In elections by the citizens, every freeman of the age of twenty-one years, having resided in the state two years next before the election, and within that time paid a state or county tax, which shall have been assessed at

> least six months before the election, shall enjoy the rights of an elector, etc.

This clause guarantees the right of suffrage to us as fully as to any of our fellow citizens whatsoever, for:

1. Such was the intention of the framers. In the original draft, reported by a committee of nine, the word "WHITE" stood before "FREEMAN." On motion of Albert Gallatin it was stricken out, for the express purpose of including colored citizens within the pale of the elective franchise. . . .

2. We are CITIZENS. This, we believe, would never have been denied had it not been for the scheme of expatriation to which we have already referred. But as our citizenship has been doubted by some who are not altogether unfriendly to us, we beg leave to submit some proof, which we think you will not hastily set aside.

We were regarded as *citizens* by those who drew up the Articles of Confederation between the states in 1778. The fourth of the said articles contains the following language: "The free inhabitants of each of these states, paupers, vagabonds, and fugitives from justice excepted, shall be entitled to all privileges and immunities of free *citizens* in the several states." That we were not excluded under the phrase "paupers, vagabonds, and fugitives from justice" any more than our white countrymen is plain from the debates that preceded the adoption of the article. For, on the 25th of June, 1778, "the delegates from South Carolina moved the following amendment *in behalf of their state*. In Article 4, between the words *free* inhabitants, insert *white*. Decided in the negative; ayes, two states; nays, eight states; one state divided." Such was the solemn decision of the revolutionary Congress, concurred in by the entire delegation from our own commonwealth.

On the adoption of the present Constitution of the United States, no change was made as to the rights of citizenship. This is explicitly proved by the *Journal* of Congress. Take, for example, the following resolution passed in the House of Representatives, December 21, 1803: "On motion; *Resolved,* that the Committee appointed to inquire and report whether any further provisions are necessary for the more effectual protection of American seamen do inquire into the expediency of granting protections to such American seamen, *citizens of the United States*, as *are free persons of color*, and that they report by bill, or otherwise." — — —*Journ. H. Rep.* 1st Sess., 8th Cong., p. 224.

Proofs might be multiplied. In almost every state we have been spoken of, either expressly or by implication, as *citizens*. In the very year before the adoption of the present constitution, 1789, the Pennsylvania Society for Promoting the Abolition of Slavery, etc., put forth an address, signed by Benjamin Franklin, President, in which they stated one of their objects to be, "to *qualify* those who have been restored to freedom, for the exercise and enjoyment of CIVIL LIBERTY." The Convention of 1790, by striking out the word "WHITE," fixed the same standard of *qualification* for all; and, in fact, granted and guaranteed "civil liberty" to all who possessed that qualification. Are we now to be told that the convention did not intend to include colored men, and that Benjamin Franklin did not know what he was about, forasmuch as it was impossible for a colored man to become a citizen of the commonwealth?

It may here be objected to us, that in point of fact we have lost by the recent decision of the [Pennsylvania] Supreme Court, in the case of *Fogg* v. *Hobbs*, whatever claim to the right of suffrage we may have had under the constitution of 1790; and hence have no reason to oppose the amended constitution. Not so. We hold our rights under the present constitution none the cheaper for that decision. The section already cited gives us all that we ask, all that we can conceive it in the power of language to convey.

Reject, fellow citizens, the partial, disfranchising constitution offered you by the Reform Convention, and we shall confidently expect that the Supreme Court will do us the justice and itself the honor to retract its decision. Should it not, our appeal will still be open to the conscience and common sense of the people, who through their chief magistrate and a majority of two-thirds of both branches of the legislature may make way to the bench of the Supreme Court for expounders of the constitution who will not do violence to its most sacred and fundamental principles.

We cannot forbear here to refer you to some points in the published opinion of the court as delivered by Chief Justice Gibson, which we believe will go far to strip it of the weight and authority ordinarily conceded to the decision of the highest tribunal (save the elections) of this commonwealth.

1. The court relies much on a decision *said to have been had* "ABOUT" forty-three years ago the claim of which to a place in the repository of Pennsylvania law is thus set forth by the court itself:

> About the year 1795, as I have it from James Gibson, Esq., of the Philadelphia bar, the very point before us was ruled by the High Court of Errors and Appeals against the right of Negro suffrage. Mr. Gibson declined an invitation to be concerned in the argument, and therefore has no memorandum of the cause to direct us to the record. I have had the office searched for it; but the papers had fallen into such disorder as to preclude a hope of its recovery. Most of them were imperfect, and many were lost or misplaced. *But Mr. Gibson's remembrance of the decision is perfect and entitled to full confidence.*

Now, suppressing doubt, and supposing such a decision actually to have emanated from the then highest tribunal of the commonwealth, does not the fact that it was so utterly forgotten as not to have regulated the polls within the memory of the present generation, nor to have been brought up against us in the Reform Convention, prove that it was virtually retracted? And if retracted, is it now to be revived to the overthrow of rights enjoyed without contradiction during the average life of man?

2. The court argues that colored men are not *freemen*, and hence not entitled by the present constitution to vote, because under laws prior to the constitution there *might be* individuals who were not slaves, and yet were not *freemen!* The deduction is that as the word "freeman" was, *before* the present constitution, used in a restricted sense, it must have been used in the same sense *in* it. The correctness of this interpretation will be tested by substituting, in Article 3, Section 1, for the word "freeman" the meaning which the court chooses to have attached to it. This meaning appears from the passages cited by the court to be *an elector*. Making the substitution, the article reads, "In elections by the citizens, every *elector*, of the age of twenty-one years, etc., shall enjoy the right of an *elector*, etc."—a proposition which sheds a very faint light upon the question of the extent of the elective franchise, and from which it would

178

appear that there may be electors who are *not* to enjoy the rights of electors.

But taking the less restricted term "citizen," which the court also seems to think of the same force with "freeman," the article will read more sensibly, that "In elections by the citizens, every *citizen* of the age of twenty-one," who has paid taxes, etc., "shall enjoy the right of an elector." To what evidence does the court refer to show that a *colored* man may not be a *citizen?* To none whatever. We have too much respect for old Pennsylvania to believe that such puerile absurdity can become her fixed and irreversible law.

3. Since the argument above referred to, such as it is, does not rest upon color, it is not less applicable to the descendants of Irish and German ancestors than to ourselves. If there ever have been within the commonwealth men, or sets of men, who though personally free were not technically *freemen*, it is unconstitutional, according to the doctrine of the court, for their descendants to exercise the right of suffrage, pay what taxes they may, till in "the discretion of the judges" their blood has "become so diluted in successive descents as to lose its distinctive character." Is this the doctrine of Pennsylvania freedom?

4. Lastly, the court openly rests its decision on the authority of a wrong which this commonwealth so long ago as 1780 solemnly acknowledged, and, to the extent of its power, forever repealed. To support the same *wrong* in *other states*, the constitution of *this*, when it uses the words "every freeman," must be understood to exclude every freeman of a certain color! The court is of opinion that the people of this commonwealth had no power to confer the rights of citizenship upon one who, were he in another state, *might be* loaded by its laws with "countless disabilities." Now, since in some of the states, men may be found in slavery who have not the slightest trace of African blood, it is difficult to see, on the doctrine of the court, how the constitution of Pennsylvania could confer the right of citizenship upon any person; and, indeed, how it could have allowed the emancipation of slaves of any color. To such vile dependence on its own ancient *wrongs,* and on the present *wrongs* of other states, is Pennsylvania reduced by this decision!

Are we then presumptuous in the hope that this grave sentence will be as incapable of resurrection fifty years hence as is that which the chief justice assures us was pronounced "*about* the year 1795"? No. The blessings of the broad and impartial charter of Pennsylvania rights can no more be wrested from us by legal subtlety than the beams of our common sun or the breathing of our common air.

What have we done to forfeit the inestimable benefits of this charter? Why should taxpaying colored men, any more than other taxpayers, be deprived of the right of voting for their representatives? It was said in the convention that this government belongs to the *whites*. We have already shown this to be false as to the past. Those who established our present government designed it equally for all. It is for you to decide whether it shall be confined to the European complexion in future.

Why should you exclude us from a fair participation in the benefits of the republic? Have we oppressed the whites? Have we used our rights to the injury of any class? Have we disgraced it by receiving bribes? Where are the charges written down, and who will swear to them? We challenge investigation. We put it to the conscience of every Pennsylvanian, whether there is, or ever has been, in the commonwealth, either a political party or religious sect which has less deserved than ourselves to be thus disfranchised. As to the charge of idleness, we fling it back indignantly. Whose brows have sweat for our livelihood but our own? As to vice, if it disqualifies us for civil liberty, why not apply the same rule to the whites, so far as they are vicious? Will you punish the innocent for the crimes of the guilty?

The execution of the laws is in the hands of the whites. If we are bad citizens let them apply the proper remedies. We do not ask the right of suffrage for the inmates of our jails and penitentiaries, but for those who honestly and industriously contribute to bear the burdens of the state. As to inferiority to the whites, if indeed we are guilty of it, either by nature or education, we trust our enjoyment of the rights of freemen will on that account be considered the less dangerous. If we are incompetent to fill the offices of state, it will be the fault of the whites only if we are suffered to disgrace them. We are in too feeble a minority to cherish a mischievous ambition. Fair protection is all that we aspire to.

We ask your attention, fellow citizens, to facts and testimonies

Free Negroes

The first black men to reach the New World were not slaves. Black explorers, craftsmen, and servants accompanied most of the early Spanish explorers, beginning as early as 1501 — indeed Estevan or "Little Steven," a Negro member of the expedition of Pánfilo de Narváez, was the first man to explore the regions now known as Arizona and New Mexico. While the overwhelming majority of the black people who lived in colonial America were slaves, free Negroes lived here and there throughout the colonies from the first. Some of them had been born free. Others bought their freedom or were freed by their masters. Still others were runaway slaves, living in constant fear of recapture. Most clustered in cities and towns where work for unskilled laborers was likely to be found; some like trapper Jean Baptiste du Sable became pioneers and moved westward. Wherever they lived, their lives were hard and severely limited by white society. In every state special laws were passed to circumscribe their freedom; black people were often denied the vote, forbidden to testify in court, not allowed to attend public schools (although they were taxed for their support), and forced to carry special passes if they wished to travel. Despite these handicaps, free Negroes managed to find jobs, raise families, and create their own institutions and organizations. Some free men, such as pioneer journalist and Abolitionist William Whipper, above, began to campaign for the freedom of their black brethren.

Black soldiers and sailors also served with distinction in the War of 1812. They were especially important in the victories on Lake Erie and at New Orleans (right); in the aftermath of both battles, the U.S. commanders singled out their black troops for special praise. Many slaves had joined the army hoping thus to win their freedom, but most were unceremoniously returned to their masters after the war.

Black Americans have served with valor in every American war. The Revolution was no exception;
more than 5,000 black men served in the Continental Army. Despite the heroism shown by
Negroes in the war's early skirmishes — Crispus Attucks, a black laboring man, was among the first
to fall in the Boston Massacre and Peter Salem, at left, fired the shot that killed Major Pitcairn,
the first British officer to breach the rebel lines during the battle of Bunker Hill — George Washington
forbade Negro enlistment for fear it would inspire slaves to desert their masters. Only when
slaves began running away to join the British army did he relent. Black companies and integrated
units fought in most of the war's major battles — including the seizure of Fort Ticonderoga and
the battles of Long Island, Brandywine, Yorktown, and Princeton.

These watercolors by Pavel Svinin, a Russian traveler, offer a
glimpse of free Negroes in the early 19th century. At top right a
fiddler plays for dancing at a wayside inn. At bottom right,
churchgoers participate in services at a Methodist church in
Philadelphia. Excluded from most white organizations (including
churches), free Negroes developed their own. Some Negro
organizations, such as the Prince Hall Masonic lodge that was
founded in 1787, have survived to the present day. Above,
craftsmen work in the streets of Philadelphia.

Prominent slaveholders like John C. Calhoun and Henry Clay saw the continued existence of large numbers of free Negroes as a constant threat to the slavery system and to the Union. African colonization, therefore, seemed to them, as well as to many prominent non-slaveholders in the North, an attractive way to solve the Negro problem. They helped form the American Colonization Society and persuaded Congress to secure land in Africa on which to establish a black republic. The new nation was named Liberia, and its first president was Joseph Roberts, above, a Virginia-born freeman. Beginning in 1822 a thin stream of Negroes set out for Liberia. But the back-to-Africa movement never caught on among black Americans — despite efforts to revive it in later years. Fewer than 15,000 Negroes ever went to Liberia. Similar schemes for black emigration to Canada and South America were even less successful. For better or worse black Americans elected to stay in the land they had been brought to as unwilling immigrants.

which go to show that, considering the circumstances in which we have been placed, our country has no reason to be ashamed of us, and that those have the most occasion to blush to whom nature has given the power.

By the careful inquiry of a committee appointed by the Pennsylvania Society for Promoting the Abolition of Slavery, it has been ascertained that the colored population of Philadelphia and its suburbs, numbering 18,768 souls, possess at the present time, of real and personal estate, not less than $1,350,000. They have paid for taxes during the last year $3,252.83; for house, water, and ground rent, $166,963.50. This committee estimate the income of the holders of real estate occupied by the colored people to be 7½ percent on a capital of about $2 million. Here is an addition to the wealth of their white brethren.

But the rents and taxes are not all; to pay them, the colored people must be employed in labor, and here is another profit to the whites, for no man employs another unless he can make his labor profitable to himself. For a similar reason, a profit is made by all the whites who sell to colored people the necessaries or luxuries of life. Though the aggregate amount of the wealth derived by the whites from our people can only be conjectured, its importance is worthy of consideration by those who would make it less by lessening our motive to accumulate for ourselves.

Nor is the profit derived from us counterbalanced by the sums which we in any way draw from the public treasures. From a statement published by order of the Guardians of the Poor of Philadelphia, in 1830, it appears that out of 549 outdoor poor relieved during the year, only 22 were persons of color, being about 4 percent of the whole number, while the ratio of our population to that of the city and suburbs exceeds 8¼ percent. By a note appended to the printed report above referred to, it appears that the colored *paupers* admitted into the almshouse for the same period did not exceed 4 percent of the whole. Thus it has been ascertained that they pay more than they receive in the support of their own poor. The various "mutual relief" societies of Philadelphia expend upward of $7,000 annually for the relief of their members when sick or disabled.

That we are not neglectful of our religious interests nor of the education of our children is shown by the fact that there are among us in Philadelphia, Pittsburgh, York, West Chester, and Columbia, 22 churches, 48 clergymen, 26 day schools, 20 Sabbath schools, 125 Sabbath school teachers, 4 literary societies, 2 public libraries, consisting of about 800 volumes, besides 8,333 volumes in private libraries, 2 tract societies, 2 Bible societies, and 7 temperance societies.

In other parts of the state we are confident our condition will compare very favorably with that in Philadelphia, although we are not furnished with accurate statistics.

Our fathers shared with yours the trials and perils of the wilderness. Among the facts which illustrate this, it is well known that the founder of your capital, from whom it bears the name of Harrisburg, was rescued by a *colored* man from a party of Indians who had captured and bound him to the stake for execution. In gratitude for this act, he *invited colored persons* to settle in his town, and offered them land on favorable terms. When our common country has been invaded by a foreign foe, colored men have hazarded their lives in its defense. Our fathers fought by the side of yours in the struggle which made us an independent republic.

Are we to be thus looked to for help in the "hour of danger," but trampled under foot in the time of peace? In which of the battles of the Revolution did not our fathers fight as bravely as yours for American liberty? Was it that their children might be disfranchised and loaded with insult that they endured the famine of Valley Forge and the horrors of the Jersey prison ship? Nay, among those from whom you are asked to wrench the birthright of CIVIL LIBERTY are those who themselves shed their blood on the snows of Jersey and faced British bayonets in the most desperate hour of the Revolution. . . .

Be it remembered, fellow citizens, that it is only for the *"industrious, peaceable, and useful"* part of the colored people that we plead. We would have the right of suffrage only as the reward of industry and worth. We care not how high the qualification be placed. All we ask is, that no man shall be excluded on account of his *color;* that the same rule shall be applied to all.

J. J. FLOURNOY
Black Workers and White Labor

Southern slaveholders frequently trained their Negroes in a trade and then hired them out to city employers by the month or the year. The rates paid for such labor were considerably less than the wages that white laborers, who had to support themselves, could afford to accept. By the time of the Civil War, skilled Negro labor had almost entirely replaced skilled white labor in many Southern cities. The following protest, addressed to the contractors for mason's and carpenter's work of Athens, Georgia, appeared in the local paper in January 1838. [Source: Southern Banner, January 13, 1838.]

I desire your candid consideration of the views I shall here express. I ask no reply to them except at your own volition. I am aware that most of you have too strong antipathy to encourage the masonry and carpentry trades of your poor white brothers, that your predilections for giving employment in your line of business to ebony workers have either so cheapened the white man's labor, or expatriated hence, with but a few solitary exceptions, all the white masons and carpenters of this town.

The white man is the only real, legal, moral, and civil proprietor of this country and state. The right of his proprietorship reaches from the date of the studies of those white men Copernicus and Galileo, who indicated from the seclusion of their closets the sphericity of the earth; which sphericity hinted to another white man, Columbus, the possibility, by a westerly course of sailing, of finding land. Hence, by white man alone was this continent discovered; by the prowess of white men alone (though not always properly or humanely exercised) were the fierce and active Indians driven occidentally. And if swarms and hordes of infuriated red men pour down now from the Northwest, like the wintry blast thereof, the white men alone, aye, those to whom you decline to give money for bread and clothes for their famishing families, in the logic matter of withholding work from them, or employing Negroes, in the sequel, to cheapen their wages to a rate that amounts to a moral and physical impossibility for them either to live here and

189

support their families—would bare their breasts to the keen and whizzing shafts of the savage crusaders—defending Negroes too in the bargain, for if left to themselves without our aid, the Indians would or can sweep the Negroes hence, "as dewdrops are shaken from the lion's mane."

The right, then, gentlemen, you will no doubt candidly admit, of the white man to employment in preference to Negroes, who *must* defer to us since they live well enough on plantations, cannot be considered impeachable by contractors. It is a right more virtual and indisputable than that of agrarianism. As masters of the polls in a majority, carrying all before them, I am surprised the poor do not elect faithful members to the legislature, who will make it penal to prefer Negro mechanic labor to white men's. But of the premises as I have now laid them down, you will candidly judge for yourselves, and draw a conclusion with me, that white bricklayers and house joiners must henceforward have ample work and remuneration; and yourselves and other contractors will set the example and pursue it for the future without deviation.

JOHN GREENLEAF WHITTIER

The Farewell

Many Abolitionists wrote stories and poems replete with sentimental and horrifying episodes in order to stir indignation against slavery. This tactic was criticized, even within their own ranks, because it was felt that the passion aroused in readers precluded a peaceful solution to the slavery question. However, the practice continued, reaching its apex, perhaps, in Harriet Beecher Stowe's Uncle Tom's Cabin *(1852). Whittier wrote stories and poems of this sort for thirty years. He had been drawn into the crusade against slavery by William Lloyd Garrison, the founder of the militant Abolitionist movement and the first editor to publish Whittier's verse. "The Farewell" is probably more effective as propaganda than as poetry.* [*Source:* Complete Poetical Works, *Cambridge Edition, Boston, 1894.*]

The Farewell

of a Virginia slave mother to her daughters
sold into Southern bondage

Gone, gone, — sold and gone,
To the rice swamp dank and lone.

There no mother's eye is near them,
There no mother's ear can hear them;
Never, when the torturing lash
Seams their back with many a gash,
Shall a mother's kindness bless them,
Or a mother's arms caress them.

Gone, gone, — sold and gone,
To the rice swamp dank and lone,
From Virginia's hills and waters;
Woe is me, my stolen daughters!

Gone, gone, — sold and gone,
To the rice swamp dank and lone.

Where the slave whip ceaseless swings,
Where the noisome insect stings,
Where the fever demon strews
Poison with the falling dews,
Where the sickly sunbeams glare
Through the hot and misty air;

Gone, gone, — sold and gone,
To the rice swamp dank and lone,
From Virginia's hills and waters;
Woe is me, my stolen daughters!

Gone, gone, — sold and gone,
To the rice swamp dank and lone.

Oh, when weary, sad, and slow,
From the fields at night they go,
Faint with toil, and racked with pain,
To their cheerless homes again,
There no brother's voice shall greet them,
There no father's welcome meet them.

191

Gone, gone, — sold and gone,
To the rice swamp dank and lone,
From Virginia's hills and waters;
Woe is me, my stolen daughters!

Gone, gone, — sold and gone,
To the rice swamp dank and lone.

From the tree whose shadow lay
On their childhood's place of play;
From the cool spring where they drank;
Rock, and hill, and rivulet bank;
From the solemn house of prayer,
And the holy counsels there;

Gone, gone, — sold and gone,
To the rice swamp dank and lone,
From Virginia's hills and waters;
Woe is me, my stolen daughters!

Gone, gone, — sold and gone,
To the rice swamp dank and lone;

Toiling through the weary day,
And at night the spoiler's prey.
Oh, that they had earlier died,
Sleeping calmly, side by side,
Where the tyrant's power is o'er,
And the fetter galls no more!

Gone, gone, — sold and gone,
To the rice swamp dank and lone,
From Virginia's hills and waters;
Woe is me, my stolen daughters!

Gone, gone, — sold and gone,
To the rice swamp dank and lone.

By the holy love He beareth;
By the bruisèd reed He spareth;
Oh, may He, to whom alone
All their cruel wrongs are known,

Still their hope and refuge prove,
With a more than mother's love.

Gone, gone, — sold and gone,
To the rice swamp dank and lone,
From Virginia's hills and waters;
Woe is me, my stolen daughters!

WILLIAM HARPER
The Inequality of Men

William Harper's Memoir on Slavery, *which first appeared in 1837 and is reprinted here in part, is regarded as one of the most important pro-slavery statements in the history of the great controversy that led up to the Civil War. Harper, also the author of the South Carolina Nullification Ordinance of 1832, converted the earlier argument of Thomas R. Dew, that slavery is a positive good for master and slave alike, into a theory of human nature and human equality that in effect reduced the second paragraph of the Declaration of Independence to a nullity. Harper's arguments were taken up by John C. Calhoun in his speeches and writings; they thus gained national fame. [*Source:* Cotton Is King, and Pro-Slavery Arguments, E. N. Elliot, ed., Augusta, Ga., 1860, pp. 549-563.]*

The institution of domestic slavery exists over far the greater portion of the inhabited earth. Until within a very few centuries, it may be said to have existed over the whole earth — at least in all those portions of it which had made any advances toward civilization. We might safely conclude, then, that it is deeply founded in the nature of man and the exigencies of human society. Yet, in the few countries in which it has been abolished — claiming, perhaps justly, to be farthest advanced in civilization and intelligence, but which have had the smallest opportunity of observing its true character and effects — it is denounced as the most intolerable of social and political evils. Its existence, and every hour of its continuance, is regarded as the crime of the communities in which it is found. Even by those in the countries alluded to, who regard it with the most indulgence or the least abhorrence, who attribute no criminality to the present generation, who found it in existence and have not yet been able to devise the means of abolishing it – it is pronounced a misfortune and a curse injurious and dangerous always, and which must be finally fatal to the societies which admit it. This is no longer regarded as a subject of argument and investigation. The opinions referred to are assumed as settled, or the truth of them as self-evident. If any voice is raised among ourselves to extenuate or to vindicate, it is unheard. The judgment is made up. We can have no hearing before the tribunal of the civilized world. . . .

President [Thomas] Dew [of the College of William and Mary] has shown that the institution of slavery is a principal cause of civilization. Perhaps nothing can be more evident than that it is the sole cause. If anything can be predicated as universally true of uncultivated man, it is that he will not labor beyond what is absolutely necessary to maintain his existence. Labor is pain to those who are unaccustomed to it, and the nature of man is averse to pain. Even with all the training, the helps, and motives of civilization, we find that this aversion cannot be overcome in many individuals of the most cultivated societies. The coercion of slavery alone is adequate to form man to habits of labor. Without it, there can be no accumulation of property, no providence for the future, no tastes for comfort or elegancies, which are the characteristics and essentials of civilization.

He who has obtained the command of another's labor first begins to accumulate and provide for the future, and the foundations of civilization are laid. We find confirmed by experience that which is so evident in theory. Since the existence of man upon the earth, with no exception whatever, either of ancient or modern times, every society which has attained civilization has advanced to it through this process.

Will those who regard slavery as immoral, or crime in itself, tell us that man was not intended for civilization, but to roam the earth as a biped brute? . . . Or will they say that the Judge of all the earth has done wrong in ordaining the means by which alone that end can be obtained? . . . The act itself is good if it promotes the good pur-

194

poses of God, and would be approved by Him, if that result only were intended.

Do they not blaspheme the Providence of God who denounce as wickedness and outrage that which is rendered indispensable to His purposes in the government of the world? Or at what stage of the progress of society will they say that slavery ceases to be necessary, and its very existence becomes sin and crime? . . .

There seems to be something in this subject which blunts the perceptions and darkens and confuses the understandings and moral feelings of men. Tell them that, of necessity, in every civilized society, there must be an infinite variety of conditions and employments, from the most eminent and intellectual to the most servile and laborious; that the Negro race, from their temperament and capacity, are peculiarly suited to the situation which they occupy, and not less happy in it than any corresponding class to be found in the world; prove incontestably that no scheme of emancipation could be carried into effect without the most intolerable mischiefs and calamities to both master and slave, or without probably throwing a large and fertile portion of the earth's surface out of the pale of civilization—and you have done nothing. They reply that whatever may be the consequence, you are bound to do *right;* that man has a right to himself, and man cannot have property in man; that if the Negro race be naturally inferior in mind and character, they are not less entitled to the rights of humanity; that if they are happy in their condition, it affords but the stronger evidence of their degradation, and renders them still more objects of commiseration. They repeat, as the fundamental maxim of our civil policy, that all men are born free and equal, and quote from our Declaration of Independence, "that men are endowed by their Creator with certain inalienable *rights,* among which are life, liberty, and the pursuit of happiness." . . .

Notwithstanding our respect for the important document which declared our independence, yet if anything be found in it, and especially in what may be regarded rather as its ornament than its substance—false, sophistical or unmeaning—that respect should not screen it from the freest examination.

All men are born free and equal. Is it not palpably nearer the truth to say that no man was ever born free, and that no two men were ever born equal? Man is born in a state of the most helpless dependence on others. He continues subject to the absolute control of others, and remains without many of the civil and all of the political privileges of his society until the period which the laws have fixed as that at which he is supposed to have attained the maturity of his faculties.

Then inequality is further developed, and becomes infinite in every society, and under whatever form of government. Wealth and poverty, fame or obscurity, strength or weakness, knowledge or ignorance, ease or labor, power or subjection, mark the endless diversity in the condition of men.

But we have not arrived at the profundity of the maxim. This inequality is, in a great measure, the result of abuses in the institutions of society. They do not speak of what exists but of what ought to exist. Everyone should be left at liberty to obtain all the advantages of society which he can compass, by the free exertion of his faculties, unimpeded by civil restraints. It may be said that this would not remedy the evils of society which are complained of. The inequalities to which I have referred, with the misery resulting from them, would exist in fact under the freest and most popular form of government that man could devise.

But what is the foundation of the bold dogma so confidently announced? Females are human and rational beings. They may be found of better faculties and better qualified to exercise political privileges, and to attain the distinctions of society, than many men; yet who complains of the order of society by which they are excluded from them? For I do not speak of the few who would desecrate them; do violence to the nature which their Creator has impressed upon them; drag them from the position which they necessarily occupy for the existence of civilized society, and in which they constitute its blessing and ornament—the only position which they have ever occupied in any human society—to place them in a situation in which they would be alike miserable and degraded. Low as we descend in combating the theories of presumptuous dogmatists, it cannot be necessary to stoop to this. . . .

We admit the existence of a moral law, binding on societies as on individuals. Society must act in good faith. No man, or body of men, has a right to inflict pain or privation on others, unless with a view,

196

after full and impartial deliberation, to prevent a greater evil. If this deliberation be had, and the decision made in good faith, there can be no imputation of moral guilt. Has any politician contended that the very existence of governments in which there are orders privileged by law constitutes a violation of morality; that their continuance is a crime, which men are bound to put an end to, without any consideration of the good or evil to result from the change? Yet this is the natural inference from the dogma of the natural equality of men as applied to our institution of slavery—an equality not to be invaded without injustice and wrong, and requiring to be restored instantly, unqualifiedly, and without reference to consequences.

This is sufficiently commonplace, but we are sometimes driven to [the] commonplace. It is no less a false and shallow than a presumptuous philosophy which theorizes on the affairs of men as a problem to be solved by some unerring rule of human reason, without reference to the designs of a superior intelligence, so far as he has been placed to indicate them in their creation and destiny. Man is born to subjection. Not only during infancy is he dependent, and under the control of others; at all ages, it is the very bias of his nature that the strong and the wise should control the weak and the ignorant.

So it has been since the days of Nimrod. The existence of some form of slavery in all ages and countries is proof enough of this. He is born to subjection as he is born in sin and ignorance.

To make any considerable progress in knowledge, the continued efforts of successive generations and the diligent training and unwearied exertions of the individual are requisite. To make progress in moral virtue, not less time and effort, aided by superior help, are necessary; and it is only by the matured exercise of his knowledge and his virtue that he can attain to civil freedom. Of all things, the existence of civil liberty is most the result of artificial institution. The proclivity of the natural man is to domineer or to be subservient.

A noble result, indeed, but in the attaining of which, as in the instances of knowledge and virtue, the Creator, for His own purposes, has set a limit beyond which we cannot go.

But he who is most advanced in knowledge is most sensible of his own ignorance, and how much must forever be unknown to man

197

in his present condition. As I have heard it expressed, the farther you extend the circle of light, the wider is the horizon of darkness. He who has made the greatest progress in moral purity is most sensible of the depravity, not only of the world around him but of his own heart, and the imperfection of his best motives; and this he knows that men must feel and lament so long as they continue men. So, when the greatest progress in civil liberty has been made, the enlightened lover of liberty will know that there must remain much inequality, much injustice, much *slavery*, which no human wisdom or virtue will ever be able wholly to prevent or redress. . . . The condition of our whole existence is but to struggle with evils; to compare them, to choose between them, and, so far as we can, to mitigate them. To say that there is evil in any institution is only to say that it is human.

And can we doubt but that this long discipline and laborious process, by which men are required to work out the elevation and improvement of their individual nature and their social condition, is imposed for a great and benevolent end? Our faculties are not adequate to the solution of the mystery why it should be so; but the truth is clear that the world was not intended for the seat of universal knowledge, or goodness, or happiness, or freedom.

Man has been endowed by his Creator with certain inalienable rights, among which are life, liberty, and the pursuit of happiness. What is meant by the *inalienable* right of liberty? Has anyone who has used the words ever asked himself this question? Does it mean that a man has no right to alienate his own liberty; to sell himself and his posterity for slaves? This would seem to be the more obvious meaning. When the word "right" is used, it has reference to some law which sanctions it and would be violated by its invasion. It must refer either to the general law of morality or the law of the country—the law of God or the law of man. If the law of any country permitted it, it would of course be absurd to say that the law of that country was violated by such alienation. If it have any meaning in this respect, it would mean that, though the law of the country permitted it, the man would be guilty of an immoral act who should thus alienate his liberty. A fit question for schoolmen to discuss, and the consequences resulting from its decision as important as from any of theirs. Yet who will say that the man pressed by famine, and in prospect of death, would be criminal for such an act? Self-pres-ervation, as is truly said, is the first law of nature. High and pecu-liar characters, by elaborate cultivation, may be taught to prefer death to slavery, but it would be folly to prescribe this as a duty to the mass of mankind.

If any rational meaning can be attributed to the sentence I have quoted, it is this: That the society or the individuals who exercise the powers of government are guilty of a violation of the law of God or of morality, when, by any law or public act, they deprive men of life or liberty, or restrain them in the pursuit of happiness. Yet every government does, and of necessity must, deprive men of life and lib-erty for offenses against society. Restrain them in the pursuit of happiness! Why, all the laws of society are intended for nothing else but to restrain men from the pursuit of happiness, according to their own ideas of happiness or advantage—which the phrase must mean if it means anything. And by what right does society punish by the loss of life or liberty? Not on account of the moral guilt of the crim-inal—not by impiously and arrogantly assuming the prerogative of the Almighty to dispense justice or suffering, according to moral desert. It is for its own protection; it is the right of self-defense. . . . Society inflicts these forfeitures for the security of the lives of its members; it inflicts them for the security of their property, the great essential of civilization; it inflicts them also for the protection of its political institutions, the forcible attempt to overturn which has al-ways been justly regarded as the greatest crime. . . .

And is it by this . . . well-sounding but unmeaning verbiage of natural equality and inalienable rights that our lives are to be put in jeopardy, our property destroyed, and our political institutions overturned or endangered? If a people had on its borders a tribe of barbarians, whom no treaties or faith could bind, and by whose attacks they were constantly endangered, against whom they could devise no security but that they should be exterminated or enslaved, would they not have the right to enslave them and keep them in slavery so long as the same danger would be incurred by their manumission? . . .

By what right is it that man exercises dominion over the beasts of the field; subdues them to painful labor, or deprives them of life for his sustenance or enjoyment? They are not rational beings. No,

199

but they are the creatures of God, sentient beings, capable of suffering and enjoyment, and entitled to enjoy according to the measure of their capacities. Does not the voice of nature inform everyone that he is guilty of wrong when he inflicts on them pain without necessity or object? If their existence be limited to the present life, it affords the stronger argument for affording them the brief enjoyment of which it is capable. It is because the greater good is effected, not only to man but to the inferior animals themselves.

The care of man gives the boon of existence to myriads who would never otherwise have enjoyed it, and the enjoyment of their existence is better provided for while it lasts. It belongs to the being of superior faculties to judge of the relations which shall subsist between himself and inferior animals, and the use he shall make of them; and he may justly consider himself, who has the greater capacity of enjoyment, in the first instance. Yet he must do this conscientiously, and no doubt, moral guilt has been incurred by the infliction of pain on these animals, with no adequate benefit to be expected.

I do no disparagement to the dignity of human nature, even in its humblest form, when I say that on the very same foundation, with the difference only of circumstance and degree, rests the right of the civilized and cultivated man over the savage and ignorant. It is the order of nature and of God that the being of superior faculties and knowledge, and therefore of superior power, should control and dispose of those who are inferior. It is as much in the order of nature that men should enslave each other as that other animals should prey upon each other. I admit that he does this under the highest moral responsibility, and is most guilty if he wantonly inflicts misery or privation on beings more capable of enjoyment or suffering than brutes, without necessity or any view to the greater good which is to result. If we conceive of society existing without government, and that one man by his superior strength, courage, or wisdom could obtain the mastery of his fellows, he would have a perfect right to do so. He would be morally responsible for the use of his power, and guilty if he failed to direct them so as to promote their happiness as well as his own.

Moralists have denounced the injustice and cruelty which have been practised toward our aboriginal Indians, by which they have

200

been driven from their native seats and exterminated, and no doubt with much justice. No doubt, much fraud and injustice has been practised in the circumstances and the manner of their removal. Yet who has contended that civilized man had no moral right to possess himself of the country? That he was bound to leave this wide and fertile continent, which is capable of sustaining uncounted myriads of a civilized race, to a few roving and ignorant barbarians? Yet if anything is certain, it is certain that there were no means by which he could possess the country without exterminating or enslaving them. Savage and civilized man cannot live together, and the savage can be tamed only by being enslaved or by having slaves. By enslaving alone could he have preserved them. And who shall take upon himself to decide that the more benevolent course, and more pleasing to God, was pursued toward them, or that it would not have been better that they had been enslaved generally, as they were in particular instances?

It is a refined philosophy, and utterly false in its application to general nature or the mass of humankind, which teaches that existence is not the greatest of all boons, and worthy of being preserved even under the most adverse circumstances. The strongest instinct of all animated beings sufficiently proclaims this. When the last red man shall have vanished from our forests, the sole remaining traces of his blood will be found among our enslaved population. The African slave trade has given, and will give, the boon of existence to millions and millions in our country who would otherwise never have enjoyed it, and the enjoyment of their existence is better provided for while it lasts. Or if, for the rights of man over inferior animals, we are referred to Revelation, which pronounces — "ye shall have dominion over the beasts of the field, and over the fowls of air," we refer to the same, which declares not the less explicitly — "Both the bondmen and bondmaids which thou shalt have shall be of the heathen that are among you. Of them shall you buy bondmen and bondmaids." . . .

Man, as I have said, is not born to civilization. He is born rude and ignorant. But it will be, I suppose, admitted that it is the design of his Creator that he should attain to civilization; that religion should be known; that the comforts and elegancies of life should be enjoyed; that letters and arts should be cultivated; in short, that there should be the greatest possible development of moral and intellectual excellence. It can hardly be necessary to say anything of those who have extolled the superior virtues and enjoyments of savage life—a life of physical wants and sufferings, of continual insecurity, of furious passions and depraved vices. Those who have praised savage life are those who have known nothing of it, or who have become savages themselves. But as I have said, so far as reason or universal experience instructs us, the institution of slavery is an essential process in emerging from savage life. It must then produce good and promote the designs of the Creator.

JOHN C. CALHOUN
The Danger of Abolitionist Petitions

In 1835 the militant Abolitionists mounted a campaign to abolish slavery and the slave trade in the District of Columbia, where, they argued, in contradistinction to the Southern states, Congress had a right to legislate concerning the subject. By 1836 thousands of petitions (over 400,000 by 1839) had been received by Congress. In the House, Northern Conservatives and Southern Democrats combined to institute the so-called Gag Rule, according to which all such petitions were laid on the table but not read. Opposition to the Gag Rule, which had to be renewed at each session of Congress, was led by John Quincy Adams, former President and now a representative from Massachusetts. At the beginning of each Congress he took the opportunity to debate on the imposition of the rule to read a number of the petitions, and thus earned the sobriquet "Old Man Eloquent." This procedure enraged the slaveholders, who tried to silence him by every means short of violence. The Senate adopted a different procedure. There, it became traditional for the petitions to be read, whereupon a motion barring the petitioners' prayer would be proposed and passed. One of numerous speeches against the petitions by John C. Calhoun, who wanted the Senate to adopt a Gag Rule similar to that of the House, is reprinted here. Delivered in February 1837, it expresses the Southern position that the very existence of the Union was endangered by abolitionism. [Source: Speeches of John C. Calhoun, New York, 1843, pp. 222-226.]

202

If the time of the Senate permitted, I should feel it to be my duty to call for the reading of the mass of petitions on the table, in order that we might know what language they hold toward the slaveholding states and their institutions; but as it will not, I have selected indiscriminately from the pile, two: one from those in manuscript and the other from the printed; and, without knowing their contents, will call for the reading of them so that we may judge, by them, of the character of the whole.

(Here the secretary, on the call of Mr. Calhoun, read the two petitions.)

Such . . . is the language held toward us and ours; the peculiar institutions of the South, that on the maintenance of which the very existence of the slaveholding states depends, is pronounced to be sinful and odious, in the sight of God and man; and this with a systematic design of rendering us hateful in the eyes of the world, with a view to a general crusade against us and our institutions. This, too, in the legislative halls of the Union, created by these confederated states for the better protection of their peace, their safety, and their respective institutions. And yet we, the representatives of twelve of these sovereign states against whom this deadly war is waged, are expected to sit here in silence, hearing ourselves and our constituents day after day denounced, without uttering a word; if we but open our lips, the charge of agitation is resounded on all sides, and we are held up as seeking to aggravate the evil which we resist. Every reflecting mind must see in all this a state of things deeply and dangerously diseased.

I do not belong . . . to the school which holds that aggression is to be met by concession. Mine is the opposite creed, which teaches that encroachments must be met at the beginning and that those who act on the opposite principle are prepared to become slaves. In this case, in particular, I hold concession or compromise to be fatal. If we concede an inch, concession would follow concession — compromise would follow compromise — until our ranks would be so broken that effectual resistance would be impossible. We must meet the enemy on the frontier, with a fixed determination of maintaining our position at every hazard. Consent to receive these insulting petitions, and the next demand will be that they be referred to a committee in order that they may be deliberated and acted upon.

At the last session, we were modestly asked to receive them simply to lay them on the table, without any view of ulterior action. I then told the senator from Pennsylvania (Mr. Buchanan), who strongly urged that course in the Senate, that it was a position that could not be maintained, as the argument in favor of acting on the petitions, if we were bound to receive, could not be resisted. I then said that the next step would be to refer the petition to a committee, and I already see indications that such is now the intention. If we yield, that will be followed by another, and we would thus proceed, step by step, to the final consummation of the object of these petitions.

We are now told that the most effectual mode of arresting the progress of Abolition is to reason it down; and, with this view, it is urged that the petitions ought to be referred to a committee. That is the very ground which was taken at the last session in the other house; but, instead of arresting its progress, it has since advanced more rapidly than ever. The most unquestionable right may be rendered doubtful if once admitted to be a subject of controversy, and that would be the case in the present instance. The subject is beyond the jurisdiction of Congress; they have no right to touch it in any shape or form or to make it the subject of deliberation or discussion.

In opposition to this view, it is urged that Congress is bound by the Constitution to receive petitions in every case and on every subject, whether within its constitutional competency or not. I hold the doctrine to be absurd and do solemnly believe that it would be as easy to prove that it has the right to abolish slavery as that it is bound to receive petitions for that purpose. The very existence of the rule that requires a question to be put on the reception of petitions is conclusive to show that there is no such obligation. It has been a standing rule from the commencement of the government and clearly shows the sense of those who formed the Constitution on this point. The question on the reception would be absurd, if, as is contended, we are bound to receive; but I do not intend to argue the question. I discussed it fully at the last session, and the arguments then advanced neither have nor can be answered.

As widely as this incendiary spirit has spread, it has not yet infected this body, or the great mass of the intelligent and business portion of the North; but unless it be speedily stopped, it will spread and work upward till it brings the two great sections of the Union into deadly conflict. This is not a new impression with me. Several years since, in a discussion with one of the senators from Massachusetts (Mr. Webster), before this fell spirit had showed itself, I then predicted that the doctrine of the proclamation and the force bill—that this government had a right, in the last resort, to determine the extent of its own powers and enforce it at the point of the bayonet, which was so warmly maintained by that senator—would at no distant day arouse the dormant spirit of Abolitionism. I told him that the doctrine was tantamount to the assumption of unlimited power on the part of the government, and that such would be the impression on the public mind in a large portion of the Union.

The consequence would be inevitable—a large portion of the Northern states believed slavery to be a sin and would believe it to be an obligation of conscience to abolish it, if they should feel themselves in any degree responsible for its continuance, and that his doctrine would necessarily lead to the belief of such responsibility. I then predicted that it would commence, as it has, with this fanatical portion of society; and that they would begin their operation on the ignorant, the weak, the young, and the thoughtless, and would gradually extend upward till they became strong enough to obtain political control, when he, and others holding the highest stations in society, would, however reluctant, be compelled to yield to their doctrine or be driven into obscurity. But four years have since elapsed, and all this is already in a course of regular fulfillment.

Standing at the point of time at which we have now arrived, it will not be more difficult to trace the course of future events now than it was then. Those who imagine that the spirit now abroad in the North will die away of itself without a shock or convulsion have formed a very inadequate conception of its real character; it will continue to rise and spread, unless prompt and efficient measures to stay its progress be adopted. Already it has taken possession of the pulpit, of the schools, and, to a considerable extent, of the press—those great instruments by which the mind of the rising generation will be formed.

However sound the great body of the nonslaveholding states are at present, in the course of a few years they will be succeeded by

205

those who will have been taught to hate the people and institutions of nearly one-half of this Union, with a hatred more deadly than one hostile nation ever entertained toward another. It is easy to see the end. By the necessary course of events, if left to themselves, we must become, finally, two people. It is impossible, under the deadly hatred which must spring up between the two great sections, if the present causes are permitted to operate unchecked, that we should continue under the same political system. The conflicting elements would burst the Union asunder, as powerful as are the links which hold it together. Abolition and the Union cannot coexist. As the friend of the Union, I openly proclaim it, and the sooner it is known the better. The former may now be controlled, but in a short time it will be beyond the power of man to arrest the course of events.

We of the South will not, cannot surrender our institutions. To maintain the existing relations between the two races inhabiting that section of the Union is indispensable to the peace and happiness of both. It cannot be subverted without drenching the country in blood and extirpating one or the other of the races. Be it good or bad, it has grown up with our society and institutions and is so interwoven with them that to destroy it would be to destroy us as a people. But let me not be understood as admitting, even by implication, that the existing relations between the two races, in the slave-holding states, is an evil. Far otherwise; I hold it to be a good, as it has thus far proved itself to be, to both, and will continue to prove so, if not disturbed by the fell spirit of Abolition.

I appeal to facts. Never before has the black race of Central Africa, from the dawn of history to the present day, attained a condition so civilized and so improved, not only physically but morally and intellectually. It came among us in a low, degraded, and savage condition, and, in the course of a few generations, it has grown up under the fostering care of our institutions, as reviled as they have been, to its present comparative civilized condition. This, with the rapid increase of numbers, is conclusive proof of the general happiness of the race, in spite of all the exaggerated tales to the contrary.

In the meantime, the white or European race has not degenerated. It has kept pace with its brethren in other sections of the Union where slavery does not exist. It is odious to make comparison; but I appeal to all sides whether the South is not equal in virtue, intelligence, patriotism, courage, disinterestedness, and all the high qualities which adorn our nature. I ask whether we have not contributed our full share of talents and political wisdom in forming and sustaining this political fabric; and whether we have not constantly inclined most strongly to the side of liberty and been the first to see and first to resist the encroachments of power. In one thing only are we inferior — the arts of gain. We acknowledge that we are less wealthy than the Northern section of this Union, but I trace this mainly to the fiscal action of this government, which has extracted much from and spent little among us. Had it been the reverse — if the exaction had been from the other section and the expenditure with us — this point of superiority would not be against us now, as it was not at the formation of this government.

But I take higher ground. I hold that, in the present state of civilization, where two races of different origin and distinguished by color and other physical differences, as well as intellectual, are brought together, the relation now existing in the slaveholding states between the two is, instead of an evil, a good — a positive good. I feel myself called upon to speak freely upon the subject, where the honor and interests of those I represent are involved. I hold, then, that there never has yet existed a wealthy and civilized society in which one portion of the community did not, in point of fact, live on the labor of the other. Broad and general as is this assertion, it is fully borne out by history.

This is not the proper occasion, but, if it were, it would not be difficult to trace the various devices by which the wealth of all civilized communities has been so unequally divided and to show by what means so small a share has been allotted to those by whose labor it was produced, and so large a share given to the nonproducing class. The devices are almost innumerable, from the brute force and gross superstition of ancient times to the subtle and artful fiscal contrivances of modern. I might well challenge a comparison between them and the more direct, simple, and patriarchal mode by which the labor of the African race is among us commanded by the European. I may say, with truth, that in few countries so much is left to the share of the laborer and so little exacted from him or where there is more kind attention to him in sickness or infirmities of age. Compare his condition with the tenants of the poorhouses in the most civilized portions of Europe—look at the sick and the old and infirm slave, on one hand, in the midst of his family and friends, under the kind superintending care of his master and mistress, and compare it with the forlorn and wretched condition of the pauper in the poorhouse.

But I will not dwell on this aspect of the question. I turn to the political; and here I fearlessly assert that the existing relation between the two races in the South, against which these blind fanatics are waging war, forms the most solid and durable foundation on which to rear free and stable political institutions. It is useless to disguise the fact. There is, and always has been, in an advanced stage of wealth and civilization, a conflict between labor and capital. The condition of society in the South exempts us from the disorders and dangers resulting from this conflict; and which explains why it is that the political condition of the slaveholding states has been so much more stable and quiet than those of the North. The advantages of the former, in this respect, will become more and more manifest if left undisturbed by interference from without, as the country advances in wealth and numbers. We have, in fact, but just entered that condition of society where the strength and durability of our political institutions are to be tested; and I venture nothing in predicting that the experience of the next generation will fully test how vastly more favorable our condition of society is to that of other sections for free and stable institutions, provided we are not disturbed by the interference of others or shall have sufficient intelligence and spirit to resist promptly and successfully such interference.

It rests with ourselves to meet and repel them. I look not for aid to this government or to the other states; not but there are kind feelings toward us on the part of the great body of the nonslaveholding states; but, as kind as their feelings may be, we may rest assured that no political party in those states will risk their ascendency for our safety. If we do not defend ourselves, none will defend us; if we yield, we will be more and more pressed as we recede; and, if we submit, we will be trampled underfoot. Be assured that emancipation itself would not satisfy these fanatics; that gained, the next step would be to raise the Negroes to a social and political equality

208

with the whites; and, that being effected, we would soon find the present condition of the two races reversed. They, and their Northern allies, would be the masters, and we the slaves; the condition of the white race in the British West India Islands, as bad as it is, would be happiness to ours; there the mother country is interested in sustaining the supremacy of the European race. It is true that the authority of the former master is destroyed, but the African will there still be a slave, not to individuals, but to the community—forced to labor, not by the authority of the overseer but by the bayonet of the soldiery and the rod of the civil magistrate.

Surrounded as the slaveholding states are with such imminent perils, I rejoice to think that our means of defense are ample if we shall prove to have the intelligence and spirit to see and apply them before it is too late. All we want is concert, to lay aside all party differences, and unite with zeal and energy in repelling approaching dangers. Let there be concert of action, and we shall find ample means of security without resorting to secession or disunion. I speak with full knowledge and a thorough examination of the subject, and, for one, see my way clearly.

One thing alarms me—the eager pursuit of gain which overspreads the land and which absorbs every faculty of the mind and every feeling of the heart. Of all passions, avarice is the most blind and compromising—the last to see and the first to yield to danger. I dare not hope that anything I can say will arouse the South to a due sense of danger. I fear it is beyond the power of mortal voice to awaken it in time from the fatal security into which it has fallen.

WILLIAM JOHNSON
Diary of a Free Negro

Before the Civil War the activities of free Negroes were severely curtailed by various laws in the Southern states. Such persons often had to carry a certificate of freedom, secure a license to sell merchandise, and observe a curfew. Throughout the South no Negro, slave or free, could vote or receive instruction. In view of these restrictions, the life of the free Negro William Johnson was somewhat remarkable. Johnson was wealthy; he owned at least three barber shops, and kept a few slaves. White men traded with him, borrowed money from him, and sought his advice. The diary that he kept for sixteen years was passed on through his family. In 1938 it was entrusted to two historians, and first published thirteen years later. [Source: William Johnson's Natchez: The Ante-Bellum Diary of a Free Negro, William R. Hogan and Edwin A. Davis, eds., Baton Rouge, 1951, pp. 71-167.]

Oct. 30, 1835. Race between Fanny Kemble & Redd Mariah — 2 Miles and Repeate — $2000 aside — Redd Mariah made 4 or five very bad starts — When they did start F. K. was held up No start Mariah ran two miles Out The 2d start they had Mariah Jumped the fence and threw the Boy — she did not Run for it. The money was given up to Fanny Kemble — My opinion was that Red Mariah would have won the Money — Rouland & a Mr. Lupton fights Luton Bruised him very much and had him Down for a ½ minute. Rouland Resiled with him & threw him & the fall Broke his Leg in someway or other.

31 I Loaned Dr. Benbrook $3.00 I went to the Race track First Race between Mr. Rich. Harrisons Little Black Rachel Jackson & a grey mare of Mr Hocket Woods. Bets were all in favor of Rachel Jackson — Single Dash of a mile. The grey or Mary won the Race with perfect Ease beating the other about 60 or 80 feet — Second Race Mr. H. Woods bay Colt & Big Indian, 2 miles Out Won by big Indian about 40 or fifty yards — I did bet one Dollar on Rachel Jackson with a Stranger & I bet one on the bay Colt against Indian — also with the Stranger, & ten Dollars with Mr. Saml. Gosien — Lost all — A Mr Simington Died at the Forks of the Road. He was a Negro trader. I paid Mr Barlow $3.75 for the Hyre 3 days of Ben. . . .

Nov. 3 Mr. Hough Leaves this place for New Orleans on S. B. Chester, I sent a Dayly paper & a Letter to Jas Miller — He Directs me to Collect the money that he Owes me from his partner Mr Skeggs — Mr Bledsoe Orders a wig to be made very Light Hair — Finds William at Mr Parkers Kitchen with his Girls Struck him with the whip 1st and then with the stick He ran home and I followed him there and whiped him well for it, having often told him about going Down there — He then Comes Out on Bill Nix and Seys that he Bought five finger Rings &c.

210

4 I took Bill Nix and gave him a whiping. He then Confessed that he had taken the Key of Side Bourd which unlocked Mothers trunk and that he had got money frequently to the amount of Eight or ten Dollars He had bought a finger Ring of Cockarill & Surie, cost $3.00, a whip from Mr Spielmans Zack, cost 1.00, a pair of Boots from Middleton, cost $2.50 He paid John for a pair of Pantaloons His Mother was greatly Hurt at the Conduct of Her Degraded Son—Mr Bledsoe teling Mr. Bradley that Capt Myres after having Settled with the owners of the Boat and given them a Receit in full for the money that they Owed him he went to New Orleans and Collected money to the amount of a thousand Dollars and kept it by saying the Boat owed Him

5 The Dayly Paper anoncees the Result of the Election Col Bingaman & Mr McMurran, Representatives, Mr Chambers, Shreriff. Miss Sarai Newman gets married to a Mr Foster of Woodville, a merchant—I paid Phill $3.00 for water Out of the pond for seven Days—Mr Duolon paid me for two months shaving $2.00 I paid Mr Mellen five Dollars for One years Subscription to the Weekly Courier & Journal for Mr Jas Miller—Mr Smith paid me for One months Shaving 1.50 I paid Mr Bledsoes Boy $11 for 2 Gunea pigs

6 I paid $2.50 for a Bundle of Shingles. The Citizens went Out to the Race track in search of the Gamblers; the Brought in Elick Piper from Mr Mardice's place—Had a meeting at the Court House for the purpose of trying him—Gridley took him from them and put him to Jail—Twas their Intention to have whipd him—Mr Bray puts up his new sign. His men all got Drunk Made a great noise.

7 Col Bingaman & Mr Chambers gives a Dinner at Mr Parkers. Underwood & John Mason fights. Underwood whiped him very Easy—I paid Mr S. Cotten $27.00 the amount Due to Dr Hunt, Deceased. I Loaned Mr Whiting $8.00 pd Mr Harrison Black mare runs a mile against Sorril mare Called the Sumpter Filly—Black M. won the Race very Easy, by 30 yards—Cryzers horse ran against the one Eyed Sorrel mare The mare won the race by Eleven feet. They ran 750 yards

8 The Fencibles [Natchez, Miss., volunteer militia] Left Here for Vicksburg on Bourd of the Steam Boat Ponchartrain. They Left here about 1 Oclock in the Evening—31 in Number—Gave William $2.00 Stephen pd me $12.00

9 I Commenced to pull Down the part of the Stable to Rebuild it up again—Paid $10.00 for 2000 Shingles—The Jone Left here at Night taking 4 or 5 more of the Fencibles to Vicksburg Mr Massy Came to buy my Land for Mr Flecheo—Mr Newman pays me $5.00 that he Borrowed Tuesday 27th day of October I Loaned Dr Benbrook $2.00

10 Mrs. Merricks House on Main street Sold at Auction and was Bought by Abby for five thousand & Eighty Dollars—Hyred— — —To Drive for me—1.50 per Day—Receid a Letter by Greenburg Wade for [from] Orleans. Mrs Miller wishes me to purchase a house & Lot Down there at $3500. Mr F. Rowland pays me $50.00 the ballance of the money Due me from Mr Robert for house Rent. I stopped Stephen in to work for Mr Rowes from 9 Oclock untill Night, tho he did not work any.

11 Maj. Miller Came to Natchez. Mr Harden took my Letter to Mrs Miller I sent $15 to get a wig for Mr Bledsoe—My mule ranaway I sent John & Stephen down to Ragleys place for him. They Could not find him Mr Rowes has my old Roan Horse all Day—I gave Mr Jackson Five Dollars. He commenced work after Dinner, worked untill night—Mr Whiting paid me $8.00 that he Borrowed on Saturday November 7th

12 Mc & myself went out to Parson Connelly Sale to Look at his Cows. They were all Dry—Stephen & John went to Rayley place for my mule Came home with him at 11 A. M. Oclock Mr M. Williams sends his sick Boy to Bourd until he returns from Red River I made Maj Dunbar a present of 2 guinea pigs

13 Bought a Sorrel Horse—Rob. Roy—at Auction for $106 cash— I thought Mc would take him when I Bought him and when he came up I asked him if wanted to buy a Horse and he told no, that food was too high—I then told him to take him to his stable and keep him to ride for his feed—He then said as above stated that corn was too high—I then proposed for him ride him on Sunday—He said no that he was agoing to ride Mr Browns Horse to try him—Mr Gilbert auditer &c. came down from Jackson—Fencibles Returned from Vicksburg They Looked very well. Higly pleased with the citizens of that place would not suffer them to pay for anything what every— Mr Barber Returned from the North—Mother Buys Mary and her Child from Mr Murcherson for $800.00. . . .

212

22 I gave old French $2.00 I did not see old Mc the whole day. Two Irishman commenced boxing in fun and then began to fight. The one kicked the other in such a seviere maner that he broke his gaul. His Head was bruised also — Hc Dicd in 8 or ten hours after the fight His name was Russell He was Killed by, — — —. He was put in Jail on Monday 23d inst

23 Mr Bledsoe gets the wig that I sent to Orleans for He pays me $15.00 for it. Tis what it cost me — I Loaned Mr. Whiting $10 I told Mr Flecheo that he could take my Land at 8 dollars per acre. I Loaned Mr Gilbert my Horse to wride out to Col Bingamans — Northern mail arrived. Brings News to Gilbert that Linch was Elected by small majority — Old Fletcheo Gets Drunk and came in the shop Play, Tour de Nesle or the Chamber of Death Margariett of Bergundy, Mrs Lyons Farce, dead Shot.

24 I Loaned Dr Hubbard One hundred and 75 dollars — Mr Baynton arrives here. The Little Dwarf arrives here. The play is Hunch Back. Master Walter by Mr Parsons — A Bear belonging [to] Mr Phiffs Killcd a Little Yellow Child Down at Mr Parkers Hotel They had to shoot him Dead to Loose him — Mc takes his horse home to his own stable — Mr Pulling and Milne has a sort of a fight about the moving of some coal. Mr P. threw a Hatchet at Mr M. and it mist him Mr M attempted to get a gun Down to shoot. . . .

May 19, 1836. The Volunteers from Madison County Left here for Texas. To Day it was that I Found Old Pagg in possession of a Black man belonging Mr Barber. The Boys name was Patrick, I Brought him Out of his yard with the Saddle, Bridle, Martingale and all on the Horse. I got on him and rode home on him, After having showed the Horse to his master he promised me that he would pay any Damage that I seen proper to Charge him for the Horse

20 Mr Barber sells the Black man Patrick that stoled my Horse, he Sold him on that account alone. To Day the Old Gentleman that Lost his Wife by her Runing away with a Big whiskered man by the name of Clayton, the old man swears that he will kill Clayton on the first site Mr Patterson paid me $10 that was due me from the Vicksburgh Volunteers — To day I Bot at Sorias Auction 12 pairs of Pantaloons at 94 cents per pair. I gave John 1 pair, Charles 1 pair, Bill Nix 1 pair, Steven 1 pair, Louis 1 pair. . . .

June 3 I Bot Moses from a man by the name of William Good, at

Least I Bot him at auction under the Hammer for four Hundred Dollars cash—I Bot also 2 Boxes of wine at 2.87 ½ per Box and 5 small Boxes of shaving soap, 43 cents per Box Mr Samuel Davis sells his Family Residence to Mr Gildart for twenty thousand Dollars. No Sail I Bot of Mr Chew all the Birds that Mr Grayson Left here and their Cages also for ten Dollars Cash. . . .

22 Buisness only Tolerably Brisk, Mr McGetrick makes a Bet with Mr Cobler to day of $25 that his Brown Horse would beat Mr Mardices Little Bay mare a ½ mile Race They gave me the $50 to hold as there stakes The winner was to have the fifty Dollars—I Loaned Dr Hubbard $400 to be paid on Monday; Some Talk about town of Lynching — — — — — — — the Painter for taking off Dr — — — s Daughter.

23 Dr Hubbard pd me $100, that being a part of Four Hundred that I Loaned him yesterday—He prescribed for John 20 grs of Calamal & 5 grs of James Powders News to day that fifteen thousand Mexicans were Marching towards Texas and that six hundred thousand Dollars were subscribed by the Mexicans in One Single Day

24 Roberson and Dr Hogg has a kind of a fight, old Dr Hogg made him Travell prety fast. Particulars are those, Roberson Owed the Dr 12 dollars for Medical Services. The Dr gave his account to Whiting to Collect for him so he presented the Acct. to Roberson & R. said that he was not the man, so Dr suied on it, & Robs. Came to his office to abuse him about it, and the old Dr told him to Leave his office. The Dr and him came to Blowes, and the Dr struck him with a chair & R. ran in the street & struck him in the Breast with a Brick, then ran up Street as Hard as he could split and the old Dr after him So Roberson run throuh Thistles Stable and came out at the Back side of the Stable and went Home The Dr & Maj Miller went around to Robs House Dr went in & struck him with his cane and R. caught the stick and the sword came out, and the Dr would have killed him if his arm had not been caught by Mr Ross—Roberson then Broke and run as hard as he could split to the Jail, and went in for Safe Keeping—In time of the fight Robs Brother Struck Maj Miller on the head with a Brick Bat and then Run and the old Maj after him as hard as he could split The Maj stumbled and fell and as he fell he made a cut at Robison and Cut him in the Butt

214

Mr. — — — — gave Dr — — the plain Talk about His Daughter &c.

26 Mc and myself wrode Out as far as the Race track. Good many young men from town were Out there Drunk Mr Debins, Mr Abona, Mr — — —, Mr S Davis, Mr Hyram Hanchet and a good many Others

July 2 Tarlton Brings my mule

4 Big marching about town The Huzars turned Out for the first time in the streets on parade — the Fencibles and the Mechanicks also — Big Dinner at Mr West tavern — Mr Calmes Died this morning Early after having been to Market, He Broke a Blood vessell and Died before Dr Hogg could get to see him

5 Mr Calmes, the Jailer, was Buried to Day by the Masons, Large procession — I sent my mule up to Spraigue & Howell to be sold but they did not sell her There were no purchasers Little William Winston came to stay with me to Lern the Barbers trade. . . .

Aug. 29 I herd to day that Last Saturday when the Bunker Hill Left here that there was on Bourd of her 100 men Bound for Texas Comanded by a Capt Williams — The Boat Landed at Peter Littles place to wood & those men went on shore and Robbed his Hen Roos and then whiped his Negro Boy — The old man his self then Came Out and they partly knocked him Down and then pouned him pretty severely — they then Left and went on Bourd of the Steam Boat taking with them all the old Fellows Chickens & Turkeys — To Day a Boy belonging to Mr S. Davis was hung on the other side of the River His name was Nim Rod — He was Hung for Killing the overseer by the name of Levels I believe, Early this Evening Mr Vannerson gets married to old Mrs Purnell. . . .

Nov. 27 I got up this morning before Day and took my gun Out to Scotts old Field and put her under a Log and Came home I got back to town at Day Break — I Rode Out in the afternoon, took my gun from under the Log and commenced Shooting Crows. I Killed 2 crows at One Shot and I Killed four at four other Single Shots, making in all Six and I Shot 1 Rice Bird, 1 gold Finch & 1 Tom Tit — Bill Nix & Simpson was with me, I then when in the old Field, made the Boys Take a Race Charles wrode my Little mare & Bill Nix wrde my Sorrill Horse Rob Roy — the Horse could Out Run her very Easy — I did not get in untill night

28 To Day we had Bloody work for a while in the streets up at Throckmortons Corner. Last night up at Mrs Rowans Bourding

215

House several gentlemen were in conversation about a Duel that was fought in South Carolina. When Mr Charles Stewart stated that those Gentlement that fought actually fought with Bullits, Mr Dalhgreen Said that they must fought with paper Bullits—Mr C. Stewart then Said if any man would say that they fought with paper Bullits that he is a Damed Lyar and a Dd Scoundrel & a Dmd Coward—this was at the Supper Table Mr Dalhgreen Jumped up and Slaped Mr C. Stewarts Cheek one very hard slapp

They were then parted so young Stewart told him that they would settle it in the morning—So this morning young Stewart took a Stand up at Carpenters Drug Store for the purpose of making the attackt upon Dalhgreen as he would be going to the Bank—Dr Hubbard at the Request of his Brother went up to Carpenters with young Stewart to see him Out in the affair Elick Stewart said that he would not take any part in the affair and he took a stand over on Sorias Corner—and as Dalhgreen past the Door Stewart steped up to him and told him that now was to Settle therr Dispute and at the Same time Struck Mr Dalhgreen with his stick, Mr D then Struck him Back with an umberralla—Stewart Struck him with the Stick again—

Mr D. then steped Back and Drew a Pistol and Fired at Mr S. and missed Him—Mr S. then Drew and Fired and the Ball Lodged under the arm in the Left Side of Mr Dalhgreen, Mr D. then steped in at Throckmortons Store S steped in at the Door but finding that D. had another Pistol he steped Back and stood in the caseing of the Door D. then advanced on him, shot Him on Left Side of the face on the Temple or uper hinge of the Jaw Bone and the instant the Ball took Effect he Droped on his Knees and Fell over on the pavement as Dead, so Dead that he Barely Breathed. At the instant he fell Mr Elick Stewart ran up and struck D. with his fist D then advanced on him with an Empty Pistol and in doing so Dr Hubbard shoved Him Back, E. S. Drew a Bouye Knife and commenced cuting at him—Mr D. had no weapon at this time and was fighting with his naked hands and Mr E. S. with the Knife—

It was one of the gamest fights that we have Ever had in Our City before—E. S. cut him twice over the Head and cut his Little finger nearly off and split his hand pretty Bad Mr R. Bledsoe and Mr Hewit has a small fist fight. After a Blow or two past, Mr Bledsoe went and

216

got his Pistols. I am told as Soon as Mr Hewit saw the pistol he Said whoorer and ran Down the street and got in a Store and Mr Bledsoe made him retract what he had Said in writing before he would Let him go—this he did from fear

29 To Day I went up to the Agricultural Bank and Received in cash Seventeen Hundred and Fifty Dollars being the amount of a note that I Received from Flecheaux given him by Mr R. Bledsoe for Land that I sold to Flecheaux which Said Flecheaux Sold to Mr R. Bledsoe—I went to day around to Dr Hubbards office to shave young Mr Stewarts head, he was quite ill—I then went on up to Mrs Rowans to Shave Dr Dalhgreens Beard off—he was very Comfortably Situated and in a thriving condition I made a mistake in this. Col. Bingaman Sent Steven in town to me to day and instead of Coming in he went under the Hill and got Drunk I Supose; I found him on a Dray and I sent Dr Hogg to see what was the matter with him and the Dr pronounced him Drunk at first site. . . .

Dec. 8 To Day about Dinner they had had a Leargquantity of Gentlemen were on the Bluff to See the car Start, They had put Down about 40 feet of Rails and had put on a Car, and they were a Runing it Backwards and fowards on the Small Road that they had constructed, There were present Gov. Quitman, Mr Vanison, W. P. Mellon, R. Fields, T. Jones, W Chambers, Rice, Holton, Capt Cotten and a greate many more To Day I Bot the improvements that Flecho put on my House, that is the window and Several other things and the Counter also—He is to Leave the House on the 16th of this month without Fail—Wheathers Bot the House that he Lives in at auction to Day, It Sold for 17 hundred Dollars I had to whip Bill Winston and Bix Nix for fighting in the shop to night when gentleman was in the Shop. I had to give it to them Both.

9 I received of Mr Proctor to Day thirty Barrels of coal, price 1 Dollar per Barrell Mc He got 20 Barrells of the same man, I gave the Carpenters to day $2 to Buy Liquor with, The[y] commenced puting on the weather Bourding to day for the first. I had to give William a few cracks this Evening for insolent Language whilst Cutting a gentlemans Hair, it was at dinner time. . . .

March 6, 1837. Col A L. Bingaman Received a challenge from Col Osburn Claibourne To fight. The Col. Came in very Early this morning and got shaved He seemed to be wraped up in thought, he

217

had nothing to say—The Roumer Says that they are to fight with Riffles—I am very Sorry to heare that they are agoing to fight—I only wish that they may be prevented from fighting for I Like them Both—Col. Clabourne has 40 of his Slaves put up to be Sold at auction, Report Seys they are sold for debt Lawyer Baker has old Armstead in Jail and gave him to day One Hundred & fifty Lashes He Seys that he stoled four Hundred Dollars from him—Mr Duffield was put in Jail Last night for debt.

Abolitionist Protest Against the President

In July 1835 a group of South Carolinians stormed the post office in Charleston and burned packages of Abolitionist literature awaiting distribution. The incident raised the issue of state interference with the delivery of the U.S. mails. In December 1835 President Jackson presented his views to Congress. He condemned what he called "wicked attempts" to "instigate the slaves to insurrection" and recommended legislation to prohibit the circulation of incendiary mail in Southern states. The Abolitionists protested the President's speech in the letter reproduced below. It was issued on December 26, 1835, and featured in the Abolitionist press. The President's bill did not become law, mainly because Congress refused to give any state or the federal government the right to censor the mail. [Source: William Jay, A View of the Action of the Federal Government in Behalf of Slavery, *New York, 1839, pp. 229-240.]*

To the President of the United States:

Sir:

In your message to Congress of the 7th instant are the following passages:

"I must also invite your attention to the painful excitement produced in the South, by attempts to circulate through the mails, inflammatory appeals, *addressed to the passions of the slaves,* in prints and in various sorts of publications, *calculated to stimulate them to insurrection and produce all the horrors of*

218

a servile war. There is, doubtless, no respectable portion of our countrymen who can be so far misled as to feel any other sentiment than that of indignant regret at conduct so destructive of the harmony and peace of the country and *so repugnant to the principles of our national compact and to the dictates of humanity and religion.*"

You remark that it is fortunate that the people of the North have "given so strong and impressive a tone to the sentiments entertained against the proceedings of the misguided persons who have engaged in these *unconstitutional and wicked attempts.*" And you proceed to suggest to Congress "the propriety of passing such a law as will prohibit, under severe penalties, the circulation in the Southern states, through the mails, of incendiary publication, *intended to instigate the slaves to insurrection.*"

A servile insurrection, as experience has shown, involves the slaughter of the whites, without respect to sex or age. Hence, sir, the purport of the information you have communicated to Congress and to the world is that there are American citizens who, in violation of the dictates of humanity and religion, have engaged in unconstitutional and wicked attempts to circulate, through the mails, inflammatory appeals addressed to the passions of the slaves, and which appeals, as is implied in the object of your proposed law, are *intended to stimulate the slaves to indiscriminate massacre.* Recent events irresistibly confine the application of your remarks to the officers and members of the American Antislavery Society and its auxiliaries.

On the 28th of March, 1834, the Senate of the United States passed the following resolution:

Resolved, that the President, in relation to the public revenue, has assumed upon himself authority and power not conferred by the Constitution and laws, but in derogation of both.

On the 5th of the ensuing month, you transmitted to that body your "solemn protest" against their decision. Instructed by your example, we now, sir, in behalf of the Society of which we are the constituted organs and in behalf of all who are associated with it, present to you this, our "solemn protest," against your grievous and unfounded accusations.

219

Should it be supposed, that in thus addressing you, we are wanting in the respect due to your exalted station, we offer, in our vindication, your own acknowledgement to the Senate: "Subject only to the restraints of truth and justice, the free people of the United States have the undoubted right as individuals or collectively, orally or in writing, at such times and in such language and form as they may think proper, to discuss his (the President's) official conduct and to express and promulgate their opinions concerning it."

In the exercise of this "undoubted right," we protest against the judgment you have pronounced against the Abolitionists.

First, because, in rendering that judgment officially, you assumed a power not belonging to your office.

You complained that the resolution censuring your conduct, "though adopted by the Senate in its legislative capacity, is, in its effects and in its characteristics, essentially *judicial*." And thus, sir, although the charges of which we complain were made by you in your executive capacity, they are, equally with the resolution, essentially *judicial*.

The Senate adjudged that your conduct was unconstitutional. You pass the same judgment on our efforts. Nay, sir, you go farther than the Senate. That body forbore to impeach your motives; but you have assumed the prerogatives, not only of a court of law but of conscience, and pronounce our efforts to be *wicked* as well as unconstitutional.

Second, we protest against the *publicity* you have given to your accusations.

You felt it to be a grievance that the charge against you was "spread upon the *Journal* of the Senate, published to the nation and to the world — made part of our enduring archives and incorporated in the history of the age. The punishment of removal from office and future disqualification does not follow the decision; but the *moral influence* of a solemn declaration by a majority of the Senate, that the accused is guilty of the offense charged upon him, has been as effectually secured as if the like declaration had been made upon an impeachment expressed in the same terms."

And is it nothing, sir, that we are officially charged by the President of the United States with wicked and unconstitutional efforts and with harboring the most execrable intentions; and, this, too, in a document spread upon the *Journals* of both houses of Congress, published to the nation and to the world, made part of our enduring archives, and incorporated in the history of the age? It is true that, although you have given judgment against us, you cannot award execution. We are not, indeed, subjected to the penalty of murder; but need we ask you, sir, what must be the *moral influence* of your declaration, that we have intended its perpetration?

Third, we protest against your condemnation of us *unheard.*

What, sir, was your complaint against the Senate? "Without notice, *unheard* and untried, I find myself charged, on the records of the Senate and in a form unknown in our country, with the high crime of violating the laws and Constitution of my country. No notice of the charge was given to the accused, and no opportunity afforded him to respond to the accusation—to meet his accusers face to face—to cross-examine the witnesses—to procure counteracting testimony or to be heard in his defense."

Had you, sir, done to others as it thus seems you would that others should do to you, no occasion would have been given for this protest. You most truly assert, in relation to the conduct of the Senate, "It is the policy of our benign system of jurisprudence to secure in all criminal proceedings, and even in the most trivial litigations, a fair, unprejudiced, and impartial trial." And by what authority, sir, do you except such of your fellow citizens as are known as Abolitionists from the benefit of this benign system? When has a fair, unprejudiced, and impartial trial been accorded to those who dare to maintain that all men are equally entitled to life, liberty, and the pursuit of happiness? What was the trial, sir, which preceded the judgment you have rendered against them?

Fourth, we protest against the *vagueness* of your charges.

We cannot more forcibly describe the injustice you have done us than by adopting your own indignant remonstrance against what you deemed similar injustice on the part of the Senate: Some of the first principles of natural right and enlightened jurisprudence have been violated in the very form of the resolution. It carefully abstains from averring in *which* of the late proceedings the President has assumed upon himself authority and power not conferred by the Constitution and laws. Why was not the certainty of the offense, the nature and cause of the accusation, set out in the manner required in the Constitution, before even the humblest individual, for the smallest crime, can be exposed to condemnation? Such a specification was due to the accused that he might direct his defense to the real points of attack. A more striking illustration of the soundness and necessity of the rules which forbid *vague and indefinite generalities* and require a reasonable certainty in all judicial allegations, and a more glaring instance of the violation of these rules has seldom been exhibited.

It has been reserved for you, sir, to exhibit a still more striking illustration of the importance of these rules and a still more glaring instance of their violation. You have accused an indefinite number of your fellow citizens, without designation of name or residence, of making unconstitutional and wicked efforts and of harboring intentions which could be entertained only by the most depraved and abandoned of mankind; and yet you carefully abstain from averring *which* article of the Constitution they have transgressed; you omit stating when, where, and by whom these wicked attempts were made; you give no specification of the inflammatory appeals which you assert have been addressed to the passions of the slaves. You well know that the *"moral influence"* of your charges will affect thousands of your countrymen, many of them your political friends—some of them heretofore honored with your confidence—most, if not all of them, of irreproachable characters; and yet, by the very vagueness of your charges, you incapacitate each one of this multitude from proving his innocence.

Fifth, we protest against your charges, because they are *untrue.* Surely, sir, the burden of proof rests upon you. If you possess evidence against us, we are, by your own showing, entitled to "an opportunity to cross-examine witnesses, to procure counteracting testimony, and to be heard in [*our*] defense." You complained that you had been denied such an opportunity. It was not to have been expected, then, that you would make the conduct of the Senate the model of your own. Conscious of the wrong done to you and protesting against it, you found yourself compelled to enter on your defense. You have placed us in similar circumstances, and we proceed to follow your example:

The substance of your various allegations may be embodied in the charge, that we have attempted to circulate, through the mails, appeals addressed to the passions of the slaves, calculated to stimulate them to insurrection, and with the intention of producing a servile war.

It is deserving of notice that the *attempt* to circulate our papers is alone charged upon us. It is not pretended that we have put our appeals into the hands of a single slave, or that, in any instance, our endeavors to excite a servile war have been crowned with success. And in what way was our most execrable attempts made? By secret agents, traversing the slave country in disguise, stealing by night into the hut of the slave, and there reading to him our inflammatory appeals? You, sir, answer this question by declaring that we attempted the mighty mischief by circulating our appeals "THROUGH THE MAILS!" And are the Southern slaves, sir, accustomed to receive periodicals by mail? Of the thousands of publications mailed from the Antislavery office for the South, did you ever hear, sir, of one solitary paper being addressed to a slave? Would you know to whom they were directed, consult the Southern newspapers, and you will find them complaining that they were sent to public officers, clergymen, and other influential citizens.

Thus it seems we are incendiaries who place the torch in the hands of him whose dwellings we would fire! We are conspiring to excite a servile war, and announce our design to the masters, and commit to their care and disposal the very instruments by which we expect to effect our purpose! It has been said that thirty or forty of our papers were received at the South, directed to free people of color. We cannot deny the assertion because these papers may have been mailed by others for the sinister purpose of charging the act upon us. We are, however, ready to make our several affidavits that not one paper, with our knowledge or by our authority, has ever been sent to any such person in a slave state. The free people of color at the South can exert no influence in behalf of the enslaved; and we have no disposition to excite odium against them by making them the recipients of our publications.

Your proposal that a law should be passed punishing the circulation, through the mails, of papers *intended to excite the slaves to insurrection* necessarily implies that such papers are now circulated; and you expressly and positively assert that we have attempted to circulate appeals addressed to passions of the slaves and *calculated to produce all the horrors of a servile war*. We trust, sir, your proposed law, so portentous to the freedom of the press, will not be enacted till you have furnished Congress with stronger evidence of its necessity than unsupported assertions. We hope you will lay before that body, for its information, the papers to which you refer. This is the more necessary as the various public journals and meetings which have denounced us for entertaining insurrectionary and murderous designs have in no instance been able to quote from our publications a single exhortation to the slaves to break their fetters or the expression of a solitary wish for a servile war.

How far our writings are "calculated" to produce insurrection is a question which will be variously decided according to the latitude in which it is discussed. When we recollect that the humble schoolbook, the tale of fiction, and the costly annual have been placed under the ban of Southern editors for trivial allusions to slavery — and that a Southern divine has warned his fellow citizens of the danger of permitting slaves to be present at the celebration of our national festival, where they might listen to the Declaration of Independence and to eulogiums on liberty — we have little hope that our disquisitions on human rights will be generally deemed safe and innocent where those rights are habitually violated. Certain writings of one of your predecessors, President Jefferson, would undoubtedly be regarded, in some places, so insurrectionary as to expose to popular violence whoever should presume to circulate them.

As, therefore, sir, there is no common standard by which the criminality of opinions respecting slavery can be tested, we acknowledge the foresight which prompted you to recommend that the "severe penalties" of your proposed law should be awarded, not according to the character of the publication but the *intention* of the writer. Still, sir, we apprehend that no trivial difficulties will be experienced in the application of your law. The writer may be anonymous or beyond the reach of prosecution, while the porter who deposits the papers in the post office and the mail carrier who transports them, having no evil intentions, cannot be visited with the "severe penalties"; and thus will your law fail in securing to the South that entire exemption from all discussion on the subject of slavery, which it so vehemently desires. The success of the attempt already made to establish a censorship of the press is not such as to invite further encroachment on the rights of the people to publish their sentiments.

In your protest, you remarked to the Senate: "The whole executive power being vested in the President, who is *responsible* for its exercise, it is a necessary consequence that he should have a right to employ agents of his *own choice,* to aid him in the performance of his duties, and to *discharge* them when he is no longer *willing* to be RESPONSIBLE for their acts. He is equally bound to take care that the laws be faithfully executed, whether they impose duties on the highest officer of state or the *lowest subordinates* in any of the departments."

It may not be uninteresting to you, sir, to be informed in what manner your "subordinate" in New York, who, on your "responsibility," is exercising the functions of Censor of the American press, discharges the arduous duties of this untried and, until now, unheard of office. We beg leave to assure you, that his task is executed with a simplicity of principle and celerity of dispatch unknown to any Censor of the press in France or Austria. Your subordinate decides upon the incendiary character of the publications committed to the post office by a glance at the wrappers or bags in which they are contained. No packages sent to be mailed from our office and directed to a slave state can escape the vigilance of this inspector of canvas and brown paper. Even your own protest, sir, if in an anti-slavery envelope, would be arrested on its progress to the South as "inflammatory, incendiary and insurrectionary in the highest degree."

No veto, however, is *as yet* imposed on the circulation of publications from any printing office but our own. Hence, when we desire to send "appeals" to the South, all that is necessary is to insert them in some newspaper that espouses our principles, pay for as many thousand copies as we think proper, and order them to be mailed according to our instructions.

Such, sir, is the worthless protection purchased for the South, by the most unblushing and dangerous usurpation of which any public officer has been guilty since the organization of our federal government. . . .

225

And now, sir, permit us respectfully to suggest to you the propriety of ascertaining the *real* designs of Abolitionists before your apprehensions of them lead you to sanction any more trifling with the LIBERTY OF THE PRESS. You assume it as a fact that Abolitionists are miscreants who are laboring to effect the massacre of their Southern brethren. Are you aware of the extent of the reproach which such an assumption casts upon the character of your countrymen? In August last, the number of Antislavery societies known to us was 263; we have *now* the names of more than 350 societies, and accessions are daily made to the multitude who embrace our principles. And can you think it possible, sir, that these citizens are deliberately plotting murder and furnishing us with funds to send publications to the South "intended to instigate the slaves to insurrection"? Is there anything in the character and manners of the free states to warrant the imputation on their citizens of such enormous wickedness? Have you ever heard, sir, of whole communities in these states subjecting obnoxious individuals to a mock trial, and, then, in contempt of law, humanity, and religion, deliberately murdering them? You have seen in the public journals great rewards offered for the perpetration of horrible crimes. We appeal to your candor and ask, were these rewards offered by Abolitionists or by men whose charges against Abolitionists you have condescended to sanction and disseminate?

And what, sir, is the character of those whom you have in your message held up to the execration of the civilized world? Their enemies being judges, they are *religious* fanatics. And what are the haunts of these plotters of murder? The pulpit, the bench, the bar, the professor's chair, the hall of legislation, the meeting for prayer, the temple of the Most High. But strange and monstrous as is this conspiracy, still you believe in its existence and call on Congress to counteract it. Be persuaded, sir, the moral sense of the community is abundantly sufficient to render this conspiracy utterly impotent the moment its machinations are exposed. Only PROVE the assertions and insinuations in your message, and you dissolve in an instant every Antislavery society in our land. Think not, sir, that we shall interpose any obstacle to an inquiry into our conduct. We invite, nay, sir, we entreat the appointment by Congress of a committee of investigation to visit the Antislavery office in New York. They shall be put in possession of copies of all the publications that have been issued from our press. Our whole correspondence shall be submitted to their inspection; our accounts of receipts and expenditures shall be spread before them, and we ourselves will cheerfully answer under oath whatever interrogatories they may put to us relating to the charges you have advanced.

Should such a committee be denied and should the law you propose, stigmatizing us as felons, be passed without inquiry into the truth of your accusation and without allowing us a hearing, then shall we make the language of your protest our own, and declare that, "If such proceedings shall be approved and sustained by an intelligent people, then will the great contest with arbitrary power which had established in statutes, in bills of rights, in sacred charters, and in constitutions of government, the right of every citizen to a notice before trial, to a hearing before condemnation, and to an impartial tribunal for deciding on the charge, have been made in VAIN."

Before we conclude, permit us, sir, to offer you the following assurances.

Our principles, our objects, and our measures are wholly uncontaminated by considerations of party policy. Whatever may be our respective opinions as citizens of men and measures, as Abolitionists we have expressed no political preferences and are pursuing no party ends. From neither of the gentlemen nominated to succeed you have we anything to hope or fear; and to neither of them do we intend, as Abolitionists, to afford any aid or influence. This declaration will, it is hoped, satisfy the partisans of the rival candidates that it is not necessary for them to assail our rights by way of convincing the South that they do not possess our favor.

We have addressed you, sir, on this occasion, with republican plainness and Christian sincerity, but with no desire to derogate from the respect that is due to you or wantonly to give you pain. . . .

When convinced that our endeavors are wrong, we shall abandon them; but such conviction must be produced by other arguments than vituperation, popular violence, or penal enactments.

Resolutions on Abolitionist Propaganda

Riled by Abolitionist literature that was flooding the mails, the South Carolina legislature passed the following resolutions in December 1835. It then petitioned the various Northern legislatures to prohibit Abolitionist activity in their states, and also asked the postmaster general to ban the literature from the mails. Other Southern states acted similarly. Abolitionists were not popular, and the petitions were extensively debated. President Jackson, himself no slavery enthusiast, recommended legislation to prohibit the circulation of incendiary material. Congress came to the conclusion in 1836 that to do so would be unconstitutional, but the practice of Southern postmasters in refusing to deliver Abolitionist propaganda was not interfered with by the federal government. [Source: Acts and Resolutions of the General Assembly of the State of South Carolina Passed in December, 1835, Columbia, 1836, pp. 26-28.]

Your Committee, desirous of making a matter of record, both of our rights and the assertion of the just expectation that they will be respected by those who are united with us in the bonds of a common Union, beg leave to offer the following resolutions for the adoption of both branches of the legislature.

1. *Resolved*, that the formation of the abolition societies, and the acts and doings of certain fanatics calling themselves Abolitionists, in the nonslaveholding states of this Confederacy, are in direct violation of the obligations of the compact of the Union, dissocial and incendiary in the extreme.

2. *Resolved*, that no state having a just regard for her own peace and security can acquiesce in a state of things by which such conspiracies are engendered within the limits of a friendly state, united to her by the bonds of a common league of political association, without either surrendering or compromising her most essential rights.

3. *Resolved*, that the legislature of South Carolina, having every confidence in the justice and friendship of the nonslaveholding states, announces to her co-states her confident expectation, and she earnestly requests that the governments of these states will promptly and effectually suppress all those associations within their

respective limits purporting to be abolition societies; and that they will make it highly penal to print, publish, and distribute newspapers, pamphlets, tracts, and pictorial representations calculated and having an obvious tendency to excite the slaves of the Southern states to insurrection and revolt.

4. *Resolved*, that, regarding the domestic slavery of the Southern states as a subject exclusively within the control of each of the said states, we shall consider every interference by any other state or the general government as a direct and unlawful interference, to be resisted at once and under every possible circumstance.

5. *Resolved*, in order that a salutary negative may be put on the mischievous and unfounded assumption of some of the Abolitionists, the nonslaveholding states are requested to disclaim by legislative declaration all right, either on the part of themselves or the government of the United States, to interfere in any manner with domestic slavery, either in the states or in the territories where it exists.

6. *Resolved*, that we should consider the abolition of slavery in the District of Columbia as a violation of the rights of the citizens of that District, derived from the implied conditions on which that territory was ceded to the general government, and as a usurpation to be at once resisted as nothing more than the commencement of a scheme of much more extensive and flagrant injustice.

7. *Resolved*, that the legislature of South Carolina regards with decided approbation the measures of security adopted by the Post Office Department of the United States in relation to the transmission of incendiary tracts. But if this highly essential and protective policy be counteracted by Congress, and the United States mail becomes a vehicle for the transmission of the mischievous documents with which it was recently freighted, we, in this contingency, expect that the chief magistrate of our state will forthwith call the legislature together that timely measures may be taken to prevent its traversing our territory.

8. *Resolved*, that the governor be requested to transmit a copy of this report and resolutions to the executives of the several states that they may be laid before their respective legislatures.

GEORGE McDUFFIE

The Natural Slavery of the Negro

At the end of the eighteenth century, informed Northerners and Southerners alike looked forward to the natural demise of slavery. But the invention of the cotton gin made cotton the basis of the Southern economy after 1800, and slaves seemed to become more and more necessary as the wealth of the region grew. A message delivered to the South Carolina legislature by Governor George McDuffie in 1835 (excerpts appear below) marked the beginning of the South's counterattack against Northern Abolitionist propaganda. The speech reflected the transition in Southern thought from the notion of slavery as a necessary evil to the notion of slavery as a positive good, for white and black alike. McDuffie's main thesis, that the Negro was "destined by providence to occupy this condition of servile dependence," was thereafter central in all defenses of slavery. [Source: American History Leaflets, Colonial and Constitutional, Albert B. Hart and Edward Channing, eds., No. 10, July 1893.]

Since your last adjournment, the public mind throughout the slave-holding states has been intensely, indignantly, and justly excited by the wanton, officious, and incendiary proceedings of certain societies and persons in some of the nonslaveholding states, who have been actively employed in attempting to circulate among us pamphlets, papers, and pictorial representations of the most offensive and inflammatory character, and eminently calculated to seduce our slaves from their fidelity and excite them to insurrection and massacre. These wicked monsters and deluded fanatics, overlooking the numerous objects in their own vicinity, who have a moral if not a legal claim upon their charitable regard, run abroad in the expansion of their hypocritical benevolence, muffled up in the saintly mantle of Christian meekness, to fulfill the fiendlike errand of mingling the blood of the master and the slave, to whose fate they are equally indifferent, with the smoldering ruins of our peaceful dwellings.

No principle of human action so utterly baffles all human calculation as that species of fanatical enthusiasm which is made of envy and ambition, assuming the guise of religious zeal and acting upon the known prejudices, religious or political, of an ignorant multitude. Under the influence of this species of voluntary madness, nothing is sacred that stands in the way of its purposes. Like all other religious impostures, it has power to consecrate every act, however atrocious, and every person, however covered with "multiplying villainies," that may promote its diabolical ends or worship at its infernal altars. By its unholy creed, murder itself becomes a labor of love and charity, and the felon renegade, who flies from the justice of his country, finds not only a refuge but becomes a sainted minister in the sanctuary of its temple. . . .

The crime which these foreign incendiaries have committed against the peace of the state is one of the very highest grade known to human laws. It not only strikes at the very existence of society but seeks to accomplish the catastrophe, by the most horrible means, celebrating the obsequies of the state in a saturnalian carnival of blood and murder, and while brutally violating all the charities of life and desecrating the very altars of religion, impiously calling upon Heaven to sanction these abominations. It is my deliberate opinion that the laws of every community should punish this species of interference by death without benefit of clergy, regarding the authors of it as "enemies of the human race." Nothing could be more appropriate than for South Carolina to set this example in the present crisis, and I trust the legislature will not adjourn till it discharges this high duty of patriotism.

It cannot be disguised, however, that any laws which may be enacted by the authority of this state, however adequate to punish and repress offenses committed within its limits, will be wholly insufficient to meet the exigencies of the present conjuncture. If we go no further than this, we had as well do nothing. . . .

It will, therefore, become our imperious duty, recurring to those great principles of international law which still exist in all their primitive force among the sovereign states of this confederacy, to demand of our sovereign associates the condign punishment of those enemies of our peace who avail themselves of the sanctuaries of their respective jurisdictions, to carry on schemes of incendiary hostility against the institutions, the safety, and the existence of the state. In performing this high duty to which we are constrained by the great law of self-preservation, let us approach to our co-states with all the fraternal mildness which becomes us as members of the same family of confederated republics and, at the same time, with that firmness and decision which becomes a sovereign state, while maintaining her dearest interests and most sacred rights.

For the institution of domestic slavery we hold ourselves responsible only to God, and it is utterly incompatible with the dignity and the safety of the state to permit any foreign authority to question our right to maintain it. It may nevertheless be appropriate, as a voluntary token of our respect for the opinions of our confederate brethren, to present some views to their consideration on this subject, calculated to disabuse their minds of false opinions and pernicious prejudices.

No human institution, in my opinion, is more manifestly consistent with the will of God than domestic slavery, and no one of His ordinances is written in more legible characters than that which consigns the African race to this condition, as more conducive to their own happiness, than any other of which they are susceptible. Whether we consult the sacred Scriptures or the lights of nature and reason, we shall find these truths as abundantly apparent as if written with a sunbeam in the heavens. Under both the Jewish and Christian dispensations of our religion, domestic slavery existed with the unequivocal sanction of its prophets, its apostles, and finally its great Author. The patriarchs themselves, those chosen instruments of God, were slaveholders. In fact, the divine sanction of this institution is so plainly written that "he who runs may read" it, and those overrighteous pretenders and Pharisees who affect to be scandalized by its existence among us would do well to inquire how much more nearly they walk in the ways of godliness than did Abraham, Isaac, and Jacob.

That the African Negro is destined by Providence to occupy this condition of servile dependence is not less manifest. It is marked on the face, stamped on the skin, and evinced by the intellectual inferiority and natural improvidence of this race. They have all the qualities that fit them for slaves, and not one of those that would fit them to be freemen. They are utterly unqualified, not only for rational freedom but for self-government of any kind. They are, in all respects, physical, moral, and political, inferior to millions of the human race who have for consecutive ages dragged out a wretched existence under a grinding political despotism, and who are doomed to this hopeless condition by the very qualities which unfit them for a better. It is utterly astonishing that any enlightened American, after contemplating all the manifold forms in which even the white race of mankind is doomed to slavery and oppression, should suppose it possible to reclaim the African race from their destiny.

The capacity to enjoy freedom is an attribute not to be communicated by human power. It is an endowment of God, and one of the rarest which it has pleased His inscrutable wisdom to bestow upon the nations of the earth. It is conferred as the reward of merit, and only upon those who are qualified to enjoy it. Until the "Ethiopian can change his skin," it will be in vain to attempt, by any human power, to make freemen of those whom God has doomed to be slaves by all their attributes.

Let not, therefore, the misguided and designing intermeddlers who seek to destroy our peace imagine that they are serving the cause of God by practically arraigning the decrees of His providence. Indeed, it would scarcely excite surprise if, with the impious audacity of those who projected the Tower of Babel, they should attempt to scale the battlements of heaven and remonstrate with the God of wisdom for having put the mark of Cain and the curse of Ham upon the African race instead of the European.

If the benevolent friends of the black race would compare the condition of that portion of them which we hold in servitude with that which still remains in Africa, totally unblessed by the lights of civilization or Christianity and groaning under a savage despotism, as utterly destitute of hope as of happiness, they would be able to form some tolerable estimate of what our blacks have lost by slavery in America and what they have gained by freedom in Africa. Greatly as their condition has been improved by their subjection to an enlightened and Christian people—the only mode under heaven by which it could have been accomplished—they are yet wholly unprepared for anything like a rational system of self-government. Emancipation would be a positive curse, depriving them of a guardianship essential to their happiness, and they may well say in the language of the Spanish proverb, "Save us from our friends and we will take care of our enemies."

If emancipated, where would they live and what would be their condition? The idea of their remaining among us is utterly visionary. Amalgamation is abhorrent to every sentiment of nature; and if they remain as a separate caste, whether endowed with equal privileges or not, they will become our masters, or we must resume the mastery over them. This state of political amalgamation and conflict, which the Abolitionists evidently aim to produce, would be the most horrible condition imaginable and would furnish Dante or Milton with the type for another chapter illustrating the horrors of the infernal regions. The only disposition, therefore, that could be made of our emancipated slaves would be their transportation to Africa, to exterminate the natives or be exterminated by them; contingencies either of which may well serve to illustrate the wisdom, if not the philanthropy, of these superserviceable madmen who in the name of humanity would desolate the fairest region of the earth and destroy the most perfect system of social and political happiness that ever has existed.

It is perfectly evident that the destiny of the Negro race is either the worst possible form of political slavery or else domestic servitude as it exists in the slaveholding states. The advantage of domestic slavery over the most favorable condition of political slavery does not admit of a question. . . .

In all respects, the comforts of our slaves are greatly superior to those of the English operatives, or the Irish and continental peasantry, to say nothing of the millions of paupers crowded together in those loathsome receptacles of starving humanity, the public poorhouses. Besides the hardships of incessant toil, too much almost for human nature to endure, and the sufferings of actual want, driving them almost to despair, these miserable creatures are perpetually annoyed by the most distressing cares for the future condition of themselves and their children.

From this excess of labor, this actual want, and these distressing cares, our slaves are entirely exempted. They habitually labor from two to four hours a day less than the operatives in other countries; and it has been truly remarked, by some writer, that a Negro cannot be made to injure himself by excessive labor. It may be safely affirmed that they usually eat as much wholesome and substantial food in one day as English operatives or Irish peasants eat in two. And as it regards concern for the future, their condition may well be envied even by their masters. There is not upon the face of the earth any class of people, high or low, so perfectly free from care and anxiety. They know that their masters will provide for them, under all circumstances, and that in the extremity of old age, instead of being driven to beggary or to seek public charity in a poorhouse, they will be comfortably accommodated and kindly treated among their relatives and associates. . . .

In a word, our slaves are cheerful, contented, and happy, much beyond the general condition of the human race, except where those foreign intruders and fatal ministers of mischief, the emancipationists, like their arch-prototype in the Garden of Eden and actuated by no less envy, have tempted them to aspire above the condition to which they have been assigned in the order of Providence. . . .

Reason and philosophy can easily explain what experience so clearly testifies. If we look into the elements of which all political communities are composed, it will be found that servitude, in some form, is one of the essential constituents. No community ever has existed without it, and we may confidently assert none ever will. In the very nature of things there must be classes of persons to discharge all the different offices of society, from the highest to the lowest. Some of those offices are regarded as degrading, though they must and will be performed; hence those manifold forms of dependent servitude which produce a sense of superiority in the masters or employers and of inferiority on the part of the servants. Where these offices are performed by members of the political community, a dangerous element is introduced into the body politic; hence the alarming tendency to violate the rights of property by agrarian legislation, which is beginning to be manifest in the older states, where universal suffrage prevails without domestic slavery, a tendency that will increase in the progress of society with the increasing inequality of wealth.

No government is worthy of the name that does not protect the rights of property, and no enlightened people will long submit to such a mockery. Hence it is that, in older countries, different political orders are established to effect this indispensable object; and it will be fortunate for the nonslaveholding states if they are not, in less than a quarter of a century, driven to the adoption of a similar institution, or to take refuge from robbery and anarchy under a military despotism.

But where the menial offices and dependent employments of

society are performed by domestic slaves, a class well defined by their color and entirely separated from the political body, the rights of property are perfectly secure without the establishment of artificial barriers. In a word, the institution of domestic slavery supersedes the necessity of an order of nobility and all the other appendages of a hereditary system of government. If our slaves were emancipated and admitted, bleached or unbleached, to an equal participation in our political privileges, what a commentary should we furnish upon the doctrines of the emancipationists, and what a revolting spectacle of republican equality should we exhibit to the mockery of the world! No rational man would consent to live in such a state of society if he could find a refuge in any other.

Domestic slavery, therefore, instead of being a political evil, is the cornerstone of our republican edifice. No patriot who justly estimates our privileges will tolerate the idea of emancipation, at any period, however remote, or on any conditions of pecuniary advantage, however favorable. I would as soon open a negotiation for selling the liberty of the state at once as for making any stipulations for the ultimate emancipation of our slaves. So deep is my conviction on this subject that, if I were doomed to die immediately after recording these sentiments, I could say in all sincerity and under all the sanctions of Christianity and patriotism, "God forbid that my descendants, in the remotest generations, should live in any other than a community having the institution of domestic slavery as it existed among the patriarchs of the primitive church and in all the free states of antiquity."

If the legislature should concur in these general views of this important element of our political and social system, our confederates should be distinctly informed, in any communications we may have occasion to make to them, that in claiming to be exempted from all foreign interference, we can recognize no distinction between ultimate and immediate emancipation.

It becomes necessary, in order to ascertain the extent of our danger, and the measures of precaution necessary to guard against it, that we examine into the real motives and ultimate purposes of the Abolition societies and their prominent agents. To justify their officious and gratuitous interference in our domestic affairs—the most insulting and insolent outrage which can be offered to a community—they profess to hold themselves responsible for the pretended sin of our domestic slavery, because, forsooth *they* tolerate its existence among *us*. If they are at all responsible for the sin of slavery, whatever that may be, it is not because they tolerate it now but because their ancestors were the agents and authors of its original introduction. These ancestors sold ours the slaves and warranted the title, and it would be a much more becoming labor of filial piety for their descendants to pray for their souls, if they are Protestants, and buy masses to redeem them from purgatory, if they are Catholics, than to assail their warranty and slander their memory by denouncing them as "man-stealers and murderers."

But this voluntary and gratuitous assumption of responsibility, in imitation of a recent and high example in our history, but imperfectly conceals a lurking principle of danger, which deserves to be examined and exposed. What is there to make the people of New York or Massachusetts responsible for slavery in South Carolina any more than the people of Great Britain? To assume that the people of those states are responsible for the continuance of this institution is distinctly to assume that they have a right to abolish it. And whatever enforced disclaimers they may make, their efforts would be worse than unprofitable on any other hypothesis. The folly of attempting to convert the slaveholders to voluntary emancipation, by a course of slander and denunciation, is too great to be ascribed even to fanaticism itself. They do not, indeed, disguise the fact that their principal object is to operate on public opinion in the nonslaveholding states. And to what purpose? They cannot suppose that the opinion of those states, however unanimous, can break the chains of slavery by some moral magic. The whole tenor of their conduct and temper of their discussions clearly demonstrate that their object is to bring the slaveholding states into universal odium, and the public opinion of the nonslaveholding to the point of emancipating our slaves by federal legislation, without the consent of their owners. Disguise it as they may, "to this complexion it must come at last."

It is in this aspect of the subject that it challenges our grave and solemn consideration. It behooves us, then, in my opinion, to demand, respectfully, of each and every one of the nonslaveholding states:

237

1. A formal and solemn disclaimer, by its legislature, of the existence of any rightful power, either in such state or the United States, in Congress assembled, to interfere in any manner whatever with the institution of domestic slavery in South Carolina.

2. The immediate passage of penal laws by such legislature, denouncing against the incendiaries of whom we complain, such punishments as will speedily and forever suppress their machinations against our peace and safety. Though the right to emancipate our slaves by coercive legislation has been very generally disclaimed by popular assemblages in the nonslaveholding states, it is nevertheless important that each of those states should give this disclaimer and the authentic and authoritative form of a legislative declaration, to be preserved as a permanent record for our future security. Our right to demand of those states the enactment of laws for the punishment of those enemies of our peace, who avail themselves of the sanctuary of their sovereign jurisdiction to wage a war of extermination against us, is founded on one of the most salutary and conservative principles of international law. Every state is under the most sacred obligations, not only to abstain from all such interference with the institutions of another as is calculated to disturb its tranquillity or endanger its safety but to prevent its citizens or subjects from such interference, either by inflicting condign punishment itself, or by delivering them up to the justice of the offending community. As between separate and independent nations, the refusal of a state to punish these offensive proceedings against another, by its citizens or subjects makes the state so refusing an accomplice in the outrage and furnishes a just cause of war.

These principles of international law are universally admitted, and none have been more sacredly observed by just and enlightened nations. The obligations of the nonslaveholding states to punish and repress the proceedings of their citizens against our domestic institutions and tranquillity are greatly increased, both by the nature of those proceedings and the fraternal relation which subsists between the states of this confederacy. For no outrage against any community can be greater than to stir up the elements of servile insurrection, and no obligation to repress it can be more sacred than that which adds to the sanctions of international law the solemn guarantee of a constitutional compact, which is at once the bond

and the condition of our Union. The liberal, enlightened, and magnanimous conduct of the people in many portions of the nonslaveholding states forbids us to anticipate a refusal on the part of those
states to fulfill these high obligations of national faith and duty.

And we have the less reason to look forward to this inauspicious
result from considering the necessary consequences which would
follow to the people of those states and of the whole commercial
world from the general emancipation of our slaves. These consequences may be presented, as an irresistible appeal, to every rational philanthropist in Europe or America. It is clearly demonstrable
that the production of cotton depends, not so much on soil and
climate as on the existence of domestic slavery. In the relaxing
latitudes where it grows, not one-half the quantity would be produced but for the existence of this institution; and every practical
planter will concur in the opinion that if all the slaves in these states
were now emancipated, the American crop would be reduced the
very next year from 1,200,000 to 600,000 bales.

No great skill in political economy will be required to estimate
how enormously the price of cotton would be increased by this
change, and no one who will consider how largely this staple con-
tributes to the wealth of manufacturing nations, and to the necessaries and comforts of the poorer classes all over the world, can fail
to perceive the disastrous effects of so great a reduction in the
quantity and so great an enhancement in the price of it. In Great
Britain, France, and the United States, the catastrophe would be
overwhelming, and it is not extravagant to say that for little more
than 2 million Negro slaves, cut loose from their tranquil moorings
and set adrift upon the untried ocean of at least a doubtful experiment, 10 million poor white people would be reduced to destitution,
pauperism, and starvation.

An anxious desire to avoid the last sad alternative of an injured
community prompts this final appeal to the interests and enlightened philanthropy of our confederate states. And we cannot permit
ourselves to believe that our just demands, thus supported by every
consideration of humanity and duty, will be rejected by states who
are united to us by so many social and political ties, and who have so
deep an interest in the preservation of that Union.

JOSEPH H. INGRAHAM

Planters and Slaves

The writings of Joseph Ingraham are rarely consulted today, except by historians. However, in the late 1830s and 1840s, his novels (many published in newspapers) were enormously popular. "A young, dark man, with soft voice," Longfellow noted in 1846. "He says he has written eighty novels, and of these twenty during the last year." While a young man, Ingraham, a New Englander, toured southwestern Mississippi, and his first book, and probably his best, The South-West, *records what he observed there. It was published anonymously (signed "By a Yankee") in 1835. Sections from it appear below. [Source:* The South-West, *New York, 1835, Vol. II, pp. 89-93, 247-255.]*

Among Northerners, Southern planters are reputed wealthy. This idea is not far from correct—as a class they are so, perhaps more so than any other body of men in America. Like our Yankee farmers, they are tillers of the soil. "But why" you may ask, "do they who are engaged in the same pursuits as the New England farmer so infinitely surpass him in the reward of his labors?" The Northern farmer cannot at the most make more than 3 percent on his farm. He labors himself, or pays for labor. He *must* do the first or he cannot live. If he does the latter, he can make nothing. If by hard labor and frugal economy the common, independent Yankee farmer, such as the traveler meets with anywhere in New England, lays up annually from $400 to $700, he is a thriving man and "getting rich." His daughters are attractive, and his sons will have something "handsome" to begin the world with. But the Southern farmer can make from 15 to 30 percent by his farm. He works on his plantation a certain number of slaves, say thirty, which are to him what the sinewy arms of the Yankee farmer are to himself.

Each slave ought to average from seven to eight bales of cotton during the season, especially on the new lands. An acre will generally average from one to two bales. Each bale averages 400 pounds, at from twelve to fifteen cents a pound. This may not be an exact estimate, but it is not far from the true one.

Deducting $2,500 for the expenses of the plantation, there will

240

remain the net income of $11,000.

Now suppose this plantation and slaves to have been purchased on a credit, paying at the rate of $600 apiece for his Negroes, the planter would be able to pay for nearly two-thirds of them the first year. The second year, he would pay for the remainder, and purchase ten or twelve more; and the third year, if he had obtained his plantation on a credit of that length of time, he would pay for that also, and commence his fourth year with a valuable plantation, and thirty-five or forty slaves, all his own property, with an increased income for the ensuing year of some thousands of dollars. Henceforward, if prudent, he will rank as an opulent planter. Success is not, however, always in proportion to the outlay or expectations of the aspirant for wealth. It is modified and varied by the wear and tear, sickness and death, fluctuations of the market, and many other ills to which all who adventure in the great lottery of life are heirs.

In the way above alluded to, numerous plantations in this state have been commenced, and thus the wealth of a great number of the opulent planters of this region has originated. Incomes of $20,000 are common here. Several individuals possess incomes of from $40,000 to $50,000 and live in a style commensurate with their wealth. The amount is generally expressed by the number of their Negroes and the number of "bales" they make at a crop. To know the number of either is to know accurately their incomes. And as this is easily ascertained, it is not difficult to form a prompt estimate of individual wealth.

To sell cotton in order to buy Negroes—to make more cotton to buy more Negroes, ad infinitum, is the aim and direct tendency of all the operations of the thoroughgoing cotton planter; his whole soul is wrapped up in the pursuit. It is, apparently, the principle by which he "lives, moves, and has his being." There are some who "work" 300 and 400 Negroes, though the average number is from 30 to 100. "This is all very fine," you say, "but the slaves!—there's the rub." True; but without slaves there could be no planters, for whites will not and cannot work cotton plantations beneath a broiling Southern sun. Without planters there could be no cotton; without cotton no wealth. Without them, Mississippi would be a wilderness and revert to the aboriginal possessors. Annihilate them tomorrow and this

241

state and every Southern state might be bought for a song. . . .

Many of the planters are Northerners. When they have conquered their prejudices, they become thorough, driving planters, generally giving themselves up to the pursuit more devotedly than the regular-bred planter. Their treatment of their slaves is also far more rigid. Northerners are entirely unaccustomed to their habits, which are perfectly understood and appreciated by Southerners, who have been familiar with Africans from childhood; whom they have had for their nurses, playfellows, and "bearers," and between whom and themselves a reciprocal and very natural attachment exists, which, on the gentleman's part, involuntarily extends to the whole dingy race, exhibited in a kindly feeling and condescending familiarity, for which he receives gratitude in return. On the part of the slave, this attachment is manifested by an affection and faithfulness which only cease with life.

Of this state of feeling, which a Southern life and education can only give, the Northerner knows nothing. Inexperience leads him to hold the reins of government over his novel subjects with an unsparing severity, which the native ruler of these domestic colonies finds wholly unnecessary. The slave always prefers a Southern master, because he knows that he will be understood by him. His kindly feelings toward, and sympathies with, slaves, as such, are as honorable to his heart as gratifying to the subjects of them. He treats with suitable allowance those peculiarities of their race which the unpractised Northerner will construe into idleness, obstinacy, laziness, revenge, or hatred. There is another cause for their difference of treatment to their slaves. The Southerner, habituated to their presence, never fears them, and laughs at the idea. It is the reverse with the Northerner: he fears them and hopes to intimidate them by severity. . . .

There are properly three distinct classes of slaves in the South. The first, and most intelligent, class is composed of the domestic slaves, or "servants," as they are properly termed, of the planters. Some of these both read and write, and possess a great degree of intelligence; and as the Negro, of all the varieties of the human species, is the most imitative, they soon learn the language and readily adopt the manners of the family to which they are attached. It is true they frequently burlesque the latter and select the high-sound-

242

ing words of the former for practice; for the Negro has an ear for euphony, which they usually misapply or mispronounce.

"Ben, how did you like the sermon today?" I once inquired of one, who, for pompous language and high-sounding epithets, was the Johnson of Negroes. "Mighty obligated wid it, master, de 'clusive 'flections werry distructive to de ignorum."

In the more fashionable families, Negroes feel it their duty—to show their aristocratic breeding—to ape manners and to use language to which the common herd cannot aspire. An aristocratic Negro, full of his master's wealth and importance which he feels to be reflected upon himself, is the most aristocratic personage in existence. He supports his own dignity and that of his own master, or "family," as he phrases it, which he deems inseparable, by a course of conduct befitting colored gentlemen. Always about the persons of their masters or mistresses, the domestic slaves obtain a better knowledge of the modes of civilized life than they could do in the field, where Negroes can rise but little above their original African state.

So identified are they with the families in which they have been "raised," and so accurate, but rough, are the copies which they individually present of their masters that were all the domestic slaves of several planters' families transferred to Liberia or Haiti, they would there constitute a by no means inferior state of African society, whose model would be found in Mississippi. Each family would be a faithful copy of that with which it was once connected; and should their former owners visit them in their new home, they would smile at its resemblance to the original. It is from this class that the friends of wisely regulated emancipation are to seek material for carrying their plans into effect.

The second class is composed of town slaves, which not only includes domestic slaves, in the families of the citizens, but also all Negro mechanics, draymen, hostlers, laborers, hucksters, and washwomen, and the heterogeneous multitude of every other occupation who fill the streets of a busy city—for slaves are trained to every kind of manual labor. The blacksmith, cabinet maker, carpenter, builder, wheelwright—all have one or more slaves laboring at their trades. The Negro is a third arm to every workingman who can possibly save money enough to purchase one. He is emphatically the "right-hand man" of every man. Even free Negroes cannot do without them; some of them own several, to whom they are the severest masters.

"To whom do you belong?" I once inquired of a Negro whom I had employed. "There's my master," he replied, pointing to a steady old Negro who had purchased himself, then his wife, and subsequently his three children, by his own manual exertions and persevering industry. He was now the owner of a comfortable house, a piece of land, and two or three slaves, to whom he could add one every three years. It is worthy of remark, and serves to illustrate one of the many singularities characteristic of the race, that the free Negro who "buys his wife's freedom," as they term it, from her master by paying him her full value ever afterward considers her in the light of property.

"Thomas, you are a free man," I remarked to one who had purchased himself and wife from his master by the profits of a poultry yard and vegetable garden, industriously attended to for many years in his leisure hours and on Sundays. "You are a free man; I suppose you will soon have Negroes of your own."

"Hi! Hab one now, master." "Who, Tom?" "Ol' Sarah, master." "Old Sarah! She is your wife." "She my nigger too; I pay master five hun'red dollar for her."

Many of the Negroes who swarm in the cities are what are called "hired servants." They belong to planters or others, who, finding them qualified for some occupation in which they cannot afford to employ them, hire them to citizens as mechanics, cooks, waiters, nurses, etc., and receive the monthly wages for their services. Some steady slaves are permitted to "hire their own time"; that is, to go into town and earn what they can as porters, laborers, gardeners, or in other ways, and pay a stipulated sum weekly to their owners, which will be regulated according to the supposed value of the slave's labor. Masters, however, who are sufficiently indulgent to allow them to "hire their time" are seldom rigorous in rating their labor very high. But whether the slave earns less or more than the specified sum, he must always pay that and neither more nor less than that to his master at the close of each week as the condition of this privilege.

Few fail in making up the sum and generally they earn more, if industrious, which is expended in little luxuries, or laid by in an old rag among the rafters of their houses, till a sufficient sum is thus accumulated to purchase their freedom. This they are seldom refused, and if a small amount is wanting to reach their value, the master makes it up out of his own purse, or rather, takes no notice of the deficiency. I have never known a planter refuse to aid, by peculiar indulgences, any of his steady and well-disposed slaves who desired to purchase their freedom. On the contrary, they often endeavor to excite emulation in them to the attainment of this end. This custom of allowing slaves to "hire their time," ensuring the master a certain sum weekly and the slave a small surplus, is mutually advantageous to both.

The majority of town servants are those who are hired to families by planters, or by those living in town who own more than they have employment for, or who can make more by hiring them out than by keeping them at home. Some families, who possess not an acre of land but own many slaves, hire them out to different individuals; the wages constituting their only income, which is often very large. There are indeed few families, however wealthy, whose incomes are not increased by the wages of hired slaves, and there are many poor people, who own one or two slaves, whose hire enables them to live comfortably. From three to five dollars a week is the hire of a female, and seventy-five cents or a dollar a day for a male. Thus, contrary to the opinion at the North, families may have good servants and yet not own one, if they are unable to buy, or are conscientious upon that ground, though there is not a shade of difference between hiring a slave, where prejudices are concerned, and owning one. Those who think otherwise, and thus compound with conscience, are only making a distinction without a difference.

Northern people, when they come to this country, who dislike either to hire or purchase, often bring free colored or white servants (helps) with them. The first soon marry with the free blacks, or become too lofty in their conceptions of things, in contrasting the situation of their fellows around them with their own, to be retained. The latter, if they are young and pretty, or even old and ugly, assume the fine lady at once, disdaining to be servants among slaves, and Hymen, in the person of some spruce overseer, soon fulfills their expectations. I have seen but one white servant, or

245

domestic, of either sex in this country, and this was the body servant of an Englishman who remained a few days in Natchez, during which time John sturdily refused to perform a single duty of his station. . . .

The third and lowest class consists of those slaves who are termed "field hands."[1] Many of them rank but little higher than the brutes that perish in the scale of intellect, and they are, in general, as a class, the last and lowest link in the chain of the human species. Secluded in the solitude of an extensive plantation, which is their world, beyond whose horizon they know nothing; their walks limited by the "quarters" and the field; their knowledge and information derived from the rude gossip of their fellows, straggling runaways, or house servants; and without seeing a white person except their master or overseer as they ride over the estate, with whom they seldom hold any conversation, they present the singular feature of African savages, disciplined to subordination and placed in the heart of a civilized community.

Mere change of place will not change the savage. Moral and intellectual culture alone will elevate him to an equality with his civilized brethren. The African transplanted from the arid soil of Ebo, Sene-Gambia, or Guinea, to the green fields of America, without mental culture, will remain still the wild African, though he may wield his ox-whip, whistle after his plough, and lift his hat when addressed, like his more civilized fellows. His children, born on the plantation to which he is attached, and suffered to grow up as ignorant as himself, will not be one degree higher in the scale of civilization than they would have been had they been born in Africa. The next generation will be no higher advanced; and though they may have thrown away the idols of their country and been taught some vague notions of God and the Christian religion, they are, in almost every sense of the word, Africans, as rude and barbarous but not so artless as their untamed brethren beyond the Atlantic.

This has been, till within a few years, the general condition of "field hands" in this country, though there have been exceptions on

1. "Field hands," "Force," "Hands," "People," and "Niggers" are terms applied to the purchased laborers of a plantation; but "Slaves"—never. "Boys" is the general term for the men, and "women," for females. It is common to address a Negro forty years of age as "boy." If much older, he is called "daddy" or "uncle"; but "mister" or "man"—never. The females, in old age, become "aunty," "granny," or "old lady."

some plantations, highly honorable to their proprietors. Within a few years, gentlemen of intelligence, humanity, and wealth, themselves the owners of great numbers of slaves, have exerted themselves and used their influence in mitigating the condition of this class. They commenced a reformation of the old system, whose chief foundation was unyielding rigor, first upon their own plantations. The influence of their example was manifest by the general change which gradually took place on other estates. This reformation is still in progress, and the condition of the plantation slave is now meliorated, so far as policy will admit, while they remain in their present relation.

JOHN GREENLEAF WHITTIER:
Man's Property in Man

The poetry of John Greenleaf Whittier was first published by William Lloyd Garrison, founder of the militant Abolitionist movement that got under way in the 1830s. Partly because of his association with Garrison, Whittier ardently espoused the Abolitionist cause. The cruelty of slavery, and the iniquity of a system that permitted one man to buy and sell another, became the ever-present subject of his poetry and prose. In May 1833, Whittier wrote and had printed at his own expense the pamphlet Justice and Expediency, *part of which is reproduced below. Five thousand copies of the pamphlet were later reissued by a wealthy merchant and humanitarian, Arthur Tappan. [*Source:* The Conflict with Slavery, etc., etc., London, 1889, pp. 9-57.]*

It may be inquired of me why I seek to agitate the subject of slavery in New England, where we all acknowledge it to be an evil. Because such an acknowledgment is not enough on our part. It is doing no more than the slave master and the slave trader. "We have found," says James Monroe in his speech on the subject before the Virginia Convention, "that this evil has preyed upon the very vitals of the Union; and has been prejudicial to all the states in which it has existed." All the states in their several constitutions and declarations

247

of rights have made a similar statement. And what has been the consequence of this general belief in the evil of human servitude? Has it sapped the foundations of the infamous system? No. Has it decreased the number of its victims? Quite the contrary. Unaccompanied by philanthropic action, it has been, in a moral point of view, worthless—a thing without vitality—sightless, soulless, dead.

But it may be said that the miserable victims of the system have our sympathies. Sympathy! the sympathy of the priest and the Levite, looking on and acknowledging, but holding itself aloof from mortal suffering. Can such hollow sympathy reach the broken of heart, and does the blessing of those who are ready to perish answer it? . . .

No! Let the truth on this subject, undisguised, naked, terrible as it is, stand out before us. Let us no longer seek to cover it; let us no longer strive to forget it; let us no more dare to palliate it. It is better to meet it here with repentance than at the bar of God. . . .

But it may be urged that New England has no participation in slavery and is not responsible for its wickedness.

Why are we thus willing to believe a lie? New England not responsible! Bound by the United States Constitution to protect the slaveholder in his sins, and yet not responsible! Joining hands with crime, covenanting with oppression, leaguing with pollution, and yet not responsible! Palliating the evil, hiding the evil, voting for the evil, do we not participate in it? Members of one confederacy, children of one family, the curse and the shame, the sin against our brother, and the sin against our God—all the iniquity of slavery which is revealed to man and all which crieth in the ear, or is manifested to the eye of Jehovah, will assuredly be visited upon all our people. . . .

Slavery is protected by the constitutional compact, by the standing army, by the militia of the free states. Let us not forget that should the slaves, goaded by wrongs unendurable, rise in desperation and pour the torrent of their brutal revenge over the beautiful Carolinas or the consecrated soil of Virginia, New England would be called upon to arrest the progress of rebellion, to tread out with the armed heel of her soldiery that spirit of freedom which knows no distinction of caste or color; which has been kindled in the heart of the black as well as in that of the white.

248

And what is this system which we are thus protecting and upholding? A system which holds 2 million of God's creatures in bondage; which leaves 1 million females without any protection, save their own feeble strength, and which makes even the exercise of that strength in resistance to outrage punishable with death; which considers rational, immortal beings as articles of traffic, vendible commodities, merchantable property; which recognizes no social obligations, no natural relations; which tears without scruple the infant from the mother, the wife from the husband, the parent from the child. In the strong but just language of another: "It is the full measure of pure, unmixed, unsophisticated wickedness; and scorning all competition or comparison, it stands without a rival in the secure, undisputed possession of its detestable preeminence."

So fearful an evil should have its remedies. The following are among the many which have been from time to time proposed:

1. Placing the slaves in the condition of the serfs of Poland and Russia, fixed to the soil, and without the right on the part of the master to sell or remove them. This was intended as a preliminary to complete emancipation at some remote period, but it is impossible to perceive either its justice or expediency.

2. Gradual abolition—an indefinite term, but which is understood to imply the draining away, drop by drop, of the great ocean of wrong; plucking off at long intervals some straggling branches of the moral Upas; holding out to unborn generations the shadow of a hope which the present may never feel; gradually ceasing to do evil; gradually refraining from robbery, lust, and murder: in brief, obeying a shortsighted and criminal policy rather than the commands of God.

3. Abstinence on the part of the people of the free states from the use of the known products of slave labor in order to render that labor profitless. Beyond a doubt, the example of conscientious individuals may have a salutary effect upon the minds of some of the slaveholders; but so long as our Confederacy exists, a commercial intercourse with slave states and a consumption of their products cannot be avoided.

4. Colonization.

The exclusive object of the American Colonization Society, according to the 2nd Article of its constitution, is to colonize the free people of color residing among us in Africa or such other place as Congress may direct. Steadily adhering to this object, it has nothing to do with slavery; and I allude to it as a remedy only because some of its friends have in view an eventual abolition or an amelioration of the evil.

Let facts speak. The Colonization Society was organized in 1817. It has 218 auxiliary societies. The legislatures of fourteen states have recommended it. Contributions have poured into its treasury from every quarter of the United States. Addresses in its favor have been heard from all our pulpits. It has been in operation sixteen years. During this period nearly 1 million human beings have died in slavery; and the number of slaves has increased more than half a million, or in round numbers, 550,000.

The Colonization Society has been busily engaged all this while in conveying the slaves to Africa; in other words, abolishing slavery. In this very charitable occupation, it has carried away of manumitted slaves, 613: balance against the society, 549,387!

But enough of its abolition tendency. What has it done for amelioration? Witness the newly enacted laws of some of the slave states, laws bloody as the Code of Draco, violating the laws of God and the unalienable rights of His children. But why talk of amelioration? Amelioration of what? Of sin, of crime unutterable, of a system of wrong and outrage horrible in the eye of God! Why seek to mark the line of a selfish policy, a carnal expediency between the criminality of hell and that repentance and its fruits enjoined of heaven?

For the principles and views of the society we must look to its own statements and admissions; to its annual reports; to those of its auxiliaries; to the speeches and writings of its advocates; and to its organ, the *African Repository*.

1. It excuses slavery and apologizes for slaveholders. . . .
2. It pledges itself not to oppose the system of slavery. . . .
3. It regards God's rational creatures as property. . . .
4. It boasts that its measures are calculated to perpetuate the detested system of slavery, to remove the fears of the slaveholder, and increase the value of his stock of human beings. . . .
5. It denies the power of Christian love to overcome an unholy prejudice against a portion of our fellow creatures. . . .

250

6. It opposes strenuously the education of the blacks in this country as useless as well as dangerous. . . .

E. B. Caldwell, the first secretary of the American Colonization Society, in his speech at its formation, recommended them to be kept "in the lowest state of ignorance and degradation, for (says he) the nearer you bring them to the condition of brutes, the better chance do you give them of possessing their apathy.". . .

I seek to do the Colonization Society no injustice, but I wish the public generally to understand its character. The tendency of the society to abolish the slave trade by means of its African colony has been strenuously urged by its friends. But the fallacy of this is now admitted by all. . . .

I come now to the only practicable, the only just scheme of emancipation—immediate abolition of slavery; an immediate acknowledgment of the great truth, that man cannot hold property in man; an immediate surrender of baneful prejudice to Christian love; an immediate practical obedience to the command of Jesus Christ: "Whatsoever ye would that men should do unto you, do ye even so to them."

A correct understanding of what is meant by immediate abolition must convince every candid mind that it is neither visionary nor dangerous; that it involves no disastrous consequences of bloodshed and desolation; but, on the contrary, that it is a safe, practicable, efficient remedy for the evils of the slave system.

The term "immediate" is used in contrast with that of "gradual." Earnestly as I wish it, I do not expect, no one expects, that the tremendous system of oppression can be instantaneously overthrown. The terrible and unrebukable indignation of a free people has not yet been sufficiently concentrated against it. The friends of abolition have not forgotten the peculiar organization of our Confederacy, the delicate division of power between the states and the general government. They see the many obstacles in their pathway; but they know that public opinion can overcome them all. They ask no aid of physical coercion. They seek to obtain their object not with the weapons of violence and blood but with those of reason and truth, prayer to God, and entreaty to man.

They seek to impress indelibly upon every human heart the true doctrines of the rights of man; to establish now and forever this

251

great and fundamental truth of human liberty – that man cannot hold property in his brother – for they believe that the general admission of this truth will utterly destroy the system of slavery, based as that system is upon a denial or disregard of it. . . .

If our fathers intended that slavery should be perpetual, that our practice should forever give the lie to our professions, why is the great constitutional compact so guardedly silent on the subject of human servitude? If state necessity demanded this perpetual violation of the laws of God and the rights of man, this continual solecism in a government of freedom, why is it not met as a necessity, incurable and inevitable, and formally and distinctly recognized as a settled part of our social system? State necessity, that imperial tyrant, seeks no disguise. . . .

What, then, is our duty? To give effect to the spirit of our Constitution; to plant ourselves upon the great declaration and declare in the face of all the world that political, religious, and legal hypocrisy shall no longer cover as with loathsome leprosy the features of American freedom; to loose at once the bands of wickedness; to undo the heavy burdens and let the oppressed go free.

We have indeed been authoritatively told in Congress and elsewhere that our brethren of the South and West will brook no further agitation of the subject of slavery. What, then! Shall we heed the unrighteous prohibition? No; by our duty as Christians, as politicians, by our duty to ourselves, to our neighbor, and to God, we are called upon to agitate this subject; to give slavery no resting place under the hallowed aegis of a government of freedom; to tear it root and branch, with all its fruits of abomination, at least from the soil of the national domain. The slaveholder may mock us; the representatives of property, merchandise, vendible commodities, may threaten us; still our duty is imperative; the spirit of the Constitution should be maintained within the exclusive jurisdiction of the government. If we cannot "provide for the general welfare," if we cannot "guarantee to each of the states a republican form of government," let us at least no longer legislate for a free nation within view of the falling whip, and within hearing of the execrations of the taskmaster and the prayer of his slave! . . .

The slave will become conscious sooner or later of his brute strength, his physical superiority, and will exert it. His torch will be

252

at the threshold and his knife at the throat of the planter. Horrible and indiscriminate will be his vengeance. Where, then, will be the pride, the beauty, and the chivalry of the South? . . .

Let the cause of insurrection be removed, then, as speedily as possible. Cease to oppress. "Let him that stole steal no more." Let the laborer have his hire. Bind him no longer by the cords of slavery, but with those of kindness and brotherly love. Watch over him for his good. Pray for him; instruct him; pour light into the darkness of his mind.

Let this be done and the horrible fears which now haunt the slumbers of the slaveholder will depart. Conscience will take down its racks and gibbets, and his soul will be at peace. His lands will no longer disappoint his hopes. Free labor will renovate them. . . .

The conflicting interests of free and slave labor furnish the only ground for fear in relation to the permanency of the Union. The line of separation between them is day by day growing broader and deeper; geographically and politically united, we are already, in a moral point of view, a divided people. But a few months ago we were on the very verge of civil war, a war of brothers, a war between the North and the South, between the slaveholder and the free laborer. The danger has been delayed for a time; this bolt has fallen without mortal injury to the Union, but the cloud from whence it came still hangs above us, reddening with the elements of destruction.

LYDIA M. CHILD
Proposals for Equal Treatment of Negroes

The militant Abolitionists in the 1830s did not only speak out against the institution of slavery in the South, they also condemned all forms of anti-Negro prejudice, which existed then, as it does now, in both North and South. But their vision of social and political equality for all contravened the prevailing sentiment everywhere, and everywhere they were unpopular. Even in the North, they were attacked and condemned and often physically assaulted. Lydia M. Child was already a prominent

253

novelist when she turned to writing on behalf of Negro equality, and
her early reform literature, a selection of which follows, was widely read.
The selection below is from a book of hers that was published in July
1833. [Source: An Appeal in Favor of That Class of Americans Called
Africans, Boston, 1833, Ch. 8.]

While we bestow our earnest disapproval on the system of slavery, let us not flatter ourselves that we are in reality any better than our brethren of the South. Thanks to our soil and climate and the early exertions of the Quakers, the *form* of slavery does not exist among us; but the very *spirit* of the hateful and mischievous thing is here in all its strength. The manner in which we use what power we have gives us ample reason to be grateful that the nature of our institutions does not entrust us with more. Our prejudices against colored people is even more inveterate than it is at the South. The planter is often attached to his Negroes, and lavishes caresses and kind words upon them, as he would on a favorite hound; but our coldhearted, ignoble prejudice admits of no exception—no intermission.

The Southerners have long continued habit, apparent interest and dreaded danger to palliate the wrong they do; but we stand without excuse. They tell us that Northern ships and Northern capital have been engaged in this wicked business; and the reproach is true. Several fortunes in this city have been made by the sale of Negro blood. If these criminal transactions are still carried on, they are done in silence and secrecy, because public opinion has made them disgraceful. But if the free states wished to cherish the system of slavery forever, they could not take a more direct course than they now do. Those who are kind and liberal on all other subjects unite with the selfish and the proud in their unrelenting efforts to keep the colored population in the lowest state of degradation; and the influence they unconsciously exert over children early infuses into their innocent minds the same strong feelings of contempt.

The intelligent and well-informed have the least share of this prejudice; and when their minds can be brought to reflect upon it, I have generally observed that they soon cease to have any at all. But such a general apathy prevails, and the subject is so seldom brought into view, that few are really aware how oppressively the influence of society is made to bear upon this injured class of the community. . . .

An unjust law exists in this commonwealth by which marriages between persons of different color is pronounced illegal. I am perfectly aware of the gross ridicule to which I may subject myself by alluding to this particular; but I have lived too long, and observed too much, to be disturbed by the world's mockery. In the first place, the government ought not to be invested with power to control the affections any more than the consciences of citizens. A man has at least as good a right to choose his wife as he has to choose his religion. His taste may not suit his neighbors; but so long as his deportment is correct, they have no right to interfere with his concerns. In the second place, this law is a *useless* disgrace to Massachusetts. Under existing circumstances, none but those whose condition in life is too low to be much affected by public opinion will form such alliances; and they, when they choose to do so, *will* make such marriages, in spite of the law.

I know two or three instances where women of the laboring class have been united to reputable, industrious colored men. These husbands regularly bring home their wages and are kind to their families. If by some of the odd chances, which not unfrequently occur in the world, their wives should become heirs to any property, the children may be wronged out of it, because the law pronounces them illegitimate. And while this injustice exists with regard to *honest*, industrious individuals, who are merely guilty of differing from us in a matter of taste, neither the legislation nor customs of slaveholding states exert their influence against *immoral* connections.

In one portion of our country this fact is shown in a very peculiar and striking manner. There is a numerous class at New Orleans, called quateroons, or quadroons, because their colored blood has for several successive generations been intermingled with the white. The women are much distinguished for personal beauty and gracefulness of motion; and their parents frequently send them to France for the advantages of an elegant education. White gentlemen of the first rank are desirous of being invited to their parties, and often become seriously in love with these fascinating but unfortunate

255

beings. Prejudice forbids matrimony, but universal custom sanctions temporary connections, to which a certain degree of respectability is allowed on account of the peculiar situation of the parties. These attachments often continue for years—sometimes for life—and instances are not unfrequent of exemplary constancy and great propriety of deportment. . . .

There is another Massachusetts law, which an enlightened community would not probably suffer to be carried into execution under any circumstances; but it still remains to disgrace the statutes of this commonwealth. It is as follows:

> No African or Negro, other than a subject of the emperor of Morocco, or a citizen of the United States (proved so by a certificate of the secretary of the state of which he is a citizen), shall tarry within this commonwealth longer than two months; and on complaint a justice shall order him to depart in ten days; and if he do not then, the justice may commit such African or Negro to the House of Correction, there to be kept at hard labor; and at the next term of the Court of C. P., he shall be tried, and if convicted of remaining as aforesaid, shall be whipped not exceeding ten lashes; and if he or she shall not *then* depart such process shall be repeated and punishment inflicted *toties quoties.*

An honorable Haitian or Brazilian, who visited this country for business or information, might come under this law, unless public opinion rendered it a mere dead letter.

There is among the colored people an increasing desire for information and a laudable ambition to be respectable in manners and appearance. Are we not foolish as well as sinful in trying to repress a tendency so salutary to themselves and so beneficial to the community? Several individuals of this class are very desirous to have persons of their own color qualified to teach something more than mere reading and writing. But in the public schools, colored children are subject to many discouragements and difficulties; and into the private schools they cannot gain admission. A very sensible and well-informed colored woman in a neighboring town, whose family have been brought up in a manner that excited universal remark and approbation, has been extremely desirous to obtain for her eldest daughter the advantages of a private school; but she has been resolutely repulsed on account of her complexion. The girl is a very light mulatto, with great modesty and propriety of manners; perhaps no young person in the commonwealth was less likely to have a bad influence on her associates. The clergyman respected the family, and he remonstrated with the instructor; but while the latter admitted the injustice of the thing, he excused himself by saying such a step would occasion the loss of all his white scholars.

In a town adjoining Boston, a well-behaved colored boy was kept out of the public school more than a year, by vote of the trustees. His mother, having some information herself, knew the importance of knowledge, and was anxious to obtain it for her family. She wrote repeatedly and urgently; and the schoolmaster himself told me that the correctness of her spelling and the neatness of her handwriting formed a curious contrast with the notes he received from many white parents. At last, this spirited woman appeared before the committee and reminded them that her husband, having for many years paid taxes as a citizen, had a right to the privileges of a citizen; and if her claim were refused, or longer postponed, she declared her determination to seek justice from a higher source. The trustees were, of course, obliged to yield to the equality of the laws, with the best grace they could. The boy was admitted, and made good progress in his studies. Had his mother been too ignorant to know her rights, or too abject to demand them, the lad would have had a fair chance to get a living out of the state as the occupant of a workhouse or penitentiary.

The attempt to establish a school for African girls at Canterbury, Connecticut, has made too much noise to need a detailed account in this volume. I do not know the lady who first formed the project, but I am told that she is a benevolent and religious woman. It certainly is difficult to imagine any other motives than good ones for an undertaking so arduous and unpopular. Yet had the pope himself attempted to establish his supremacy over that commonwealth, he could hardly have been repelled with more determined and angry resistance. Town meetings were held, the records of which are not highly creditable to the parties concerned. Petitions were sent to the legislature, beseeching that no African school might be allowed to admit individuals not residing in the town where said school was

257

established; and strange to relate, this law, which makes it impossible to collect a sufficient number of pupils, was sanctioned by the state. A colored girl who availed herself of this opportunity to gain instruction was warned out of town, and fined for not complying; and the instructress was imprisoned for persevering in her benevolent plan.

It is said, in excuse, that Canterbury will be inundated with vicious characters who will corrupt the morals of the young men; that such a school will break down the distinctions between black and white; and that marriages between people of different colors will be the probable result. Yet they seem to assume the ground that colored people *must* always be an inferior and degraded class — that the prejudice against them *must* be eternal, being deeply founded in the laws of God and nature. Finally, they endeavored to represent the school as one of the *incendiary* proceedings of the Anti-slavery Society; and they appeal to the Colonization Society, as an aggrieved child is wont to appeal to its parent.

The objection with regard to the introduction of vicious characters into a village certainly has some force; but are such persons likely to leave cities for a quiet country town in search of moral and intellectual improvement? Is it not obvious that the *best* portion of the colored class are the very ones to prize such an opportunity for instruction? Grant that a large proportion of these unfortunate people *are* vicious, is it not our duty, and of course our wisest policy, to try to make them otherwise? And what will so effectually elevate their character and condition as knowledge? I beseech you, my countrymen, think of these things wisely and in season.

As for intermarriages, if there be such a repugnance between the two races, founded in the laws of *nature*, methinks there is small reason to dread their frequency.

The breaking down of distinctions in society, by means of extended information, is an objection which appropriately belongs to the emperor of Austria, or the sultan of Egypt.

I do not know how the affair at Canterbury is *generally* considered; but I have heard individuals of all parties and all opinions speak of it — and never without merriment or indignation. Fifty years hence, the *black* laws of Connecticut will be a greater source of amusement to the antiquarian than her famous *blue* laws.

258

A similar though less violent opposition arose in consequence of the attempt to establish a college for colored people at New Haven. A young colored man who tried to obtain education at the Wesleyan College in Middleton was obliged to relinquish the attempt on account of the persecution of his fellow students. Some collegians from the South objected to a colored associate in their recitations; and those from New England promptly and zealously joined in the hue and cry. A small but firm party were in favor of giving the colored man a chance to pursue his studies without insult or interruption; and I am told that this manly and disinterested band were all Southerners. As for those individuals who exerted their influence to exclude an unoffending fellow citizen from privileges which ought to be equally open to all, it is to be hoped that age will make them wiser; and that they will learn, before they die, to be ashamed of a step attended with more important results than usually belong to youthful follies. . . .

Let us seriously consider what injury a Negro college could possibly do us. It is certainly a fair presumption that the scholars would be from the better portion of the colored population; and it is an equally fair presumption that knowledge would improve their characters. There are already many hundreds of colored people in the city of Boston. In the street they generally appear neat and respectable; and in our houses they do not "come between the wind and our nobility." Would the addition of one or two hundred more even be perceived? As for giving offense to the Southerners by allowing such establishments — they have no right to interfere with our internal concerns any more than we have with theirs. Why should they not give up slavery to please us, by the same rule that we must refrain from educating the Negroes to please them? If they are at liberty to do wrong, we certainly ought to be at liberty to do right. They may talk and publish as much about us as they please; and we ask for no other influence over them.

It is a fact not generally known that the brave Kosciuszko left a fund for the establishment of a Negro college in the United States. Little did he think he had been fighting for a people who would not grant one rood of their vast territory for the benevolent purpose!

According to present appearances, a college for colored persons will be established in Canada; and thus, by means of our foolish and wicked pride, the credit of this philanthropic enterprise will be transferred to our mother country.

In Boston there is an infant school, three primary schools, and a grammar school. The two last are, I believe, supported by the public; and this fact is highly creditable. A building for the colored grammar school is not supplied by the city, though such provision is always made for similar institutions for white boys. The apartment is close and uncomfortable, and many pupils stay away who would gladly attend under more convenient circumstances. There ought likewise to be a colored teacher instead of a white one. Under the dominion of existing prejudices, it is difficult to find a white man, well qualified to teach such a school, who feels the interest he ought to feel in these Pariahs of our republic. The parents would repose more confidence in a colored instructor; and he, both from sympathy and pride, would be better fitted for his task.

It is peculiarly incumbent on the city authorities to supply a commodious building for the colored grammar school, because public prejudice excludes these oppressed people from all lucrative employments, and they cannot, therefore, be supposed to have ample funds of their own.

I was much pleased with the late resolution awarding Franklin medals to the colored pupils of the grammar school; and I was still more pleased with the laudable project, originated by Josiah Holbrook, Esq., for the establishment of a colored lyceum. Surely a better spirit *is* beginning to work in this cause; and when once begun, the good sense and good feeling of the community will bid it go on and prosper. . . .

In the theater, it is not possible for respectable colored people to obtain a decent seat. They must either be excluded, or herd with the vicious.

A fierce excitement prevailed, not long since, because a colored man had bought a pew in one of our churches. I heard a very kind-hearted and zealous democrat declare his opinion that "the fellow ought to be turned out by constables, if he dared to occupy the pew he had purchased." Even at the communion table, the mockery of human pride is mingled with the worship of Jehovah. Again and again have I seen a solitary Negro come up to the altar, meekly and timidly, after all the white communicants had retired. One Episcopal clergyman of this city forms an honorable exception to this remark. When there is room at the altar, Mr. − − − often makes a signal to the colored members of his church to kneel beside their white brethren; and once, when two white infants and one colored one were to be baptized, and the parents of the latter bashfully lingered far behind the others, he silently rebuked the unchristian spirit of pride by first administering the Holy Ordinance to the little dark-skinned child of God. . . .

A well-known country representative, who makes a very loud noise about his democracy, once attended the Catholic Church. A pious Negro requested him to take off his hat while he stood in the presence of the Virgin Mary. The white man rudely shoved him aside, saying, "You son of an Ethiopian, do you dare to speak to me!" I more than once heard the hero repeat this story; and he seemed to take peculiar satisfaction in telling it. Had he been less ignorant, he would not have chosen "son of an *Ethiopian*" as an *ignoble* epithet; to have called the African his own equal would have been abundantly more sarcastic. The same republican dismissed a strong, industrious colored man who had been employed on the farm during his absence. "I am too great a democrat," quoth he, "to have anybody in my house who don't sit at my table; and I'll be hanged if I ever eat with the son of an Ethiopian."

Men whose education leaves them less excuse for illiberality are yet vulgar enough to join in this ridiculous prejudice. The colored woman, whose daughter has been mentioned as excluded from a private school, was once smuggled into a stage, upon the supposition that she was a white woman with a sallow complexion. Her manners were modest and prepossessing, and the gentlemen were very polite to her. But when she stopped at her own door, and was handed out by her curly headed husband, they were at once surprised and angry to find they had been riding with a mulatto — and had, in their ignorance, been really civil to her! . . .

Mr. Garrison was the first person who dared to edit a newspaper in which slavery was spoken of as altogether wicked and inexcusable. For this crime the legislature of Georgia have offered $5,000 to anyone who will "arrest and prosecute him to conviction *under the laws of that state*." An association of gentlemen in South Carolina have likewise offered a large reward for the same object. It is, to say

261

the least, a very remarkable step for one state in this Union to promulgate such a law concerning a citizen of another state, merely for publishing his opinions boldly. The disciples of Fanny Wright promulgate the most zealous and virulent attacks upon Christianity without any hindrance from the civil authorities; and this is done upon the truly rational ground that individual freedom of opinion ought to be respected—that what is false cannot stand, and what is true cannot be overthrown. We leave Christianity to take care of itself; but slavery is a "delicate subject," and whoever attacks that must be punished. Mr. Garrison is a disinterested, intelligent, and remarkably pure-minded man, whose only fault is that he cannot be moderate on a subject which it is exceedingly difficult for an honest mind to examine with calmness. Many who highly respect his character and motives regret his tendency to use wholesale and unqualified expressions; but it is something to have the truth told, even if it be not in the most judicious way.

Where an evil is powerfully supported by the self-interest and prejudice of the community, none but an ardent individual will venture to meddle with it. Luther was deemed indiscreet even by those who liked him best; yet a more prudent man would never have given an impetus sufficiently powerful to heave the great mass of corruption under which the church was buried. Mr. Garrison has certainly the merit of having first called public attention to a neglected and very important subject. I believe whoever fairly and dispassionately examines the question will be more than disposed to forgive the occasional faults of an ardent temperament, in consideration of the difficulty of the undertaking and the violence with which it has been opposed. . .

We are told that the Southerners will of themselves do away slavery, and they alone understand how to do it. But it is an obvious fact that all their measures have tended to perpetuate the system; and even if we have the fullest faith that they mean to do their duty, the belief by no means absolves us from doing ours. The evil is gigantic; and its removal requires every heart and head in the community.

It is said that our sympathies ought to be given to the masters, who are abundantly more to be pitied than the slaves. If this be the case, the planters are singularly disinterested not to change places with their bondmen. Our sympathies *have* been given to the masters—and to those masters who seemed most desirous to remain forever in their pitiable condition. There are hearts at the South sincerely desirous of doing right in this cause; but their generous impulses are checked by the laws of their respective states and the strong disapprobation of their neighbors. I know a lady in Georgia who would, I believe, make any personal sacrifice to instruct her slaves and give them freedom; but if she were found guilty of teaching the alphabet or manumitting her slaves, fines and imprisonment would be the consequence; if she sold them, they would be likely to fall into hands less merciful than her own. Of such slave owners we cannot speak with too much respect and tenderness. They are comparatively few in number, and stand in a most perplexing situation; it is a duty to give all our sympathy to *them*. It is mere mockery to say what is so often said, that the Southerners, as a body, really wish to abolish slavery. If they wished it, they certainly would make the attempt. When the majority heartily desire a change, it is effected, be the difficulties what they may. The Americans are peculiarly responsible for the example they give; for in no other country does the unchecked voice of the people constitute the whole of government. . . .

The strongest and best reason that can be given for our supineness on the subject of slavery is the fear of dissolving the Union. The Constitution of the United States demands our highest reverence. Those who approve, and those who disapprove of particular portions, are equally bound to yield implicit obedience to its authority. But we must not forget that the Constitution provides for any change that may be required for the general good. The great machine is constructed with a safety valve by which any rapidly increasing evil may be expelled whenever the people desire it.

If the Southern politicians are determined to make a Siamese question of this also—if they insist that the Union shall not exist without slavery—it can only be said that they join two things which have no affinity with each other and which cannot permanently exist together. They chain the living and vigorous to the diseased and dying; and the former will assuredly perish in the infected neighborhood.

Declaration of the American Anti-Slavery Society

Prior to the 1830s, American Abolition societies were typically small and timid, and most Abolitionists supported schemes to "colonize" the Negroes, that is, to settle them in geographically isolated communities. William Lloyd Garrison injected a militant tone into the Abolitionist movement. He declared moral war on the slaveholders and demanded that they immediately and without compensation grant the Negroes freedom and political and social equality within the white society. He had the effect of goading into action those already convinced of the injustice of slavery and provoking the violent response of those who opposed his views. The American Anti-Slavery Society, which convened for the first time in early December 1833, expressed the new Abolitionist sentiment. The Society was designed to give doctrinal and administrative coherence to the movement. Garrison drafted the following declaration for the Society; it was adopted with minor revisions on December 6. Within five years the Society had 1,350 local chapters. [Source: First Annual Report of the American Anti-Slavery Society, etc., etc., New York, 1834: "Declaration of the National Anti-Slavery Convention."]

The convention, assembled in the city of Philadelphia to organize a National Anti-Slavery Society, promptly seize the opportunity to promulgate the following Declaration of Sentiments, as cherished by them in relation to the enslavement of one-sixth portion of the American people.

More than fifty-seven years have elapsed since a band of patriots convened in this place to devise measures for the deliverance of this country from a foreign yoke. The cornerstone upon which they founded the temple of freedom was broadly this: "That all men are created equal; and they are endowed by their Creator with certain inalienable rights; that among these are life, LIBERTY, and the pursuit of happiness." At the sound of their trumpet call 3 million people rose up as from the sleep of death and rushed to the strife of blood, deeming it more glorious to die instantly as freemen than desirable to live one hour as slaves. They were few in number, poor in resources; but the honest conviction that TRUTH, JUSTICE, and RIGHT were on their side made them invincible.

264

We have met together for the achievement of an enterprise, without which that of our fathers is incomplete; and which, for its magnitude, solemnity, and probable results upon the destiny of the world as far transcends theirs as moral truth does physical force.

In purity of motive, in earnestness of zeal, in decision of purpose, in intrepidity of action, in steadfastness of faith, in sincerity of spirit, we would not be inferior to them.

Their principles led them to wage war against their oppressors and to spill human blood like water in order to be free. *Ours* forbid the doing of evil that good may come and lead us to reject, and to entreat the oppressed to reject the use of all carnal weapons for deliverance from bondage, relying solely upon those which are spiritual and mighty through God to the pulling down of strongholds.

Their measures were physical resistance—the marshaling in arms, the hostile array, the mortal encounter. *Ours* shall be such as only the opposition of moral purity to moral corruption—the destruction of error by the potency of truth, the overthrow of prejudice by the power of love, and the abolition of slavery by the spirit of repentance.

Their grievances, great as they were, were trifling in comparison with the wrongs and sufferings of those for whom we plead. Our fathers were never slaves; never bought and sold like cattle; never shut out from the light of knowledge and religion; never subjected to the lash of brutal taskmasters.

But those for whose emancipation we are striving, constituting at the present time at least one-sixth part of our countrymen, are recognized by the law and treated by their fellow beings as marketable commodities, as goods and chattels, as brute beasts; are plundered daily of the fruits of their toil without redress; really enjoying no constitutional nor legal protection from licentious and murderous outrages upon their persons; are ruthlessly torn asunder—the tender babe from the arms of its frantic mother, the heartbroken wife from her weeping husband—at the caprice or pleasure of irresponsible tyrants.

For the crime of having a dark complexion, they suffer the pangs of hunger, the infliction of stripes, and the ignominy of brutal servitude. They are kept in heathenish darkness by laws expressly enacted to make their instruction a criminal offense.

These are the prominent circumstances in the condition of more than 2 million of our people, the proof of which may be found in thousands of indisputable facts and in the laws of the slaveholding states.

Hence we maintain that in view of the civil and religious privileges of this nation, the guilt of its oppression is unequaled by any other on the face of the earth; and, therefore, that it is bound to repent instantly, to undo the heavy burden, to break every yoke, and to let the oppressed go free.

We further maintain that no man has a right to enslave or imbrute his brother; to hold or acknowledge him, for one moment, as a piece of merchandise; to keep back his hire by fraud; or to brutalize his mind by denying him the means of intellectual, social, and moral improvement.

The right to enjoy liberty is inalienable. To invade it is to usurp the prerogative of Jehovah. Every man has a right to his own body, to the products of his own labor, to the protection of law, and to the common advantages of society. It is piracy to buy or steal a native African and subject him to servitude. Surely the sin is as great to enslave an American as an African.

Therefore, we believe and affirm:

That there is no difference, *in principle*, between the African slave trade and American slavery.

That every American citizen who retains a human being in involuntary bondage as his property is (according to Scripture) a MAN STEALER.

That the slaves ought instantly to be set free and brought under the protection of law.

That if they had lived from the time of Pharaoh down to the present period, and had been entailed through successive generations, their right to be free could never have been alienated, but their claims would have constantly risen in solemnity.

That all those laws which are now in force, admitting the right of slavery, are, therefore, before God, utterly null and void, being an audacious usurpation of the Divine prerogative; a daring infringement on the the law of nature; a base overthrow of the very foundations of the social compact; a complete extinction of all the rela-

266

tions, endearments, and obligations of mankind; and a presumptuous transgression of all the holy commandments; and that, therefore, they ought instantly to be abrogated.

We further believe and affirm that all persons of color who possess the qualifications which are demanded of others ought to be admitted forthwith to the enjoyment of the same privileges, and the exercise of the same prerogatives, as others; and that the paths of preferment, of wealth, and of intelligence should be opened as widely to them as to persons of a white complexion.

We maintain that no compensation should be given to the planters emancipating their slaves:

Because it would be a surrender of the great fundamental principle, that man cannot hold property in man;

Because SLAVERY IS A CRIME, AND THEREFORE IS NOT AN ARTICLE TO BE SOLD;

Because the holders of slaves are not the just proprietors of what they claim; freeing the slaves is not depriving them of property but restoring it to its rightful owner; it is not wronging the master, but righting the slave—restoring him to himself;

Because immediate and general emancipation would only destroy nominal, not real, property; it would not amputate a limb or break a bone of the slaves, but by infusing motives into their breasts would make them doubly valuable to the masters as free laborers; and

Because, if compensation is to be given at all, it should be given to the outraged and guiltless slaves and not to those who have plundered and abused them.

We regard as delusive, cruel, and dangerous any scheme of expatriation which pretends to aid, either directly or indirectly, in the emancipation of the slaves, or to be a substitute for the immediate and total abolition of slavery.

We fully and unanimously recognize the sovereignty of each state to legislate exclusively on the subject of the slavery which is tolerated within its limits; we concede that Congress, *under the present national compact*, has no right to interfere with any of the slave states, in relation to this momentous subject.

But we maintain that Congress has a right, and is solemnly bound, to suppress the domestic slave trade between the several states, and to abolish slavery in those portions of our territory which the Constitution has placed under its exclusive jurisdiction.

We also maintain that there are, at the present time, the highest obligations resting upon the people of the free states to remove slavery by moral and political action as prescribed in the Constitution of the United States. They are now living under a pledge of their tremendous physical force to fasten the galling fetters of tyranny upon the limbs of millions in the Southern states; they are liable to be called at any moment to suppress a general insurrection of the slaves; they authorize the slave owner to vote on three-fifths of his slaves as property, and thus enable him to perpetuate his oppression; they support a standing army at the South for its protection; and they seize the slave who has escaped into their territories and send him back to be tortured by an enraged master or a brutal driver. This relation to slavery is criminal and full of danger: IT MUST BE BROKEN UP.

These are our views and principles; these our designs and measures. With entire confidence in the overruling justice of God, we plant ourselves upon the declaration of our independence and the truths of Divine Revelation as upon the Everlasting Rock.

We shall organize antislavery societies, if possible, in every city, town, and village in our land.

We shall send forth agents to lift up the voice of remonstrance, of warning, of entreaty, and rebuke.

We shall circulate, unsparingly and extensively, antislavery tracts and periodicals.

We shall enlist the pulpit and the press in the cause of the suffering and the dumb.

We shall aim at a purification of the churches from all participation in the guilt of slavery.

We shall encourage the labor of freemen rather than that of slaves by giving a preference to their productions. . . .

We shall spare no exertions nor means to bring the whole nation to speedy repentance.

Our trust for victory is solely in God. We may be personally defeated, but our principles never. TRUTH, JUSTICE, REASON, HUMANITY must and will gloriously triumph. Already a host is coming up to the help of the Lord against the mighty, and the prospect before

268

us is full of encouragement.

Submitting this declaration to the candid examination of the people of this country, and of the friends of liberty throughout the world, we hereby affix our signatures to it, pledging ourselves that, under the guidance and by the help of Almighty God, we will do all that in us lies, consistently with this declaration of our principles, to overthrow the most execrable system of slavery that has ever been witnessed upon earth; to deliver our land from its deadliest curse; to wipe out the foulest stain which rests upon our national escutcheon; and to secure to the colored population of the United States all the rights and privileges which belong to them as men and as Americans—come what may to our persons, our interests, or our reputations, whether we live to witness the triumph of LIBERTY, JUSTICE, and HUMANITY, or perish untimely as martyrs in this great, benevolent, and holy cause.

THOMAS R. DEW
Pro-Slavery Arguments

Virginia's Constitutional Convention of 1829, moved both by scruple and the declining economic value of Negroes, argued seriously a proposal to abolish slavery in the state. In 1831-1832 the legislature debated the same question, inspired largely by Nat Turner's slave rebellion of 1831, which cast doubt on the safety of the institution. Shortly afterward, in a critique of this debate, Thomas R. Dew, professor of political economy at the College of William and Mary, published a defense of the slave economy that stiffened sentiment in its favor. Dew's book became a major source for pro-slavery argument throughout the South. [Source: The Pro-Slavery Argument, Philadelphia, 1853, pp. 451-462.]

It is said slavery is wrong, in the *abstract* at least, and contrary to the spirit of Christianity. To this we answer . . . that any question must be determined by its circumstances, and if, as really is the case, we cannot get rid of slavery without producing a greater injury to both the masters and slaves, there is no rule of conscience or revealed law of God which *can* condemn us. The physician will not order the spreading cancer to be extirpated although it will eventually cause the death of his patient, because he would thereby hasten the fatal issue.

So, if slavery had commenced even contrary to the laws of God and man, and the sin of its introduction rested upon our heads, and it was even carrying forward the nation by slow degrees to final ruin – yet, if it were *certain* that an attempt to remove it would only hasten and heighten the final catastrophe – that it was, in fact, a *vulnus immedicabile* on the body politic which no legislation could safely remove, then we would not only not be found to attempt the extirpation but we would stand guilty of a high offense in the sight of both God and man if we should rashly make the effort. But the original sin of introduction rests not on our heads, and we shall soon see that all those dreadful calamities which the false prophets of our day are pointing to will never, in all probability, occur.

With regard to the assertion that slavery is against the spirit of Christianity, we are ready to admit the general assertion, but deny most positively that there is anything in the Old or New Testament which would go to show that slavery, when once introduced, ought at all events to be abrogated, or that the master commits any offense in holding slaves. The children of Israel themselves were slaveholders and were not condemned for it. All the patriarchs themselves were slaveholders; Abraham had more than 300; Isaac had a "great store" of them; and even the patient and meek Job himself had "a very great household." When the children of Israel conquered the land of Canaan, they made one whole tribe "hewers of wood and drawers of water," and they were at that very time under the special guidance of Jehovah; they were permitted expressly to purchase slaves of the heathen and keep them as an inheritance for their posterity; and even the children of Israel might be enslaved for six years.

When we turn to the New Testament, we find not one single passage at all calculated to disturb the conscience of an honest slaveholder. No one can read it without seeing and admiring that the meek and humble Savior of the world in no instance meddled with the established institutions of mankind; he came to save a

270

fallen world, and not to excite the black passions of men and array them in deadly hostility against each other. From no one did he turn away; his plan was offered alike to all—to the monarch and the subject, the rich and the poor, the master and the slave. He was born in the Roman world, a world in which the most galling slavery existed, a thousand times more cruel than the slavery in our own country; and yet he nowhere encourages insurrection; he nowhere fosters discontent; but exhorts *always* to implicit obedience and fidelity.

What a rebuke does the practice of the Redeemer of mankind imply upon the conduct of some of his nominal disciples of the day, who seek to destroy the contentment of the slaves, to rouse their most deadly passions, to break up the deep foundations of society, and to lead on to a night of darkness and confusion! "Let every man" (says Paul) "abide in the same calling wherein he is called. Art thou called *being* a servant? Care not for it; but if thou mayest be made free, use *it* rather" (I Cor. 7:20,21). Again: "Let as many servants as are under the yoke count their own masters worthy of all honor, that the name of God and His doctrines be not blasphemed; and they that have believing masters, let them not despise *them*, because they are brethren, but rather do them service, because they are faithful and beloved partakers of the benefit. These things teach and exhort" (I Tim. 6:1,2). Servants are even commanded in Scripture to be faithful and obedient to unkind masters. "Servants," (says Peter) "be subject to your masters with all fear; not only to the good and gentle but to the froward. For what glory is it if when ye shall be buffeted for your faults ye take it patiently; but if when ye do well and suffer for it, ye take it patiently, this is acceptable with God" (I Pet. 2:18,20). These and many other passages in the New Testament most convincingly prove that slavery in the Roman world was nowhere charged as a fault or crime upon the holder, and everywhere is the most implicit obedience enjoined.

We beg leave . . . to address a few remarks to those who have conscientious scruples about the holding of slaves, and therefore consider themselves under an obligation to break all the ties of friendship and kindred—dissolve all the associations of happier days to flee to a land where this evil does not exist. We cannot condemn the conscientious actions of mankind, but we must be per-

271

mitted to say that if the assumption even of these pious gentlemen be correct, we do consider their conduct as very unphilosophical. And we will go further still—we look upon it as even immoral upon their own principles.

Let us admit that slavery is an evil; and what then? Why, it has been entailed upon us by no fault of ours, and must we shrink from the charge which devolves upon us, and throw the slave, in consequence, into the hands of those who have no scruples of conscience—those who will not perhaps treat him so kindly? No! This is not philosophy, it is not morality; we must recollect that the unprofitable man was thrown into utter darkness. To the slaveholder has truly been entrusted the five talents. Let him but recollect the exhortation of the apostle—"Masters, give unto your servants that which is just and equal; knowing that ye also have a Master in heaven"; and in the final day he shall have nothing on this score with which his conscience need be smitten, and he may expect the welcome plaudit—"Well done thou good and faithful servant, thou hast been faithful over a few things, I will make thee ruler over many things; enter thou into the joy of thy Lord." . . .

It is further said that the moral effects of slavery are of the most deleterious and hurtful kind. And as Mr. Jefferson has given the sanction of his great name to this charge, we shall proceed to examine it with all that respectful deference to which every sentiment of so pure and philanthropic a heart is justly entitled.

> The whole commerce between master and slave . . . is a perpetual exercise of the most boisterous passions; the most unremitting despotism on the one part, and degrading submission on the other. Our children see this and learn to imitate it, for man is an imitative animal—this quality is the germ of education in him. From his cradle to his grave, he is learning what he sees others do. If a parent had no other motive, either in his own philanthropy or self-love, for restraining the intemperance of passion toward his slave, it should always be a sufficient one that his child is present. But generally it is not sufficient. The parent storms, the child looks on, catches the lineaments of wrath, puts on the same airs in the circle of smaller slaves, gives a loose to his worst of passions, and thus

nursed, educated, and daily exercised in the worst of tyranny, cannot but be stamped by it with odious peculiarities.

Now we boldly assert that the fact does not bear Mr. Jefferson out in his conclusions. He has supposed the master in a continual passion—in the constant exercise of the most odious tyranny—and the child, a creature of imitation, looking on and learning. But is not this master sometimes kind and indulgent to his slaves? Does he not mete out to them, for faithful service, the reward of his cordial approbation? Is it not his interest to do it? And when thus acting humanely and speaking kindly, where is the child, the creature of imitation, that he does not look on and learn? We may rest assured, in this intercourse between a good master and his servant, more good than evil *may* be taught the child; the exalted principles of morality and religion may thereby be sometimes indelibly inculcated upon his mind, and instead of being reared a selfish, contracted being, with nought but self to look to, he acquires a more exalted benevolence, a greater generosity and elevation of soul, and embraces for the sphere of his generous actions a much wider field.

Look to the slaveholding population of our country and you everywhere find them characterized by noble and elevated sentiments, by humane and virtuous feelings. We do not find among them that cold, contracted, calculating selfishness, which withers and repels everything around it, and lessens or destroys all the multiplied enjoyments of social intercourse. Go into our national councils and ask for the most generous, the most disinterested, the most conscientious, and the least unjust and oppressive in their principles, and see whether the slaveholder will be passed by in the selection. . . .

Is it not a fact known to every man in the South that the most cruel masters are those who have been unaccustomed to slavery. It is well known that Northern gentlemen who marry Southern heiresses are much severer masters than Southern gentlemen. And yet, if Mr. Jefferson's reasoning were correct, they ought to be milder; in fact, it follows from his reasoning that the authority which the father is called on to exercise over his children must be seriously detrimental; and yet we know that this is not the case; that, on the contrary, there is nothing which so much humanizes and softens the heart as this *very authority*. And there are none, even among those who have no children themselves, so disposed to pardon the follies and indiscretion of youth as those who have seen most of them and suffered greatest annoyance. There may be many cruel masters, and there are unkind and cruel fathers too; but both the one and the other make all those around them shudder with horror. We are disposed to think that their example ... tends rather to strengthen than weaken the principle of benevolence and humanity.

Let us now look a moment to the slave and contemplate his position. Mr. Jefferson has described him as hating rather than loving his master, and as losing, too, all that *amor patriae* which characterizes the true patriot. We assert again that Mr. Jefferson is not borne out by the fact. We are well convinced that there is nothing but the mere relations of husband and wife, parent and child, brother and sister which produce a closer tie than the relation of master and servant. We have no hesitation in affirming that, throughout the whole slaveholding country, the slaves of a good master are his warmest, most constant, and most devoted friends; they have been accustomed to look up to him as their supporter, director, and defender.

Everyone acquainted with Southern slaves knows that the slave rejoices in the elevation and prosperity of his master; and the heart of no one is more gladdened at the successful debut of young master or miss on the great theater of the world than that of either the young slave who has grown up with them and shared in all their sports, and even partaken of all their delicacies, or the aged one who has looked on and watched them from birth to manhood, with the kindest and most affectionate solicitude, and has ever met from them all the kind treatment and generous sympathies of feeling, tender hearts. Judge Smith, in his able speech on Foote's Resolutions in the Senate, said, in an emergency he would rely upon his own slaves for his defense—he would put arms into their hands, and he had no doubt they would defend him faithfully. In the late Southampton insurrection, we know that many actually convened their slaves and armed them for defense, although slaves were here the cause of the evil which was to be repelled.

We have often heard slaveholders affirm that they would sooner rely upon their slaves' fidelity and attachment in the hour of danger and severe trial than on any other equal number of individuals; and

274

we all know that the son or daughter who has been long absent from the parental roof, on returning to the scenes of infancy, never fails to be greeted with the kindest welcome and the most sincere and heartfelt congratulations from those slaves among whom he has been reared to manhood. . . .

In the debate in the Virginia legislature, no speaker *insinuated even,* we believe, that the slaves in Virginia were not treated kindly; and all, too, agree that they were most abundantly fed; and we have no doubt but that they form the happiest portion of our society. A merrier being does not exist on the face of the globe than the Negro slave of the United States. Even Captain Hall himself, with his thick "crust of prejudice," is obliged to allow that they are happy and contented, and the master much less cruel than is generally imagined. Why, then, since the slave is happy, and happiness is the great object of all animated creation, should we endeavor to disturb his contentment by infusing into his mind a vain and indefinite desire for liberty—a something which he cannot comprehend, and which must inevitably dry up the very sources of his happiness.

The fact is that all of us, and the great author of the Declaration of Independence is like us in this respect, are too prone to judge of the happiness of others by ourselves—we make *self* the standard and endeavor to draw down everyone to its dimensions—not recollecting that the benevolence of the Omnipotent has made the mind of man pliant and susceptible of happiness in almost every situation and employment. We might rather die than be the obscure slave that waits at our back—our education and our habits generate an ambition that makes us aspire at something loftier and disposes us to look upon the slave as unsusceptible of happiness in his humble sphere, when he may indeed be much happier than we are, and have his ambition too; but his ambition is to excel all his other slaves in the performance of his servile duties, to please and to gratify his master, and to command the praise of all. . . .

Let the wily philanthropist but come and whisper into the ears of such a slave that his situation is degrading and his lot a miserable one; let him but light up the dungeon in which he persuades the slave that he is caged, and that moment, like the serpent that entered the Garden of Eden, he destroys his happiness and his usefulness. We cannot, therefore, agree with Mr. Jefferson in the opinion that slavery makes the unfeeling tyrant and ungrateful

275

dependent. And in regard to Virginia, especially, we are almost disposed, judging from the official returns of crimes and convictions, to assert . . . "that the whole population of Virginia, consisting of three *castes* — of free white, free colored, and slave colored population, is the soundest and most moral of any other. . . ."

It has been contended that slavery is unfavorable to a republican spirit; but the whole history of the world proves that this is far from being the case. In the ancient republics of Greece and Rome, where the spirit of liberty glowed with most intensity, the slaves were more numerous than the freemen. Aristotle and the great men of antiquity believed slavery necessary to keep alive the spirit of freedom. In Sparta the freemen were even forbidden to perform the offices of slaves, lest [they] might lose the spirit of independence. In modern times, too, liberty has always been more ardently desired by slaveholding communities. "Such," says Burke, "were our Gothic ancestors; such, in our days, were the Poles; and such will be all masters of slaves who are not slaves themselves." "These people of the southern (American) colonies are much more strongly, and with a higher and more stubborn spirit, attached to liberty than those of the northward." And from the time of Burke down to the present day, the Southern states have always borne the same honorable distinction. Burke says, "it is because freedom is to them not only an enjoyment but a kind of rank and privilege." Another, and perhaps more efficient cause of this is the perfect spirit of equality so prevalent among the whites of all the slaveholding states. . . .

We believe slavery in the United States has accomplished this, in regard to the whites, as nearly as can be expected or even desired in this world. The menial and low offices being all performed by the blacks, there is at once taken away the greatest cause of distinction and separation of the ranks of society. The man to the North will not shake hands familiarly with his servant, and converse and laugh and dine with him, no matter how honest and respectable he may be. But go to the South, and you will find that no white man feels such inferiority of rank as to be unworthy of association with those around him. Color alone is here the badge of distinction, the true mark of aristocracy, and all who are white are equal in spite of the variety of occupation. . . . It is this spirit of equality which is both the generator and preserver of the genuine spirit of liberty.

276

4. A Firebell in the Night

1820 - 1831

NAT TURNER

Confession

Nat Turner led the best known of all Southern slave revolts, which occurred on August 21, 1831, and climaxed a three-year period of unrest among the slaves during which time Turner had been successful in convincing his followers that he was divinely appointed to lead them from bondage. The statistics of the revolt were themselves sufficient to alarm the whole South: sixty whites killed by Turner's men, and at least one hundred Negroes killed in suppressing the revolt. But the details of the episode as Turner described it in the following confession struck the slaveholding South with even greater fear and put an end to the work of the emancipation societies there. Of the sixty or seventy men and one woman involved in the revolt, twenty-eight were convicted, thirteen (including Turner and the woman) were hanged, and the rest deported. The confession was dictated to Turner's attorney Thomas R. Gray, who asked the questions in the text and included an occasional comment of his own. [Source: Anglo-African Magazine, December 1859.]

Agreeable to his own appointment, on the evening he was committed to prison, with permission of the jailer, I visited Nat on Tuesday the 1st of November, when, without being questioned at all, he commenced his narrative in the following words:

Sir, you have asked me to give a history of the motives which induced me to undertake the late insurrection, as you call it. To do so I must go back to the days of my infancy, and even before I was born. I was thirty-one years of age the 2nd of October last and born the property of Benj. Turner, of this county. In my childhood a circumstance occurred which made an indelible impression on my mind and laid the groundwork of that enthusiasm which has terminated so fatally to many both white and black, and for which I am about to atone at the gallows. It is here necessary to relate this circumstance, trifling as it may seem; it was the commencement of that belief which has grown with time, and even now, sir, in this dungeon, helpless and forsaken as I am, I cannot divest myself of. Being at play with other children, when three or four years old, I was telling them something, which my mother overhearing, said it had happened before I was born; I stuck to my story, however, and related some things which went in the opinion to confirm it; others being called on were greatly astonished, knowing that these things had happened, and caused them to say in my hearing, I surely would be a prophet, as the Lord had shown me things that had happened before my birth. And my father and mother strengthened me in this my first impression, saying in my presence, I was intended for some great purpose, which they had always thought from certain marks on my head and breast [a parcel of excrescences which I believe are not at all uncommon, particularly among Negroes, as I have seen several with the same. In this case he has either cut them off, or they have nearly disappeared].

My grandmother, who was very religious and to whom I was much attached, my master, who belonged to the church, and other religious persons who visited the house, and whom I often saw at prayers, noticing the singularity of my manners, I suppose, and my uncommon intelligence for a child, remarked I had too much sense to be raised and if I was, I would never be of any service to anyone as a slave. To a mind like mine, restless, inquisitive and observant of everything that was passing, it was easy to suppose that religion was the subject to which it would be directed, and although this subject principally occupied my thoughts, there was nothing that I saw or heard of to which my attention was not directed. The manner in which I learned to read and write not only had great influence on my own mind—as I acquired it with the most perfect ease; so much so, that I have no recollection whatever of learning the alphabet— but to the astonishment of the family, one day, when a book was shown to me to keep me from crying, I began spelling the names of different objects. This was a source of wonder to all in the neighborhood, particularly the blacks; and this learning was constantly improved at all opportunities. When I got large enough to go to work, while employed, I was reflecting on many things that would present themselves to my imagination, and, whenever an opportunity occurred of looking at a book, when the school children were getting their lessons, I would find many things that the fertility of my own imagination had depicted to me before; all my time not devoted to my master's service was spent either in prayer, or in making experiments in casting different things in molds made of earth, in attempting to make paper, gunpowder, and many other experiments that, although I could not perfect, yet convinced me of its practicability if I had the means.

I was not addicted to stealing in my youth, nor have ever been. Yet such was the confidence of the Negroes in the neighborhood, even at this early period of my life, in my superior judgment, that they would often carry me with them when they were going on any roguery, to plan for them. Growing up among them, with this confidence in my superior judgment, and when this, in their opinions, was perfected by Divine inspiration, from the circumstances already alluded to in my infancy, and which belief was ever afterwards zealously inculcated by the austerity of my life and manners, which became the subject of remark with white and black.

Having soon discovered to be great, I must appear so and, therefore, studiously avoided mixing in society and wrapped myself in mystery, devoting my time to fasting and prayer. By this time, having arrived to man's estate and hearing the Scriptures commented on at meetings, I was struck with that particular passage which says: "Seek ye the kingdom of Heaven and all things shall be added unto you." I reflected much on this passage and prayed daily for light on this subject: As I was praying one day at my plow, the Spirit spoke to me, saying "Seek ye the kingdom of Heaven and all things shall be added unto you."

Question: What do you mean by the Spirit?

Answer: The Spirit that spoke to the prophets in former days.

And I was greatly astonished and for two years prayed continually, whenever my duty would permit. And then again I had the same revelation, which fully confirmed me in the impression that I was ordained for some great purpose in the hands of the Almighty.

Several years rolled round, in which many events occurred to strengthen me in this belief. At this time I reverted in my mind to the remarks made of me in my childhood, and the things that had been shown me, and as it had been said of me in my childhood by those by whom I had been taught to pray, both white and black, and in whom I had the greatest confidence, that I had too much sense to be raised, and if I was I would never be of any use to anyone as a slave. Now finding I had arrived to man's estate and was a slave, and these revelations being made known to me, I began to direct my attention to this great object, to fulfill the purpose for which, by this time, I felt assured I was intended. Knowing the influence I had obtained over the minds of my fellow servants, (not by the means of conjuring and such like tricks, for to them I always spoke of such things with contempt) but by the communion of the Spirit whose revelations I often communicated to them, and they believed and said my wisdom came from God. I now began to prepare them for my purpose, by telling them something was about to happen that would terminate in fulfilling the great promise that had been made to me.

About this time I was placed under an overseer, from whom I ran away; and after remaining in the woods thirty days, I returned, to the astonishment of the Negroes on the plantation, who thought I had made my escape to some other part of the country, as my father had done before. But the reason of my return was, that the Spirit appeared to me and said I had my wishes directed to the things of this world, and not to the kingdom of Heaven, and that I should return to the service of my earthly master, "For he who knoweth his Master's will, and doeth it not, shall be beaten with many stripes, and thus have I chastened you." And the Negroes found fault, and murmured against me, saying that if they had my sense they would not serve any master in the world. And about this time I had a vision, and I saw white spirits and black spirits engaged in battle, and the sun was darkened, the thunder rolled in the heavens, and blood flowed in streams, and I heard a voice saying, "Such is your luck, such you are called to see, and let it come rough or smooth, you must surely bear it."

I now withdrew myself as much as my situation would permit from the intercourse of my fellow servants, for the avowed purpose of serving the Spirit more fully, and it appeared to me, and reminded me of the things it had already shown me, and that it would then reveal to me the knowledge of the elements, the revolution of the planets, the operation of tides, and changes of the seasons. After this revelation in the year 1825 and the knowledge of the elements being made known to me, I sought more than ever to obtain true holiness before the great day of judgment should appear, and then I began to receive the true knowledge of faith. And from the first steps of righteousness until the last, was I made perfect; and the Holy Ghost was with me, and said "Behold me as I stand in the Heavens," and I looked and saw the forms of men in different

282

attitudes, and there were lights in the sky to which the children of darkness gave other names than what they really were, for they were the lights of the Savior's hands, stretched forth from east to west, even as they were extended on the cross on Calvary for the redemption of sinners. And I wondered greatly at these miracles, and prayed to be informed of a certainty of the meaning thereof, and shortly afterwards, while laboring in the field, I discovered drops of blood on the corn, as though it were dew from heaven, and I communicated it to many, both white and black in the neighborhood; and I then found on the leaves in the woods hieroglyphic characters and numbers, with the forms of men in different attitudes, portrayed in blood, and representing the figures I had seen before in the heavens. And now the Holy Ghost had revealed itself to me and made plain the miracles it had shown me. For as the blood of Christ had been shed on this earth, and had ascended to heaven for the salvation of sinners, and was now returning to earth again in the form of dew, and as the leaves on the trees bore the impression of the figures I had seen in the heavens, it was plain to me that the Savior was about to lay down the yoke He had borne for the sins of men, and the great day of judgment was at hand.

About this time, I told these things to a white man (Etheldred T. Brantley) on whom it had a wonderful effect, and he ceased from his wickedness and was attacked immediately with a cutaneous eruption, and blood oozed from the pores of his skin, and after praying and fasting nine days, he was healed, and the Spirit appeared to me again and said, as the Savior had been baptized, so should we be also; and when the white people would not let us be baptized by the church, we went down into the water together, in the sight of many who reviled us, and were baptized by the Spirit. After this I rejoiced greatly, and gave thanks to God. And on May 12, 1828, I heard a loud noise in the heavens, and the Spirit instantly appeared to me and said the Serpent was loosened, and Christ had laid down the yoke He had borne for the sins of men, and that I should take it on and fight against the Serpent, for the time was fast approaching, when the first should be last and the last should be first.

Question: Do you not find yourself mistaken now?

Answer: Was not Christ crucified?

And by signs in the heavens that it would make known to me

when I should commence the great work, and until the first sign appeared, I should conceal it from the knowledge of men. And on the appearance of the sign, (the eclipse of the sun last February) I should arise and prepare myself and slay my enemies with their own weapons. And immediately on the sign appearing in the heavens, the seal was removed from my lips, and I communicated the great work laid out for me to do, to four in whom I had the greatest confidence (Henry, Hark, Nelson, and Sam). It was intended by us to have begun the work of death on the 4th of July last. Many were the plans formed and rejected by us, and it affected my mind to such a degree that I fell sick, and the time passed without our coming to any determination how to commence; still forming new schemes and rejecting them, when the sign appeared again, which determined me not to wait longer.

Since the commencement of 1830, I had been living with Mr. Joseph Travis, who was to me a kind master and placed the greatest confidence in me; in fact, I had no cause to complain of his treatment to me. On Saturday evening, the 20th of August, it was agreed between Henry, Hark and myself, to prepare a dinner the next day for the men we expected, and then to concert a plan, as we had not yet determined on any. Hark on the following morning brought a pig, and Henry brandy, and being joined by Sam, Nelson, Will, and Jack, they prepared in the woods a dinner, where, about three o'clock, I joined them.

Question: Why were you so backward in joining them?

Answer: The same reason that had caused me not to mix with them for years before.

I saluted them on coming up and asked Will how came he there; he answered, his life was worth no more than others, and his liberty as dear to him. I asked him if he thought to obtain it? He said he would, or lose his life. This was enough to put him in full confidence. Jack, I knew, was only a tool in the hands of Hark, it was quickly agreed we should commence at home (Mr. J. Travis') on that night, and until we had armed and equipped ourselves and gathered sufficient force, neither age nor sex was to be spared (which was invariably adhered to).

We remained at the feast until about two hours in the night, when we went to the house and found Austin; they all went to the

284

Slavery on American Soil

Even though slavery was legal throughout the colonies, most slaves lived and worked in the Southern colonies—from Maryland to the Carolinas—and labored on the vast tobacco, rice, and indigo plantations that were the source of the region's wealth. For the most part, slaves were the perquisites of the rich and well-born, such as Lord Calvert, shown above in a 1761 painting by John Hesselius; although still a child, the young lord had his own body servant. In 1792 Eli Whitney invented the cotton gin, an ingenious device that greatly simplified the task of readying cotton for spinning. Southern soil was ideally suited for cotton-growing. Within a few years, cotton became the South's chief crop and the demand for additional slaves to grow and tend it multiplied many times. In a single year, 1803, more than 20,000 new slaves were brought to the South to serve "King Cotton."

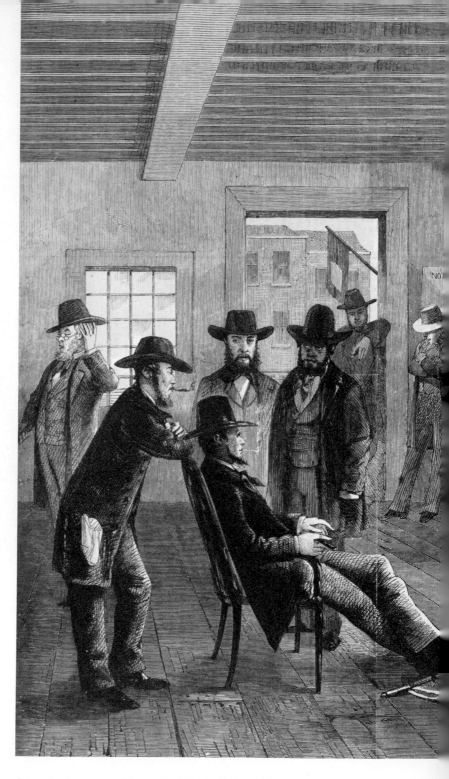

Those slaves who survived capture and the psychological and physical horrors of the "Middle Passage" were herded ashore at Southern ports, paraded before an auctioneer and his customers, and then sold to the highest bidder. This slave sale was sketched by an English artist in Richmond, Virginia, in 1856. Among the cruelest features of this traffic was its attack on the black family: the father might be sold to one buyer, the mother to another, and their children to still a third.

NEGROES
FOR SALE
AT AUCTION
TH'S DAY
AT 1 O'CLOCK

THE NEW YORK HER...

This idyllic scene, painted by an unknown artist about 1825, shows a Southern plantation—the usual destination of newly bought slaves. The big house in which the master and his family lived sits atop the hill. The small buildings along the hillside housed the slaves. The painting shows the plantation system as nostalgic whites would like to remember it; the reality was very different.

Joseph Cinque, a Mendi chieftain who had been seized and sold into slavery, led a revolt on the slave ship Amistad *in 1839. His followers killed most of the crew and ordered the survivors to sail back to Africa. The white sailors tricked Cinque and made for Long Island where the ship was seized and Cinque was arrested and tried for murder. Former President John Quincy Adams defended Cinque and won his freedom.*

Robbed of their culture, shorn of their religion, torn from their families, treated like beasts of burden, it is astonishing that any slaves had the will to resist the system. Yet thousands fought back. Countless slaves ran away from their masters, preferring to brave the dangers of swamps and slave-catchers to the day-to-day degradation of slavery itself. Still others took up arms against it. Some scholars believe that more than 250 slave rebellions took place in the South prior to the Civil War.

Perhaps the best-known slave revolt was led by Nat Turner in Virginia in 1831. He and a small band of followers, shown above in a romanticized version, wandered the countryside, killing more than 60 whites before being captured by a force of some 3,000 armed men. Turner was hanged and more than 100 slaves were killed by vengeful whites.

Some runaway slaves joined forces with another oppressed people, the American Indians. During the Seminole Wars in Florida, more than a thousand black people fought alongside the Indians. Many were killed in the fighting and more than 500 were re-enslaved after the wars.

There were two classes among slaves—those who worked in the fields, called "field hands," and a sort of elite who worked in the master's home. The house servants cooked, waited on table, raised the master's children, cleaned and laundered. Being close to the family kitchen, they ate fairly well, their housing was often better than that of the field hands, and they were given their master's cast-off clothing. They repaid this relative kindness by scorning their less fortunate fellows. The two slaves shown here were especially prized members of this elite: at left is Caesar, an elderly slave who had already been the property of three generations of the same family when he was photographed about 1850; at right is Jane, a young slave nurse photographed with her infant charge in 1858.

Men, women, and children (as soon as they were old enough to use tools) toiled in the fields under the watchful, often brutal eye of an overseer. The overseer and slaves shown above were sketched by Benjamin Latrobe; at left, an English tobacco label of about 1700 shows three white colonists smoking and drinking in the shade while slaves work in the tobacco fields.

LONDON'S VIRGINIA.

The conditions under which slaves lived and worked depended on the enlightenment of their master. The Negro had no recourse at law, and much of the "kindness" that sympathetic historians describe was simply good business. Slaves who were fed, clothed, and housed adequately lived longer and did more work than those who were not. These slave quarters, photographed on a South Carolina plantation in 1860, were better than average.

Slavery was not confined to the settled eastern seaboard. These slaves accompanied their master to the California gold fields in 1852.

cider press and drank, except myself. On returning to the house, Hark went to the door with an axe, for the purpose of breaking it open, as we knew we were strong enough to murder the family, if they were awaked by the noise; but, reflecting that it might create an alarm in the neighborhood, we determined to enter the house secretly and murder them while sleeping. Hark got a ladder and set it against the chimney on which I ascended and, hoisting a window, entered and came down stairs, unbarred the door, and removed the guns from their places. It was then observed that I must spill the first blood. On which, armed with a hatchet and accompanied by Will, I entered my master's chamber. It being dark, I could not give a death blow; the hatchet glanced from his head; he sprang from the bed and called his wife. It was his last word. Will laid him dead with a blow of his axe, and Mrs. Travis shared the same fate, as she lay in bed.

The murder of this family, five in number, was the work of a moment, not one of them awoke; there was a little infant, sleeping in a cradle, that was forgotten until we had left the house and gone some distance, when Henry and Will returned and killed it; we got here four guns that would shoot and several old muskets, with a pound or two of powder. We remained some time at the barn, where we paraded; I formed them in a line as soldiers and, after carrying them through all the maneuvers I was master of, marched them off to Mr. Salathul Francis', about 600 yards distant. Sam and Will went to the door and knocked. Mr. Francis asked who was there; Sam replied it was him and he had a letter for him, on which he got up and came to the door; they immediately seized him, and dragging him out a little from the door, he was dispatched by repeated blows on the head; there was no other white person in the family.

We started from there for Mrs. Reese's, maintaining the most perfect silence on our march, where finding the door unlocked, we entered and murdered Mrs. Reese in her bed, while sleeping; her son awoke, but it was only to sleep the sleep of death. He had only time to say who is that, and he was no more. From Mrs. Reese's we went to Mrs. Turner's, a mile distant, which we reached about sunrise on Monday morning. Henry, Austin, and Sam went to the still, where, finding Mr. Peebles, Austin shot him, and the rest of us went to the house; as we approached, the family discovered us and shut the door. Vain hope! Will, with one stroke of his axe, opened it, and we entered and found Mrs. Turner and Mrs. Newsome in the middle of a room almost frightened to death. Will immediately killed Mrs. Turner with one blow of his axe. I took Mrs. Newsome by the hand, and with the sword I had when I was apprehended, I struck her several blows over the head, but not being able to kill her, as the sword was dull. Will turning around and discovering it, dispatched her also.

A general destruction of property and search for money and ammunition always succeeded the murders. By this time my company amounted to fifteen, and nine men mounted, who started for Mrs. Whitehead's (the other six were to go through a by way to Mr. Bryant's and rejoin us at Mrs. Whitehead's). As we approached the house we discovered Mr. Richard Whitehead standing in the cotton patch, near the lane fence; we called him over into the lane, and Will, the executioner, was near at hand, with his fatal axe, to send him to an untimely grave. As we pushed on to the house, I discovered some one run round the garden, and, thinking it was some of the white family, I pursued them, but finding it was a servant girl belonging to the house, I returned to commence the work of death, but they whom I left had not been idle; all the family were already murdered but Mrs. Whitehead and her daughter Margaret. As I came round to the door I saw Will pulling Mrs. Whitehead out of the house, and at the step he nearly severed her head from her body with his broad axe. Miss Margaret, when I discovered her, had concealed herself in the corner formed by the projection of the cellar cap from the house; on my approach she fled, but was soon overtaken, and after repeated blows with a sword, I killed her by a blow on the head with a fence rail. By this time, the six who had gone by Mr. Bryant's rejoined us and informed me they had done the work of death assigned them.

We again divided, part going to Mr. Richard Porter's, and from thence to Nathaniel Francis', the others to Mr. Howell Harris' and Mr. T. Doyle's. On my reaching Mr. Porter's, he had escaped with his family. I understood there, that the alarm had already spread, and I immediately returned to bring up those sent to Mr. Doyle's and Mr. Howell Harris'; the party I left going on to Mr. Francis', having told them I would join them in that neighborhood. I met these sent to Mr.

Doyle's and Mr. Harris' returning, having met Mr. Doyle on the road and killed him; and learning from some who joined them that Mr. Harris was from home, I immediately pursued the course taken by the party gone on before; but knowing they would complete the work of death and pillage at Mr. Francis' before I could get there, I went to Mr. Peter Edwards', expecting to find them there, but they had been here also. I then went to Mr. John T. Barrow's; they had been here and murdered him. I pursued on their track to Capt. Newit Harris', where I found the greater part mounted and ready to start; the men, now amounting to about forty, shouted and hurrahed as I rode up; some were in the yard, loading their guns, others drinking. They said Captain Harris and his family had escaped, the property in the house they destroyed, robbing him of money and other valuables. I ordered them to mount and march instantly, this was about nine or ten o'clock Monday morning.

I proceeded to Mr. Levi Waller's, two or three miles distant. I took my station in the rear, and as it was my object to carry terror and devastation wherever we went, I placed fifteen or twenty of the best mounted and most to be relied on in front, who generally approached the houses as fast as their horses could run; this was for two purposes, to prevent their escape and strike terror to the inhabitants; on this account I never got to the houses, after leaving Mrs. Whitehead's until the murders were committed, except in one case. I sometimes got in sight in time to see the work of death completed, viewed the mangled bodies as they lay, in silent satisfaction, and immediately started in quest of other victims.

Having murdered Mrs. Waller and ten children, we started for Mr. William Williams'; having killed him and two little boys that were there; while engaged in this, Mrs. Williams fled and got some distance from the house, but she was pursued, overtaken, and compelled to get up behind one of the company, who brought her back, and after showing her the mangled body of her lifeless husband, she was told to get down and lay by his side, where she was shot dead. I then started for Mr. Jacob Williams', where the family were murdered. Here we found a young man named Drury, who had come on business with Mr. Williams; he was pursued, overtaken and shot. Mrs. Vaughan's was the next place we visited, and, after murdering the family here, I determined on starting for Jerusalem.

299

Our number amounted now to fifty or sixty, all mounted and armed with guns, axes, swords, and clubs.

On reaching Mr. James W. Parker's gate, immediately on the road leading to Jerusalem and about three miles distant, it was proposed to me to call there, but I objected, as I knew he was gone to Jerusalem, and my object was to reach there as soon as possible; but some of the men having relations at Mr. Parker's, it was agreed that they might call and get his people. I remained at the gate on the road with seven or eight; the others going across the field to the house about half a mile off. After waiting some time for them, I became impatient and started to the house for them, and on our return we were met by a party of white men, who had pursued our blood-stained track, and who had fired on those at the gate and dispersed them, which I knew nothing of, not having been at that time rejoined by any of them.

Immediately on discovering the whites, I ordered my men to halt and form, as they appeared to be alarmed. The white men, eighteen in number, approached us in about one hundred yards, when one of them fired (this was against the positive orders of Captain Alexander P. Peete, who commanded, and who had directed the men to reserve their fire until within thirty paces). And I discovered about half of them retreating. I then ordered my men to fire and rush on them; the few remaining stood their ground until we approached within fifty yards, when they fired and retreated. We pursued and overtook some of them who we thought we left dead (they were not killed); after pursuing them about two hundred yards and rising a little hill, I discovered they were met by another party, and had halted and were reloading their guns. (This was a small party from Jerusalem who knew the Negroes were in the field and had just tied their horses to await their return to the road knowing that Mr. Parker and family were in Jerusalem, but knew nothing of the party that had gone in with Captain Peete. On hearing the firing they immediately rushed to the spot and arrived just in time to arrest the progress of these barbarous villains and save the lives of their friends and fellow citizens.)

Thinking that those who retreated first, and the party who fired on us at fifty or sixty yards distant, had all only fallen back to meet others with ammunition. As I saw them reloading their guns, and

300

more coming up than I saw at first, and several of my bravest men being wounded, the others became panic struck and scattered over the field; the white men pursued and fired on us several times. Hark had his horse shot under him, and I caught another for him as it was running by me; five or six of my men were wounded, but none left on the field; finding myself defeated here I instantly determined to go through a private way and cross the Nottoway River at the Cypress Bridge, three miles below Jerusalem, and attack that place in the rear, as I expected they would look for me on the other road, and I had a great desire to get there to procure arms and ammunition. After going a short distance in this private way, accompanied by about twenty men, I overtook two or three who told me the others were dispersed in every direction. After trying in vain to collect a sufficient force to proceed to Jerusalem, I determined to return, as I was sure they would make back to their old neighborhood, where they would rejoin me, make new recruits, and come down again. On my way back, I called at Mrs. Thomas', Mrs. Spencer's, and several other places, the white families having fled; we found no more victims to gratify our thirst for blood. We stopped at Maj. Ridley's quarter for the night, and being joined by four of his men, with the recruits made since my defeat, we mustered now about forty strong.

After placing out sentinels, I laid down to sleep, but was quickly roused by a great racket; starting up, I found some mounted and others in great confusion; one of the sentinels having given the alarm that we were about to be attacked, I ordered some to ride around and reconnoiter, and on their return the others being more alarmed, not knowing who they were, fled in different ways, so that I was reduced to about twenty again, with this I determined to attempt to recruit, and proceed on to rally in the neighborhood I had left. Dr. Blunt's was the nearest house, which we reached just before day; on riding up the yard, Hark fired a gun. We expected Dr. Blunt and his family were at Maj. Ridley's, as I knew there was a company of men there; the gun was fired to ascertain if any of the family were at home; we were immediately fired upon and retreated leaving several of my men. I do not know what became of them, as I never saw them afterwards.

Pursuing our course back and coming in sight of Captain Harris', where we had been the day before, we discovered a party of white men at the house, on which all deserted me but two (Jacob and Nat). We concealed ourselves in the woods until near night, when I sent them in search of Henry, Sam, Nelson, and Hark, and directed them to rally all they could at the place we had had our dinner the Sunday before, where they would find me, and I accordingly returned there as soon as it was dark and remained until Wednesday evening, when discovering white men riding around the place as though they were looking for some one, and none of my men joining me, I concluded Jacob and Nat had been taken and compelled to betray me.

On this I gave up all hope for the present; and on Thursday night, after having supplied myself with provisions from Mr. Travis', I scratched a hole under a pile of fence rails in a field, where I concealed myself for six weeks, never leaving my hiding place but for a few minutes in the dead of night to get water, which was very near. Thinking by this time I could venture out, I began to go about in the night and eavesdrop the houses in the neighborhood; pursuing this course for about a fortnight and gathering little or no intelligence, afraid of speaking to any human being, and returning every morning to my cave before the dawn of day. I know not how long I might have led this life, if accident had not betrayed me. A dog in the neighborhood, passing by my hiding place one night while I was out, was attracted by some meat I had in my cave, and crawled in and stole it, and was coming out just as I returned. A few nights after, two Negroes having started to go hunting with the same dog, and passed that way, the dog came again to the place, and having just gone out to walk about, discovered me and barked, on which thinking myself discovered, I spoke to them to beg concealment. On making myself known, they fled from me. Knowing then they would betray me, I immediately left my hiding place and was pursued almost incessantly until I was taken a fortnight afterwards by Mr. Benjamin Phipps, in a little hole I had dug out with my sword, for the purpose of concealment, under the top of a fallen tree. On Mr. Phipps discovering the place of my concealment, he cocked his gun and aimed at me. I requested him not to shoot, and I would give up, upon which he demanded my sword. I delivered it to him, and he brought me to prison. During the time I was pursued, I had many hairbreadth escapes, which your time will not permit you to relate. I am here loaded with chains, and willing to suffer the fate that awaits me.

I here proceeded to make some inquiries of him, after assuring him of the certain death that awaited him, and that concealment would only bring destruction on the innocent as well as guilty, of his own color, if he knew of any extensive or concerted plan. His answer was, I do not. When I questioned him as to the insurrection in North Carolina happening about the same time, he denied any knowledge of it; and when I looked him in the face as though I would search his inmost thoughts, he replied, "I see sir, you doubt my word; but can you not think the same ideas and strange appearances about this time in the heavens might prompt others, as well as myself, to this undertaking." I now had much conversation with and asked him many questions, having forborne to do so previously, except in the cases noted in parentheses; but during his statement, I had, unnoticed by him, taken notes as to some particular circumstances, and, having the advantage of his statement before me in writing, on the evening of the third day that I had been with him, I began a cross examination and found his statement corroborated by every circumstance coming within my own knowledge, or the confessions of others who had been either killed or executed and whom he had not seen or had any knowledge since 22nd of August last. He expressed himself fully satisfied as to the impracticability of his attempt.

It has been said he was ignorant and cowardly, and that his object was to murder and rob for the purpose of obtaining money to make his escape. It is notorious, that he was never known to have a dollar in his life, to swear an oath, or drink a drop of spirits. As to his ignorance, he certainly never had the advantages of education, but he can read and write (it was taught him by his parents) and for natural intelligence and quickness of apprehension is surpassed by few men I have ever seen. As to his being a coward, his reason as given for not resisting Mr. Phipps shows the decision of his character. When he saw Mr. Phipps present his gun, he said he knew it was impossible for him to escape, as the woods were full of men; he therefore thought it was better to surrender and trust to fortune for his escape. He is a complete fanatic, or plays his part most admirably.

On other subjects he possesses an uncommon share of intelligence, with a mind capable of attaining anything; but warped and perverted by the influence of early impressions. He is below the ordinary stature, though strong and active, having the true Negro face, every feature of which is strongly marked. I shall not attempt to describe the effect of his narrative, as told and commented on by himself, in the condemned hole of the prison. The calm, deliberate composure with which he spoke of his late deeds and intentions, the expression of his fiendlike face when excited by enthusiasm, still bearing the stains of the blood of helpless innocence about him; clothed with rags and covered with chains; yet daring to raise his manacled hands to heaven, with a spirit soaring above the attributes of man; I looked on him and my blood curdled in my veins.

I will not shock the feelings of humanity, nor wound afresh the bosoms of the disconsolate sufferers in this unparalleled and inhuman massacre, by detailing the deeds of their fiendlike barbarity. There were two or three who were in the power of these wretches, had they known it, and who escaped in the most providential manner. There were two whom they thought they had left dead on the field at Mr. Parker's, but who were only stunned by the blows of their guns, as they did not take time to reload when they charged on them.

The escape of a little girl who went to school at Mr. Waller's, and where the children were collecting for that purpose, excited general sympathy. As their teacher had not arrived, they were at play in the yard, and, seeing the Negroes approach, she ran up on a dirt chimney (such as are common to log houses) and remained there unnoticed during the massacre of the eleven that were killed at this place. She remained on her hiding place till just before the arrival of a party, who were in pursuit of the murderers, when she came down and fled to a swamp, where, a mere child as she was, with the horrors of the late scene before her, she lay concealed until the next day, when seeing a party go up to the house, she came up and, on being asked how she escaped, replied with the utmost simplicity: The Lord helped her. She was taken up behind a gentleman of the party and returned to the arms of her weeping mother.

Miss Whitehead concealed herself between the bed and the mat that supported it, while they murdered her sister in the same room, without discovering her. She was afterwards carried off and concealed for protection by a slave of the family, who gave evidence against several of them on their trial. Mrs. Nathaniel Francis, while concealed in a closet heard their blows and the shrieks of the victims of these ruthless savages; they then entered the closet where she was concealed, and went out without discovering her. While in this hiding place she heard two of her women in a quarrel about the division of her clothes. Mr. John T. Baron, discovering them approaching his house, told his wife to make her escape and, scorning to fly, fell fighting on his own threshold. After firing his rifle, he discharged his gun at them and then broke it over the villain who first approached him, but he was overpowered and slain. His bravery, however, saved from the hands of these monsters his lovely and amiable wife, who will long lament a husband as deserving of her love. As directed by him, she attempted to escape through the garden, when she was caught and held by one of her servant girls, but another coming to her rescue, she fled to the woods and concealed herself. Few indeed, were those who escaped their work of death. But fortunate for society, the hand of retributive justice has overtaken them; and not one that was known to be concerned has escaped.

The Commonwealth v. *Nat Turner:*

Charged with making insurrection, and plotting to take away the lives of divers free white persons, etc., on the 22nd of August, 1831. The court composed of — — —, having met for the trial of Nat Turner, the prisoner was brought in and arraigned, and upon his arraignment pleaded *not guilty*; saying to his counsel, that he did not feel so.

On the part of the Commonwealth, Levi Waller was introduced, who being sworn, deposed as follows: (*agreeably to Nat's own Confession*). Col Trezvant [the committing magistrate] was then introduced, who being sworn, numerated Nat's Confession to him, as follows: (*his Confession as given to Mr. Gray*). The prisoner introduced no evidence, and the case was submitted without argument to the court, who having found him guilty, Jeremiah Cobb, Esq., chairman, pronounced the sentence of the court, in the following words: "Nat Turner! Stand up. Have you anything to say why sentence of death should not be pronounced against you?"

Answer: I have not. I have made a full confession to Mr. Gray, and I have nothing more to say.

"Attend then to the sentence of the court. You have been arraigned and tried before this court, and convicted of one of the highest crimes in our criminal code. You have been convicted of plotting in cold blood the indiscriminate destruction of men, of helpless women, and of infant children. The evidence before us leaves not a shadow of doubt, but that your hands were often imbrued in the blood of the innocent; and your own confession tells us that they were stained with the blood of a master, in your own language, too indulgent. Could I stop here, your crime would be sufficiently aggravated. But the original contriver of a plan, deep and deadly, one that never can be effected, you managed so far to put it into execution, as to deprive us of many of our most valuable citizens; and this was done when they were asleep, and defenseless, under circumstances shocking to humanity. And while upon this part of the subject, I cannot but call your attention to the poor misguided wretches who have gone before you. They are not few in number; they were your bosom associates; and the blood of all cries aloud, and calls upon you, as the author of their misfortune. Yes! You forced them unprepared, from Time to Eternity. Borne down by this load of guilt, your only justification is, that you were led away by fanaticism. If this be true, from my soul I pity you; and while you have my sympathies, I am, nevertheless, called upon to pass the sentence of the court. The time between this and your execution will necessarily be very short; and your only hope but must be in another world. The judgment of the court is, that you be taken hence to the jail from whence you came, thence to the place of execution, and on Friday next, between the hours of 10 A.M. and 2 P.M., be hung by the neck until you are dead! dead! dead! and may the Lord have mercy upon your soul."

A Negro View of Negro Prospects

While the Abolitionist movement dedicated its efforts to freeing slaves in the South, free Negroes in the North found that in most states they were regarded as second-class citizens. Gustave de Beaumont, who toured America with

306

Alexis de Tocqueville, noted in his novel Marie, *published in 1835, that free Negroes throughout most of the states were prohibited from voting, from serving as judge, juror, or constable, from entering theaters, hotels, or public dining rooms (except as servants), from enrolling in schools, and in some states from reading or teaching their children to read. In response to such restrictions on their civil rights, a Negro convention met at Philadelphia, June 6-11, 1831, and issued the following address to the nation. [Source:* Liberator, *October 22, 1831.]*

Respected Brethren and Fellow Citizens:

In accordance with a resolution of the last Convention, we have again assembled in order to discharge those duties which have devolved upon us by your unanimous voices.

Our attention has been called to investigate the political standing of our brethren, wherever dispersed, but more particularly the situation of those in this great republic.

Abroad, we have been cheered with pleasant views of humanity and the steady, firm, and uncompromising march of equal liberty to the human family. Despotism, tyranny, and injustice have had to retreat in order to make way for the inalienable rights of man. Truth has conquered prejudice, and mankind are about to rise in the majesty and splendor of their native dignity.

The cause of general emancipation is gaining powerful and able friends abroad. Britain and Denmark have performed such deeds as will immortalize them for their humanity in the breasts of the philanthropists of the present day; while, as a just tribute to their virtues, after ages will yet erect imperishable monuments to their memory. (Would to God we could say thus of our own native soil!)

And it is only when we look to our own native land, to the birth-place of our *fathers*, to the land for whose prosperity their blood and our sweat have been shed and cruelly extorted, that the Convention has had cause to hang its head and blush. Laws, as cruel in themselves as they were unconstitutional and unjust, have in many places been enacted aginst our poor, unfriended, and unoffending brethren; laws (without a shadow of provocation on our part) at whose bare recital the very savage draws him up for fear of the contagion—looks noble and prides himself because he bears not the name of a Christian.

307

But the Convention would not wish to dwell long on this subject, and it is one that is too sensibly felt to need description.

We would wish to turn you from this scene with an eye of pity and a breast glowing with mercy, praying that the recording angel may drop a tear which shall obliterate forever the remembrance of so foul a stain upon the national escutcheon of this great republic.

This spirit of persecution was the cause of our Convention. It was that first induced us to seek an asylum in the Canadas; and the Convention feel happy to report to their brethren that our efforts to establish a settlement in that province have not been made in vain. Our prospects are cheering; our friends and funds are daily increasing; wonders have been performed far exceeding our most sanguine expectations; already have our brethren purchased 800 acres of land — and 2,000 of them have left the soil of their birth, crossed the lines, and laid the foundation for a structure which promises to prove an asylum for the colored population of these United States. They have erected 200 log houses and have 500 acres under cultivation.

And now it is to your fostering care the Convention appeal, and we appeal to you as to men and brethren yet to enlarge their borders.

We therefore ask of you, brethren, we ask of you, philanthropists, of every color and of every kindred, to assist us in this undertaking. We look to a kind Providence and to you to say whether our desires shall be realized and our labors crowned with success.

The Convention has done its duty, and it now remains for you, brethren, to do yours. Various obstacles have been thrown in our way by those opposed to the elevation of the human species; but, thanks to an all-wise Providence, His goodness has yet cleared the way, and our advance has been slow but steady. The only thing now wanted is an accumulation of funds, in order to enable us to make a purchase agreeably to the direction of the first Convention; and, to effect that purpose, the Convention has recommended to the different societies engaged in that cause to persevere and prosecute their designs with doubled energy; and we would earnestly recommend to every colored man (who feels the weight of his degradation) to consider himself in duty bound to contribute his mite toward this great object. We would say to all that the prosperity of the rising generation mainly depends upon our active exertions.

Yes, it is with us to say whether they shall assume a rank and standing among the nations of the earth, as men and freemen, or whether they shall still be prized and held at market price. Oh, then, by a brother's love, and by all that makes man dear to man—awake in time! Be wise! Be free! Endeavor to walk with circumspection; be obedient to the laws of our common country; honor and respect its lawmakers and lawgivers; and, through all, let us not forget to respect ourselves.

During the deliberations of this Convention, we had the favor of advising and consulting with some of our most eminent and tried philanthropists—men of unblemished character and of acknowledged rank and standing. Our sufferings have excited their sympathy; our ignorance appealed to their humanity; and, brethren, we feel that gratitude is due to a kind and benevolent Creator, that our excitement and appeal have neither been in vain.

A plan has been proposed to the Convention for the erection of a college for the instruction of young men of color, on the manual labor system, by which the children of the poor may receive a regular classical education, as well as those of their more opulent brethren, and the charge will be so regulated as to put it within the reach of all. In support of this plan, a benevolent individual has offered the sum of $1,000, provided that we can obtain subscriptions to the amount of $19,000 in one year. The Convention has viewed the plan with considerable interest, and, after mature deliberation, on a candid investigation, feel strictly justified in recommending the same to the liberal patronage of our brethren, and respectfully solicit the aid of those philanthropists who feel an interest in sending light, knowledge, and truth to all of the human species.

To the friends of general education, we do believe that our appeal will not be in vain; for the present ignorant and degraded condition of many of our brethren in these United States (which has been a subject of much concern to the Convention) can excite no astonishment (although used by our enemies to show our inferiority in the scale of human beings); for, what opportunities have they possessed for mental cultivation or improvement? Mere ignorance, however, in a people divested of the means of acquiring information by books, or an extensive connection with the world, is no just criterion of their intellectual incapacity; and it has been actually seen, in various remarkable instances, that the degradation of the mind and character, which has been too hastily imputed to a people kept, as we are, at a distance from those sources of knowledge which abound in civilized and enlightened communities, has resulted from no other causes than our unhappy situation and circumstances.

True philanthropy disdains to adopt those prejudices against any people which have no better foundation than accidental diversities of color, and refuses to determine without substantial evidence and incontestable fact as the basis of her judgment. And it is in order to remove these prejudices, which are the actual causes of our ignorance, that we have appealed to our friends in support of the contemplated institution.

The Convention has not been unmindful of the operations of the American Colonization Society, and it would respectfully suggest to that august body of learning, talent, and worth that, in our humble opinion, strengthened, too, by the opinions of eminent men in this country as well as in Europe, that they are pursuing the direct road to perpetuate slavery, with all its unchristianlike concomitants, in this boasted land of freedom; and as citizens and men whose best blood is sapped to gain popularity for that institution, we would, in the most feeling manner, beg of them to desist, or, if we must be sacrificed to their philanthropy, we would rather die at home. Many of our fathers, and some of us, have fought and bled for the liberty, independence, and peace which you now enjoy and, surely, it would be ungenerous and unfeeling in you to deny us a humble and quiet grave in that country which gave us birth!

In conclusion, the Convention would remind our brethren that knowledge is power, and to that end we call on you to sustain and support by all honorable, energetic, and necessary means those presses which are devoted to our instruction and elevation; to foster and encourage the mechanical arts and sciences among our brethren; to encourage simplicity, neatness, temperance, and economy in our habits, taking due care always to give the preference to the production of freemen wherever it can be had. Of the utility of a general fund, the Convention believes there can exist but one sentiment, and that is for a speedy establishment of the same. Finally, we trust our brethren will pay due care to take such measures as will ensure a general and equal representation in the next Convention.

WILLIAM LLOYD GARRISON
For Immediate Abolition

*Sometime during the year 1829, William Lloyd Garrison changed his mind
about Negro slavery. He had always advocated its abolition, but he had been
a gradualist, holding that a slow, steady movement in the direction of freedom
would be better for whites and Negroes alike. But now he rejected this
position, which he came to condemn; for "has not the experience of two
centuries," he could say with his new understanding, "shown that gradualism
in theory is perpetuity in practice?" The change of heart would not be
important if it had not, for all practical purposes, launched the movement
known as militant Abolitionism. Probably the most influential organ of this
movement was the* Liberator, *the Boston weekly that Garrison edited from its
first issue, in January 1831, to its last, in December 1865 — the month that saw
the ratification of the Thirteenth Amendment outlawing slavery. Portions of
the famous salutatory of the* Liberator's *first issue are reprinted below.*

In the month of August I issued proposals for publishing the *Libera-*
tor in Washington City; but the enterprise, though hailed in different sections of the country, was palsied by public indifference. Since
that time, the removal of the *Genius of Universal Emancipation* to
the seat of government has rendered less imperious the establishment of a similar periodical in that quarter.

During my recent tour for the purpose of exciting the minds of
the people by a series of discourses on the subject of slavery, every
place that I visited gave fresh evidence of the fact that a greater
revolution in public sentiment was to be effected in the free
states—*and particularly in New England*—than at the South. I
found contempt more bitter, opposition more active, detraction
more relentless, prejudice more stubborn, and apathy more frozen
than among slaveowners themselves. Of course, there were individual exceptions to the contrary. This state of things afflicted but did
not dishearten me. I determined, at every hazard, to lift up the
standard of emancipation in the eyes of the nation, *within sight of*
Bunker Hill and in the birthplace of liberty. That standard is now
unfurled; and long may it float, unhurt by the spoliations of time or
the missiles of a desperate foe—yea, till every chain be broken and

every bondman set free! Let Southern oppressors tremble; let their secret abettors tremble; let their Northern apologists tremble; let all the enemies of the persecuted blacks tremble.

I deem the publication of my original prospectus unnecessary, as it has obtained a wide circulation. The principles therein inculcated will be steadily pursued in this paper, excepting that I shall not array myself as the political partisan of any man. In defending the great cause of human rights, I wish to derive the assistance of all religions and of all parties.

Assenting to the "self-evident truth" maintained in the American Declaration of Independence, "that all men are created equal and endowed by their Creator with certain inalienable rights, among which are life, liberty, and the pursuit of happiness," I shall strenuously contend for the immediate enfranchisement of our slave population. In Park Street Church, on the Fourth of July, 1829, in an address on slavery, I unreflectingly assented to the popular but pernicious doctrine of *gradual* abolition. I seize this opportunity to make a full and unequivocal recantation, and thus publicly to ask pardon of my God, of my country, and of my brethren, the poor slaves, for having uttered a sentiment so full of timidity, injustice, and absurdity. A similar recantation from my pen was published in the *Genius of Universal Emancipation* at Baltimore, in September 1829. My conscience is now satisfied.

I am aware that many object to the severity of my language; but is there not cause for severity? I *will be* as harsh as truth and as uncompromising as justice. On this subject I do not wish to think, or speak, or write with moderation. No! No! Tell a man whose house is on fire to give a moderate alarm; tell him to moderately rescue his wife from the hands of the ravisher; tell the mother to gradually extricate her babe from the fire into which it has fallen—but urge me not to use moderation in a cause like the present. I am in earnest; I will not equivocate; I will not excuse; I will not retreat a single inch—AND I WILL BE HEARD. The apathy of the people is enough to make every statue leap from its pedestal and to hasten the resurrection of the dead.

It is pretended that I am retarding the cause of emancipation by the coarseness of my invective and the precipitancy of my measures. *The charge is not true.* On this question my influence, humble as it is, is felt at this moment to a considerable extent, and shall be felt in coming years—not perniciously but beneficially: not as a curse but as a blessing—and posterity will bear testimony that I was right. I desire to thank God that IIe enables me to disregard "the fear of man which bringeth a snare," and to speak His truth in its simplicity and power.

WILLIAM LLOYD GARRISON:

The Dangers of Slavery

*Antislavery movements had existed in the United States since the Revolution. They had even received occasional support in the South, on moral grounds; but the invention of the cotton gin in 1793 made slavery a seeming economic necessity. In addition, Negro revolts like the Nat Turner uprising of 1831 stirred old fears among Southern whites, entangling the slavery question in a web of moral, social, and economic issues. As the South was uniting to defend and preserve slavery, William Lloyd Garrison began to preach a new kind of abolitionism in the North. Rejecting the efforts of colonization societies to deport freed slaves to Africa, Garrison insisted on the gradual emancipation of the slaves. His address on "The Dangers of the Nation," delivered on July 4, 1829, when he was only twenty-four years old, is reprinted in part below. [*Source: Old South Leaflets, No. 180, Boston, n. d.]*

It is natural that the return of a day which established the liberties of a brave people should be hailed by them with more than ordinary joy; and it is their duty as Christians and patriots to celebrate it with signal tokens of thanksgiving.

Fifty-three years ago, the Fourth of July was a proud day for our country. It clearly and accurately defined the rights of man; it made no vulgar alterations in the established usages of society; it presented a revelation adapted to the common sense of mankind; it vindicated the omnipotence of public opinion over the machinery of kingly government; it shook, as with the voice of a great earthquake, thrones which were seemingly propped up with atlantean pillars; it gave an impulse to the heart of the world, which yet thrills to its extremities. . . .

I speak not as a partisan or an opponent of any man or measures when I say that our politics are rotten to the core. *We* boast of our freedom, who go shackled to the polls, year after year, by tens and hundreds and thousands! *We* talk of free agency, who are the veriest machines, the merest automata, in the hands of unprincipled jugglers! *We* prate of integrity and virtue and independence, who sell our birthright for office, and who, nine times in ten, do not get Esau's bargain—no, not even a mess of pottage!

Is it republicanism to say that the majority can do no wrong? Then I am not a republican. Is it aristocracy to say that the people sometimes shamefully abuse their high trust? Then I am an aristocrat.

It is not the appreciation but the abuse of liberty to withdraw altogether from the polls, or to visit them merely as a matter of form, without carefully investigating the merits of candidates. The republic does not bear a charmed life; our prescriptions, administered through the medium of the ballot box—the mouth of the political body—may kill or cure, according to the nature of the disease and our wisdom in applying the remedy. It is possible that a people may bear the title of freemen who execute the work of slaves. To the dullest observers of the signs of the times, it must be apparent that we are rapidly approximating to this condition. . . .

But there is another evil which, if we had to contend against nothing else, should make us quake for the issue. It is gangrene preying upon our vitals, an earthquake rumbling under our feet, a mine accumulating materials for a national catastrophe. It should make this a day of fasting and prayer, not of boisterous merriment and idle pageantry; a day of great lamentation, not of congratulatory joy. It should spike every cannon and haul down every banner. Our garb should be sackcloth, our heads bowed in the dust, our supplications for the pardon and assistance of Heaven.

Last week this city was made breathless by a trial of considerable magnitude. The court chamber was inundated for hours, day after day, with a dense and living tide which swept along like the rush of a mountain torrent. Tiers of human bodies were piled up to the walls, with almost miraculous condensation and ingenuity. It

314

seemed as if men abhorred a vacuum equally with nature; they would suspend themselves, as it were, by a nail and stand upon air with the aid of a peg. Although it was a barren, ineloquent subject, and the crowd immense, there was no perceptible want of interest, no evidence of impatience. The cause was important, involving the reputation of a distinguished citizen. There was a struggle for mastery between two giants, a test of strength in tossing mountains of law. The excitement was natural.

I stand up here in a more solemn court, to assist in a far greater cause; not to impeach the character of one man but of a whole people; not to recover the sum of $100,000 but to obtain the liberation of 2 million of wretched, degraded beings, who are pining in hopeless bondage, over whose sufferings scarcely an eye weeps or a heart melts or a tongue pleads either to God or man. I regret that a better advocate had not been found to enchain your attention and to warm your blood. Whatever fallacy, however, may appear in the argument, there is no flaw in the indictment; what the speaker lacks, the cause will supply.

Sirs, I am not come to tell you that slavery is a curse, debasing in its effect, cruel in its operation, fatal in its continuance. The day and the occasion require no such revelation. I do not claim the discovery as my own, that "all men are created equal," and that among their inalienable rights are "life, liberty, and the pursuit of happiness." Were I addressing any other than a free and Christian assembly, the enforcement of this truth might be pertinent. Neither do I intend to analyze the horrors of slavery for your inspection, nor to freeze your blood with authentic recitals of savage cruelty. Nor will time allow me to explore even a furlong of that immense wilderness of suffering which remains unsubdued in our land. I take it for granted that the existence of these evils is acknowledged, if not rightly understood. My object is to define and enforce our duty as Christians and philanthropists. . . .

I assume as distinct and defensible propositions:

1. That the slaves of this country, whether we consider their moral, intellectual, or social condition, are preeminently entitled to the prayers and sympathies and charities of the American people; and their claims for redress are as strong as those of any Americans could be in a similar condition.

315

2. That as the free states, by which I mean nonslaveholding states, are constitutionally involved in the guilt of slavery by adhering to a national compact that sanctions it, and in the danger by liability to be called upon for aid in case of insurrection, they have the right to remonstrate against its continuance and it is their duty to assist in its overthrow.

3. That no justificative plea for the perpetuity of slavery can be found in the condition of its victims, and no barrier against our righteous interference in the laws which authorize the buying, selling, and possessing of slaves, nor in the hazard of a collision with slaveholders.

4. That education and freedom will elevate our colored population to a rank with the whites, making them useful, intelligent, and peaceable citizens.

In the first place, it will be readily admitted that it is the duty of every nation primarily to administer relief to its own necessities, to cure its own maladies, to instruct its own children, and to watch over its own interests. He is "worse than an infidel" who neglects his own household and squanders his earnings upon strangers; and the policy of that nation is unwise which seeks to proselyte other portions of the globe at the expense of its safety and happiness. . . .

The condition of the slaves, in a religious point of view, is deplorable, entitling them to a higher consideration, on our part, than any other race . . . higher than our red men of the forest, for we do not bind them with gyves [shackles] nor treat them as chattels.

And here let me ask—What has Christianity done, by direct effort, for our slave population? Comparatively nothing. She has explored the isles of the ocean for objects of commiseration; but, amazing stupidity, she can gaze without emotion on a multitude of miserable beings at home, large enough to constitute a nation of freemen, whom tyranny has heathenized by law. In her public services they are seldom remembered, and in her private donations they are forgotten. . . .

I have said that the claims of the slaves for redress are as strong as those of any Americans could be in a similar condition. Does any man deny the position? The proof, then, is found in the fact that a very large proportion of our colored population were born on our soil and are therefore entitled to all the privileges of American citizens. This is their country by birth, not by adoption. Their children possess the same inherent and inalienable rights as ours; and it is a crime of the blackest dye to load them with fetters.

Every Fourth of July, our Declaration of Independence is produced, with a sublime indignation, to set forth the tyranny of the mother country and to challenge the admiration of the world. But what a pitiful detail of grievances does this document present in comparison with the wrongs which our slaves endure! In the one case, it is hardly the plucking of a hair from the head; in the other, it is the crushing of a live body on the wheel — the stings of the wasp contrasted with the tortures of the Inquisition. Before God, I must say that such a glaring contradiction as exists between our creed and practice the annals of 6,000 years cannot parallel. In view of it, I am ashamed of my country.

I am sick of our unmeaning declamation in praise of liberty and equality; of our hypocritical cant about the inalienable rights of man. I could not, for my right hand, stand up before a European assembly and exult that I am an American citizen, and denounce the usurpations of a kingly government as wicked and unjust; or, should I make the attempt, the recollection of my country's barbarity and despotism would blister my lips and cover my cheeks with burning blushes of shame.

Will this be termed a rhetorical flourish? Will any man coldly accuse me of intemperate zeal? I will borrow, then, a ray of humanity from one of the brightest stars in our American galaxy, whose light will gather new effulgence to the end of time. "This, sirs, is a cause that would be dishonored and betrayed if I contented myself with appealing only to the understanding. It is too cold and its processes are too slow for the occasion. I desire to thank God that, since He has given me an intellect so fallible, He has impressed upon me an instinct that is sure. On a question of shame and honor — liberty and oppression — reasoning is sometimes useless, and worse. I feel the decision in my pulse: if it throws no light upon the brain, it kindles a fire at the heart." . . .

I come to my second proposition, the right of the free states to remonstrate against the continuance and to assist in the overthrow of slavery.

This, I am aware, is a delicate subject, surrounded with many formidable difficulties. But if delay only adds to its intricacy, wherefore shun an immediate investigation? I know that we of the North

317

affectedly believe that we have no local interest in the removal of this great evil; that the slave states can take care of themselves, and that any proffered assistance on our part would be rejected as impertinent, dictatorial, or meddlesome; and that we have no right to lift up even a note of remonstrance. But I believe that these opinions are crude, preposterous, dishonorable, unjust. Sirs, this is a business in which, as members of one great family, we have a common interest; but we take no responsibility, either individually or collectively. Our hearts are cold, our blood stagnates in our veins. We act, in relation to the slaves, as if they were something lower than the brutes that perish.

On this question I ask no support from the injunction of Holy Writ which says, "Therefore all things whatsoever ye would that men should do to you, do ye even so to them: for this is the law and the prophets." I throw aside the common dictates of humanity. I assert the right of the free states to demand a gradual abolition of slavery, because, by its continuance, they participate in the guilt thereof and are threatened with ultimate destruction; because they are bound to watch over the interests of the whole country without reference to territorial divisions; because their white population is nearly double that of the slave states, and the voice of this overwhelming majority should be potential; because they are now deprived of their just influence in the councils of the nation; because it is absurd and anti-republican to suffer property to be represented as men and vice versa; because it gives the South an unjust ascendancy over other portions of territory, and a power that may be perverted on every occasion. . . .

Now I say that, on the broad system of equal rights, this monstrous inequality should no longer be tolerated. If it cannot be speedily put down, not by force but by fair persuasion; if we are always to remain shackled by unjust constitutional provisions when the emergency that imposed them has long since passed away; if we must share in the guilt and danger of destroying the bodies and souls of men *as the price of our Union;* if the slave states will haughtily spurn our assistance and refuse to consult in the general welfare, then the fault is not ours if a separation eventually takes place. . . .

It may be objected that the laws of the slave states form insurmountable barriers to any interference on our part.

Answer: I grant that we have not the right, and I trust not the disposition, to use coercive measures. But do these laws hinder our prayers or obstruct the flow of our sympathies? Cannot our charities alleviate the condition of the slave, and perhaps break his fetters? Can we not operate upon public sentiment (the lever that can move the moral world) by way of remonstrance, advice, or entreaty? . . .

Suppose that, by a miracle, the slaves should suddenly become white. Would you shut your eyes upon their sufferings and calmly talk of constitutional limitations? No, your voice would peal in the ears of the taskmasters like deep thunder; you would carry the Constitution by force if it could not be taken by treaty; patriotic assemblies would congregate at the corners of every street; the old cradle of liberty would rock to a deeper tone than ever echoed therein at British aggression; the pulpit would acquire new and unusual eloquence from our holy religion. The argument that these white slaves are degraded would not then obtain. You would say: It is enough that they are white and in bondage, and they ought immediately to be set free. You would multiply your schools of instruction and your temples of worship, and rely on them for security. . . .

But the plea is prevalent that any interference by the free states, however benevolent or cautious it might be, would only irritate and inflame the jealousies of the South and retard the cause of emancipation.

If any man believes that slavery can be abolished without a struggle with the worst passions of human nature, quietly, harmoniously, he cherishes a delusion. It can never be done unless the age of miracles returns. No, we must expect a collision full of sharp asperities and bitterness. We shall have to contend with the insolence and pride and selfishness of many a heartless being. But these can be easily conquered by meekness and perseverance and prayer. . . .

If it be still objected that it would be dangerous to liberate the present race of blacks, I answer [that] the emancipation of all the slaves of this generation is most assuredly out of the question. The fabric which now towers above the Alps must be taken away brick by brick and foot by foot, till it is reduced so low that it may be overturned without burying the nation in its ruins. Years may elapse before the completion of the achievement; generations of blacks may go down to the grave, manacled and lacerated, without a hope for their children; the philanthropists who are now pleading in behalf of the oppressed may not live to witness the dawn which will precede the glorious day of universal emancipation; but the work will go on, laborers in the cause will multiply, new resources will be discovered, the victory will be obtained, worth the desperate struggle of a thousand years. Or, if defeat follow, woe to the safety of this people! The nation will be shaken as if by a mighty earthquake. . . . The terrible judgments of an incensed God will complete the catastrophe of republican America.

And since so much is to be done for our country; since so many prejudices are to be dispelled, obstacles vanquished, interests secured, blessings obtained; since the cause of emancipation must progress heavily and meet with much unhallowed opposition, why delay the work? There must be a beginning and now is a propitious time, perhaps the last opportunity that will be granted us by a long-suffering God. . . . Let us not look coldly on and see our Southern brethren contending single-handed against an all-powerful foe: faint, weary, borne down to the earth. We are all alike guilty. Slavery is strictly a national sin. New England money has been expended in buying human flesh; New England ships have been freighted with sable victims; New England men have assisted in forging the fetters of those who groan in bondage. . . .

I will say, finally, that I despair of the republic while slavery exists therein. If I look up to God for success, no smile of mercy or forgiveness dispels the gloom of futurity. . . . Why should we slumber at this momentous crisis? . . . If we had any regard for our safety and happiness, we should strive to crush the vampire which is feeding upon our lifeblood. All the selfishness of our nature cries aloud for a better security. Our own vices are too strong for us and keep us in perpetual alarm. How, in addition to these, shall we be able to contend successfully with millions of armed and desperate men, as we must eventually if slavery does not cease?

THOMAS DARTMOUTH RICE

Jump, Jim Crow

"Jim Crow," the Negro stereotype who was a famous minstrel show personality throughout the nineteenth century and whose name came later to stand for the segregation of Negroes, is said to have been created in 1828 by the showman, Thomas ("Daddy") Rice. Rice blackened his face, wore old clothes, and performed a song and dance routine in which he imitated the jerky movements and unintelligible utterances of a decrepit and malformed Negro he claimed he had once seen. The act was immediately popular and was widely copied by other entertainers. Rice published a version of "Jump, Jim Crow" in 1830, but the song underwent numerous alterations, taking on topical references like the Calypso songs of today. The version printed here makes reference to some political and other events of the Jacksonian period. [Source: Brown University, Harris Collection of American Poetry and Plays, Series of Old American Songs, No. 15.]

Come listen all you girls and boys
    I'm just from Tuckahoe;
I'm going to sing a little song—
    My name's Jim Crow.

    Chorus:
    Wheel about, turn about,
    Do just so;
    Every time I wheel about
    I jump Jim Crow.

I'm a roarer on the fiddle,
    And down in old Virginny,
They say I play the skientific
    Like Massa Pagganninny.

Then I go to Washington
    With bank memorial;
But find they talk such nonsense
    I spend my time with Sal.

Then I go to the President
　He ask me what I do;
I put the veto on the boot
　And nullify the shoe.

Then I go to New York,
　To put them right all there;
But find so many tick heads,
　I give up in despair.

I walk down to the Battery
　With Dina by my side;
And there we see Miss Watson,
　The Paganini bride.

She sing so lovely that my heart
　Go pit a pat just so;
I wish she'd fall in love with me,
　I'd let Miss Dina go.

SAMUEL CORNISH and JOHN RUSSWURM
The First Negro Newspaper

The Abolitionist movement of the 1830s was antedated by numerous organizations and newspapers dedicated not only to the emancipation of slaves in the Southern states but also to gaining equal opportunities and respect for the free Negroes in the Northern states. The first Negro graduate of Bowdoin College, John Russwurm, joined with Samuel Cornish in founding the earliest newspaper written by and for the Negroes of America. The first issue of Freedom's Journal *appeared on March 16, 1827, in New York City, and contained the following Abolitionist editorial. Though Russwurm and Cornish originally opposed efforts to establish an African colony for American Negroes, they finally succumbed to the unrelenting prejudices of U.S. society,*

*writing in the end: "We consider it mere waste of words to talk of ever
enjoying citizenship in this country." Russwurm himself later
emigrated to Liberia.*

To Our Patrons:

In presenting our first number to our patrons, we feel all the
diffidence of persons entering upon a new and untried line of business. But a moment's reflection upon the noble objects which we
have in view by the publication of this journal; the expediency of its
appearance at this time, when so many schemes are in action
concerning our people, encourage us to come boldly before an
enlightened public. For we believe that a paper devoted to the
dissemination of useful knowledge among our brethren, and to their
moral and religious improvement, must meet with the cordial
approbation of every friend to humanity.

The peculiarities of this journal render it important that we
should advertise to the world our motives by which we are actuated
and the objects which we contemplate.

We wish to plead our own cause. Too long have others spoken for
us. Too long has the public been deceived by misrepresentations in
things which concern us dearly, though, in the estimation of some,
mere trifles; for though there are many in society who exercise
toward us benevolent feelings, still (with sorrow we confess it) there
are others who make it their business to enlarge upon the least trifle
which tends to the discredit of any person of color, and pronounce
anathemas and denounce our whole body for the misconduct of this
guilty one. We are aware that there are many instances of vice
among us, but we avow that it is because no one has taught its
subjects to be virtuous; many instances of poverty, because no
sufficient efforts accommodated to minds contracted by slavery and
deprived of early education have been made, to teach them how to
husband their hard earnings and to secure to themselves comforts.

Education being an object of the highest importance to the
welfare of society, we shall endeavor to present just and adequate
views of it, and to urge upon our brethren the necessity and expediency of training their children, while young, to habits of industry,
and thus forming them for becoming useful members of society. It
is surely time that we should awake from this lethargy of years and

323

make a concentrated effort for the education of our youth. We form a spoke in the human wheel, and it is necessary that we should understand our [de]pendence on the different parts, and theirs on us, in order to perform our part with propriety.

Though not desirous of dictating, we shall feel it our incumbent duty to dwell occasionally upon the general principles and rules of economy. The world has grown too enlightened to estimate any man's character by his personal appearance. Though all men acknowledge the excellency of Franklin's maxims, yet comparatively few practise upon them. We may deplore, when it is too late, the neglect of these self-evident truths, but it avails little to mourn. Ours will be the task of admonishing our brethren on these points.

The civil rights of a people being of the greatest value, it shall ever be our duty to vindicate our brethren, when oppressed, and to lay the case before the public. We shall also urge upon our brethren (who are qualified by the laws of the different states) the expediency of using their elective franchise, and of making an independent use of the same. We wish them not to become the tools of party.

And as much time is frequently lost, and wrong principles instilled, by the perusal of works of trivial importance, we shall consider it a part of our duty to recommend to our young readers such authors as will not only enlarge their stock of useful knowledge but such as will also serve to stimulate them to higher attainments in science.

We trust, also, that through the columns of the *Freedom's Journal* many practical pieces, having for their bases the improvement of our brethren, will be presented to them from the pens of many of our respected friends, who have kindly promised their assistance.

It is our earnest wish to make our journal a medium of intercourse between our brethren in the different states of this great confederacy; that through its columns an expression of our sentiments on many interesting subjects which concern us may be offered to the public; that plans which apparently are beneficial may be candidly discussed and properly weighed; if worthy, receive our cordial approbation, if not, our marked disapprobation.

Useful knowledge of every kind and everything that relates to Africa shall find a ready admission into our columns; and as that vast continent becomes daily more known, we trust that many things will come to light proving that the natives of it are neither so ignorant nor stupid as they have generally been supposed to be.

And while these important subjects shall occupy the columns of the *Freedom's Journal,* we would not be unmindful of our brethren who are still in the iron fetters of bondage. They are our kindred by all the ties of nature; and though but little can be effected by us, still let our sympathies be poured forth, and our prayers in their behalf ascend to Him who is able to succor them.

From the press and the pulpit we have suffered much by being incorrectly represented. Men whom we equally love and admire have not hesitated to represent us disadvantageously without becoming personally acquainted with the true state of things, nor discerning between virtue and vice among us. The virtuous part of our people feel themselves sorely aggrieved under the existing state of things – they are not appreciated.

Our vices and our degradation are ever arrayed against us, but our virtues are passed by unnoticed. And what is still more lamentable, our friends, to whom we concede all the principles of humanity and religion, from these very causes seem to have fallen into the current of popular feeling and are imperceptibly floating on the stream – actually living in the practice of prejudice, while they abjure it in theory and feel it not in their hearts. Is it not very desirable that such should know more of our actual condition, and of our efforts and feelings, that in forming or advocating plans for our amelioration, they may do it more understandingly? In the spirit of candor and humility we intend by a simple representation of facts to lay our case before the public, with a view to arrest the progress of prejudice and to shield ourselves against the consequent evils. We wish to conciliate all and to irritate none, yet we must be firm and unwavering in our principles and persevering in our efforts.

If ignorance, poverty, and degradation have hitherto been our unhappy lot, has the eternal decree gone forth that our race alone are to remain in this state, while knowledge and civilization are shedding their enlivening rays over the rest of the human family? The recent travels of Denham and Clapperton in the interior of Africa, and the interesting narrative which they have published; the establishment of the republic of Haiti after years of sanguinary warfare; its subsequent progress in all the arts of civilization; and

325

the advancement of liberal ideas in South America, where despotism has given place to free governments and where many of our brethren now fill important civil and military stations, prove the contrary.

The interesting fact that there are 500,000 free persons of color, one-half of whom might peruse, and the whole be benefited by the publication of the *Journal;* that no publication, as yet, has been devoted exclusively to their improvement; that many selections from approved standard authors, which are within the reach of few, may occasionally be made; and, more important still, that this large body of our citizens have no public channel — all serve to prove the real necessity, at present, for the appearance of the *Freedom's Journal.*

It shall ever be our desire so to conduct the editorial department of our paper as to give offense to none of our patrons, as nothing is further from us than to make it the advocate of any partial views, either in politics or religion. What few days we can number have been devoted to the improvement of our brethren; and it is our earnest wish that the remainder may be spent in the same delightful service.

In conclusion, whatever concerns us as a people will ever find a ready admission into the *Freedom's Journal,* interwoven with all the principal news of the day.

And while everything in our power shall be performed to support the character of our journal, we would respectfully invite our numerous friends to assist by their communications, and our colored brethren to strengthen our hands by their subscriptions, as our labor is one of common cause and worthy of their consideration and support. And we most earnestly solicit the latter, that if at any time we should seem to be zealous or too pointed in the inculcation of any important lesson, they will remember that they are equally interested in the cause in which we are engaged, and attribute our zeal to the peculiarities of our situation and our earnest engagedness in their well-being.

Anonymous: On Educating Negro Women

Freedom's Journal, the first Negro newspaper, served not only as a forum for the Abolitionist sentiments of educated Negroes, but also as an official sounding board for the average Negro whose views heretofore had seldom been published. The August 10, 1827, issue of the paper carried the following letter, in which an anonymous author, "Matilda," made a humble plea for female education. It is noteworthy not only as one of the earliest entreaties for women's rights made by a Negro but also because it was written when Emma Hart Willard and Catharine Beecher were just beginning their crusades.

Messrs. Editors,

Will you allow a female to offer a few remarks upon a subject that you must allow to be all-important? I don't know that in any of your papers you have said sufficient upon the education of females. I hope you are not to be classed with those who think that our mathematical knowledge should be limited to "fathoming the dish-kettle," and that we have acquired enough of history if we know that our grandfather's father lived and died. It is true the time has been when to darn a stocking and cook a pudding well was considered the end and aim of a woman's being. But those were days when ignorance blinded men's eyes. The diffusion of knowledge has destroyed those degrading opinions, and men of the present age allow that we have minds that are capable and deserving of culture.

There are difficulties, and great difficulties, in the way of our advancement; but that should only stir us to greater efforts. We possess not the advantages with those of our sex whose skins are not colored like our own, but we can improve what little we have and make our one talent produce twofold. The influence that we have over the male sex demands that our minds should be instructed and improved with the principles of education and religion, in order that this influence should be properly directed. Ignorant ourselves, how can we be expected to form the minds of our youth and conduct them in the paths of knowledge? How can we "teach the young *idea* how to shoot" if we have none ourselves? There is a great responsibility resting somewhere, and it is time for us to be up and doing.

I would address myself to all mothers, and say to them that while it is necessary to possess a knowledge of cookery and the various mysteries of pudding making, something more is requisite. It is their bounden duty to store their daughters' minds with useful learning. They should be made to devote their leisure time to reading books, whence they would derive valuable information which could never be taken from them.

I will not longer trespass on your time and patience. I merely throw out these hints in order that some more able pen will take up the subject.

Matilda

RICHARD FURMAN
A Religious Defense of Slavery

Slavery was defended in the South not only on economic but also on religious grounds, and many preachers found justification for the "peculiar institution" in the Bible. They pointed out that the Old Testament told, apparently without censure, of the ownership of slaves by the patriarchs, and they cited passages in the New Testament that seemed to support slavery in the Roman Empire. To clergymen such as Richard Furman, the Bible, which was the book of the highest law, gave divine sanction to the American practice. Representing the South Carolina Baptists, Furman in 1822 wrote and presented the following declaration to the governor of the state, who responded with unqualified praise. The significant portions of the declaration appear below. [Source: Rev. Dr. Richard Furman's Exposition of the Views of the Baptists, Relative to the Coloured Population of the United States, in a Communication to the Governor of South-Carolina, Charleston, 1823, pp. 7-16.]

On the lawfulness of holding slaves, considering it in a moral and religious view, the convention think it their duty to exhibit their sentiments on the present occasion before Your Excellency, because they consider their duty to God, the peace of the state, the satisfaction of scrupulous consciences, and the welfare of the slaves themselves as intimately connected with a right view of the subject. The rather, because certain writers on politics, morals, and religion, and some of them highly respectable, have advanced positions and inculcated sentiments very unfriendly to the principle and practice of holding slaves; and, by some, these sentiments have been advanced among us, tending in their nature *directly* to disturb the domestic peace of the state, to produce insubordination and rebellion among the slaves, and to infringe the rights of our citizens; and *indirectly* to deprive the slaves of religious privileges by awakening in the minds of their masters a fear that acquaintance with the Scriptures and the enjoyment of these privileges would naturally produce the aforementioned effects; because the sentiments in opposition to the holding of slaves have been attributed by their advocates to the Holy Scriptures and to the genius of Christianity.

These sentiments, the convention, on whose behalf I address Your Excellency, cannot think just or well-founded; for the right of holding slaves is clearly established in the Holy Scriptures, both by precept and example. In the Old Testament, the Israelites were directed to purchase their bondmen and bondmaids of the heathen nations; except they were of the Canaanites, for these were to be destroyed. And it is declared that the persons purchased were to be their "bondmen forever," and an "inheritance for them and their children." They were not to go out free in the year of jubilee, as the Hebrews, who had been purchased, were; the line being clearly drawn between them. . . .

Had the holding of slaves been a moral evil, it cannot be supposed that the inspired apostles, who feared not the faces of men and were ready to lay down their lives in the cause of their God, would have tolerated it for a moment in the Christian Church. If they had done so on a principle of accommodation, in cases where the masters remained heathen, to avoid offenses and civil commotion, yet, surely, where both master and servant were Christian, as in the case before us, they would have enforced the law of Christ and required that the master should liberate his slave in the first instance. But, instead of this, they let the relationship remain untouched as being lawful and right, and insist on the relative duties.

In proving this subject justifiable by scriptural authority, its morality is also proved; for the Divine Law never sanctions immoral actions.

The Christian Golden Rule of doing to others as we would they should do to us has been urged as an unanswerable argument against holding slaves. But surely this rule is never to be urged against that order of things which the Divine Government has established; nor do our desires become a standard to us, under this rule, unless they have a due regard to justice, propriety, and the general good. . . .

If the holding of slaves is lawful, or according to the Scriptures, then this scriptural rule can be considered as requiring no more of the master, in respect of justice (whatever it may do in point of generosity) than what he, if a slave, could consistently wish to be done to himself, while the relationship between master and servant should be still continued.

In this argument, the advocates for emancipation blend the ideas of injustice and cruelty with those which respect the existence of slavery, and consider them as inseparable. But, surely, they may be separated. A bond-servant may be treated with justice and humanity as a servant; and a master may, in an important sense, be the guardian and even father of his slaves. . . .

That Christian nations have not done all they might, or should have done, on a principle of Christian benevolence for the civilization and conversion of the Africans; that much cruelty has been practised in the slave trade, as the benevolent Wilberforce and others have shown; that much tyranny has been exercised by individuals, as masters over their slaves, and that the religious interests of the latter have been too much neglected by many cannot, will not be denied. But the fullest proof of these facts will not also prove that the holding men in subjection, as slaves, is a moral evil and inconsistent with Christianity. Magistrates, husbands, and fathers have proved tyrants. This does not prove that magistracy, the husband's right to govern, and parental authority are unlawful and wicked. The individual who abuses his authority and acts with cruelty must answer for it at the Divine Tribunal, and civil authority should interpose to prevent or punish it; but neither civil nor ecclesiastical authority can consistently interfere with the possession and legitimate exercise of a right given by the Divine Law. . . .

It appears to be equally clear that those, who by reasoning on abstract principles, are induced to favor the scheme of general emancipation, and who ascribe their sentiments to Christianity, should be particularly careful, however benevolent their intentions may be, that they do not by a perversion of the scriptural doctrine, through their wrong views of it, not only invade the domestic and religious peace and rights of our citizens on this subject but, also by an intemperate zeal, prevent indirectly the religious improvement of the people they design, professedly, to benefit; and, perhaps, become, evidently, the means of producing in our country scenes of anarchy and blood. And all this in a vain attempt to bring about a state of things which, if arrived at, would not probably better the state of that people; which is thought by men of observation to be generally true of the Negroes in the Northern states who have been liberated.

To pious minds it has given pain to hear men, respectable for intelligence and morals, sometimes say that holding slaves is indeed indefensible, but that to us it is necessary and must be supported. On this principle, mere politicians, unmindful of morals, may act. But surely, in a moral and religious view of the subject, this principle is inadmissible. It cannot be said that theft, falsehood, adultery, and murder are become necessary and must be supported. Yet there is reason to believe that some of honest and pious intentions have found their minds embarrassed, if not perverted, on this subject by this plausible but unsound argument. From such embarrassment the view exhibited above affords relief.

The convention, sir, are far from thinking that Christianity fails to inspire the minds of its subjects with benevolent and generous sentiments; or that liberty, rightly understood or enjoyed, is a blessing of little moment. The contrary of these positions they maintain. But they also consider benevolence as consulting the truest and best interests of its objects; and view the happiness of liberty as well as of religion as consisting not in the name or form but in the reality. While men remain in the chains of ignorance and error, and under the dominion of tyrant lusts and passions, they cannot be free. And the more freedom of action they have in this state, they are but the more qualified by it to do injury both to themselves and others. It is, therefore, firmly believed that general emancipation to the Negroes in this country would not, in present circumstances, be for their own happiness, as a body; while it would be extremely injurious to the community at large in various ways; and, if so, then it is not required even by benevolence.

But acts of benevolence and generosity must be free and volun-tary; no man has a right to compel another to the performance of them. This is a concern which lies between a man and his God. If a man has obtained slaves by purchase, or inheritance, and the hold-ing of them as such is justifiable by the law of God, why should he be required to liberate them, because it would be a generous action, rather than another, on the same principle, to release his debtors or sell his lands and houses and distribute the proceeds among the poor? These also would be generous actions. Are they, therefore, obligatory? Or, if obligatory, in certain circumstances, as personal, voluntary acts of piety and benevolence, has any man or body of men, civil or ecclesiastic, a right to require them? Surely those who are advocates for compulsory or strenuous measures to bring about emancipation should duly weigh this consideration.

Should, however, a time arrive when the Africans in our country might be found qualified to enjoy freedom, and, when they might obtain it in a manner consistent with the interest and peace of the community at large, the convention would be happy in seeing them free. And so they would, in seeing the state of the poor, the ignorant, and the oppressed of every description and of every country mel-iorated; so that the reputed free might be free, indeed, and happy. But there seems to be just reason to conclude that a considerable part of the human race, whether they bear openly the character of slaves or are reputed freemen, will continue in such circumstances, with mere shades of variation, while the world continues. . . .

And here I am brought to a part of the general subject which, I confess to Your Excellency, the convention, from a sense of their duty as a body of men to whom important concerns of religion are confided, have particularly at heart, and wish it may be seriously considered by all our citizens: This is the religious interests of the Negroes. For though they are slaves, they are also men; and are with ourselves accountable creatures, having immortal souls and being destined to future eternal award. Their religious interests claim a regard from their masters of the most serious nature; and it is indispensable. Nor can the community at large, in a right esti-mate of their duty and happiness, be indifferent on this subject. To the truly benevolent it must be pleasing to know that a number of masters, as well as ministers and pious individuals of various Christian denominations among us, do conscientiously regard this duty; but there is great reason to believe that it is neglected and disregarded by many.

The convention are particularly unhappy in considering that an idea of the Bible's teaching the doctrine of emancipation as necessary, and, tending to make servants insubordinate to proper authority, has obtained access to any mind; both on account of its direct influence on those who admit it, and the fear it excites in others, producing the effects before noticed. But it is hoped it has been evinced that the idea is an erroneous one, and that it will be seen that the influence of a right acquaintance with that Holy Book tends directly and powerfully, by promoting the fear and love of God, together with just and peaceful sentiments toward men, to produce one of the best securities to the public for the internal and domestic peace of the state.

PETER JAY
Against Disfranchising Negro Freemen in New York

Property ownership as a qualification for voting had seldom been challenged before the 1820s. However, as merchants, manufacturers, craftsmen, and small plot farmers became more numerous, and as the large estates that had been associated with the propertied class were divided into smaller holdings, many pressed for universal suffrage. In September 1821 the New York State constitutional convention met and formed a committee to review the electoral laws of the state. The discussion that ensued revealed a wide range of viewpoints during a month of hard debate. Nathan Sanford introduced and defended a resolution, ultimately adopted, that extended suffrage to all white taxpayers regardless of their property holdings. This democratic sentiment did not, however, extend to the free Negro, who, ironically, was now threatened with disfranchisement. Peter Jay, the son of John Jay, spoke up in the

333

convention in defense of Negro voting rights, but in the end these rights were
curtailed rather than extended in the new constitution. [*Source:* Reports
of the Proceedings and Debates of the Convention of 1821, Assembled for
the Purpose of Amending the Constitution of the State of New-York, *Albany,*
1821, pp. 183-185.]

The chairman of the select committee has given a fair and candid
exposition of the reasons that induced them to make the report now
under consideration, and of the motives by which they were governed. He has clearly stated why they were desirous of extending
the right of suffrage to some who did not at present enjoy it, but he
has wholly omitted to explain why they deny it to others who actually possess it. The omission, however, has been supplied by one of
his colleagues, who informed us that all who were not white ought
to be excluded from political rights, because such persons were
incapable of exercising them discreetly, and because they were
peculiarly liable to be influenced and corrupted. These reasons, sir, I
shall notice presently.

When this Convention was first assembled, it was generally
understood that provisions would be made to extend the right
of suffrage, and some were apprehensive that it might be extended
to a degree which they could not approve. But, sir, it was not expected that this right was in any instance to be restricted, much less
was it anticipated, or desired, that a single person was to be disfranchised. Why, sir, are these men to be excluded from rights
which they possess in common with their countrymen? What crime
have they committed for which they are to be punished? Why are
they, who were born as free as ourselves, natives of the same
country, and deriving from nature and our political institutions
the same rights and privileges which we have, now to be deprived
of all those rights, and doomed to remain forever as aliens among
us?

We are told, in reply, that other states have set us the example.
It is true that other states treat this race of men with cruelty and
injustice, and that we have hitherto manifested toward them a
disposition to be just and liberal. Yet, even in Virginia and North
Carolina, free people of color are permitted to vote, and, if I am
correctly informed, exercise that privilege. In Pennsylvania, they

334

are much more numerous than they are here, and there they are not disfranchised, nor has any inconvenience been felt from extending to all men the rights which ought to be common to all. In Connecticut, it is true, they have, for the last three years, adopted a new constitution, which prevents people of color from acquiring the right of suffrage in future, yet even there they have preserved the right of all those who previously possessed it.

Mr. Chairman, I would submit to the consideration of the committee whether the proposition of the gentleman from Saratoga is consistent with the Constitution of the United States. That instrument provides that "citizens of each state shall be entitled to all the privileges and immunities of citizens in the several states." No longer ago than last November, the legislature of this state almost unanimously resolved that "if the provisions contained in any proposed constitution of a new state deny to any citizens of the existing states the privileges and immunities of citizens of such new state, that such proposed constitution should not be accepted or confirmed; the same in the opinion of this legislature being void by the Constitution of the United States." Now, sir, is not the right of suffrage a privilege? And can you deny it to a citizen of Pennsylvania, who comes here and complies with your laws, merely because he is not six feet high, or because he is of a dark complexion?

But we are told by one of the select committee that people of color are incapable of exercising the right of suffrage. I may have misunderstood that gentleman; but I thought he meant to say that they labored under a physical disability. It is true that some philosophers have held that the intellect of a black man is naturally inferior to that of a white one; but this idea has been so completely refuted, and is now so universally exploded, that I did not expect to have heard of it in an assembly so enlightened as this, nor do I now think it necessary to disprove it.

That in general the people of color are inferior to the whites in knowledge and in industry, I shall not deny. You made them slaves, and nothing is more true than the ancient saying, "The day you make a man a slave takes half his worth away." Unaccustomed to provide for themselves, and habituated to regard labor as an evil, it is no wonder that when set free, they should be improvident and idle, and that their children should be brought up without education, and without prudence or forethought. But will you punish the children for your own crimes; for the injuries which you have inflicted upon their parents? Besides, sir, this state of things is fast passing away. Schools have been opened for them, and it will, I am sure, give pleasure to this committee to know that in these schools there is discovered a thirst for instruction, and a progress in learning, seldom to be seen in the other schools of the state. They have also churches of their own, and clergymen of their own color, who conduct their public worship with perfect decency and order, and not without ability.

[This state, Mr. Chairman, has taken high ground against slavery and all its degrading consequences and accompaniments. There are gentlemen on this floor who, to their immortal honor, have defended the cause of] this oppressed people in Congress, and I trust they will not now desert them. Adopt the amendment now proposed, and you will hear a shout of triumph and a hiss of scorn from the Southern part of the Union, which I confess will mortify me — I shall shrink at the sound because I fear it will be deserved. But it has been said that this measure is necessary to preserve the purity of your elections. I do not deny that necessity has no law, and that self-preservation may justify in states, as well as in individuals, an infringement of the rights of others. Were I a citizen of one of the Southern states, I would not (much as I abhor slavery) advise an immediate and universal emancipation.

But where is the necessity in the present instance? The whole number of colored people in the state, whether free or in bondage, amounts to less than a fortieth part of the whole population. When your numbers are to theirs as forty to one, do you still fear them? To assert this would be to pay them a compliment, which, I am sure, you do not think they deserve. But there are a greater number in the city of New York. How many? Sir, in even that city, the whites are to the blacks as ten to one. And even of the tenth which is composed of the black population, how few are there that are entitled to vote? It has also been said that their numbers are rapidly increasing. The very reverse is the fact. During the last ten years, in which the white population has advanced with astonishing rapidity, the colored population of the state has been stationary. This fact appears from the official returns of the last and the preceding census, and completely refutes the arguments which are founded upon this misstatement. Will you, then, without necessity, and merely to gratify an unreasonable prejudice, stain the constitution you are about to form, with a provision equally odious and unjust, and in direct violation of the principles which you profess, and upon which you intend to form it? I trust, I am sure, you will not.

ANONYMOUS

Motives for Stopping the Domestic Slave Trade

Although smuggling of Negro slaves persisted until about 1860, the importation of slaves into the United States had been strictly forbidden by legislation passed during the first two decades of the century. These regulations did not prohibit the slave trade within the U. S. borders, and, consequently, the domestic slave business boomed. Opposition to commerce in slaves was frequently based on other than humanitarian motives. Many Southerners, such as the anonymous author of the following piece, were fearful of Negro insurrections and believed that it was in the best interest of slave owners to regulate the interstate slave trade. This letter was sent by a "citizen" to the editor of a Georgia newspaper. [Source: Journal (Milledgeville, Ga.), December 4, 1821.]

The policy of prohibiting the further introduction of slaves for the purpose of speculation is so obvious that it seems almost preposterous to attempt its proof. The arguments in its support are so numerous and so strong as almost to overwhelm us. We scarcely know where to begin or where to end them. It is difficult to imagine a clearer truth than that it is inexpedient to increase an acknowledged evil. The following are some of the considerations which forbid the introduction of slaves for the purpose of speculation.

Every man knows that speculators would constantly introduce

337

into the state the dregs of the colored population of the states north of us; that the jails of North and South Carolina, Maryland, and Virginia would be disgorged upon this deluded state. Negro speculators, many of whom would come from other states, and would fear none of the calamities they might bring on us, would naturally introduce among us Negroes of the worst character, because, in many instances, they would purchase them for half price; and the villain who might attempt the assassination of his master, the rape of his mistress, or the conflagration of a city, might, in a few days, be transported to Georgia and sold to an unsuspecting citizen for the hard earnings of his honest labor. To the dealer in human flesh, it would be a matter of little consequence if the next day he perpetrated any or all those crimes!

But not only would speculators constantly introduce firebrands among our colored people; but they would, in very many instances, inveigle and run off the slaves of our fellow citizens north of us; they would, by fraud and violence, tear from the dearest associations and sell among us persons as much entitled to personal liberty by the laws of the land as the reader who kindly gives me his attention while I endeavor to show him the magnitude of one of the greatest calamities which would afflict this state; I mean, an unrestricted domestic slave trade! It is perhaps needless to detail instances of the stealing of Negroes, bond and free, which might easily be cited. The reader's memory will easily supply them; as well as some notable instances in which men from the South have expiated these offenses by the most ignominious punishments in the North; thus casting the blackness of their character on the section of country to which they belonged.

Who sees not the progress of society? Who sees not the spirit of the age? Can anyone be insensible of the increasing disposition of Virginia, Maryland, and some other states to throw off their colored population? When they have made any considerable advance toward this object, will they not assume the tone of the Northern states? Will they not join in the imposition of "restrictions" upon the slaveholding states? May they not promote *abolition* in the South? Insensible as they may become in process of time to the difficulties and dangers of the South, may they not pursue a course of conduct tending to produce a state of things too horrible to contemplate? It is clearly incumbent on Georgia to persevere in her countervailing policy; it is clearly incumbent on her to refuse to receive in her bosom the colored population of states who, after relieving themselves of the greatest weight that presses on them, may, at some remote period, join in a general crusade against the South.

We should forbear to increase the aggregate amount of investments in property, which, by the progress of society, by the operations of a spirit which is evidently gone abroad in Christendom, may become not only worthless but dangerous. Nor ought it to destroy the force of this reasoning, that these consequences may be remote. He who confines his views to the present moment, he who endeavors not to avert from future generations the calamities which threaten them, is alike unworthy of the name of a parent and of a politician.

The late discussions on the subject of slavery with reference to Missouri shook our political fabric to its foundations. Will the citizens of Georgia consent to increase an evil which so lately threatened a dissolution of the Union and the annihilation of the best hopes of man? . . .

We know the vast excess of colored people in the West Indies. Within a few years, we have seen a government established in one of the largest of them, which is constantly increasing in numbers and intelligence, in physical and moral and political importance and which portends the most terrible convulsions in the West Indies. Constituted and situated as the Southern states are, can they hope to remain entirely undisturbed by those convulsions? And is it not one of the plainest dictates of policy, nay, of *common sense*, not to *increase* the numbers of an enemy already too numerous! I say, *enemy;* for such, in the nature of man, they necessarily are; and let it be remembered, too, *that they overspread our entire country and occupy the most commanding positions.* . . .

If the great state of South Carolina has pursued an oscillating policy in relation to the slave trade, it may furnish ground for regret, but certainly furnishes no matter for the imitation of other states. It remains for Georgia, placed as she is between the old and the new slaveholding states, to exhibit an example of steady and enlightened policy; which, while it shall prevent the increase of an acknowledged evil by suppressing *the speculation* in slaves, shall yet allow

339

to citizens and to emigrants the right to introduce them for their own use, or the use of their children; and shall extend to our colored population all the comfort that is consistent with their situation and the good of the community. In this way, she might, from her circumstances and her local situation, exert the most benign influence on the fate of unborn millions of both colors: She might secure the applause and the benedictions of the world.

But, it may possibly be supposed that an increase of the number of our slaves is necessary on account of the late acquisitions and of further contemplated acquisitions of territory. This is denied. We have already laborers enough to cut down and exhaust our territory as fast as we can extinguish the Indian title. But suppose an increase of laborers necessary; citizens and emigrants already have the right to make this increase for their own use. And though the permanent interests of the community might perhaps require an adoption of the Virginia policy, yet, perhaps, for the blindness of our mind and the hardness of our heart, it might be better to continue, for the present, the policy of permitting citizens or real emigrants to introduce slaves for their own use, and only to direct our efforts against the colossal evil of the *speculation* in slaves.

Yet the Virginia policy may demand consideration. They have closed every avenue to the further introduction of slaves; and they afford every facility gradually to drain off a population, for whose introduction they now reproach the memory of their ancestors—a population which has exhausted their soil, deteriorated their morals, and endangered their repose. This policy is sanctioned by their Washingtons and Henrys and Jeffersons and Monroes. It is not for me to decide whether a policy adapted to the situation of Virginia is suited to the circumstances of Georgia; or whether the great principles which constitute the best support of her policy are equally applicable to all nations, all times, and all circumstances.

340

JOHN QUINCY ADAMS

Slavery and the Constitution

*The complexity of the issues involved in the debate about the Missouri Compromise is revealed in the selection that appears below from the diary of John Quincy Adams, dated March 3, 1820, only three days before the Missouri Enabling Act went into effect. President Monroe had assembled his cabinet (Adams was secretary of state) for advice before signing the bills admitting Maine and Missouri, and Adams recommended their acceptance. He did so despite the fact that he believed that slavery was a profound moral evil. At the same time, however, he was convinced that the Constitution did not give the federal government the power to abolish the institution. "The abolition of slavery where it is established must be left entirely to the people of the state itself," he declared in a letter of the same date to Governor Jonathan Jennings of Indiana. "The healthy have no right to reproach or to prescribe for the diseased." [*Source:* Memoirs of John Quincy Adams, Comprising Portions of his Diary from 1795 to 1848, Charles Francis Adams, ed., Vol. V, Philadelphia, 1875, pp. 4-12.]*

When I came this day to my office, I found there a note requesting me to call at one o'clock at the President's house. It was then one, and I immediately went over. He expected that the two bills—for the admission of Maine, and to enable Missouri to make a constitution—would have been brought to him for his signature, and he had summoned all the members of the administration to ask their opinions, in writing, to be deposited in the Department of State, upon two questions: (1) whether Congress had a constitutional right to prohibit slavery in a territory; and (2) whether the 8th Section of the Missouri bill (which interdicts slavery *forever* in the territory north of thirty-six and a half latitude) was applicable only to the territorial state, or could extend to it after it should become a state.

As to the first question, it was unanimously agreed that Congress have the power to prohibit slavery in the Territories; and yet neither Crawford, Calhoun, nor Wirt could find any express power to that effect given in the Constitution; and Wirt declared himself very decidedly against the admission of any implied powers. The progress of this discussion has so totally merged in passion all the reasoning faculties of the slave-holders, that these gentlemen, in the simplicity of their hearts, had come to a conclusion in direct opposition to their premises, without being aware or conscious of inconsistency. They insisted upon it that the clause in the Constitution, which gives Congress power to dispose of and make all *needful* rules and regulations respecting the territory and other property of the United States, had reference to it only as land, and conferred no authority to make rules binding upon its inhabitants; and Wirt added the notable Virginian objection, that Congress could make only *needful* rules and regulations, and that a prohibition of slavery was not *needful.*

Their argument, as Randolph said of it in the House, covered the whole ground, and their compromise, measured by their own principles, is a sacrifice of what they hold to be the Constitution. I had no doubt of the right of Congress to interdict slavery in the Territories, and urged that the power contained in the term "dispose of" included the authority to do everything that could be done with it as mere property, and that the additional words, authorizing needful rules and regulations respecting it, must have reference to persons connected with it, or could have no meaning at all. As to the force of the term needful, I observed, it was relative, and must always be supposed to have reference to some end. Needful to what end? Needful in the Constitution of the United States to any of the ends for which that compact was formed. Those ends are declared in its preamble; to establish justice, for example. What can be more needful for the establishment of justice than the interdiction of slavery where it does not exist? . . .

After this meeting, I walked home with Calhoun, who said that . . . in the Southern country . . . domestic labor was confined to the blacks; and such was the prejudice that if he, who was the most popular man in his district, were to keep a white servant in his house, his character and reputation would be irretrievably ruined.

I said that this confounding of the ideas of servitude and labor was one of the bad effects of slavery; but he thought it attended with many excellent consequences. It did not apply to all kinds of labor—not, for example, to farming. He himself had often held the plough; so had his father. Manufacturing and mechanical labor

342

was not degrading. It was only manual labor — the proper work of slaves. No white person could descend to that. And it was the best guarantee to equality among the whites. It produced an unvarying level among them. It not only did not excite but did not even admit of inequalities, by which one white man could domineer . . .

I told Calhoun I could not see things in the same light. It is, in truth, all perverted sentiment — mistaking labor for slavery, and dominion for freedom. The discussion of this Missouri question has betrayed the secret of their souls. In the abstract they admit that slavery is an evil, they disclaim all participation in the introduction of it, and cast it all upon the shoulders of our old Grandam Britain. But when probed to the quick upon it, they show at the bottom of their souls pride and vainglory in their condition of masterdom. They fancy themselves more generous and noblehearted than the plain freemen who labor for subsistence. They look down upon the simplicity of a Yankee's manners, because he has no habits of overbearing like theirs and cannot treat Negroes like dogs.

It is among the evils of slavery that it taints the very sources of moral principle. It establishes false estimates of virtue and vice; for what can be more false and heartless than this doctrine which makes the first and holiest rights of humanity to depend upon the color of the skin? It perverts human reason, and reduces man endowed with logical powers to maintain that slavery is sanctioned by the Christian religion, that slaves are happy and contented in their condition, that between master and slave there are ties of mutual attachment and affection, that the virtues of the master are refined and exalted by the degradation of the slave; while at the same time they vent execrations upon the slave trade, curse Britain for having given them slaves, burn at the stake Negroes convicted of crimes for the terror of the example, and writhe in agonies of fear at the very mention of human rights as applicable to men of color. The impression produced upon my mind by the progress of this discussion is that the bargain between freedom and slavery contained in the Constitution of the United States is morally and politically vicious, inconsistent with the principles upon which alone our Revolution can be justified; cruel and oppressive, by riveting the chains of slavery, by pledging the faith of freedom to maintain and perpetuate the tyranny of the master; and grossly unequal and impolitic, by admitting that slaves are at once enemies to be kept in subjection, property to be secured or restored to their owners, and persons not to be represented themselves, but for whom their masters are privileged with nearly a double share of representation. The consequence has been that this slave representation has governed the Union.

Benjamin portioned above his brethren has ravined as a wolf. In the morning he has devoured the prey, and at night he has divided the spoil. It would be no difficult matter to prove, by reviewing the history of the Union under this Constitution, that almost everything which has contributed to the honor and welfare of the nation has been accomplished in spite of them or forced upon them, and that everything unpropitious and dishonorable, including the blunders and follies of their adversaries, may be traced to them.

I have favored this Missouri Compromise, believing it to be all that could be effected under the present Constitution, and from extreme unwillingness to put the Union at hazard. But perhaps it would have been a wiser as well as a bolder course to have persisted in the restriction upon Missouri, till it should have terminated in a convention of the states to revise and amend the Constitution. This would have produced a new Union of thirteen or fourteen States, unpolluted with slavery, with a great and glorious object to effect; namely, that of rallying to their standard the other states by the universal emancipation of their slaves. If the Union must be dissolved, slavery is precisely the question upon which it ought to break. For the present, however, this contest is laid asleep.

THOMAS JEFFERSON

A Firebell in the Night

The Missouri Compromise, by the terms of which slavery was henceforth excluded from the territories north of latitude 36°30' (the southern boundary of Missouri), alarmed Thomas Jefferson, as he told John Holmes in this famous letter, "like a firebell in the night." The vividness of the image was in keeping

*with the passions of the time. Jefferson disapproved deeply of slavery; but he
even more strongly disapproved of any action on the part of Congress that, in
his view, exceeded its constitutional authority. Slavery, Jefferson felt, would die
a natural death if left alone; but the very life of the Union depended on
maintaining a due measure in legislative acts. In addition, the Compromise
had drawn a line across the country on the basis of a principle, and not of
geography; such a line, held up, as Jefferson put it, to the angry passions of
men, could have no other ultimate effect than the disastrous rending of the
body politic. Holmes, a Massachusetts man, was one of the few Northern
congressmen to vote against the Tallmadge Amendment that would have
excluded slavery from Missouri itself; Jefferson's prophetic letter to him was
written April 22, 1820, a short month after the passage of the Missouri
Compromise. [*Source: Memoirs, Correspondence, and Private Papers of
Thomas Jefferson, *Thomas Jefferson Randolph, ed., London, 1829, vol IV, pp.
323-333.*]*

I thank you, dear sir, for the copy you have been so kind as to send
me of the letter to your constituents on the Missouri question. It is a
perfect justification to them. I had for a long time ceased to read
newspapers, or pay any attention to public affairs, confident they
were in good hands, and content to be a passenger in our bark to the
shore from which I am not distant. But this momentous question,
like a firebell in the night, awakened and filled me with terror. I
considered it at once as the knell of the Union. It is hushed, indeed,
for the moment. But this is a reprieve only, not a final sentence. A
geographical line, coinciding with a marked principle, moral and
political, once conceived and held up to the angry passions of men,
will never be obliterated; and every new irritation will mark it
deeper and deeper. I can say, with conscious truth, that there is not
a man on earth who would sacrifice more than I would to relieve us
from this heavy reproach, in any *practicable* way.

The cession of that kind of property, for so it is misnamed, is a
bagatelle which would not cost me a second thought, if, in that way,
a general emancipation and *expatriation* could be effected; and
gradually, and with due sacrifices, I think it might be. But as it is,
we have the wolf by the ears, and we can neither hold him, nor
safely let him go. Justice is in one scale, and self-preservation in the
other. Of one thing I am certain, that as the passage of slaves from

one state to another would not make a slave of a single human being who would not be so without it, so their diffusion over a greater surface would make them individually happier, and proportionally facilitate the accomplishment of their emancipation, by dividing the burden on a greater number of coadjutors. An abstinence too, from this act of power, would remove the jealousy excited by the undertaking of Congress to regulate the condition of the different descriptions of men composing a state. This certainly is the exclusive right of every state, which nothing in the Constitution has taken from them and given to the general government. Could Congress, for example, say that the non-freemen of Connecticut shall be freemen, or that they shall not emigrate into any other state?

I regret that I am now to die in the belief that the useless sacrifice of themselves by the generation of 1776, to acquire self-government and happiness to their country, is to be thrown away by the unwise and unworthy passions of their sons, and that my only consolation is to be that I live not to weep over it. If they would but dispassionately weigh the blessings they will throw away against an abstract principle more likely to be effected by union than by scission, they would pause before they would perpetrate this act of suicide on themselves, and of treason against the hopes of the world. To yourself, as the faithful advocate of the Union, I tender the offering of my high esteem and respect.

5. The New Nation

1777 - 1819

RUFUS KING

Against the Extension of Slavery to the New States

Slavery was permitted by French and Spanish laws in the territory of the Louisiana Purchase. After the War of 1812, therefore, no opposition arose when Southern slave owners took their property into the region. Nor did they hesitate to include slavery in their constitution when they asked to be admitted to the Union as the State of Missouri. But when a bill for this purpose came before the House in February 1819, James Tallmadge of New York surprised and angered the Southern members by offering an amendment prohibiting the further introduction of slaves into the area, and providing for the eventual emancipation of those who were already there. The amended bill passed the House but was lost in the Senate, and thus was put over to the next session of Congress. What was at stake was the tacit political balance between North and South that had prevailed since 1787. The North in the interval had drawn ahead in population, and therefore in the number of members it sent to the House. But the balance was maintained in the Senate, which in the admission of new states to the Union had always accepted free and slave states alternately; after the admission of Alabama in 1819 there were just eleven of each kind. The Missouri debate was not on the morals of slavery but on the question of sectional power and prestige. Senator Rufus King of New York, who in the following remarks argued for the Missouri restriction, was an old Federalist. He but uttered the long-standing resentment of his party at the dominance of the South, particularly Virginia, in national politics. King sent the substance of two of his speeches on the Missouri bill to Hezekiah Niles, who published them in his popular journal. [Source: Niles' Weekly Register, December 4, 1819.]

The Constitution declares "that Congress shall have power to dispose of, and make all needful rules and regulations respecting the territory and other property of the United States." Under this power, Congress have passed laws for the survey and sale of the public lands, for the division of the same into separate territories; and have ordained for each of them a constitution, a place of temporary government, whereby the civil and political rights of the inhabitants are regulated, and the rights of conscience and other natural rights are protected.

The power to make all needful regulations includes the power to determine what regulations are needful; and if a regulation prohibiting slavery within any territory of the United States be, as it has been, deemed needful, Congress possess the power to make the same, and, moreover, to pass all laws necessary to carry this power into execution.

The territory of Missouri is a portion of Louisiana, which was purchased of France, and belongs to the United States in full dominion; in the language of the Constitution, Missouri is their territory, or property, and is subject, like other territories of the United States, to the regulations and temporary government which has been, or shall be, prescribed by Congress. The clause of the Constitution, which grants this power to Congress, is so comprehensive and unambiguous, and its purpose so manifest, that commentary will not render the power, or the object of its establishment, more explicit or plain.

The Constitution further provides, that "new states may be admitted by Congress into the Union."

As this power is conferred without limitation, the time, terms, and circumstances of the admission of new states are referred to the discretion of Congress, which may admit new states, but are not obliged to do so—of right no new state can demand admission into the Union unless such demand be founded upon some previous engagement with the United States.

When admitted by Congress into the Union, whether by compact or otherwise, the new state becomes entitled to the enjoyment of the same rights, and bound to perform the like duties, as the other states, and its citizens will be entitled to all privileges and immunities of citizens in the several states.

The citizens of each state possess rights and owe duties that are peculiar to and arise out of the constitution and laws of the several states. These rights and duties differ from each other in the different states, and among these differences, none is so remarkable or important as that which proceeds from the constitution and laws of the several states respecting slavery; the same being permitted in some states, and forbidden in others.

The question respecting slavery in the old thirteen states had been decided and settled before the adoption of the Constitution, which grants no power to Congress to interfere with or to change what had been previously settled. The slave states, therefore, are free to continue or to abolish slavery. Since the year 1808, Congress has possessed power to prohibit, and have prohibited, the further migration or importation of slaves into any of the old thirteen states, and at all times under the Constitution have had power to prohibit such migration or importation into any of the new states or territories of the United States. The Constitution contains no express provisions respecting slavery in a new state that may be admitted into the Union; every regulation upon this subject belongs to the power whose consent is necessary to the formation and admission of such state. Congress may, therefore, make it a condition of the admission of a new state that slavery shall be forever prohibited within the same. We may, with the more confidence, pronounce this to be the construction of the Constitution, as it has been so amply confirmed by the past decisions of Congress. . . .

Although Congress possess the power of making the exclusion of slavery a part or condition of the act admitting a new state into the Union, they may, in special cases, and for sufficient reasons, forbear to exercise this power. Thus, Kentucky and Vermont were admitted as new states into the Union without making the abolition of slavery the condition of their admission. In Vermont, slavery never existed, her laws excluding the same. Kentucky was formed out of, and settled by, Virginia, and the inhabitants of Kentucky, equally with those of Virginia, by fair interpretation of the Constitution, were exempt from all such interference of Congress as might disturb or impair the security of their property in slaves. . . .

If Congress possess the power to exclude slavery from Missouri, it still remains to be shown that they ought to do so. The examination of this branch of the subject, for obvious reasons, is attended with peculiar difficulty, and cannot be made without passing over arguments which to some of us might appear to be decisive, but the use of which, in this place, would call up feelings the influence of which would disturb, if not defeat, the impartial consideration of the subject.

Slavery unhappily exists within the United States. Enlightened

351

men in the states where it is permitted, and everywhere out of them, regret its existence among us, and seek for the means of limiting and of mitigating it. The first introduction of slaves is not imputable to the present generation, nor even to their ancestors. Before the year 1642, the trade and ports of the colonies were open to foreigners equally as those of the mother country, and as early as 1620, a few years only after planting the colony of Virginia, and the same in which the first settlement was made in the old colony of Plymouth, a cargo of Negroes was brought into and sold as slaves in Virginia by a foreign ship. From this beginning the importation of slaves was continued for nearly two centuries. To her honor, Virginia, while a colony, opposed the importation of slaves, and was the first state to prohibit the same by a law passed for this purpose in 1778, thirty years before the general prohibition enacted by Congress in 1808. The laws and customs of the states in which slavery has existed for so long a period must have had their influence on the opinions and habits of the citizens, which ought not to be disregarded on the present occasion.

Omitting, therefore, the arguments which might be urged, and which by all of us might be deemed conclusive, were this an original question, the reasons which shall be offered in favor of the interposition of the power of Congress to exclude slavery from Missouri shall be only such as respect the common defense, the general welfare, and that wise administration of government which as far as possible may produce the impartial distribution of benefits and burdens throughout the Union.

By the Articles of Confederation, the common treasury was to be supplied by the several states according to the value of the land, with the houses and improvements thereon, within the respective states. From the difficulty in making this valuation, the old Congress were unable to apportion the requisitions for the supply of the general treasury, and obliged the states to propose an alteration of the Articles of Confederation, by which the whole number of free persons, with three-fifths of the slaves contained in the respective states, should become the rule of such apportionment of the taxes. A majority of the states approved of this alteration, but some of them disagreed to the same; and for want of a practicable rule of apportionment, the whole of the requisitions of taxes made by Congress

352

during the Revolutionary War, and afterward, up to the establishment of the Constitution of the United States, were merely provisional and subject to revision and correction as soon as such rules should be adopted. The several states were credited for their supplies, and charged for the advances made to them by Congress, but no settlement of their accounts could be made, for the want of a rule of apportionment, until the establishment of the Constitution.

When the general convention that formed the Constitution took the subject into their consideration, the whole question was once more examined; and while it was agreed that all contributions to the common treasury should be made according to the ability of the several states to furnish the same, the old difficulty recurred in agreeing upon a rule whereby such ability should be ascertained, there being no simple standard by which the ability of individuals to pay taxes can be ascertained. A diversity in the selection of taxes has been deemed requisite to their equalization. Between communities this difficulty is less considerable, and although the rule of relative numbers would not accurately measure the wealth of nations, in states in the circumstances of the United States, whose institutions, laws, and employments are so much alike, the rule of number is probably as nearly equal as any other simple and practicable rule can be expected to be (though between the old and new states its equity is defective). These considerations, added to the approbation which had already been given to the rule by a majority of the states, induced the convention to agree that direct taxes should be apportioned among the states according to the whole number of free persons, and three-fifths of the slaves which they might respectively contain.

The rule for apportionment of taxes is not necessarily the most equitable rule for the apportionment of representatives among the states; property must not be disregarded in the composition of the first rule, but frequently is overlooked in the establishment of the second. A rule which might be approved in respect to taxes would be disapproved in respect to representatives; one individual, possessing twice as much property as another, might be required to pay double the taxes of such other; but no man has two votes to another's one; rich or poor, each has but one vote in the choice of representatives.

In the dispute between England and the colonies, the latter denied the right of the former to tax them, because they were not represented in the English Parliament. They contended that, according to the law of the land, taxation and representation were inseparable. The rule of taxation being agreed upon by the convention, it is possible that the maxim with which we successfully opposed the claim of England may have had an influence in procuring the adoption of the same rule for the apportionment of representatives. The true meaning, however, of this principle of the English constitution is that a colony or district is not to be taxed which is not represented; not that its number or representative shall be ascertained by its quota of taxes. If three-fifths of the slaves are virtually represented, or their owners obtain a disproportionate power in legislation and in the appointment of the president of the United States, why should not other property be virtually represented, and its owners obtain a like power in legislation and in the choice of the President? Property is not confined to slaves but exists in houses, stores, ships, capital in trade, and manufactures. To secure to the owners of property in slaves, greater political power than is allowed to the owners of other and equivalent property seems to be contrary to our theory of the equality of personal rights, inasmuch as the citizens of some states thereby become entitled to other and greater political power than citizens of other states.

The present House of Representatives consists of 181 members, which are apportioned among the states in a ratio of 1 representative for every 35,000 federal members, which are ascertained by adding to the whole number of free persons three-fifths of the slaves. According to the last census, the whole number of slaves within the United States was 1,191,364, which entitled the states possessing the same to 20 representatives and 20 presidential electors, more than they would be entitled to were the slaves excluded. By the last census, Virginia contained 582,104 free persons and 392,518 slaves. In any of the states where slavery is excluded, 582,104 free persons would be entitled to elect only 16 representatives, while in Virginia, 582,104 free persons, by the addition of three-fifths of her slaves, become entitled to elect, and do in fact elect, 23 representatives, being 7 additional ones on account of her slaves. Thus, while 35,000 free persons are requisite to elect 1 representative in a state where slavery is prohibited, 25,559 free persons in Virginia may, and do, elect a representative—so that 5 free persons in Virginia have as much power in the choice of representatives to Congress, and in the appointment of presidential electors, as 7 free persons in any of the states in which slavery does not exist.

This inequality in the apportionment of representatives was not misunderstood at the adoption of the Constitution, but as no one anticipated the fact that the whole of the revenue of the United States would be derived from indirect taxes (which cannot be supposed to spread themselves over the several states, according to the rule for the apportionment of direct taxes), but it was believed that a part of the contribution to the common treasury would be apportioned among the states by the rule for the apportionment of representatives. The states in which slavery is prohibited, ultimately, though with reluctance, acquiesced in the disproportionate number of representatives and electors that was secured to the slaveholding states. The concession was, at the time, believed to be a great one, and has proved to have been the greatest which was made to secure the adoption of the Constitution.

Great, however, as this concession was, it was definite, and its full extent was comprehended. It was a settlement between the thirteen states. The considerations arising out of their actual condition, their past connection, and the obligation which all felt to promote a reformation in the federal government were peculiar to the time and to the parties, and are not applicable to the new states, which Congress may now be willing to admit into the Union.

The equality of rights, which includes an equality of burdens, is a vital principle in our theory of government, and its jealous preservation is the best security of public and individual freedom; the departure from this principle in the disproportionate power and influence, allowed to the slaveholding states, was a necessary sacrifice to the establishment of the Constitution. The effect of this Constitution has been obvious to the preponderance it has given to the slaveholding states over the other states. Nevertheless, it is an ancient settlement, and faith and honor stand pledged not to disturb it. But the extension of this disproportionate power to the new states would be unjust and odious. The states whose power would be abridged, and whose burdens would be increased by the measure, cannot be expected to consent to it; and we may hope that the other states are too magnanimous to insist on it.

The existence of slavery impairs the industry and the power of a nation; and it does so in proportion to the multiplication of its slaves: where the manual labor of a country is performed by slaves, labor dishonors the hands of freemen.

If her laborers are slaves, Missouri may be able to pay money taxes, but will be unable to raise soldiers or to recruit seamen; and experience seems to have proved that manufactures do not prosper where the artificers are slaves. In case of foreign war or domestic insurrection, misfortunes from which no states are exempt, and against which all should be seasonably prepared, slaves not only do not add to but diminish the faculty of self-defense; instead of increasing the public strength, they lessen it, by the whole number of free persons whose place they occupy, increased by the number of freemen that may be employed as guards over them.

The motives for the admission of new states into the Union are the extension of the principles of our free government; the equalizing of the public burdens; and the consolidation of the power of the confederated nation. Unless these objects be promoted by the admission of new states, no such admission can be expedient or justified.

The states in which slavery already exists are contiguous to each other; they are also the portion of the United States nearest to the European colonies in the West Indies — colonies whose future condition can hardly be regarded as problematical. If Missouri, and the other states that may be formed to the west of the River Mississippi, are permitted to introduce and establish slavery, the repose, if not the security, of the Union may be endangered; all the states south of the River Ohio and west of Pennsylvania and Delaware, will be peopled with slaves, and the establishment of new states west of the River Mississippi will serve to extend slavery instead of freedom over that boundless region.

Such increase of the states, whatever other interests it may promote, will be sure to add nothing to the security of the public liberties; and can hardly fail hereafter to require and produce a change in our government.

356

On the other hand, if slavery be excluded from Missouri, and the other new states which may be formed in this quarter, not only will the slave markets be broken up, and the principles of freedom be extended and strengthened, but an exposed and important frontier will present a barrier which will check and keep back foreign assailants, who may be as brave and, as we hope, will be as free as ourselves. Surrounded in this manner by connected bodies of freemen, the states where slavery is allowed will be made more secure against domestic insurrection, and less liable to be affected by what may take place in the neighboring colonies.

It ought not to be forgotten that the first and main object of the negotiation which led to the acquisition of Louisiana was the free navigation of the Mississippi—a river that forms the sole passage from the Western states to the ocean. This navigation, although of general benefit, has been always valued and desired as of peculiar advantage to the Western states, whose demands to obtain it were neither equivocal nor unreasonable. But with the River Mississippi, by a sort of coercion, we acquired by ill or good fortune, as our future measures shall determine, the whole province of Louisiana. As this acquisition was made at the common expense, it is very fairly urged that the advantages to be derived from it should also be common. This, it is said, will not happen if slavery be excluded from Missouri, as the citizens of states where slavery is permitted will be shut out, and none but citizens of states where slavery is prohibited can become inhabitants of Missouri.

But this consequence will not arise from the proposed exclusion of slavery. The citizens of states in which slavery is allowed, like all other citizens, will be free to become the inhabitants of the Missouri, in like manner as they have become inhabitants of Ohio, Indiana, and Illinois, in which slavery is forbidden. The exclusion of slavery from Missouri will not, therefore, operate unequally among the citizens of the United States. The Constitution provides "that the citizens of each state shall be entitled to enjoy all the rights and immunities of citizens of the several states"—every citizen may therefore remove from one to another state, and there enjoy the rights and immunities of its citizens—the proposed provision excludes slaves, not citizens, whose rights it will not and cannot impair.

357

Besides, there is nothing new or peculiar in a provision for the exclusion of slavery; it has been established in the states northwest of the River Ohio, and has existed from the beginning in the old states where slavery is forbidden. The citizens of states where slavery is allowed may become inhabitants of Missouri, but cannot hold slaves there, nor in any other state where slavery is prohibited. As well might the laws prohibiting slavery in the old states become the subject of complaint as the proposed exclusion of slavery in Missouri; but there is no foundation for such complaint in either case. It is further urged that the admission of slaves into Missouri would be limited to the slaves already within the United States; that their health and comfort would be promoted by their dispersion; and that their numbers would be the same, whether they remain confined to the states where slavery exists, or are dispersed over the new states that are admitted into the Union.

That none but domestic slaves would be introduced into Missouri, and the other new and frontier states, is most fully disproved by the thousands of fresh slaves which, in violation of our laws, are annually imported into Alabama, Louisiana, and Mississippi.

We may renew our efforts, and enact new laws with heavier penalties, against the importation of slaves; the revenue cutters may more diligently watch our shores; and the naval force may be employed on the coast of Africa and on the ocean to break up the slave trade, but these means will not put an end to it. So long as markets are open to the purchase of slaves, so long they will be supplied; and so long as we permit the existence of slavery in our new and frontier states, so long slave markets will exist. The plea of humanity is equally inadmissible; since no one who has ever witnessed the experiment will believe that the condition of slaves is made better by the breaking up and separation of their families, nor by their removal from the old states to the new ones; and the objection to the provision of the bill, excluding slavery from Missouri, is equally applicable to the like prohibition of the old states; these should be revoked in order that the slaves, now confined to certain states, may, for their health and comfort and multiplication be spread over the whole Union.

That the condition of slaves within the United States has been improved, and the rigors of slavery mitigated by the establishment

358

and progress of our free governments, is a fact that imparts consolation to all who have taken pains to inquire concerning it. The disproportionate increase of free persons of color can be explained only by the supposition that the practice of emancipation is gaining ground; a practice which there is reason to believe would become more general if a plan could be devised by which the comforts and morals of the emancipated slaves could be satisfactorily provided for. For it is not to be doubted that public opinion everywhere, and especially in the oldest state of the Union, is less favorable than formerly to the existence of slavery. Generous and enlightened men in the states where slavery exists have discovered much solicitude on the subject, a desire has been manifested that emancipation might be encouraged by the establishment of a place or colony, without the United States, to which free persons of color might be removed; and great efforts for that purpose are making, with corresponding anxiety for their success. Those persons, enlightened and humane as they are known to be, surely will be unwilling to promote the removal of slaves from the old states to the new ones, where their comforts will not be multiplied, and where their fetters may be riveted forever.

Slavery cannot exist in Missouri without the consent of Congress; the question may, therefore, be considered, in certain lights, as a new one, it being the first instance in which an inquiry respecting slavery, in a case so free from the influence of the ancient laws and usages of the country, has come before the Senate.

The territory of Missouri is beyond our ancient limits, and the inquiry whether slavery shall exist there is open to many of the arguments that might be employed had slavery never existed within the United States. It is a question of no ordinary importance. Freedom and slavery are the parties which stand this day before the Senate; and upon its decision the empire of the one or the other will be established in the new state which we are about to admit into the Union.

If slavery be permitted in Missouri, with the climate and soil and in the circumstances of this territory, what hope can be entertained that it will ever be prohibited in any of the new states that will be formed in the immense region west of the Mississippi? Will the coextensive establishment of slavery and of new states throughout this region lessen the danger of domestic insurrection or of foreign aggression? Will this manner of executing the great trust of admitting new states into the Union contribute to assimilate our manners and usages, to increase our mutual affection and confidence, and to establish that equality of benefits and burdens which constitutes the true basis of our strength and union? Will the militia of the nation, which must furnish our soldiers and seamen, increase as slaves increase; will the actual disproportion in the military service of the nation be thereby diminished—a disproportion that will be, as it has been, readily borne, as between the original states, because it arises out of their compact of union, but which may become a badge of inferiority, if required for the protection of those who, being free to choose, persist in the establishment of maxims, the inevitable effect of which will deprive them of the power to contribute to the common defense, and even of the ability to protect themselves?

There are limits within which our federal system must stop; no one has supposed that it could be indefinitely extended—we are now about to pass our original boundary; if this can be done without affecting the principles of our free government, it can be accomplished only by the most vigilant attention to plant, cherish, and sustain the principles of liberty in the new states that may be formed beyond our ancient limits. With our utmost caution in this respect, it may still be justly apprehended that the general government must be made stronger as we become more extended.

But if, instead of freedom, slavery is to prevail and spread as we extend our dominion, can any reflecting man fail to see the necessity of giving to the general government greater powers; to enable it to afford the protection that will be demanded of it; powers that will be difficult to control and which may prove fatal to the public liberties?

ANONYMOUS

Against Restriction of Slavery to the Southern States

The antislavery speeches of Rufus King on the Missouri bill excited a barrage of bitter comments in the Southern press. The Richmond Enquirer, *one of the most influential newspapers in the South, ran a series of articles opposing King's position. According to the Southern view, the Constitution guaranteed new states the same rights as it did the old, and, consequently, Congress had no right to ban slavery as a qualification for admission. Though moral issues were certainly involved, many Southerners, like the anonymous author of the following selection, believed that the Northern Federalists were using the Missouri question to enhance the position of their party. The article, which appeared in the* Enquirer *on December 23, 1819, was signed "A Southron."*

The Congress of the United States have again before them the deeply interesting Missouri question. In my judgment, the petty concern of an acquisition of barren territory and even the danger of a war with a decrepit foe, in comparison with it, sink into insignificance. The matter is to preserve the happiness we already possess; to perpetuate this noble confederacy; to brighten the chain which binds together a band of brothers, instead of lighting up the torch of discord which will blaze like a bale fire from one end of the continent to the other. The harmony of the present moment, the happiness of the future, the independence of the states, the continuance of their Union, even the preservation of the unimpaired sovereignty of this ancient and venerable member of the confederacy may perhaps hang upon the decision to this interesting question.

Let not then a disgraceful supineness possess us; let not "the fatal coma," which has been eloquently declared to have seized upon the people, overcome us longer with lethargic slumber; let not a legislative body, which has hitherto been distinguished "for auguring maladministration at a distance and scenting the approach of tyranny in every tainted breeze," sleep upon their posts at this interesting moment when the enemies of our institutions are throwing up outworks which, at a period not remote, may be used

361

for the subversion of our sovereignty and independence.

It were charity to hope that the motives which have dictated the late attempt to introduce restrictions into the constitution of Missouri were as praiseworthy as they affect to be. But we cannot "wink so hard" as to be insensible to the political object which some of the statesmen of the East would fain conceal. The pretexts of humanity and a love of liberty are too flimsy a veil to hide from our view the political hostility which governs these.

Humanity! Where is the humanity of resisting the only feasible plan of future emancipation? Can we expect an event so desirable in the Southern states, while their numbers so far exceed the numbers of whites? Shall we oppose that dispersion of them through the Western states, which, by lessening the excess, may at a future day render practicable the schemes of philanthropy for their relief? Shall we adopt the barbarous principles of affected benevolence in imposing a check on the increase of black population by excluding them from an emigration to a country more salubrious and fertile than they now inhabit, and affording more abundantly the means of subsistence and comfort? Admirable philanthropists, who have religion and humanity on their lips, and look to the diminution of slave population from the combined operations of pestilence and famine!

But while humanity cannot offer an apology for this outrage upon the rights of the South, it is easily explained by the antipathies of certain politicians, and their jealousy of the influence of the Southern states in the councils of the nation. Rob us of our just portion of the territory which has been jointly purchased by the treasures of the nation and the valley of the Mississippi will be settled by the sons of the Eastern people, the inheritors of their fathers' prejudices; new states will spring up, emulous of setting new limits to Southern domination; swarms of "Southern slave-holders" will no longer crowd the halls of Congress and "sear the eyeballs" of their jealous countrymen; "the scepter will depart from Judah"; and Virginia influence—so magnified and deprecated—will be heard of no more!

If rumor has not deceived us, there may be other objects more immediate to be attained by this modern crusade against the rights of the people of the South. Some master spirit of the North may

362

expect to ride on this popular wave to the lofty pinnacle of his ambition. Whatever is indecorous in personality or unparliamentary in abuse has been abundantly poured forth by those frothy declaimers against the unavoidable domestic slavery of the South. They have assumed to themselves the power of making a form of government for others, and have supported so insolent a pretension by arguments and language no less insolent and offensive.

And when they have succeeded in excluding from the Western settlements every Southern man, and shall have sent forth in every direction swarms from the Northern hive, and missionary preachers against the cruelties and inhumanities of Southern slavery, a universal emancipation may be the next scheme suggested by visionary philanthropists or promoted by designing politicians.

With dangers such as these in prospect, can Virginia look on with stoical indifference because it is not her own case? Shall she console herself with the hope that she may be the last to be devoured? Shall she be silent when the great principles of the Constitution are assailed, when the rights of her sons, now peopling a western clime, are invaded, and principles asserted which may one day be turned with fatal effect against her own institutions?

I am not one of those who upon every trivial occasion would have the legislative body exert its rights as a member of the confederacy to protest against the acts of the general government. I would not, it is true, make this medicine of the Constitution our daily bread. But I have known no subject more important than the present, none on which the firm yet dignified and moderate language of this sovereignty was more imperiously demanded. . . .

It behooves us to contest at the threshold a pretension which violates the compact of the states; which sets at nought the great principle of self-government; which will prove an apple of discord among the sisters of this confederacy, and threaten to subvert our free and happy Constitution by a deadly blow at the rights of a part of the nation, and a destruction of the harmony and tranquility of the whole.

A Christian Indictment of Slavery

Many Christians in both North and South could not in good conscience reconcile their faith with the institution of slavery. During the nineteenth century the Presbyterian Church played a leading role in the Abolitionist movement. As early as 1787, the Presbyterian Synod of New York and Philadelphia had officially opposed slavery, and in May 1818, the General Assembly of the church issued the following revised and more adamant demand for abolition. The Assembly, which included many Southern members, adopted the report unanimously. Prior to 1820 there was significant antislavery sentiment in the South, hence the fact that wholehearted support for the Assembly's position came from the Southern members was not unusual. [Source: A Collection of the Acts, Deliverances, and Testimonies of the Supreme Judicatory of the Presbyterian Church, *Samuel J. Baird, ed., Philadelphia, 1855, pp. 820-822.]*

The General Assembly of the Presbyterian Church, having taken into consideration the subject of slavery, think proper to make known their sentiments upon it to the churches and people under their care.

We consider the voluntary enslaving of one part of the human race by another as a gross violation of the most precious and sacred rights of human nature; as utterly inconsistent with the law of God which requires us to love our neighbor as ourselves; and as totally irreconcilable with the spirit and principles of the Gospel of Christ, which enjoin that "all things whatsoever ye would that men should do to you, do ye even so to them." Slavery creates a paradox in the moral system. It exhibits rational, accountable, and immortal beings in such circumstances as scarcely to leave them the power of moral action. It exhibits them as dependent on the will of others whether they shall receive religious instruction, whether they shall know and worship the true God, whether they shall enjoy the ordinances of the gospel, whether they shall perform the duties and cherish the endearments of husbands and wives, parents and children, neighbors and friends, whether they shall preserve their chastity and purity, or regard the dictates of justice and humanity. Such are some of the consequences of slavery, consequences not imaginary but which connect themselves with its very existence.

364

The evils to which the slave is *always* exposed, often take place in fact, and in their very worst degree and form; and where all of them do not take place, as we rejoice to say that in many instances, through the influence of the principles of humanity and religion on the minds of masters they do not, still the slave is deprived of his natural right, degraded as a human being, and exposed to the danger of passing into the hands of a master who may inflict upon him all the hardships and injuries which inhumanity and avarice may suggest.

From this view of the consequences resulting from the practice into which Christian people have most inconsistently fallen of enslaving a portion of their brethren of mankind, for "God hath made of one blood all nations of men to dwell on the face of the earth," it is manifestly the duty of all Christians who enjoy the light of the present day, when the inconsistency of slavery, both with the dictates of humanity and religion, has been demonstrated, and is generally seen and acknowledged, to use their honest, earnest, and unwearied endeavors to correct the errors of former times, and as speedily as possible to efface this blot on our holy religion, and to obtain the complete abolition of slavery throughout Christendom, and if possible throughout the world.

We rejoice that the church to which we belong commenced as early as any other in this country the good work of endeavoring to put an end to slavery, and that in the same work, many of its members have ever since been, and now are, among the most active, vigorous, and efficient laborers. We do, indeed, tenderly sympathize with those portions of our church and our country where the evil of slavery has been entailed upon them; where a great, and the most virtuous part of the community abhor slavery and wish its extermination as sincerely as any others, but where the number of slaves, their ignorance, and their vicious habits generally render an immediate and universal emancipation inconsistent alike with the safety and happiness of the master and the slave. With those who are thus circumstanced, we repeat that we tenderly sympathize. At the same time, we earnestly exhort them to continue and, if possible, to increase their exertions to effect a total abolition of slavery. We exhort them to suffer no greater delay to take place in this most interesting concern than a regard to the public welfare truly and indispensably demands.

As our country has inflicted a most grievous injury upon the unhappy Africans by bringing them into slavery, we cannot, indeed, urge that we should add a second injury to the first by emancipating them in such manner as that they will be likely to destroy themselves or others. But we do think that our country ought to be governed in this matter by no other consideration than an honest and impartial regard to the happiness of the injured party; uninfluenced by the expense or inconvenience which such a regard may involve. We therefore warn all who belong to our denomination of Christians against unduly extending this plea of necessity, against making it a cover for the love and practice of slavery, or a pretense for not using efforts that are lawful and practicable to extinguish the evil.

And we, at the same time, exhort others to forbear harsh censures and uncharitable reflections on their brethren who unhappily live among slaves whom they cannot immediately set free, but who, at the same time, are really using all their influence, and all their endeavors, to bring them into a state of freedom as soon as a door for it can be safely opened.

Having thus expressed our views of slavery, and of the duty indispensably incumbent on all Christians to labor for its complete extinction, we proceed to recommend (and we do it with all the earnestness and solemnity which this momentous subject demands) a particular attention to the following points.

1. We recommend to all our people to patronize and encourage the society, lately formed, for colonizing in Africa, the land of their ancestors, the free people of color in our country. We hope that much good may result from the plans and efforts of this society. And while we exceedingly rejoice to have witnessed its origin and organization among the holders of slaves, as giving an unequivocal pledge of their desires to deliver themselves and their country from the calamity of slavery; we hope that those portions of the American Union whose inhabitants are by a gracious Providence more favorably circumstanced will cordially, and liberally, and earnestly cooperate with their brethren in bringing about the great end contemplated.

2. We recommend to all the members of our religious denomination not only to permit but to facilitate and encourage the instruc-

tion of their slaves in the principles and duties of the Christian religion, by granting them liberty to attend on the preaching of the gospel when they have the opportunity, by favoring the instruction of them in Sabbath schools, wherever those schools can be formed, and by giving them all other proper advantages for acquiring the knowledge of their duty both to God and man. We are perfectly satisfied that as it is incumbent on all Christians to communicate religious instruction to those who are under their authority, so that the doing of this in the case before us, so far from operating, as some have apprehended that it might, as an excitement to insubordination and insurrection would, on the contrary, operate as the most powerful means for the prevention of those evils.

3. We enjoin it on all church sessions and presbyteries, under the care of this Assembly, to discountenance, and, as far as possible, to prevent, all cruelty of whatever kind in the treatment of slaves; especially the cruelty of separating husband and wife, parents and children, and that which consists in selling slaves to those who will either themselves deprive these unhappy people of the blessings of the gospel, or who will transport them to places where the gospel is not proclaimed, or where it is forbidden to slaves to attend upon its institutions.

And if it shall ever happen that a Christian professor in our communion shall sell a slave who is also in communion and good standing with our church contrary to his or her will and inclination, it ought immediately to claim the particular attention of the proper church judicature; and unless there be such peculiar circumstances attending the case as can but seldom happen, it ought to be followed, without delay, by a suspension of the offender from all the privileges of the church till he repent and make all the reparation in his power to the injured party.

Displacement of Free Negroes

For those who recognized the threat to the Union posed by the institution of slavery, the possibility of colonizing the Negro often seemed a solution. Jefferson considered the idea in 1801 but felt it should be left to the state governments to execute. The American Colonization Society was formed in December 1816 for the purpose of transporting free Negroes to Africa to be colonized in the state of Liberia. The Society, composed of many prominent white people from both North and South, was supported by local groups, churches, and some state legislatures. Though designed to colonize only "free people of color," the Society opened an easy and safe channel for emancipation to those masters (and there were some) who desired to free their slaves. The Negroes themselves were, for the most part, opposed to deportation to a land no longer familiar to their people. The following selection is an account of the organizational meeting of the Society on December 21, 1816. [Source: Isaac V. Brown, Biography of the Rev. Robert Finley, *2nd edition, Philadelphia, 1857, pp. 103-120.]*

At the first meeting in the Congressional Hall, on the 21st of December, the Hon. Henry Clay was called to the chair. Before taking his seat, he addressed the meeting in the following terms, as reported in the *Intelligencer*, viz.:

> He understood the object of the present meeting to be to consider the propriety and practicability of colonizing the *free people of color* in the United States, and of forming an association in relation to that object. That class of the mixed population of our country was peculiarly situated. They neither enjoyed the immunities of freemen nor were they subject to the incapacities of slaves, but partook in some degree of the qualities of both. From their condition, and the unconquerable prejudices resulting from their color, they never could amalgamate with the free whites of this country. It was desirable, therefore, both as it respected them and the residue of the population of the country to draw them off.
>
> Various schemes of colonization had been thought of, and a part of our own continent, it was thought by some, might furnish a suitable establishment for them, but for his part he had

a decided preference for some part of the coast of Africa. There, ample provision might be made for the colony itself, and it might be rendered instrumental to the introduction into that extensive quarter of the globe of the arts, civilization, and Christianity. There was a peculiar, a moral fitness, in restoring them to the land of their fathers. And if, instead of the evils and sufferings which we have been the innocent cause of inflicting upon the inhabitants of Africa, we can transmit to her the blessings of our arts, our civilization, and our religion, may we not hope that America will extinguish a great portion of that moral debt which she has contracted to that unfortunate continent?

We should derive much encouragement in the prosecution of the object which had assembled us together by the success which had attended the colony at Sierra Leone. The establishment had commenced about twenty or twenty-five years ago under the patronage of private individuals in Great Britain. The basis of the population of the colony consisted of the fugitive slaves of the Southern states during the Revolutionary War, who had first been carried to Nova Scotia, and who afterward, about the year 1792, upon their own application, almost en masse, had been transferred to the western coast of Africa. The colony, after struggling with the most unheard of difficulties—difficulties resulting from the ignorance, barbarity, and prejudice of the natives, from the climate (which were however found to be not at all insurmountable), from wars, African as well as European, and such as are incidental to all new settlements, had made a gradual and steady progress until it has acquired a strength and stability which promises to crown the efforts of its founders with complete success. We have their experience before us; and can there be a nobler cause than that which, while it proposes to rid our own country of a useless and pernicious if not a dangerous portion of its population, contemplates the spreading of the arts of civilized life, and the possible redemption from ignorance and barbarism of a benighted portion of the globe?

It was proper and necessary distinctly to state that he understood it constituted no part of the object of this meeting to touch or agitate in the slightest degree a delicate question connected with another portion of the colored population of our country. It was not proposed to deliberate on, or consider at all, any question of emancipation, or that which was connected with the abolition of slavery. It was upon that condition alone, he was sure, that many gentlemen from the South and West whom he saw present had attended, or could be expected to cooperate. It was upon that condition that he himself attended.

He would only further add that he hoped in their deliberations they would be guided by that moderation, politeness, and deference for the opinion of each other which were essential to any useful result. But when he looked around and saw the respectable assemblage, and recollected the humane and benevolent purpose which had produced it, he felt it unnecessary to insist further on this topic.

Elias B. Caldwell, Esq., secretary of the Supreme Court of the United States, next addressed the meeting in substance as follows, viz.:

I feel peculiar embarrassment in obtruding myself upon the notice of so large and respectable a meeting in which I find some of the most distinguished characters of our country. I ask your indulgence in offering to the consideration of the meeting the resolution which I hold in my hand, and to a few explanatory observations. The objects of the meeting have been feelingly and correctly stated by the honorable chairman. The subject seems to be divided into first, the expediency; and second, the practicability of the proposed plan.

The expediency of colonizing the free people of color in the United States may be considered in reference to its influence on our civil institutions, on the morals and habits of the people, and on the future happiness of the free people of color. It has been a subject of unceasing regret and anxious solicitude, among many of our best patriots and wisest statesmen, from the first establishment of our independence, that this class of people should remain a monument of reproach to those sacred principles of civil liberty which constitute the foundations of all our constitutions. We say in the Declaration of Independence "that all men are created equal, and have certain unalienable rights." Yet it is considered impossible, consistently with the safety of the state, and it is certainly impossible with the present feelings toward these people, that they can ever be placed upon this equality or admitted to the enjoyment of these "unalienable rights" while they remain mixed with us.

Some persons may declaim and call it prejudice. No matter! Prejudice is as powerful a motive, and will as certainly exclude them, as the soundest reason. Others may say they are free enough. If this is a matter of opinion, let them judge—if of reason, let it be decided by our repeated and solemn declarations in all our public acts. This state of society unquestionably tends, in various ways, to injure the morals and destroy the habits of industry among our people. This will be acknowledged by every person who has paid any attention to the subject, and it seems to be so generally admitted that it would promote the happiness and the interests of the people to provide a place where these people might be settled by themselves that it is unnecessary to dwell on this branch of the subject.

As to the blacks, it is manifest that their interest and happiness would be promoted by collecting them together where they would enjoy equal rights and privileges with those around them. A state of degradation is necessarily a state of unhappiness. It debases the mind, it damps the energies of the soul, and represses every vigorous effort toward moral or intellectual greatness. How can you expect from them anything great or noble without the motives to stimulate or the rewards to crown great and noble achievements? It not only prevents their climbing the steep and rugged paths of fame but it prevents the enjoyment of the true happiness of calm contentment, satisfied with enjoying but a part of what we possess, of using only a portion of what is in our power. Take away, however, the portion that is not used, and it immediately becomes the object of our fondest desires.

The more you endeavor to improve the condition of these people, the more you cultivate their minds (unless by religious instruction), the more miserable you make them, in their present state. You give them a higher relish for those privileges which they can never attain, and you turn what we intend for a blessing into a curse. No, if they must remain in their present situation, keep them in the lowest state of degradation and ignorance. The more you bring them to the condition of brutes, the better chance do you give them of possessing their apathy. Surely, Americans ought to be the last people on earth to advocate such slavish doctrines; to cry peace and contentment to those who are deprived of the privileges of civil liberty. They who have so largely partaken of its blessings, who know so well how to estimate its value, ought to be the foremost to extend it to others. . . .

I will consider the practicability of colonization under three heads – the territory, the expense, and the probability of obtaining their consent.

1. The territory. Various plans have been mentioned by different persons. A situation within our own territory would certainly possess some considerable advantage. It would be more immediately under the eye and control of our own government. But there are some real and some apprehended evils to encounter. Many apprehend that they might hereafter join the Indians, or the nations bordering on our frontiers, in case of war, if they were placed so near us – that the colony would become the asylum of fugitives and runaway slaves. Added to these difficulties, there are inveterate prejudices against such a plan, in so large a portion of the country, which it would be impossible to overcome or remove. Upon mature reflection, with all the light that has yet been shed upon the subject, I believe it will be found that Africa will be liable to the fewest objections. A territory might, no doubt, be procured there; the climate is best adapted to their constitution, and they could live cheaper.

But, Mr. Chairman, I have a greater and nobler object in view in desiring them to be placed in Africa. It is the belief that through them civilization and the Christian religion would be introduced into that benighted quarter of the world. It is the hope of redeeming many millions from the lowest state of superstition and ignorance, and restoring them to the knowledge and worship of the true God. Great and powerful as are the other motives of this measure (and I acknowledge them to be of sufficient magnitude to attract the attention and to call for the united efforts of this nation), in my opinion, and you will find it the opinion of a large class of the community, all other motives are small and trifling compared with the hope of spreading among them the knowledge of the Gospel.

From the importance of this view of the subject, permit me to enlarge a little upon it. Whatever may be the difference of opinion among the different denominations of Christians, I believe they will all be found to unite in the belief that the Scriptures predict a time when the Gospel of Jesus Christ shall be spread over every part of the world — shall be acknowledged by every nation, and perhaps shall influence every heart. The opinion is perhaps as general that this glorious and happy day is near at hand. The great movements and mighty efforts in the moral and religious world seem to indicate some great design of Providence on the eve of accomplishment. The unexampled and astonishing success attending the numerous and various plans which have been devised, and which are in operation now in different parts of the world, and the union and harmony with which Christians of different denominations unite in promoting these plans, clearly indicate a divine hand in their direction.

Nay, sir, the subject on which we are now deliberating has been brought to public view, nearly at the same time, in different parts of our country. In New Jersey, New York, Indiana, Tennessee, Virginia, and perhaps other places not known to me, the public attention seems to have been awakened, as from a slumber, to this subject. The belief that I have mentioned leads Christians to look with anxious solicitude and joyful hope to every movement which they believe to be instrumental in accomplishing the great designs of Providence. They will receive your proposal with joy and support it with zeal; and, permit me to say, that it will be of no small consequence to gain the zealous support and cooperation of this portion of the community.

On the subject of expense, I should hope there would not be much difference of opinion. All are interested, though some portions are more immediately so than others. We should consider that what affects a part of our country is interesting to the whole. Besides, it is a great national object and ought to be supported by a national purse. And, as has been justly observed by the honorable gentlemen in the chair, there ought to be a national atonement for the wrongs and injuries which Africa has suffered. For, although the state legislatures commenced early after our independence to put a stop to the slave trade, and the national government interfered as soon as the Constitution would permit, yet as a nation we cannot rid ourselves entirely from the guilt and disgrace attending that iniquitous traffic until we, as a nation, have made every reparation in our power. If, however, more funds are wanting than it is thought expedient to appropriate out of the public treasury, the liberality and humanity of our citizens will not suffer it to fail for want of pecuniary aid. I should be sorry, however, to see our government dividing any part of the glory and honor which cannot fail of attending the accomplishment of a work so great, so interesting, and which will tend so much to diffuse the blessings of civil liberty and promote the happiness of man.

Among the objections which have been made, I must confess that I am most surprised at one which seems to be prevalent, to wit, that these people will be unwilling to be colonized. What, sir, are they not men? Will they not be actuated by the same motives of interest and ambition which influence other men? Or will they prefer remaining in a hopeless state of degradation for themselves and their children, to the prospect of the full enjoyment of their civil rights and a state of equality? What brought our ancestors to these shores? They had no friendly hand to lead them—no powerful arm to protect them. They left the land of their nativity, the sepulchers of their fathers, the comforts of civilized society, and all the endearments of friends and relatives and early associations to traverse the ocean, to clear the forests, to encounter all the hardships of a new settlement, and to brave the dangers of the tomahawk and scalping knife. How many were destroyed!

Sometimes whole settlements cut off by disease and hunger, by the treachery and cruelty of the savages; yet were they not discouraged.

What is it impels many Europeans daily to seek our shores and to sell themselves — for the prime of their life — to defray the expenses of their passages? It is that ruling, imperious desire planted in the breast of every man — the desire of liberty, of standing upon an equality with his fellowmen. If we were to add to these motives, the offer of land, and to aid in the expense of emigration and of first settling — they cannot be so blind to their own interests, so devoid of every generous and noble feeling, as to hesitate about accepting the offer. It is not a matter of speculation and opinion only. It has been satisfactorily ascertained that numbers will gladly accept of the invitation. And when once the colony is formed and flourishing, all other obstacles will be easily removed.

It is for us to make the experiment and the offer; we shall then, and not till then, have discharged our duty. It is a plan in which all interests, all classes and descriptions of people may unite, in which all discord and feelings may be lost in those of humanity — in promoting "peace on earth and goodwill to men."

This speaker having concluded, the Hon. John Randolph followed, and began by saying:

That it had been properly observed by the chairman that there was nothing in the proposition submitted to consideration which, in the smallest degree, touched another very important and delicate question which ought to be left as much out of view as possible. But it appeared to him that it had not been sufficiently insisted on, with a view to obtain the cooperation of all the citizens of the United States — not only that this meeting does not, in anywise, affect the question of Negro slavery but, as far as it goes, must materially tend to secure the property of every master in the United States over his slaves. It appeared to him that this aspect of the question had not been sufficiently presented to the public view. It was a notorious fact that the existence of this mixed and intermediate population of free

Negroes was viewed by every slaveholder as one of the greatest sources of the insecurity and unprofitableness of slave property; that they serve to excite in their fellow beings a feeling of discontent, of repining at their situation, and they act as channels of communication, not only between different slaves but between the slaves of different districts — that they are the depositories of stolen goods and the promoters of mischief.

In a worldly point of view, then, without entering into the general question, and apart from those higher and nobler motives which had been presented to the meeting, the owners of slaves were interested in providing a retreat for this part of our population. There was no fear that this proposition would alarm them; they had been accustomed to think seriously of the subject. There was a popular work on agriculture by John Taylor, of Caroline County, which was widely circulated and much confided in, in Virginia. In that book, much read, because coming from a practical man, this description of people was pointed out as a great evil. If a place could be provided for their reception, and a mode of sending them hence, there were hundreds, nay, thousands of citizens who would, by manumitting their slaves, relieve themselves from the cares attendant upon their possession.

The Hon. Robert Wright of Maryland added a few remarks, as follows:

That he could not withhold his approbation from a measure that had for its object the melioration of the lot of any portion of the human race, particularly of the free people of color, whose degraded state robs them of the happiness of self-government, so dear to the American people. And . . . as I discover the most delicate regard to the rights of property, I shall with great pleasure lend my aid to restore this unfortunate people to the enjoyment of their liberty; but I fear gentlemen are too sanguine in their expectations — that they would be willing to abandon the land of their nativity, so dear to man. However, I have the disposition to give them that election by furnishing all the means contemplated. But while we wish to promote the happiness of these free people of color, we ought to take care not to furnish the means of transporting out of the reach of the master his property.

These addresses being concluded, Elias B. Caldwell, Esq., offered the following resolutions, to wit:

Resolved, that an association or society be formed for the purpose of collecting information and to assist in the formation and execution of a plan for the colonization of the free people of color, with their consent, in Africa, or elsewhere, as may be thought most advisable by the constituted authorities of the country.

Resolved, that Elias B. Caldwell, John Randolph, Richard Rush, Walter Jones, Francis S. Key, Robert Wright, James H. Blake, and John Peter be a committee to present a respectful memorial to Congress requesting them to adopt such measures as may be thought most advisable for procuring a territory in Africa, or elsewhere, suitable for the colonization of the free people of color.

Resolved, that Francis S. Key, Bushrod Washington, Elias B. Caldwell, James Breckinridge, Walter Jones, Richard Rush, and William G. D. Worthington be a committee to prepare a constitution and rules for the government of the association or society above-mentioned, and report the same to the next meeting for consideration.

Act to Prohibit the Importation of Slaves

In his initial draft of the Declaration of Independence, Jefferson had condemned the slave trade, but the clause was struck from the final version. The matter was raised again in the Federal Convention of 1787, when several delegates urged constitutional abolition of the importation of slaves, but Southern slave owners, who were joined by Northern slave traders, won a stay of twenty years. As the end of this period approached, Jefferson, now President,

*urged Congress to act. "I congratulate you, fellow citizens," he declared in
his sixth annual message (1806), "on the approach of the period at which
you may interpose your authority constitutionally to withdraw the citizens of
the United States from all further participation in these violations of human
rights, which have been so long continued on the inoffending inhabitants of
Africa." Several bills were accordingly introduced in the House, and the
following one was passed on March 2, 1807. The new law, though it made
the slave trade illegal, did not end it; the smuggling of slaves, who grew more
and more valuable as the supply dwindled, continued sporadically until
1860. [Source:* The Public Statutes at Large of the United States of America,
Vol. III, Boston, 1856, pp. 426-430.]

*Be it enacted, by the Senate and House of Representatives of the
United States of America in Congress assembled,* that from and
after the 1st day of January, 1808, it shall not be lawful to import or
bring into the United States or the territories thereof, from any
foreign kingdom, place, or country, any Negro, mulatto, or person of
color with intent to hold, sell, or dispose of such Negro, mulatto, or
person of color as a slave, or to be held to service or labor.

Section 2. *And be it further enacted,* that no citizen or citizens of
the United States, or any other person, shall, from and after the 1st
day of January, in the year of Our Lord 1808, for himself, or themselves, or any other person whatsoever, either as master, factor, or
owner, build, fit, equip, load, or otherwise prepare any ship or vessel,
in any port or place within the jurisdiction of the United States, nor
shall cause any ship or vessel to sail from any port or place within
the same, for the purpose of procuring any Negro, mulatto, or person of color from any foreign kingdom, place, or country, to be
transported to any port or place whatsoever within the jurisdiction
of the United States, to be held, sold, or disposed of as slaves, or to be
held to service or labor. And if any ship or vessel shall be so fitted out
for the purpose aforesaid, or shall be caused to sail so as aforesaid,
every such ship or vessel, her tackle, apparel, and furniture shall be
forfeited to the United States and shall be liable to be seized, prosecuted, and condemned in any of the circuit courts or district courts
for the district where the said ship or vessel may be found or
seized. . . .

Section 4. *And be it further enacted,* if any citizen or citizens of

378

the United States, or any person resident within the jurisdiction of the same, shall, from and after the 1st day of January, 1808, take on board, receive, or transport from any of the coasts or kingdoms of Africa, or from any other foreign kingdom, place, or country, any Negro, mulatto, or person of color, in any ship or vessel, for the purpose of selling them in any port or place within the jurisdiction of the United States as slaves, or to be held to service or labor, or shall be in any ways aiding or abetting therein, such citizen or citizens, or person, shall severally forfeit and pay $5,000, one moiety thereof to the use of any person or persons who shall sue for and prosecute the same to effect. And every such ship or vessel in which such Negro, mulatto, or person of color shall have been taken on board, received, or transported as aforesaid, her tackle, apparel, and furniture, and the goods and effects which shall be found on board the same shall be forfeited to the United States and shall be liable to be seized, prosecuted, and condemned in any of the circuit courts or district courts in the district where the said ship or vessel may be found or seized.

And neither the importer, nor any person or persons claiming from or under him, shall hold any right or title whatsoever to any Negro, mulatto, or person of color, nor to the service or labor thereof, who may be imported or brought within the United States, or territories thereof, in violation of this law, but the same shall remain subject to any regulations not contravening the provisions of this act, which the legislatures of the several states or territories at any time hereafter may make for disposing of any such Negro, mulatto, or person of color.

Section 5. *And be it further enacted,* that if any citizen or citizens of the United States, or any other person resident within the jurisdiction of the same, shall, from and after the 1st day of January, 1808, contrary to the true intent and meaning of this act, take on board any ship or vessel from any of the coasts or kingdoms of Africa, or from any other foreign kingdom, place, or country, any Negro, mulatto, or person of color with intent to sell him, her, or them for a slave, or slaves, or to be held to service or labor, and shall transport the same to any port or place within the jurisdiction of the United States and there sell such Negro, mulatto, or person of color so transported as aforesaid for a slave, or to be held to service or

379

labor, every such offender shall be deemed guilty of a high misdemeanor and, being thereof convicted before any court having
competent jurisdiction, shall suffer imprisonment for not more than
ten years nor less than five years, and be fined not exceeding
$10,000, nor less than $1,000.

Section 6. *And be it further enacted*, that if any person or persons
whatsoever shall, from and after the 1st day of January, 1808,
purchase or sell any Negro, mulatto, or person of color for a slave, or
to be held to service or labor, who shall have been imported or
brought from any foreign kingdom, place, or country, or from the
dominions of any foreign state immediately adjoining to the United
States into any port or place within the jurisdiction of the United
States, after the last day of December, 1807, knowing at the time of
such purchase or sale such Negro, mulatto, or person of color was so
brought within the jurisdiction of the United States, as aforesaid,
such purchaser and seller shall severally forfeit and pay for every
Negro, mulatto, or person of color so purchased or sold as aforesaid
$800, one moiety thereof to the United States and the other moiety
to the use of any person or persons who shall sue for and prosecute
the same to effect: *Provided*, that the aforesaid forfeiture shall not
extend to the seller or purchaser of any Negro, mulatto, or person of
color who may be sold or disposed of in virtue of any regulation
which may hereafter be made by any of the legislatures of the
several states in that respect, in pursuance of this act, and the
Constitution of the United States.

Section 7. *And be it further enacted*, that if any ship or vessel
shall be found, from and after the 1st day of January, 1808, in any
river, port, bay, or harbor, or on the high seas, within the jurisdic-
tional limits of the United States, or hovering on the coast thereof,
having on board any Negro, mulatto, or person of color for the
purpose of selling them as slaves, or with intent to land the same in
any port or place within the jurisdiction of the United States, contrary to the prohibition of this act, every such ship or vessel, together
with her tackle, apparel, and furniture, and the goods or effects
which shall be found on board the same, shall be forfeited to the use
of the United States and may be seized, prosecuted, and condemned
in any court of the United States having jurisdiction thereof.

And it shall be lawful for the President of the United States, and he is hereby authorized, should he deem it expedient, to cause any of the armed vessels of the United States to be manned and employed to cruise on any part of the coast of the United States, or territories thereof, where he may judge attempts will be made to violate the provisions of this act, and to instruct and direct the commanders of armed vessels of the United States to seize, take, and bring into any port of the United States all such ships or vessels, and moreover to seize, take, and bring into any port of the United States all ships or vessels of the United States, wheresoever found on the high seas, contravening the provisions of this act, to be proceeded against according to law. And the captain, master, or commander of every such ship or vessel so found and seized as aforesaid shall be deemed guilty of a high misdemeanor, and shall be liable to be prosecuted before any court of the United States having jurisdiction thereof; and being thereof convicted, shall be fined not exceeding $10,000, and be imprisoned not less than two years and not exceeding four years.

GUSTAVUS VASSA
The Slave Ship

Olaudah Equiano was taken as a child from his African village, Benin, located near the present-day country of Nigeria, and shipped to the West Indies as a slave. His fate was not to be that of an ordinary slave, as he traveled extensively, eventually exploring the Arctic. On one of his many sea voyages, a captain named him Gustavus Vassa, for the sixteenth-century Swedish king, Gustavus I (Gustavus Vasa), and he was eventually baptized with that name. He was one of the few slaves who became educated and thus was equipped to write his journal, The Interesting Narrative of the Life of Gustavus Vassa, The African; *it is a rare auto-biographical account of the life of an eighteenth-century slave. The work depicts not only Gustavus' trials and sorrows, but also the miseries of other Africans who were abducted into slavery. Excerpts are reprinted here.*

381

[*Source:* The Life of Olaudah Equiano or Gustavus Vassa, The African, *Boston, 1837, pp. 30-52.*]

I hope the reader will not think I have trespassed on his patience in introducing myself to him with some account of the manners and customs of my country. They had been implanted in me with great care, and made an impression on my mind, which time could not erase, and which all the adversity and variety of fortune I have since experienced served only to rivet and record; for, whether the love of one's country be real or imaginary, or a lesson of reason, or an instinct of nature, I still look back with pleasure on the first scenes of my life, though that pleasure has been for the most part mingled with sorrow. . . .

My father, besides many slaves, had a numerous family, of which seven lived to grow up, including myself and a sister, who was the only daughter. As I was the youngest of the sons, I became, of course, the greatest favorite with my mother, and was always with her; and she used to take particular pains to form my mind. I was trained up from my earliest years in the art of war; my daily exercise was shooting and throwing javelins; and my mother adorned me with emblems, after the manner of our greatest warriors.

In this way I grew up till I was turned the age of eleven, when an end was put to my happiness in the following manner. Generally, when the grown people in the neighborhood were gone far in the fields to labor, the children assembled together in some of the neighboring premises to play; and, commonly, some of us used to get up a tree to look out for any assailant, or kidnapper, that might come upon us—for they sometimes took those opportunities of our parents' absence to attack and carry off as many as they could seize. One day, as I was watching at the top of a tree in our yard, I saw one of those people come into the yard of our next neighbor but one to kidnap, there being many stout young people in it. Immediately on this I gave the alarm of the rogue, and he was surrounded by the stoutest of them, who entangled him with cords, so that he could not escape till some of the grown people came and secured him.

But, alas! ere long it was my fate to be thus attacked, and to be carried off, when none of the grown people were nigh. One day, when all our people were gone out to their works as usual, and only I and my dear sister were left to mind the house, two men and a woman got over our walls, and in a moment seized us both, and, without giving us time to cry out or make resistance, they stopped our mouths and ran off with us into the nearest wood. Here they tied our hands, and continued to carry us as far as they could, till night came on, when we reached a small house where the robbers halted for refreshment and spent the night. We were then unbound, but were unable to take any food; and, being quite overpowered by fatigue and grief, our only relief was some sleep, which allayed our misfortune for a short time. The next morning we left the house, and continued traveling all the day.

For a long time we had kept the woods, but at last we came into a road which I believed I knew. I had now some hopes of being delivered; for we had advanced but a little way before I discovered some people at a distance on which I began to cry out for their assistance; but my cries had no other effect than to make them tie me faster and stop my mouth, and then they put me into a large sack. They also stopped my sister's mouth and tied her hands; and in this manner we proceeded till we were out of sight of these people. When we went to rest the following night, they offered us some victuals, but we refused it; and the only comfort we had was in being in one another's arms all that night, and bathing each other with our tears. But, alas! we were soon deprived of even the small comfort of weeping together. The next day proved a day of greater sorrow than I had yet experienced; for my sister and I were then separated, while we lay clasped in each other's arms. It was in vain that we besought them not to part us; she was torn from me and immediately carried away, while I was left in a state of distraction not to be described. I cried and grieved continually; and for several days did not eat anything but what they forced into my mouth.

At length, after many days traveling, during which I had often changed masters, I got into the hands of a chieftain in a very pleasant country. This man had two wives and some children, and they all used me extremely well, and did all they could to comfort me;

383

particularly the first wife, who was something like my mother. Although I was a great many days' journey from my father's house, yet these people spoke exactly the same language with us. This first master of mine, as I may call him, was a smith, and my principal employment was working his bellows, which were the same kind as I had seen in my vicinity. They were in some respects not unlike the stoves here in gentlemen's kitchens, and were covered over with leather; and in the middle of that leather a stick was fixed, and a person stood up and worked it in the same manner as is done to pump water out of a cask with a hand pump. I believe it was gold he worked, for it was of a lovely bright yellow color, and was worn by the women on their wrists and ankles.

I was there, I suppose, about a month, and they at last used to trust me some little distance from the house. This liberty I used in embracing every opportunity to inquire the way to my own home; and I also sometimes, for the same purpose, went with the maidens, in the cool of the evenings, to bring pitchers of water from the springs for the use of the house. I had also remarked where the sun rose in the morning and set in the evening as I had traveled along; and I had observed that my father's house was toward the rising of the sun. I therefore determined to seize the first opportunity of making my escape, and to shape my course for that quarter; for I was quite oppressed and weighed down by grief after my mother and friends; and my love of liberty, ever great, was strengthened by the mortifying circumstance of not daring to eat with the freeborn children, although I was mostly their companion.

While I was projecting my escape one day, an unlucky event happened, which quite disconcerted my plan and put an end to my hopes. I used to be sometimes employed in assisting an elderly slave to cook and take care of the poultry; and one morning, while I was feeding some chickens, I happened to toss a small pebble at one of them, which hit it on the middle and directly killed it. The old slave, having soon after missed the chicken, inquired after it; and on my relating the accident (for I told her the truth, for my mother would never suffer me to tell a lie), she flew into a violent passion and threatened that I should suffer for it; and, my master being out, she immediately went and told her mistress what I had done. This alarmed me very much, and I expected an instant flogging, which to

384

me was uncommonly dreadful, for I had seldom been beaten at home. I therefore resolved to fly; and accordingly I ran into a thicket that was hard by, and hid myself in the bushes. Soon afterward my mistress and the slave returned, and, not seeing me, they searched all the house, but not finding me, and I not making answer when they called to me, they thought I had run away, and the whole neighborhood was raised in the pursuit of me.

In that part of the country, as in ours, the houses and villages were skirted with woods, or shrubberies, and the bushes were so thick that a man could readily conceal himself in them so as to elude the strictest search. The neighbors continued the whole day looking for me, and several times many of them came within a few yards of the place where I lay hid. I expected every moment when I heard a rustling among the trees to be found out and punished by my master; but they never discovered me, though they were often so near that I even heard their conjectures as they were looking about for me; and I now learned from them that any attempts to return home would be hopeless. Most of them supposed I had fled toward home; but the distance was so great, and the way so intricate, that they thought I could never reach it, and that I should be lost in the woods. When I heard this, I was seized with a violent panic and abandoned myself to despair. Night, too, began to approach, and aggravated all my fears. I had before entertained hopes of getting home, and had determined when it should be dark to make the attempt; but I was now convinced it was fruitless, and began to consider that, if possibly I could escape all other animals, I could not those of the human kind; and that, not knowing the way, I must perish in the woods. Thus was I like the hunted deer:

> Every leaf and every whisp'ring breath,
> Conveyed a foe, and every foe a death.

I heard frequent rustlings among the leaves, and being pretty sure they were snakes, I expected every instant to be stung by them. This increased my anguish, and the horror of my situation became now quite insupportable. I at length quitted the thicket, very faint and hungry, for I had not eaten or drank anything all the day, and crept to my master's kitchen, from whence I set out at first, which was an open shed, and laid myself down in the ashes with an anxious wish for death, to relieve me from all my pains. I was scarcely awake in the morning when the old woman slave, who was the first up, came to light the fire, and saw me in the fireplace. She was very much surprised to see me, and could scarcely believe her own eyes. She now promised to intercede for me, and went for her master, who soon after came, and, having slightly reprimanded me, ordered me to be taken care of and not ill-treated.

Soon after this, my master's only daughter, and child by his first wife, sickened and died, which affected him so much that for some time he was almost frantic, and really would have killed himself had he not been watched and prevented. However, in a short time afterward he recovered, and I was again sold.

I was now carried to the left of the sun's rising, through many dreary wastes and dismal woods, amidst the hideous roarings of wild beasts. The people I was sold to used to carry me very often, when I was tired, either on their shoulders or on their backs. I saw many convenient well-built sheds along the road at proper distances to accommodate the merchants and travelers who lay in those buildings along with their wives, who often accompany them; and they always go well armed.

From the time I left my own nation, I always found somebody that understood me till I came to the seacoast. The languages of different nations did not totally differ, nor were they so copious as those of the Europeans, particularly the English. They were therefore easily learned; and, while I was journeying thus through Africa, I acquired two or three different tongues.

In this manner I had been traveling for a considerable time, when, one evening, to my great surprise, whom should I see brought to the house where I was but my dear sister! As soon as she saw me, she gave a loud shriek and ran into my arms – I was quite overpowered; neither of us could speak, but, for a considerable time, clung to each other in mutual embraces, unable to do anything but weep. Our meeting affected all who saw us; and, indeed, I must acknowledge, in honor of those sable destroyers of human rights, that I never met with any ill-treatment, or saw any offered to their slaves, except tying them, when necessary, to keep them from running away. When these people knew we were brother and sister, they indulged us to be together; and the man to whom I supposed we

386

The African Homeland and Slave Trade

Of all the immigrant peoples who have come to America, only the blacks were brought here against their will. The rich culture of Africa — a culture that produced such artifacts as this 16th-century ivory pendant from the kingdom of Benin — was torn from them and they were forbidden to adopt the culture of their captors in its place. These facts lie at the heart of the black man's experience in America; slavery and the century of racial repression that followed it circumscribed his life and narrowed his hopes. That slavery took root and flourished in American soil is probably the nation's greatest shame; that black people fought against slavery from the first, helped overthrow it, and continue to struggle against its legacy of bigotry should be the black American's greatest source of pride.

The CITY of LOANGO
from Dapper

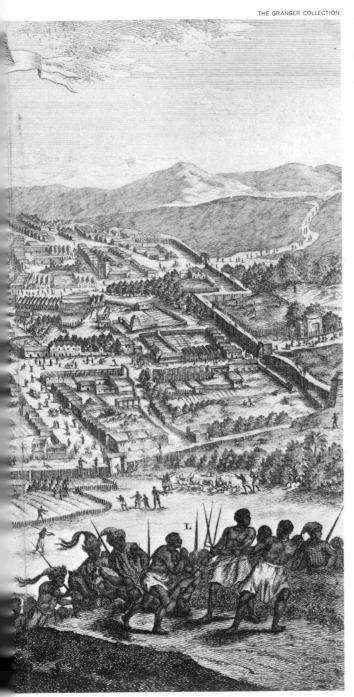

The vast and varied continent from which the black man came was never merely the dark jungle of barbarism and superstition that many Western writers have traditionally described. Some kind of civilization in Africa is very old and even the oldest known remains of a human prototype were found in northern Tanzania. African history is as complex as that of Europe (and more difficult to trace because there are no written records), but scholars now know that over the centuries countless African kingdoms and states, large and small, have arisen, quarreled with one another, and been replaced by others. Ethiopia, Nubia (whose kings once ruled from the throne of Egypt), Ashanti, Dahomey, Mali, Benin, are only a few of the kingdoms that have held sway in various parts of Africa. On the West coast, the region from which the ancestors of most black Americans came, three large black states — Ghana, Mali, and Songhai — flourished in turn. All three were based on trade and commerce. Their powerful rulers meted out justice, commanded great armies, and lived in palaces surrounded by retinues of courtiers, servants, and slaves taken in battle. West African artists and craftsmen produced a wealth of art, and local scholars were sought out by European and Asian students for their knowledge of astronomy and mathematics. This 18th-century engraving, made from a sketch by an English traveler, shows the formally laid out city of Loango, which stood near the mouth of the Congo River on the West African coast.

The European slave trade began on a small scale. In 1441 a Portuguese sea captain landed on what was soon to be called the Slave Coast (see map at right) and seized twelve men whom he took home as a present for his sovereign, Prince Henry the Navigator. The prince was pleased with his gift and urged his other captains to gather more Africans. Slave-catching in Africa was not new; Muslim slavers had been selling black slaves to Middle Eastern buyers for centuries. But black slaves were a novelty in Europe, and soon after the first slaves arrived in Portugal it became fashionable among the well-born of southern Europe to own black pages and serving girls. The trade became brisk when the colonization of the New World turned it into an enormously profitable business. Clearing land, building settlements and missions, planting, tending, and reaping crops in the New World all required cheap labor. At first native Indians were enslaved to do the white man's bidding, but the size of the task, the small number of available Indians, and their susceptibility to European diseases quickly made more workers necessary. When white convicts and indentured servants were also found inadequate (partly because they were white and could disappear into the surrounding population), the colonists turned to Africa. Soon, European slavers were raiding all along some 3,000 miles of coastline. The trade flourished for about 350 years; during that period somewhere between 15 and 24 million of West Africa's most able-bodied men, women, and children were taken from their homes and spirited across the sea. Most of them went to the West Indies and South America. Some 500,000 had been brought to colonial America by 1777: at the time of the American Revolution, one out of six Americans was a slave.

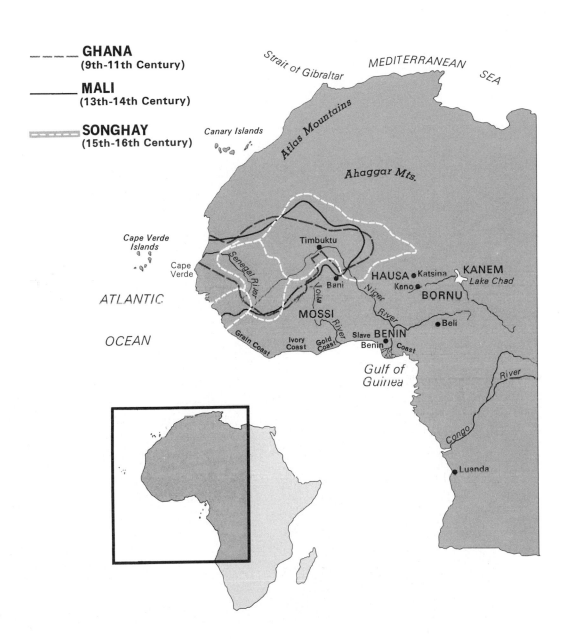

Strait of Gibraltar

MEDITERRANEAN SEA

Atlas Mountains

Canary Islands

Ahaggar Mts.

Cape Verde Islands

Cape Verde

Timbuktu

Senegal River

Bani

HAUSA

Kano

Katsina

KANEM

Lake Chad

BORNU

ATLANTIC

OCEAN

Volta

Niger River

MOSSI

River

Beli

Grain Coast

Ivory Coast

Gold Coast

Slave Coast

BENIN

Benin

Gulf of Guinea

River

Congo

Luanda

In the early days of the slave trade unsuspecting blacks were simply seized at the water's edge, but, as the coastal peoples grew more wary and the demand for slaves grew, more efficient schemes for slave-gathering were developed. Muslim slave traders and greedy black chiefs stole men, women, and children from their homes (often with great loss of life) and marched them to the coast where forts and trading posts had been built by the European slave powers. In exchange for trinkets and gold they handed over their captives. Before beginning their long journey to the New World, slaves were examined for possible diseases and branded for identification. It was here, with the painful imposition of a white man's name, that the slave's sense of and feeling for his own culture first came under attack.

The journey aboard the slave ships across the Atlantic Middle Passage was a nightmare of horrors almost impossible to exaggerate. Slaves were crowded into the dark airless hull of the ship and shackled together in long rows. The journey to the West Indies took about five weeks; the trip to New England and Chesapeake Bay, the chief American landing points, took several more. Water was stagnant, food was always scarce and often rotten. The sick or feeble were often thrown overboard. Many went mad. Others survived the trip but were never able to regain their health. Many slaves fought back, battling with their armed captors until overwhelmed. Still others threw themselves into the sea rather than succumb to slavery. More than 20 percent of the black people who set out from Africa never reached their destination. At the right is a view of the interior of a 19th-century slave ship; below is a French diagram from the same period showing the loading plan of a slave deck.

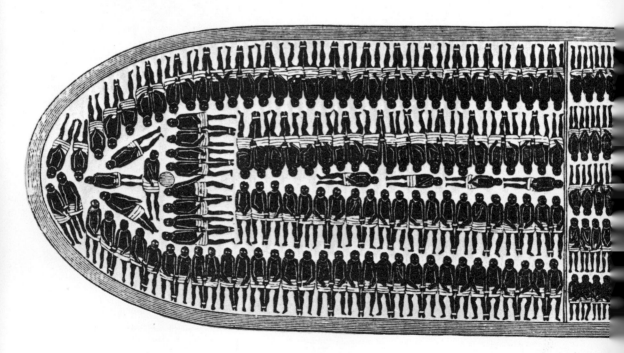

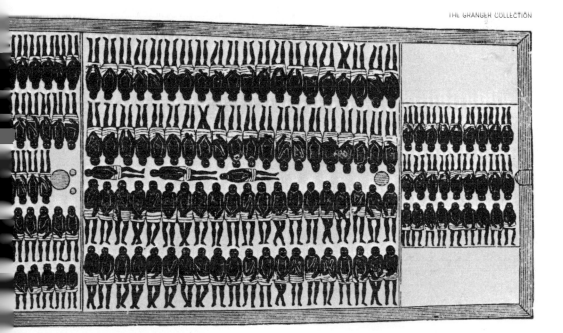

TO BE SOLD, on board the Ship *Bance-Island*, on tuesday the 6th of *May* next, at *Ashley-Ferry*; a choice cargo of about 250 fine healthy NEGROES, juft arrived from the Windward & Rice Coaft. ——The utmoft care has already been taken, and fhall be continued, to keep them free from the leaft danger of being infected with the SMALL-POX, no boat having been on board, and all other communication with people from *Charles-Town* prevented.

Auftin, Laurens, & Appleby.

N. B. Full one Half of the above Negroes have had the SMALL-POX in their own Country.

On reaching America, slaves were usually put in stockades to await sale. This poster announces a slave auction in Charleston, South Carolina, during a smallpox epidemic in the spring of 1784; prospective buyers are reassured that the human merchandise will stay healthy.

belonged lay with us, he in the middle, while she and I held one another by the hands across his breast all night; and thus, for a while, we forgot our misfortunes in the joy of being together. But even this small comfort was soon to have an end; for scarcely had the fatal morning appeared when she was again torn from me forever!

I was now more miserable, if possible, than before. The small relief which her presence gave me from pain was gone, and the wretchedness of my situation was redoubled by my anxiety after her fate, and my apprehensions lest her sufferings should be greater than mine, when I could not be with her to alleviate them. Yes, thou dear partner of all my childish sports! thou sharer of my joys and sorrows! happy should I have ever esteemed myself to encounter every misery for you and to procure your freedom by the sacrifice of my own. Though you were early forced from my arms, your image has been always riveted in my heart, from which neither time nor fortune have been able to remove it; so that, while the thoughts of your sufferings have damped my prosperity, they have mingled with adversity and increased its bitterness. To that Heaven which protects the weak from the strong, I commit the care of your innocence and virtues, if they have not already received their full reward, and if your youth and delicacy have not long since fallen victims to the violence of the African trader, the pestilential stench of a Guinea ship, the seasoning in the European colonies, or the lash and lust of a brutal and unrelenting overseer.

I did not long remain after my sister. I was again sold and carried through a number of places, till after traveling a considerable time I came to a town called Tinmah, in the most beautiful country I had yet seen in Africa. It was extremely rich, and there were many rivulets which flowed through it, and supplied a large pond in the center of the town, where the people washed. Here I first saw and tasted coconuts, which I thought superior to any nuts I had ever tasted before; and the trees which were loaded were also interspersed among the houses, which had commodious shades adjoining, and were in the same manner as ours, the insides being neatly plastered and whitewashed. Here I also saw and tasted, for the first time, sugarcane.

Their money consisted of little white shells, the size of the fingernail. I was sold here for 172 of them by a merchant who lived and brought me there. I had been about two or three days at his house when a wealthy widow, a neighbor of his, came there one evening and brought with her an only son, a young gentleman about my own age and size. Here they saw me; and, having taken a fancy to me, I was bought of the merchant and went home with them. Her house and premises were situated close to one of those rivulets I have mentioned, and were the finest I ever saw in Africa; they were very extensive, and she had a number of slaves to attend her. The next day I was washed and perfumed; and when mealtime came, I was led into the presence of my mistress, and ate and drank before her with her son. This filled me with astonishment; and I could scarce help expressing my surprise that the young gentleman should suffer me, who was bound, to eat with him who was free; and not only so, but that he would not at any time either eat or drink till I had taken first, because I was the eldest, which was agreeable to our custom.

Indeed, everything here, and all their treatment of me, made me forget that I was a slave. The language of these people resembled ours so nearly that we understood each other perfectly. They had also the very same customs as we. There were likewise slaves daily to attend us, while my young master and I, with other boys, sported with our darts and bows and arrows, as I had been used to do at home. In this resemblance to my former happy state, I passed about two months; and I now began to think I was to be adopted into the family, and was beginning to be reconciled to my situation and to forget by degrees my misfortunes, when all at once the delusion vanished; for, without the least previous knowledge, one morning early, while my dear master and companion was still asleep, I was awakened out of my reverie to fresh sorrow, and hurried away even among the uncircumcised.

Thus, at the very moment I dreamed of the greatest happiness, I found myself most miserable; and it seemed as if fortune wished to give me this taste of joy only to render the reverse more poignant. The change I now experienced was as painful as it was sudden and unexpected. It was a change, indeed, from a state of bliss to a scene which is inexpressible by me, as it discovered to me an element I had never before beheld, and till then had no idea of, and wherein such instances of hardship and cruelty continually occurred as I can never reflect on but with horror.

All the nations and people I had hitherto passed through resembled our own in their manners, customs, and language; but I came at length to a country, the inhabitants of which differed from us in all those particulars. I was very much struck with this difference, especially when I came among a people who did not circumcise, and ate without washing their hands. They cooked also in iron pots, and had European cutlasses and crossbows, which were unknown to us, and fought with their fists among themselves. Their women were not so modest as ours, for they ate and drank and slept with their men. But above all, I was amazed to see no sacrifices or offerings among them. In some of those places the people ornamented themselves with scars, and likewise filed their teeth very sharp. They wanted sometimes to ornament me in the same manner, but I would not suffer them; hoping that I might some time be among a people who did not thus disfigure themselves, as I thought they did.

At last I came to the banks of a large river which was covered with canoes, in which the people appeared to live with their household utensils and provisions of all kinds. I was beyond measure astonished at this, as I had never before seen any water larger than a pond or a rivulet; and my surprise was mingled with no small fear when I was put into one of these canoes, and we began to paddle and move along the river. We continued going on thus till night, and when we came to land and made fires on the banks, each family by themselves, some dragged their canoes on shore, others stayed and cooked in theirs, and laid in them all night. Those on the land had mats, of which they made tents, some in the shape of little houses; in these we slept; and after the morning meal, we embarked again and proceeded as before. I was often very much astonished to see some of the women, as well as the men, jump into the water, dive to the bottom, come up again, and swim about.

Thus I continued to travel, sometimes by land, sometimes by water, through different countries and various nations, till, at the end of six or seven months after I had been kidnapped, I arrived at the seacoast. It would be tedious and uninteresting to relate all the incidents which befell me during this journey, and which I have not yet forgotten; of the various hands I passed through, and the manners and customs of all the different people among whom I lived. I shall, therefore, only observe that in all the places where I was, the soil was exceedingly rich; the pumpkins, eadas, plantains, yams, etc., were in great abundance and of incredible size. There were also vast quantities of different gums, though not used for any purpose, and everywhere a great deal of tobacco. The cotton even grew quite wild, and there was plenty of redwood. I saw no mechanics whatever in all the way, except such as I have mentioned. The chief employment in all these countries was agriculture, and both the males and females, as with us, were brought up to it, and trained in the arts of war.

The first object which saluted my eyes when I arrived on the coast was the sea, and a slave ship, which was then riding at anchor and waiting for its cargo. These filled me with astonishment, which was soon converted into terror when I was carried on board. I was immediately handled and tossed up to see if I were sound by some of the crew; and I was now persuaded that I had gotten into a world of bad spirits, and that they were going to kill me. Their complexions, too, differing so much from ours, their long hair, and the language they spoke (which was very different from any I had ever heard) united to confirm me in this belief. Indeed, such were the horrors of my views and fears at the moment that, if 10,000 worlds had been my own, I would have freely parted with them all to have exchanged my condition with that of the meanest slave in my own country. When I looked round the ship, too, and saw a large furnace of copper boiling, and a multitude of black people of every description chained together, every one of their countenances expressing dejection and sorrow, I no longer doubted of my fate; and, quite overpowered with horror and anguish, I fell motionless on the deck and fainted.

When I recovered a little, I found some black people about me, who I believed were some of those who had brought me on board and had been receiving their pay; they talked to me in order to cheer me, but all in vain. I asked them if we were not to be eaten by those white men with horrible looks, red faces, and long hair. They told me I was not; and one of the crew brought me a small portion of spirituous liquor in a wine glass, but, being afraid of him, I would not take it out of his hand. One of the blacks, therefore, took it from him and gave it to me, and I took a little down my palate, which, instead of reviving me, as they thought it would, threw me into the greatest consternation at the strange feeling it produced, having never tasted any such liquor before. Soon after this, the blacks who brought me on board went off and left me abandoned to despair.

I now saw myself deprived of all chance of returning to my native country, or even the least glimpse of hope of gaining the shore, which I now considered as friendly; and I even wished for my former slavery in preference to my present situation, which was filled with horrors of every kind, still heightened by my ignorance of what I was to undergo. I was not long suffered to indulge my grief. I was soon put down under the decks, and there I received such a salutation in my nostrils as I had never experienced in my life; so that, with the loathsomeness of the stench and crying together, I became so sick and low that I was not able to eat, nor had I the least desire to taste anything. I now wished for the last friend, death, to relieve me; but soon, to my grief, two of the white men offered me eatables; and, on my refusing to eat, one of them held me fast by the hands and laid me across, I think, the windlass, and tied my feet, while the other flogged me severely.

I had never experienced anything of this kind before, and although not being used to the water, I naturally feared that element the first time I saw it, yet, nevertheless, could I have got over the nettings, I would have jumped over the side, but I could not; and, besides, the crew used to watch us very closely who were not chained down to the decks lest we should leap into the water. And I have seen some of these poor African prisoners most severely cut for attempting to do so, and hourly whipped for not eating. This, indeed, was often the case with myself. In a little time after, among the poor chained men, I found some of my own nation, which in a small degree gave ease to my mind. I inquired of these what was to be done with us? They gave me to understand we were to be carried to these white people's country to work for them. I then was a little revived, and thought, if it were no worse than working, my situation was not so desperate; but still I feared I should be put to death, the white people looked and acted, as I thought, in so savage a manner; for I had never seen among any people such instances of brutal

401

cruelty; and this not only shown toward us blacks but also to some of the whites themselves. One white man in particular I saw, when we were permitted to be on deck, flogged so unmercifully with a large rope near the foremast that he died in consequence of it; and they tossed him over the side as they would have done a brute. This made me fear these people the more; and I expected nothing less than to be treated in the same manner.

I could not help expressing my fears and apprehensions to some of my countrymen; I asked them if these people had no country, but lived in this hollow place (the ship). They told me they did not, but came from a distant one. "Then," said I, "how comes it in all our country we never heard of them?" They told me because they lived so very far off. I then asked where were their women? had they any like themselves? I was told they had. "And why," said I, "do we not see them?" They answered, because they were left behind. I asked how the vessel could go? They told me they could not tell; but that there was cloth put upon the masts by the help of the ropes I saw, and then the vessel went on; and the white men had some spell or magic they put in the water when they liked in order to stop the vessel. I was exceedingly amazed at this account, and really thought they were spirits. I therefore wished much to be from among them, for I expected they would sacrifice me; but my wishes were vain, for we were so quartered that it was impossible for any of us to make our escape.

While we stayed on the coast, I was mostly on deck; and one day, to my great astonishment, I saw one of these vessels coming in with the sails up. As soon as the whites saw it, they gave a great shout, at which we were amazed; and the more so as the vessel appeared larger by approaching nearer. At last, she came to an anchor in my sight, and when the anchor was let go, I and my countrymen who saw it were lost in astonishment to observe the vessel stop—and were now convinced it was done by magic. Soon after this the other ship got her boats out, and they came on board of us, and the people of both ships seemed very glad to see each other. Several of the strangers also shook hands with us black people, and made motions with their hands, signifying, I suppose, we were to go to their country, but we did not understand them.

402

At last, when the ship we were in had got in all her cargo, they made ready with many fearful noises, and we were all put under deck, so that we could not see how they managed the vessel. But this disappointment was the least of my sorrow. The stench of the hold while we were on the coast was so intolerably loathsome that it was dangerous to remain there for any time, and some of us had been permitted to stay on the deck for the fresh air; but now that the whole ship's cargo were confined together, it became absolutely pestilential. The closeness of the place and the heat of the climate, added to the number in the ship, which was so crowded that each had scarcely room to turn himself, almost suffocated us. This produced copious perspirations, so that the air soon became unfit for respiration, from a variety of loathsome smells, and brought on a sickness among the slaves, of which many died—thus falling victims to the improvident avarice, as I may call it, of their purchasers. This wretched situation was again aggravated by the galling of the chains, now become insupportable; and the filth of the necessary tubs, into which the children often fell and were almost suffocated. The shrieks of the women and the groans of the dying rendered the whole a scene of horror almost inconceivable.

Happily, perhaps, for myself, I was soon reduced so low here that it was thought necessary to keep me almost always on deck; and from my extreme youth I was not put in fetters. In this situation I expected every hour to share the fate of my companions, some of whom were almost daily brought upon deck at the point of death, which I began to hope would soon put an end to my miseries. Often did I think many of the inhabitants of the deep much more happy than myself. I envied them the freedom they enjoyed, and as often wished I could change my condition for theirs. Every circumstance I met with served only to render my state more painful, and heightened my apprehensions and my opinion of the cruelty of the whites.

One day they had taken a number of fishes; and when they had killed and satisfied themselves with as many as they thought fit, to our astonishment who were on deck, rather than give any of them to us to eat, as we expected, they tossed the remaining fish into the sea again, although we begged and prayed for some as well as we could, but in vain; and some of my countrymen, being pressed by hunger, took an opportunity, when they thought no one saw them, of trying to get a little privately. But they were discovered, and the attempt procured them some very severe floggings. One day, when we had a smooth sea and moderate wind, two of my wearied countrymen who were chained together (I was near them at the time), preferring death to such a life of misery, somehow made through the nettings and jumped into the sea. Immediately, another quite dejected fellow, who, on account of his illness, was suffered to be out of irons, also followed their example; and I believe many more would very soon have done the same if they had not been prevented by the ship's crew, who were instantly alarmed. Those of us that were the most active were in a moment put down under the deck, and there was such a noise and confusion among the people of the ship, as I never heard before, to stop her and get the boat out to go after the slaves. However, two of the wretches were drowned, but they got the other, and afterward flogged him unmercifully for thus attempting to prefer death to slavery.

In this manner we continued to undergo more hardships than I can now relate, hardships which are inseparable from this accursed trade. Many a time we were near suffocation from the want of fresh air, which we were often without for whole days together. This, and the stench of the necessary tubs, carried off many.

During our passage, I first saw flying fishes, which surprised me very much; they used frequently to fly across the ship, and many of them fell on the deck. I also now first saw the use of the quadrant; I had often with astonishment seen the mariners make observations with it, and I could not think what it meant. They at last took notice of my surprise; and one of them, willing to increase it as well as to gratify my curiosity, made me one day look through it. The clouds appeared to me to be land, which disappeared as they passed along. This heightened my wonder; and I was now more persuaded than ever that I was in another world, and that everything about me was magic.

At last, we came in sight of the island of Barbados, at which the whites on board gave a great shout and made many signs of joy to us. We did not know what to think of this; but as the vessel drew nearer, we plainly saw the harbor, and other ships of different kinds and sizes, and we soon anchored among them, off Bridgetown.

Many merchants and planters now came on board, though it was in the evening. They put us in separate parcels and examined us attentively. They also made us jump, and pointed to the land, signifying we were to go there. We thought by this we should be eaten by these ugly men, as they appeared to us; and, when soon after we were all put down under the deck again, there was much dread and trembling among us, and nothing but bitter cries to be heard all the night from these apprehensions, insomuch that at last the white people got some old slaves from the land to pacify us. They told us we were not to be eaten but to work, and were soon to go on land, where we should see many of our countrypeople. This report eased us much. And sure enough, soon after we were landed, there came to us Africans of all languages.

We were conducted immediately to the merchant's yard, where we were all pent up together, like so many sheep in a fold, without regard to sex or age. As every object was new to me, everything I saw filled me with surprise. What struck me first was that the houses were built with bricks and stories, and in every other respect different from those I had seen in Africa; but I was still more astonished on seeing people on horseback. I did not know what this could mean; and, indeed, I thought these people were full of nothing but magical arts. While I was in this astonishment, one of my fellow prisoners spoke to a countryman of his about the horses, who said they were the same kind they had in their country. I understood them, though they were from a distant part of Africa; and I thought it odd I had not seen any horses there; but afterward, when I came to converse with different Africans, I found they had many horses among them, and much larger than those I then saw.

We were not many days in the merchant's custody before we were sold after their usual manner, which is this. On a signal given (as the beat of a drum), the buyers rush at once into the yard where the slaves are confined and make choice of that parcel they like best. The noise and clamor with which this is attended, and the eagerness visible in the countenances of the buyers, serve not a little to increase the apprehension of terrified Africans, who may well be supposed to consider them as the ministers of that destruction to which they think themselves devoted. In this manner, without scruple, are relations and friends separated, most of them never

405

to see each other again. I remember, in the vessel in which I was brought over, in the men's apartment, there were several brothers, who, in the sale, were sold in different lots; and it was very moving, on this occasion, to see and hear their cries at parting.

O, ye nominal Christians! might not an African ask you— Learned you this from your God, who says unto you, "Do unto all men as you would men should do unto you"? Is it not enough that we are torn from our country and friends to toil for your luxury and lust of gain? Must every tender feeling be likewise sacrificed to your avarice? Are the dearest friends and relations, now rendered more dear by their separation from their kindred, still to be parted from each other, and thus prevented from cheering the gloom of slavery, with the small comfort of being together and mingling their sufferings and sorrows? Why are parents to lose their children, brothers their sisters, or husbands their wives? Surely, this is a new refinement in cruelty which, while it has no advantage to atone for it, thus aggravates distress and adds fresh horrors even to the wretchedness of slavery.

Petition by Free Negroes for Equality Under the Law

Before the emancipation of the slaves after the Civil War, Negroes were severely restricted by laws in both the South and the North. Many states had laws prohibiting them from bringing a suit against another party, or even testifying under oath in a court. One of the earliest protests against these laws is reprinted below. It was presented, January 1791, to the South Carolina legislature by the free Negroes of Charleston. [Source: Manuscript in Slavery File No. 1, Free Persons of Colour, Historical Commission of South Carolina, Columbia.]

To the Honorable David Ramsay, Esquire, president, and to the rest of the honorable new members of the Senate of the state of South Carolina.

The memorial of Thomas Cole, bricklayer, P. B. Mathews and Mathew Webb, butchers, on behalf of themselves and others, free men of color, humbly shows:

That in the enumeration of free citizens by the Constitution of the United States for the purpose of representation of the Southern states in Congress your memorialists have been considered under that description as part of the citizens of this state.

Although by the fourteenth and twenty-ninth clauses in an Act of Assembly made in the year 1740 and entitled an Act for the Better Ordering and Governing Negroes and Other Slaves in this Province, commonly called the Negro Act, now in force, your memorialists are deprived of the rights and privileges of citizens by not having it in their power to give testimony on oath in prosecutions on behalf of the state; from which cause many culprits have escaped the punishment due to their atrocious crimes, nor can they give their testimony in recovering debts due to them, or in establishing agreements made by them within the meaning of the Statutes of Frauds and Perjuries in force in this state except in cases where persons of color are concerned, whereby they are subject to great losses and repeated injuries without any means of redress.

That by the said clauses in the said Act, they are debarred of the rights of free citizens by being subject to a trial without the benefit of a jury and subject to prosecution by testimony of slaves without oath by which they are placed on the same footing.

Your memorialists show that they have at all times since the independence of the United States contributed and do now contribute to the support of the government by cheerfully paying their taxes proportionable to their property with others who have been during such period, and now are, in full enjoyment of the rights and immunities of citizens, inhabitants of a free independent state.

That as your memorialists have been and are considered as free citizens of this state, they hope to be treated as such; they are ready and willing to take and subscribe to such oath of allegiance to the states as shall be prescribed by this honorable House, and are also willing to take upon them any duty for the preservation of the peace in the city or any other occasion if called on.

Your memorialists do not presume to hope that they shall be put on an equal footing with the free white citizens of the state in general. They only humbly solicit such indulgence as the wisdom and humanity of this honorable House shall dictate in their favor by repealing the clauses in the Act beforementioned, and substituting such a clause as will effectually redress the grievances which your memorialists humbly submit in this their memorial, but under such restrictions as to your honorable House shall seem proper.

May it therefore please Your Honors to take your memorialists' case into tender consideration, and make such Acts or insert such clauses for the purpose of relieving your memorialists from the unremitted grievance they now labor under as in your wisdom shall seem meet.

BENJAMIN FRANKLIN
Against the Slave Trade

On March 25, 1790, an essay against the slave trade written by Benjamin Franklin and signed "Historicus" appeared in the Federal Gazette. *The article was occasioned by a speech of James Jackson, a U.S. senator from Georgia, who argued in favor of Negro slavery. Franklin parodied Jackson's arguments, satirically claiming that his essay was an old African speech that the Senator "perhaps [had] not seen." [Source:* The Works of Benjamin Franklin . . . , *Jared Sparks, ed., Vol. II, Boston, 1840, pp. 517-521.]*

Reading last night in your excellent paper the speech of Mr. Jackson in Congress against their meddling with the affair of slavery, or attempting to mend the condition of the slaves, it put me in mind of a similar one made about 100 years since by Sidi Mehemet Ibrahim, a member of the Divan of Algiers, which may be seen in Martin's Account of his Consulship, *anno* 1687. It was against granting the petition of the sect called Erika, or Purists, who prayed for the abolition of piracy and slavery as being unjust. Mr. Jackson does not quote it; perhaps he has not seen it. If, therefore, some of its reasonings are to be found in his eloquent speech, it may only show that

408

men's interests and intellects operate and are operated on with surprising similarity in all countries and climates, whenever they are under similar circumstances. The African's speech, as translated, is as follows.

Allah Bismillah, etc., God is great, and Mahomet is his Prophet.

Have these Erika considered the consequences of granting their petition? If we cease our cruises against the Christians, how shall we be furnished with the commodities their countries produce and which are so necessary for us? If we forbear to make slaves of their people, who in this hot climate are to cultivate our lands? Who are to perform the common labors of our city and in our families? Must we not then be our own slaves? And is there not more compassion and more favor due to us as Mussulmen, than to these Christian dogs? We have now above 50,000 slaves in and near Algiers. This number, if not kept up by fresh supplies, will soon diminish, and be gradually annihilated. If we then cease taking and plundering the infidel ships, and making slaves of the seamen and passengers, our lands will become of no value for want of cultivation; the rents of houses in the city will sink one-half; and the revenue of government arising from its share of prizes be totally destroyed! And for what? To gratify the whims of a whimsical sect, who would have us not only forbear making more slaves, but even manumit those we have.

But who is to indemnify their masters for the loss? Will the state do it? Is our treasury sufficient? Will the Erika do it? Can they do it? Or would they, to do what they think justice to the slaves, do a greater injustice to the owners? And if we set our slaves free, what is to be done with them? Few of them will return to their countries; they know too well the greater hardships they must there be subject to; they will not embrace our holy religion; they will not adopt our manners; our people will not pollute themselves by intermarrying with them. Must we maintain them as beggars in our streets, or suffer our properties to be the prey of their pillage? For men accustomed to slavery will not work for a livelihood when not compelled. And what is

409

there so pitiable in their present condition? Were they not slaves in their own countries?

Are not Spain, Portugal, France, and the Italian states governed by despots, who hold all their subjects in slavery without exception? Even England treats its sailors as slaves; for they are, whenever the government pleases, seized, and confined in ships of war, condemned not only to work, but to fight, for small wages or a mere subsistence, not better than our slaves are allowed by us. Is their condition then made worse by their falling into our hands? No; they have only exchanged one slavery for another, and I may say a better; for here they are brought into a land where the sun of Islamism gives forth its light, and shines in full splendor, and they have an opportunity of making themselves acquainted with the true doctrine, and thereby saving their immortal souls. Those who remain at home have not that happiness. Sending the slaves home then would be sending them out of light into darkness.

I repeat the question: What is to be done with them? I have heard it suggested that they be planted in the wilderness, where there is plenty of land for them to subsist on and where they may flourish as a free state; but they are, I doubt, too little disposed to labor without compulsion, as well as too ignorant to establish a good government; and the wild Arabs would soon molest and destroy or again enslave them. While serving us, we take care to provide them with everything, and they are treated with humanity. The laborers in their own country are, as I am well informed, worse fed, lodged, and clothed. The condition of most of them is therefore already mended and requires no further improvement. Here their lives are in safety. They are not liable to be impressed for soldiers, and forced to cut one another's Christian throats, as in the wars of their own countries. If some of the religious mad bigots, who now tease us with their silly petitions, have in a fit of blind zeal freed their slaves, it was not generosity, it was not humanity, that moved them to the action; it was from the conscious burden of a load of sins, and a hope, from the supposed merits of so good a work, to be excused from damnation.

How grossly are they mistaken to suppose slavery to be

disallowed by the Alcoran! Are not the two precepts (to quote no more): "Masters, treat your slaves with kindness; Slaves, serve your masters with cheerfulness and fidelity," clear proofs to the contrary? Nor can the plundering of infidels be in that sacred book forbidden, since it is well known from it that God has given the world, and all that it contains, to His faithful Mussulmen, who are to enjoy it of right as fast as they conquer it. Let us then hear no more of this detestable proposition, the manumission of Christian slaves, the adoption of which would, by depreciating our lands and houses and thereby depriving so many good citizens of their properties, create universal discontent and provoke insurrections to the endangering of government and producing [of] general confusion. I have therefore no doubt, but this wise council will prefer the comfort and happiness of a whole nation of true believers to the whim of a few Erika and dismiss their petition.

The result was, as Martin tells us, that the Divan came to this resolution: "The doctrine that plundering and enslaving the Christians is unjust is at best problematical; but that it is the interest of this state to continue the practice is clear; therefore let the petition be rejected."

And it was rejected accordingly.

And since like motives are apt to produce in the minds of men like opinions and resolutions, may we not, Mr. Brown, venture to predict from this account that the petitions to the Parliament of England for abolishing the slave trade, to say nothing of other legislatures, and the debates upon them, will have a similar conclusion? I am, sir, your constant reader and humble servant,

HISTORICUS

411

WILLIAM CUSHING

The Quock Walker Case—Slavery Unconstitutional in Massachusetts

Slavery was not expressly forbidden by the constitution of Massachusetts. However, its first article was patterned after the Virginia Declaration of Rights and copied the language of the Declaration of Independence. Accordingly, when in 1783 one Nathaniel Jennison, indicted for assault on Quock Walker, a Negro, defended the assault on the grounds that Walker was his slave, his defense was rejected by the Superior Court on the ground that slavery was by inference unconstitutional in the Commonwealth of Massachusetts. While the case was never reported officially, the opinion of Chief Justice Cushing, part of which is reprinted here, was preserved in his private notebook. [Source: Proceedings of Massachusetts Historical Society, Vol. XIII, Boston, 1875, p. 294.]

As to the doctrine of slavery and the right of Christians to hold Africans in perpetual servitude, and sell and treat them as we do our horses and cattle, that (it is true) has been heretofore countenanced by the province laws formerly, but nowhere is it expressly enacted or established. It has been a usage—a usage which took its origin from the practice of some of the European nations, and the regulations of British government respecting the then colonies, for the benefit of trade and wealth. But whatever sentiments have formerly prevailed in this particular or slid in upon us by the example of others, a different idea has taken place with the people of America, more favorable to the natural rights of mankind, and to that natural, innate desire of liberty, which with heaven (without regard to color, complexion, or shape of noses)... has inspired all the human race. And upon this ground our constitution of government, by which the people of this commonwealth have solemnly bound themselves, sets out with declaring that all men are born free and equal—and that every subject is entitled to liberty, and to have it guarded by the laws, as well as life and property—and in short is totally repugnant to the idea of being born slaves. This being the case, I think the idea of slavery is inconsistent with our own conduct and constitution; and there can be no such thing as perpetual servitude of a rational creature, unless his liberty is forfeited by some criminal conduct or given up by personal consent or contract.

Verdict: Guilty.

ALEXANDER HAMILTON

A Proposal to Arm and Then Free the Negroes

The success of the British in Georgia and South Carolina in early 1779 threatened to sever the southern states from the Union. The Continental Army could spare few troops for the southern theater of war. In a letter of March 14, 1779, to John Jay, Alexander Hamilton proposed the arming of Negro slaves to make up for the shortage. [Source: The Correspondence and Public Papers of John Jay, *Henry P. Johnston, ed., Vol. I, New York, 1890, pp. 191-193.]*

Colonel Laurens, who will have the honor of delivering you this letter, is on his way to South Carolina, on a project which I think, in the present situation of affairs there, is a very good one and deserves every kind of support and encouragement. This is to raise two, three, or four battalions of Negroes, with the assistance of the government of that state, by contributions from the owners in proportion to the number they possess. If you should think proper to enter upon the subject with him, he will give you a detail of his plan. He wishes to have it recommended by Congress to the state; and, as an inducement, that they would engage to take those battalions into continental pay.

It appears to me that an expedient of this kind, in the present state of Southern affairs, is the most rational that can be adopted, and promises very important advantages. Indeed, I hardly see how a sufficient force can be collected in that quarter without it; and the enemy's operations there are growing infinitely serious and formidable. I have not the least doubt that the Negroes will make very excellent soldiers, with proper management; and I will venture to pronounce that they cannot be put into better hands than those of Mr. Laurens. He has all the zeal, intelligence, enterprise, and every other qualification necessary to succeed in such an undertaking. It is a maxim with some great military judges that with sensible officers soldiers can hardly be too stupid; and on this principle it is thought that the Russians would make the best troops in the world if they were under other officers than their own. The king of Prussia is among the number who maintain this doctrine and has a very emphatical saying on the occasion, which I do not exactly recollect. I mention this because I frequently hear it objected to the scheme of embodying Negroes that they are too stupid to make soldiers. This is so far from appearing to me a valid objection that I think their want of cultivation (for their natural faculties are probably as good as ours), joined to that habit of subordination which they acquire from a life of servitude, will make them sooner become soldiers than our white inhabitants. Let officers be men of sense and sentiment, and the nearer the soldiers approach to machines perhaps the better.

I foresee that this project will have to combat much opposition from prejudice and self-interest. The contempt we have been taught to entertain for the blacks makes us fancy many things that are founded neither in reason nor experience; and unwillingness to part with property of so valuable a kind will furnish a thousand arguments to show the impracticability or pernicious tendency of a scheme which requires such a sacrifice. But it should be considered that if we do not make use of them in this way, the enemy probably will; and that the best way to counteract the temptations they will hold out will be to offer them ourselves. An essential part of the plan is to give them their freedom with their muskets. This will secure their fidelity, animate their courage, and I believe will have a good influence upon those who remain, by opening a door to their emancipation. This circumstance, I confess, has no small weight in inducing me to wish the success of the project; for the dictates of humanity and true policy equally interest me in favor of this unfortunate class of men.

414

Negro Voices Raised for Freedom

Negroes in America took the words of the Declaration of Independence seriously. It seemed to many of them to verge on hypocrisy that 700,000 people should be held in bondage while the nation fought a war under the banner of liberty and equality. The following petition against slavery was presented to the Massachusetts House of Representatives on January 13, 1777. [Source: Collections, Massachusetts Historical Society, 2nd series, Vol. III, pp. 436-437.]

The petition of a great number of blacks detained in a state of slavery in the bowels of a free and Christian country humbly shows that your petitioners apprehend that they have in common with all other men a natural and unalienable right to that freedom which the Great Parent of the universe has bestowed equally on all mankind and which they have never forfeited by any compact or agreement whatever. But they were unjustly dragged by the hand of cruel power from their dearest friends and some of them even torn from the embraces of their tender parents, from a populous, pleasant, and plentiful country and in violation of laws of nature and of nations and in defiance of all the tender feelings of humanity, brought here either to be sold like beasts of burden and, like them, condemned to slavery for life—among a people professing the mild religion of Jesus; a people not insensible of the secrets of rational being, nor without spirit to resent the unjust endeavors of others to reduce them to a state of bondage and subjection. Your Honor need not be informed that a life of slavery like that of your petitioners, deprived of every social privilege, of everything requisite to render life tolerable, is far worse than nonexistence.

In imitation of the laudable example of the good people of these states, your petitioners have long and patiently awaited the event of petition after petition presented by them to the legislative body of this state, and cannot but with grief reflect that their success has been but too similar. They cannot but express their astonishment that it has never been considered that every principle from which America has acted in the course of their unhappy difficulties with Great Britain pleads stronger than a thousand arguments in favor of your petitioners.

They therefore humbly beseech Your Honors to give this petition
its due weight and consideration, and cause an act of legislation to
be passed whereby they may be restored to the enjoyments of that
which is the natural right of all men, and that their children, who
were born in this land of liberty, may not be held as slaves after they
arrive at the age of twenty-one years. So may the inhabitants of this
state, no longer chargeable with the inconsistency of acting themselves the part which they condemn and oppose in others, be prospered in their present glorious struggle for liberty and have those
blessings for themselves.

6. Traffic of Mens-body

1567-1758

JOHN WOOLMAN

Journal Entries on Slavery

John Woolman was the most influential American Quaker of his day. A tailor by trade, and always prosperous in his affairs, he cared little for business but devoted the better portion of his life to social and moral causes. For thirty years he traveled from his native New Jersey throughout the colonies, writing and talking against the slave trade, protesting unjust treatment of the Indians, and arguing against war. The Journal *by which he is best known is often compared to Jonathan Edwards'* Personal Narrative, *of which it is the equal in religious devotion, and which reports a similar youthful conversion. Woolman lacked both the brilliance and the passion of Edwards, but he possessed an unfailingly generous and gentle temper and a quiet radiance of spirit. Woolman's sincere, often eloquent, espousal of Quaker doctrine is particularly evident in the following entries from his* Journal. *They were written between 1756 and 1758. [Source:* The Journal of John Woolman, *Boston, 1871, pp. 86-138.]*

Scrupling to do writings relative to keeping slaves has been a means of sundry small trials to me, in which I have so evidently felt my own will set aside that I think it good to mention a few of them. Tradesmen and retailers of goods, who depend on their business for a living, are naturally inclined to keep the goodwill of their customers; nor is it a pleasant thing for young men to be under any necessity to question the judgment or honesty of elderly men, and more especially of such as have a fair reputation. Deep-rooted customs, though wrong, are not easily altered; but it is the duty of all to be firm in that which they certainly know is right for them. A charitable, benevolent man, well-acquainted with a Negro, may, I believe, under some circumstances, keep him in his family as a servant on no other motives than the Negro's good; but man, as man, knows not what shall be after him, nor hath he any assurance that his children will attain to that perfection in wisdom and goodness necessary rightly to exercise such power; hence it is clear to me that I ought not to be the scribe where wills are drawn in which some children are made ales masters over others during life.

About this time an ancient man of good esteem in the neighborhood came to my house to get his will written. He had young Negroes, and I asked him privately how he purposed to dispose of them. He told me; I then said, "I cannot write thy will without breaking my own peace," and respectfully gave him my reasons for it. He signified that he had a choice that I should have written it, but as I could not, consistently with my conscience, he did not desire it, and so he got it written by some other person. A few years after, there being great alterations in his family, he came again to get me to write his will. His Negroes were yet young, and his son, to whom he intended to give them, was, since he first spoke to me, from a libertine become a sober young man, and he supposed that I would have been free on that account to write it. We had much friendly talk on the subject, and then deferred it. A few days after he came again and directed their freedom, and I then wrote his will.

Near the time that the last-mentioned Friend first spoke to me, a neighbor received a bad bruise in his body and sent for me to bleed him, which having done, he desired me to write his will. I took notes, and amongst other things he told me to which of his children he gave his young Negro. I considered the pain and distress he was in, and knew not how it would end, so I wrote his will, save only that part concerning his slave, and carrying it to his bedside read it to him. I then told him in a friendly way that I could not write any instruments by which my fellow creatures were made slaves without bringing trouble on my own mind. I let him know that I charged nothing for what I had done, and desired to be excused from doing the other part in the way he proposed. We then had a serious conference on the subject; at length, he agreeing to set her free, I finished his will.

Having found drawings in my mind to visit Friends on Long Island, after obtaining a certificate from our Monthly Meeting, I set off May 12, 1756. . . . My mind was deeply engaged in this visit, both in public and private, and at several places where I was, on observing that they had slaves, I found myself under a necessity, in a friendly way, to labor with them on that subject; expressing, as way opened, the inconsistency of that practice with the purity of the Christian religion, and the ill effects of it manifested amongst us. . . .

Feeling the exercise in relation to a visit to the Southern provinces to increase upon me, I acquainted our Monthly Meeting therewith and obtained their certificate. Expecting to go alone, one of my brothers who lived in Philadelphia, having some business in North Carolina, proposed going with me part of the way; but as he had a view of some outward affairs, to accept of him as a companion was some difficulty with me, whereupon I had conversation with him at sundry times. At length feeling easy in my mind, I had conversation with several elderly Friends of Philadelphia on the subject, and he obtaining a certificate suitable to the occasion, we set off in May 1757. . . .

Soon after I entered this province, a deep and painful exercise came upon me, which I often had some feeling of, since my mind was drawn toward these parts, and with which I had acquainted my brother before we agreed to join as companions. As the people in this and the Southern provinces live much on the labor of slaves, many of whom are used hardly, my concern was that I might attend with singleness of heart to the voice of the true Shepherd, and be so supported as to remain unmoved at the faces of men.

As it is common for Friends on such a visit to have entertainment free of cost, a difficulty arose in my mind with respect to saving my money by kindness received from what appeared to me to be the gain of oppression. Receiving a gift, considered as a gift, brings the receiver under obligations to the benefactor, and has a natural tendency to draw the obliged into a party with the giver. To prevent difficulties of this kind, and to preserve the minds of judges from any bias, was that divine prohibition: "Thou shalt not receive any gift; for a gift blindeth the wise, and perverteth the words of the righteous" (Ex. 23:8). As the disciples were sent forth without any provision for their journey, and our Lord said the workman is worthy of his meat, their labor in the gospel was considered as a reward for their entertainment, and therefore not received as a gift; yet, in regard to my present journey, I could not see my way clear in that respect. The difference appeared thus: the entertainment the disciples met with was from them whose hearts God had opened to receive them, from a love to them and the truth they published; but we, considered as members of the same religious society, look upon it as a piece of civility to receive each other in such visits; and such reception, at times, is partly in regard to reputation and not from an

421

inward unity of heart and spirit. Conduct is more convincing than language, and where people, by their actions, manifest that the slave trade is not so disagreeable to their principles but that it may be encouraged, there is not a sound uniting with some Friends who visit them.

The prospect of so weighty a work, and of being so distinguished from many whom I esteemed before myself, brought me very low, and such were the conflicts of my soul that I had a near sympathy with the prophet, in the time of his weakness, when he said: "If thou deal thus with me, kill me, I pray thee, if I have found favor in thy sight" (Num. 11:15). But I soon saw that this proceeded from the want of a full resignation to the divine will. Many were the afflictions which attended me, and in great abasement, with many tears, my cries were to the Almighty for His gracious and fatherly assistance, and after a time of deep trial I was favored to understand the state mentioned by the Psalmist more clearly than ever I had done before, to wit: "My soul is even as a weaned child" (Ps. 131:2). Being thus helped to sink down into resignation, I felt a deliverance from that tempest in which I had been sorely exercised, and in calmness of mind went forward, trusting that the Lord Jesus Christ, as I faithfully attended to him, would be a counselor to me in all difficulties, and that by his strength I should be enabled even to leave money with the members of society where I had entertainment, when I found that omitting it would obstruct that work to which I believed He had called me.

As I copy this after my return, I may here add that oftentimes I did so under a sense of duty. The way in which I did it was thus: When I expected soon to leave a Friend's house where I had entertainment, if I believed that I should not keep clear from the gain of oppression without leaving money, I spoke to one of the heads of the family privately, and desired them to accept of those pieces of silver and give them to such of their Negroes as they believed would make the best use of them; and at other times I gave them to the Negroes myself, as the way looked clearest to me. Before I came out, I had provided a large number of small pieces for this purpose, and thus offering them to some who appeared to be wealthy people was a trial both to me and them. But the fear of the Lord so covered me at times that my way was made easier than I expected; and few, if any, manifested any resentment at the offer, and most of them, after some conversation, accepted of them.

May 9. A Friend at whose house we breakfasted setting us a little on our way, I had conversation with him, in the fear of the Lord, concerning his slaves, in which my heart was tender. I used much plainness of speech with him, and he appeared to take it kindly. We pursued our journey without appointing meetings, being pressed in my mind to be at the Yearly Meeting in Virginia. In my traveling on the road, I often felt a cry rise from the center of my mind, thus: "O Lord, I am a stranger on the earth, hide not Thy face from me." On the 11th, we crossed the rivers Patowmack [Potomac] and Rapahannock and lodged at Port Royal. On the way we had the company of a colonel of the militia, who appeared to be a thoughtful man. I took occasion to remark on the difference in general between a people used to labor moderately for their living, training up their children in frugality and business, and those who live on the labor of slaves; the former, in my view, being the most happy life. He concurred in the remark, and mentioned the trouble arising from the untoward, slothful disposition of the Negroes, adding that one of our laborers would do as much in a day as two of their slaves. I replied that free men, whose minds were properly on their business, found a satisfaction in improving, cultivating, and providing for their families; but Negroes, laboring to support others who claim them as their property, and expecting nothing but slavery during life, had not the like inducement to be industrious.

After some further conversation, I said that men having power too often misapplied it; that though we made slaves of the Negroes, and the Turks made slaves of the Christians, I believed that liberty was the natural right of all men equally. This he did not deny, but said the lives of the Negroes were so wretched in their own country that many of them lived better here than there. I replied, "There is great odds in regard to us on what principle we act"; and so the conversation on that subject ended.

I may here add that another person, some time afterward, mentioned the wretchedness of the Negroes, occasioned by their intestine wars, as an argument in favor of our fetching them away for slaves. To which I replied, if compassion for the Africans, on account of their domestic troubles, was the real motive of our purchasing them, that spirit of tenderness being attended to would incite us to use them kindly that, as strangers brought out of affliction, their lives might be happy among us. And as they are human creatures, whose souls are as precious as ours, and who may receive the same help and comfort from the Holy Scriptures as we do, we could not omit suitable endeavors to instruct them therein; but that while we manifest by our conduct that our views in purchasing them are to advance ourselves, and while our buying captives taken in war animates those parties to push on the war and increase desolation amongst them, to say they live unhappily in Africa is far from being an argument in our favor. I further said the present circumstances of these provinces to me appear difficult; the slaves look like a burdensome stone to such as burden themselves with them; and that if the white people retain a resolution to prefer their outward prospects of gain to all other considerations and do not act conscientiously toward them as fellow creatures, I believe that burden will grow heavier and heavier, until times change in a way disagreeable to us. The person appeared very serious, and owned that in considering their condition and the manner of their treatment in these provinces, he had sometimes thought it might be just in the Almighty so to order it.

Having traveled through Maryland, we came amongst Friends at Cedar Creek in Virginia, on the 12th; and the next day rode, in company with several of them, a day's journey to Camp Creek. As I was riding along in the morning, my mind was deeply affected in a sense I had of the need of divine aid to support me in the various difficulties which attended me, and in uncommon distress of mind I cried in secret to the Most High, "O Lord be merciful, I beseech Thee, to Thy poor afflicted creature!" After some time, I felt inward relief, and, soon after, a Friend in company began to talk in support of the slave trade, and said the Negroes were understood to be the offspring of Cain, their blackness being the mark which God set upon him after he murdered Abel his brother; that it was the design of Providence they should be slaves as a condition proper to the race of so wicked a man as Cain was. Then another spoke in support of what had been said.

To all which I replied in substance as follows: That Noah and his family were all who survived the flood, according to Scripture; and

424

as Noah was of Seth's race, the family of Cain was wholly destroyed. One of them said that after the flood Ham went to the land of Nod and took a wife; that Nod was a land far distant, inhabited by Cain's race, and that the flood did not reach it; and as Ham was sentenced to be a servant of servants to his brethren, these two families, being thus joined, were undoubtedly fit only for slaves. I replied the flood was judgment upon the world for their abominations, and it was granted that Cain's stock was the most wicked, and therefore unreasonable to suppose that they were spared. As to Ham's going to the land of Nod for a wife, no time being fixed, Nod might be inhabited by some of Noah's family before Ham married a second time; moreover the text saith "That all flesh died that moved upon the earth" (Gen. 7:21).

I further reminded them how the prophets repeatedly declare "that the son shall not suffer for the iniquity of the father, but everyone be answerable for his own sins." I was troubled to perceive the darkness of their imaginations, and in some pressure of spirit said, "The love of ease and gain are the motives in general of keeping slaves, and men are wont to take hold of weak arguments to support a cause which is unreasonable. I have no interest on either side, save only the interest which I desire to have in the truth. I believe liberty is their right, and as I see they are not only deprived of it but treated in other respects with inhumanity in many places, I believe He who is a refuge for the oppressed will, in His own time, plead their cause, and happy will it be for such as walk in uprightness before Him." And thus our conversation ended.

May 14. I was this day at Camp Creek Monthly Meeting and then rode to the mountains up James River and had a meeting at a Friend's house, in both which I felt sorrow of heart, and my tears were poured out before the Lord, who was pleased to afford a degree of strength by which way was opened to clear my mind amongst Friends in those places. . . .

The sense I had of the state of the churches brought a weight of distress upon me. The gold to me appeared dim, and the fine gold changed, and though this is the case too generally, yet the sense of it in these parts hath in a particular manner borne heavy upon me. It appeared to me that through the prevailing of the spirit of this world the minds of many were brought to an inward desolation, and

425

instead of the spirit of meekness, gentleness, and heavenly wisdom, which are the necessary companions of the true sheep of Christ, a spirit of fierceness and the love of dominion too generally prevailed. From small beginnings in error great buildings by degrees are raised, and from one age to another are more and more strengthened by the general concurrence of the people; and as men obtain reputation by their profession of the truth, their virtues are mentioned as arguments in favor of general error; and those of less note, to justify themselves, say, such and such good men did the like. By what other steps could the people of Judah arise to that height in wickedness as to give just ground for the prophet Isaiah to declare, in the name of the Lord, "that none calleth for justice, nor any pleadeth for truth" (Isa. 59:4), or for the Almighty to call upon the great city of Jerusalem just before the Babylonish captivity, "If ye can find a man, if there be any who executeth judgment, that seeketh the truth, and I will pardon it" (Jer. 5:1).

The prospect of a way being open to the same degeneracy in some parts of this newly settled land of America in respect to our conduct toward the Negroes hath deeply bowed my mind in this journey, and though briefly to relate how these people are treated is no agreeable work; yet, after often reading over the notes I made as I traveled, I find my mind engaged to preserve them. Many of the white people in those provinces take little or no care of Negro marriages; and when Negroes marry after their own way, some make so little account of those marriages that with views of outward interest they often part men from their wives by selling them far asunder, which is common when estates are sold by executors at vendue. Many whose labor is heavy being followed at their business in the field by a man with a whip, hired for that purpose, have in common little else allowed but one peck of Indian corn and some salt, for one week, with a few potatoes; the potatoes they commonly raise by their labor on the first day of the week. The correction ensuing on their disobedience to overseers, or slothfulness in business, is often very severe and sometimes desperate.

Men and women have many times scarcely clothes sufficient to hide their nakedness, and boys and girls ten and twelve years old are often quite naked amongst their master's children. Some of our Society, and some of the society called Newlights, use some endeav-

426

ors to instruct those they have in reading; but in common this is not only neglected but disapproved. These are the people by whose labor the other inhabitants are in a great measure supported, and many of them in the luxuries of life. These are the people who have made no agreement to serve us, and who have not forfeited their liberty that we know of. These are the souls for whom Christ died, and for our conduct toward them we must answer before Him who is no respecter of persons. They who know the only true God, and Jesus Christ whom He hath sent, and are thus acquainted with the merciful, benevolent, gospel spirit, will therein perceive that the indignation of God is kindled against oppression and cruelty, and in beholding the great distress of so numerous a people will find cause for mourning.

From my lodgings I went to Burleigh Meeting. . . . The next meeting we had was at Black-Water, and from thence went to the Yearly Meeting at the Western Branch. When business began, some queries were introduced by some of their members for consideration, and, if approved, they were to be answered hereafter by their respective Monthly Meetings. They were the Pennsylvania queries, which had been examined by a committee of Virginia Yearly Meeting appointed the last year, who made some alterations in them, one of which alterations was made in favor of a custom which troubled me. The query was, "Are there any concerned in the importation of Negroes, or in buying them after imported?" which was thus altered, "Are there any concerned in the importation of Negroes, or buying them to trade in?" As one query admitted with unanimity was, "Are any concerned in buying or vending goods unlawfully imported, or prize goods?" I found my mind engaged to say that as we profess the truth and were there assembled to support the testimony of it, it was necessary for us to dwell deep and act in that wisdom which is pure, or otherwise we could not prosper. I then mentioned their alteration, and, referring to the last-mentioned query, added that as purchasing any merchandise taken by the sword was always allowed to be inconsistent with our principles, so Negroes being captives of war, or taken by stealth, it was inconsistent with our testimony to buy them; and their being our fellow creatures and sold as slaves added greatly to the iniquity. Friends appeared attentive to what was said; some expressed a care and concern about their

427

Negroes; none made any objection, by way of reply to what I said, but the query was admitted as they had altered it.

As some of their members have heretofore traded in Negroes, as in other merchandise, this query being admitted will be one step further than they have hitherto gone, and I did not see it my duty to press for an alteration, but felt easy to leave it all to Him who alone is able to turn the hearts of the mighty and make way for the spreading of truth on the earth, by means agreeable to His infinite wisdom. In regard to those they already had, I felt my mind engaged to labor with them and said that as we believe the Scriptures were given forth by holy men, as they were moved by the Holy Ghost, and many of us know by experience that they are often helpful and comfortable, and believe ourselves bound in duty to teach our children to read them, I believed that if we were divested of all selfish views, the same good spirit that gave them forth would engage us to teach the Negroes to read that they might have the benefit of them. Some present manifested a concern to take more care in the education of their Negroes.

May 29. At the house where I lodged was a meeting of ministers and elders. I found an engagement to speak freely and plainly to them concerning their slaves; mentioning how they, as the first rank in the Society, whose conduct in that case was much noticed by others, were under the stronger obligations to look carefully to themselves. Expressing how needful it was for them in that situation to be thoroughly divested of all selfish views; that living in the pure truth and acting conscientiously toward those people in their education and otherwise, they might be instrumental in helping forward a work so exceedingly necessary, and so much neglected amongst them. . . .

The Monthly Meeting of Philadelphia having been under a concern on account of some Friends, who this summer (1758) had bought Negro slaves, proposed to their Quarterly Meeting to have the minute reconsidered in the Yearly Meeting, which was made last on that subject, and the said Quarterly Meeting appointed a committee to consider it and to report to their next. This committee having met once and adjourned, and I, going to Philadelphia to meet a committee of the Yearly Meeting, was in town the evening on which the Quarterly Meeting's committee met the second time;

428

and finding an inclination to sit with them, I, with some others, was admitted, and Friends had a weighty conference on the subject. Soon after their next Quarterly Meeting I heard that the case was coming to our Yearly Meeting. This brought a weighty exercise upon me, and under a sense of my own infirmities, and the great danger I felt of turning aside from perfect purity, my mind was often drawn to retire alone and put up my prayers to the Lord that He would be graciously pleased to strengthen me; that setting aside all views of self-interest and the friendship of this world, I might stand fully resigned to His holy will.

In this Yearly Meeting several weighty matters were considered, and, toward the last, that in relation to dealing with persons who purchase slaves. During the several sittings of the said meeting, my mind was frequently covered with inward prayer, and I could say with David "that tears were my meat day and night." The case of slavekeeping lay heavy upon me, nor did I find any engagement to speak directly to any other matter before the meeting.

Now, when this case was opened, several faithful Friends spoke weightily thereto, with which I was comforted; and feeling a concern to cast in my mite, I said in substance as follows: "In the difficulties attending us in this life, nothing is more precious than the mind of truth inwardly manifested; and it is my earnest desire that in this weighty matter we may be so truly humbled as to be favored with a clear understanding of the mind of truth, and follow it; this would be of more advantage to the Society than any medium not in the clearness of divine wisdom. The case is difficult to some who have slaves, but if such set aside all self-interest and come to be weaned from the desire of getting estates, or even from holding them together, when truth requires the contrary, I believe way will so open that they will know how to steer through those difficulties."

Many Friends appeared to be deeply bowed under the weight of the work and manifested much firmness in their love to the cause of truth and universal righteousness on the earth. And though none did openly justify the practice of slave-keeping in general, yet some appeared concerned lest the meeting should go into such measures as might give uneasiness to many brethren, alleging that if Friends patiently continued under the exercise, the Lord, in His time, might open a way for the deliverance of these people. Finding an engage-

429

ment to speak, I said, "My mind is often led to consider the purity of the Divine Being and the justice of His judgments; and herein my soul is covered with awfulness. I cannot omit to hint of some cases where people have not been treated with the purity of justice, and the event hath been lamentable. Many slaves on this continent are oppressed, and their cries have reached the ears of the Most High. Such are the purity and certainty of His judgments that He cannot be partial in our favor. In infinite love and goodness He hath opened our understanding from one time to another concerning our duty toward this people, and it is not a time for delay. Should we now be sensible of what He requires of us, and through a respect to the private interest of some persons, or through a regard to some friend-ships which do not stand on an immutable foundation, neglect to do our duty in firmness and constancy, still waiting for some extraor-dinary means to bring about their deliverance, God may by terrible things in righteousness answer us in this matter."

Many faithful brethren labored with great firmness, and the love of truth in a good degree prevailed. Several who had Negroes ex-pressed their desire that a rule might be made to deal with such Friends as offenders who bought slaves in future. To this it was answered that the root of this evil would never be effectually struck at until a thorough search was made in the circumstances of such Friends as kept Negroes, with respect to the righteousness of their motives in keeping them, that impartial justice might be adminis-tered throughout. Several Friends expressed their desire that a visit might be made to such Friends as kept slaves, and many others said that they believed liberty was the Negro's right; to which, at length, no opposition was publicly made. A minute was made more full on that subject than any heretofore; and the names of several Friends entered who were free to join in a visit to such as kept slaves.

430

PETER FONTAINE
A Defense of Slavery in Virginia

*By the middle of the eighteenth century, slaves had become an indispensable
commodity on the tobacco, indigo, and rice plantations of Maryland,
Virginia, and South Carolina. Not yet established as a social institution — many
slaveholders deplored the ethics of the practice — the use of slave labor was
defended as an economic necessity by such respected leaders as the
Reverend Peter Fontaine of Westover, Virginia, who discussed the subject in
the following letter of March 30, 1757, to his brother Moses. [Source:
Memoirs of a Huguenot Family, Ann Maury, ed., New York, 1853, pp.
348-353.]*

Now, to answer your first query — whether by our breach of treaties
we have not justly exasperated the bordering nations of Indians
against us, and drawn upon ourselves the barbarous usage we meet
with from them and the French? To answer this fully would take up
much time. I shall only hint at some things which we ought to have
done, and which we did not do at our first settlement among them,
and which we might have learned long since from the practice of
our enemies the French.

I am persuaded we were not deficient in the observation of
treaties, but, as we got the land by concession and not by conquest,
we ought to have intermarried with them, which would have incorporated us with them effectually, and made of them staunch
friends, and, which is of still more consequence, made many of
them good Christians. But this our wise politicians at home put an
effectual stop to at the beginning of our settlement here, for, when
they heard that Rolfe had married Pocahontas, it was deliberated in
Council whether he had not committed high treason by so doing,
that is, marrying an Indian Princess. And had not some troubles
intervened which put a stop to the inquiry, the poor man might have
been hanged up for doing the most just, the most natural, the most
generous and politic action that ever was done this side of the water.
This put an effectual stop to all intermarriages afterward.

Our Indian traders have indeed their squaws, alias whores, at
the Indian towns where they trade, but leave their offspring like

bulls or boars to be provided for at random by their mothers. As might be expected, some of these bastards have been the leading men or war captains that have done us so much mischief. This ill treatment was sufficient to create jealousy in the natural man's breast, and made the Indians look upon us as false and deceitful friends, and cause all our endeavors to convert them to be ineffectual. But here, methinks, I can hear you observe—What! Englishmen intermarry with Indians? But I can convince you that they are guilty of much more heinous practices, more unjustifiable in the sight of God and man (if that, indeed, may be called a bad practice), for many base wretches among us take up with Negro women, by which means the country swarms with mulatto bastards, and these mulattoes, if but three generations removed from the black father or mother, may, by the indulgence of the laws of the country, intermarry with the white people, and actually do every day so marry.

Now, if, instead of this abominable practice which has polluted the blood of many among us, we had taken Indian wives in the first place, it would have made them some compensation for their lands. They are a free people, and the offspring would not be born in a state of slavery. We should become rightful heirs to their lands and should not have smutted our blood; for the Indian children when born are as white as Spaniards or Portuguese, and were it not for the practice of going naked in the summer and besmearing themselves with bears' grease, etc., they would continue white. And had we thought fit to make them our wives, they would readily have complied with our fashion of wearing clothes all the year round; and, by doing justice to these poor, benighted heathen, we should have introduced Christianity among them.

Your own reflections upon these hints will be a sufficient answer to your first query. I shall only add that General Johnson's success was owing, under God, to his fidelity to the Indians and his generous conduct to his Indian wife, by whom he has several hopeful sons, who are all war captains, the bulwarks with him of the Five Nations, and loyal subjects to their mother country.

As to your second query, if enslaving our fellow creatures be a practice agreeable to Christianity, it is answered in a great measure in many treatises at home, to which I refer you. I shall only mention something of our present state here.

Like Adam, we are all apt to shift off the blame from ourselves and lay it upon others, how justly in our case you may judge. The Negroes are enslaved by the Negroes themselves before they are purchased by the masters of the ships who bring them here. It is, to be sure, at our choice whether we buy them or not, so this then is our crime, folly, or whatever you will please to call it.

But our Assembly, foreseeing the ill consequences of importing such numbers among us, has often attempted to lay a duty upon them which would amount to a prohibition, such as £10 or £20 a head; but no governor dare pass such a law, having instructions to the contrary from the Board of Trade at home. By this means they are forced upon us, whether we will or will not. This plainly shows the African Company has the advantage of the colonies, and may do as it pleases with the Ministry.

Indeed, since we have been exhausted of our little stock of cash by the war, the importation has stopped; our poverty then is our best security. There is no more picking for their ravenous jaws upon bare bones; but should we begin to thrive, they will be at the same again. All our taxes are now laid upon slaves and on shippers of tobacco, which they wink at while we are in danger of being torn from them, but we dare not do it in time of peace, it being looked upon as the highest presumption to lay any burden upon trade. This is our part of the grievance, but to live in Virginia without slaves is morally impossible.

Before our troubles, you could not hire a servant or slave for love or money, so that, unless robust enough to cut wood, to go to mill, to work at the hoe, etc., you must starve or board in some family where they both fleece and half starve you. There is no set price upon corn, wheat, and provisions; so they take advantage of the necessities of strangers, who are thus obliged to purchase some slaves and land. This, of course, draws us all into the original sin and curse of the country of purchasing slaves, and this is the reason we have no merchants, traders, or artificers of any sort but what become planters in a short time.

A common laborer, white or black, if you can be so much favored as to hire one, is 1s. sterling or 15d. currency per day; a bungling carpenter, 2s. or 2s. 6d. per day; besides diet and lodging. That is, for a lazy fellow to get wood and water, £19 16s. 3d. current per annum; add to this £7 or £8 more and you have a slave for life.

433

SAMUEL HOPKINS
The Inconsistency of Slavery

In 1776, Samuel Hopkins published A Dialogue Concerning the Slavery of the Africans, *which he directed at the Continental Congress, urging it to abolish the institution of slavery. The act required some courage on Hopkins' part, for at the time Newport, Rhode Island, was one of the centers of the slaveholding interest, and many of his congregation were either slaveholders themselves or at least financially involved in the slave trade. A portion of his* Dialogue, *one of the earliest antislavery protests from the Congregational ministry, is reprinted here. [Source: The Works of Samuel Hopkins, Boston, 1854, Vol. II, pp. 551-588.]*

The slavery that now takes place is in a Christian land, and without the express sanction of civil government; and it is all of the same kind and from one original, which is most notoriously unjust. And if it be unrighteous in one instance, it is so in almost every instance; and the unrighteousness of it is most apparent, and most masters have no color of claim to hold their servants in bondage. And this is become a general and crying sin for which we are under the awful frowns of heaven. These things . . . make it duty to oppose and bear testimony, both in public and more privately, against this evil practice, which is so evidently injurious to individuals, and threatens our ruin as a people. . . .

It has always been the way of tyrants to take great pains to keep their vassals in ignorance, especially to hide from them the tyranny and oppression of which they are the subjects; and for this reason they are enemies to the liberty of the press, and are greatly provoked when their conduct is set in a true light before the public and the unrighteousness they practise properly exposed. The complaint we are now considering seems to be of the same kind with this, and well becomes all those petty tyrants who have slaves in their possession, which they are conscious they cannot vindicate, but the unrighteousness will be detected if free inquiry and freedom of speech cannot be suppressed. And this complaint is of the same kind with the conduct of the masters of slaves in the West Indies in opposing their being taught anything of Christianity, because they know every gleam of this light carries a discovery of the unrighteousness of the treatment they receive.

The present situation of our public affairs and our struggle for liberty, and the abundant conversation this occasions in all companies — while the poor Negroes look on and hear what an aversion we have to slavery and how much liberty is prized, they often hearing it declared publicly and in private, as the voice of all, that slavery is more to be dreaded than death, and we are resolved to live free or die, etc. — this, I say, necessarily leads them to attend to their own wretched situation more than otherwise they could. They see themselves deprived of all liberty and property, and their children after them, to the latest posterity, subject to the will of those who appear to have no feeling for their misery, and are guilty of many instances of hardheartedness and cruelty toward them, while they think themselves very kind; and, therefore, to make the least complaint, would be deemed the height of arrogance and abuse; and often if they have a comparatively good master now, with constant dread they see a young one growing up, who bids fair to rule over them, or their children, with rigor. . . .

No wonder there are many and great difficulties in reforming an evil practice of this kind, which has got such deep root by length of time and is become so common. But it does not yet appear that they cannot be removed by the united wisdom and strength of the American colonies, without any injury to the slaves or disadvantage to the public. Yea, the contrary is most certain, as the slaves cannot be put into a more wretched situation, ourselves being judges, and the community cannot take a more likely step to escape ruin and obtain the smiles and protection of Heaven. This matter ought, doubtless, to be attended to by the general assemblies, and continental and provincial congresses; and if they were as much united and engaged in devising ways and means to set at liberty these injured slaves as they are to defend themselves from tyranny, it would soon be effected. . . . Surely we have no reason to conclude it cannot be done till we see a suitable zeal and resolution among all orders of men, and answerable attempts are thoroughly made.

Let this iniquity be viewed in its true magnitude and in the shocking light in which it has been set in this conversation; let the wretched case of the poor blacks be considered with proper pity and

435

benevolence, together with the probably dreadful consequence to this land of retaining them in bondage, and all objections against liberating them would vanish. . . .

If parents have a son pressed on board a king's ship, how greatly are they affected with it! They are filled with grief and distress, and will cheerfully be at almost any cost and pains to procure his liberty; and we wonder not at it, but think their exercises and engagedness for his deliverance very just, and stand ready to condemn him who has no feeling for them and their son, and is not ready to afford all the assistance in his power in order to recover him. At the same time, we behold vast numbers of blacks among us, torn from their native country and all their relations, not to serve on board a man-of-war for a few years but to be abject, despised slaves for life, and their children after them, and yet have not the least feelings for them or desire of their freedom. These very parents, perhaps, have a number of Negro slaves on whom they have not the least pity, and stand ready highly to resent it if anyone espouses their cause so much as to propose they should be set at liberty. What reason for this partiality? Ought this so to be? An impartial person, who is not under the prejudices of interest, education, and custom, is shocked with it beyond all expression. The poor Negroes have sense enough to see and feel it, but have no friend to speak a word for them, none to whom they may complain. . . .

The slaves who are become unprofitable to their masters by the present calamitous state of our country will be with the less reluctance set at liberty, it is hoped; and if no public provision be made for them that they may be transported to Africa, where they might probably live better than in any other country, or be removed into those places in this land where they may have profitable business and are wanted, now so many are called from their farms to defend our country; I say, if this be not done, the masters, by freeing them, would lose nothing by it, even though they continue to support them, till some way shall be open for them to help themselves. I must here again desire every owner of slaves to make their case his own, and consider, if he or his children were unjustly in a state of slavery, whether he should think such an objection against their being set at liberty of any weight.

Would he not rather think it reasonable that the masters who had

436

held them in bondage against all right and reason would consider their being, by an extraordinary Providence, rendered unprofitable to them, as an admonition to break off their sins by righteousness and their iniquity by showing mercy to these poor; and that it ought to be a greater satisfaction to them thus to do justice without delay and relieve these oppressed poor than to possess all the riches, honors, and pleasures of this world? And if these masters should disregard such an admonition and neglect this opportunity to set them at liberty, putting it off to a more convenient season, would it not be very grievous to him and overwhelm him in despair of their ever doing it? Is it not very certain that they who make this objection against freeing their slaves without delay would not free them if the times should change and they again become profitable? If they must maintain them, can they not do it as well when they are free as while they are slaves, and ought they not to do it with much more satisfaction? . . .

But if we obstinately refuse to reform what we have implicitly declared to be wrong, and engaged to put away the holding the Africans in slavery, which is so particularly pointed out by the evil with which we are threatened and is such a glaring contradiction to our professed aversion to slavery and struggle for civil liberty, and improve the favor God is showing us as an argument in favor of this iniquity and encouragement to persist in it . . . have we not the greatest reason to fear, yea, may we not with great certainty conclude, God will yet withdraw His kind protection from us and punish us yet seven times more? This has been God's usual way of dealing with His professing people; and who can say it is not most reasonable and wise?

He, then, acts the most friendly part to these colonies and to the masters of slaves, as well as to the slaves themselves, who does his utmost to effect a general emancipation of the Africans among us. And, in this view, I could wish the conversation we have now had on this subject, if nothing better is like to be done, were published and spread through all the colonies, and had the attentive perusal of every American.

SAMUEL SEWALL

The Selling of Joseph

*Samuel Sewall is remembered chiefly for his diary. In it for fifty-seven years,
he set down the events of his own and other lives in Boston — revealing in the
process all of his many crotchets and vanities, but showing, too, the courage
that led him, on January 14, 1697, to have his pastor read from the pulpit of
his church his repentance for having concurred in the sentences that had
lately condemned nineteen persons to death as witches. Sewall was among
other things a judge, with a concern for the unfortunate that was not always
belated. His protest against slavery in the province of Massachusetts, called*
The Selling of Joseph, *was first printed in Boston in 1700.*

*Forasmuch as liberty is in real value next unto life, none ought to
part with it themselves, or deprive others of it, but upon most mature
consideration.*

The numerousness of slaves at this day in the province, and the
uneasiness of them under their slavery, has put many upon thinking whether the foundation of it be firmly and well laid, so as to
sustain the vast weight that is built upon it. It is most certain that
all men, as they are the sons of Adam, are coheirs, and have equal
right unto liberty, and all other outward comforts of life. "God hath
given the earth (with all its commodities) unto the sons of Adam"
(Ps. 115:16). "And hath made of one blood, all nations of men, for to
dwell on all the face of the earth, and hath determined the times
before appointed, and the bounds of their habitation, that they
should seek the Lord. Forasmuch then as we are the offspring of
God," etc. (Acts 17:26, 27, 29).

Now, although the title given by the last Adam does infinitely
better men's estates respecting God and themselves, and grants
them a most beneficial and inviolable lease under the broad seal of
heaven, who were before only tenants at will; yet, through the
indulgence of God to our first parents after the Fall, the outward
estate of all and every of their children remains the same as to one
another; so that, originally and naturally, there is no such thing as
slavery. Joseph was rightfully no more a slave to his brethren than
they were to him; and they had no more authority to sell him than

438

they had to slay him. And if they had nothing to do to sell him, the Ishmaelites bargaining with them and paying down twenty pieces of silver, could not make a title. Neither could Potiphar have any better interest in him than the Ishmaelites had (Gen. 37:20, 27, 28); for he that shall in this case plead alteration of property seems to have forfeited a great part of his own claim to humanity. There is no proportion between twenty pieces of silver and *liberty*. The commodity itself is the claimer. If Arabian gold be imported in any quantities, most are afraid to meddle with it, though they might have it at easy rates, lest if it should have been wrongfully taken from the owners, it should kindle a fire to the consumption of their whole estate.

'Tis pity there should be more caution used in buying a horse or a little lifeless dust than there is in purchasing men and women. Whenas they are the offspring of God, and their liberty is *Auro pretiosior omni* [more precious than all gold].

And seeing God has said, "He that stealeth a man and selleth him, or if he be found in his hand, he shall surely be put to death" (Ex. 21:16). This law being of everlasting equity, wherein man-stealing is ranked among the most atrocious of capital crimes, what louder cry can there be made of that celebrated warning, *Caveat emptor!* [Let the buyer beware.]

And all things considered, it would conduce more to the welfare of the province to have white servants for a term of years than to have slaves for life. Few can endure to hear of a Negro's being made free, and indeed they can seldom use their freedom well; yet their continual aspiring after their forbidden liberty renders them unwilling servants. And there is such a disparity in their conditions, color, and hair that they can never embody with us and grow up into orderly families, to the peopling of the land, but still remain in our body politic as a kind of extravasat[ed] blood. As many Negro men as there are among us, so many empty places there are in our train bands, and the places taken up of men that might make husbands for our daughters. And the sons and daughters of New England would become more like Jacob and Rachel, if this slavery were thrust quite out-of-doors. Moreover, it is too well known what temptations masters are under to connive at the fornication of their slaves, lest they should be obliged to find them wives, or pay their fines. It seems to be practically pleaded that they might be lawless; 'tis thought much of, that the law should have satisfaction for their thefts and other immoralities; by which means, holiness to the Lord is more rarely engraven upon this sort of servitude.

It is likewise most lamentable to think, how in taking Negroes out of Africa and selling of them here, that which God has joined together men do boldly rend asunder—men from their country, husbands from their wives, parents from their children. How horrible is the uncleanness, mortality, if not murder, that the ships are guilty of that bring great crowds of these miserable men and women. Methinks, when we are bemoaning the barbarous usage of our friends and kinfolk in Africa, it might not be unseasonable to inquire whether we are not culpable in forcing the Africans to become slaves among ourselves. And it may be a question whether all the benefit received by Negro slaves will balance the account of cash laid out upon them, and for the redemption of our own enslaved friends out of Africa, besides all the persons and estates that have perished there.

Objection 1. These blackamoors are of the posterity of Ham, and therefore are under the curse of slavery (Gen. 9:25-27).

Answer. Of all offices, one would not beg this; viz., uncalled for, to be an executioner of the vindictive wrath of God, the extent and duration of which is to us uncertain. If this ever was a commission, how do we know but that it is long since out of date? Many have found it to their cost that a prophetical denunciation of judgment against a person or people would not warrant them to inflict that evil. If it would, Hazael might justify himself in all he did against his Master and the Israelites, from II Kings 8:10, 12.

But it is possible that by cursory reading this text may have been mistaken. For Canaan is the person cursed three times over, without the mentioning of Ham. Good expositors suppose the curse entailed on him, and that this prophesy was accomplished in the extirpation of the Canaanites and in the servitude of the Gibeonites. *Vide pareum* [see Pareus]. Whereas the blackamoors are not descended of Canaan but of Cush (Ps. 68:31). Princes shall come out of Egypt (Mizraim), Ethiopia (Cush) shall soon stretch out her hands unto God; under which names all Africa may be comprehended, and their promised conversion ought to be prayed for (Jer. 13:23). Can

440

the Ethiopian change his skin? This shows that black men are the posterity of Cush, who time out of mind have been distinguished by their color. And for want of the true, Ovid assigns a fabulous cause of it.

> *Sanguine tum credunt in corpora summa vocato Aethiopum populus nigrum traxisse colorem* [It was then, as men think, that the peoples of Ethiopia became black-skinned, since the blood was drawn to the surface of their bodies by the heat; *Metamorphoses*, II].

Objection 2. The Negroes are brought out of a pagan country into places where the Gospel is preached.

Answer. Evil must not be done that good may come of it. The extraordinary and comprehensive benefit accruing to the Church of God, and to Joseph personally, did not rectify his brethren's sale of him.

Objection 3. The Africans have wars one with another. Our ships bring lawful captives taken in those wars.

Answer. For ought is known, their wars are much such as were between Jacob's sons and their brother Joseph. If they be between town and town, provincial or national, every war is upon one side unjust. An unlawful war can't make lawful captives. And by receiving, we are in danger to promote and partake in their barbarous cruelties. I am sure, if some gentlemen should go down to the Brewster's to take the air, and fish, and a stronger party from Hull should surprise them and sell them for slaves to a ship outward bound, they would think themselves unjustly dealt with — both by sellers and buyers. And yet 'tis to be feared, we have no other kind of title to our Negroes. "Therefore, all things whatsoever ye would that men should do to you, do ye even so to them; for this is the Law and the Prophets" (Matt. 7:12).

Objection 4. Abraham had servants bought with his money and born in his house.

Answer. Until the circumstances of Abraham's purchase be recorded, no argument can be drawn from it. In the meantime, charity obliges us to conclude that he knew it was lawful and good.

It is observable that the Israelites were strictly forbidden the buying or selling one another for slaves (Lev. 25:39, 46; Jer. 34:8-

441

22). And God gaged [pledged] His blessing in lieu of any loss they might conceive they suffered thereby (Deut. 15:18). And since the partition wall is broken down, inordinate self-love should likewise be demolished. God expects that Christians should be of a more ingenuous and benign frame of spirit. Christians should carry it to all the world, as the Israelites were to carry it one toward another. And for men obstinately to persist in holding their neighbors and brethren under the rigor of perpetual bondage seems to be no proper way of gaining assurance that God has given them spiritual freedom.

Our Blessed Savior has altered the measures of the ancient love song and set it to a most excellent new tune, which all ought to be ambitious of learning (Matt. 5:43, 44; John 13:34). These Ethiopians, as black as they are, seeing they are the sons and daughters of the first Adam, the brethren and sisters of the last Adam, and the offspring of God, they ought to be treated with a respect agreeable.

Against the Traffic of Mens-body

The first Negro slaves brought to the English colonies in America by Dutch traders arrived in Virginia in 1619, though slavery as an institution was not formally recognized by the colony until 1661. While the number of slaves remained small throughout the seventeenth century, their status inspired protests from various quarters, notably the Quakers and the kindred Mennonite Germans of Pennsylvania. The Mennonites, a radical Protestant sect whose members settled at Germantown near Philadelphia in 1683, were especially critical of the institution, for reasons set forth in the following resolutions of their monthly meeting of February 1688. It is the earliest known protest of its kind in the American colonies. [Source: The Pennsylvania Magazine of History and Biography, *Philadelphia, 1880, Vol. IV, pp. 28-30.]*

This is to the Monthly Meeting held at Rigert Worrell's.
These are the reasons why we are against the traffic of mens-body as follows: Is there any that would be done or handled at this manner, viz., to be sold or made a slave for all the time of his life?

How fearful and fainthearted are many on sea when they see a strange vessel, being afraid it should be a Turk, and they should be taken and sold for slaves in Turkey. Now what is this better done as Turks do? Yea, rather is it worse for them which say they are Christians, for we hear that the most part of such Negroes are brought hither against their will and consent, and that many of them are stolen. Now, though they are black, we cannot conceive there is more liberty to have them slaves as it is to have other white ones. There is a saying that we shall do to all men like as we will be done ourselves, making no difference of what generation, descent, or color they are. And those who steal or rob men, and those who buy or purchase them, are they not all alike? Here is liberty of conscience, which is right and reasonable. Here ought to be likewise liberty of the body, except of evildoers, which is another case. But to bring men hither, or to rob and sell them against their will, we stand against.

In Europe there are many oppressed for conscience sake; and here there are those oppressed which are of a black color. And we, who know that men must not commit adultery, some do commit adultery in others, separating wives from their husbands and giving them to others, and some sell the children of those poor creatures to other men. Oh! do consider well this thing, you who do it, if you would be done at this manner, and if it is done according [to] Christianity? You surpass Holland and Germany in this thing. This makes an ill report in all those countries of Europe, where they hear of that the Quakers do here handle men like they handle there the cattle. And for that reason some have no mind or inclination to come hither.

And who shall maintain this your cause or plead for it? Truly we cannot do so except you shall inform us better hereof, viz., that Christians have liberty to practise these things. Pray! What thing in the world can be done worse toward us than if men should rob or steal us away and sell us for slaves to strange countries, separating husbands from their wives and children.

Being now this is not done at that manner we will be done at, therefore, we contradict and are against this traffic of mens-bodies. And we who profess that it is not lawful to steal must likewise avoid to purchase such things as are stolen, but rather help to stop this

443

robbing and stealing if possible and such men ought to be delivered out of the hands of the robbers and set free as well as in Europe. Then is Pennsylvania to have a good report; instead it has now a bad one for this sake in other countries. Especially whereas the Europeans are desirous to know in what manner the Quakers do rule in their province, and most of them do look upon us with an envious eye. But if this is done well, what shall we say is done evil?

If once these slaves (which they say are so wicked and stubborn men) should join themselves, fight for their freedom and handle their masters and mistresses as they did handle them before, will these masters and mistresses take the sword at hand and war against these poor slaves, like we are able to believe some will not refuse to do? Or have these Negroes not as much right to fight for their freedom as you have to keep them slaves?

Now consider well this thing, if it is good or bad. And in case you find it to be good to handle these blacks at that manner, we desire and require you hereby lovingly that you may inform us herein, which at this time never was done, viz., that Christians have liberty to do so, to the end we shall be satisfied in this point, and satisfy likewise our good friends and acquaintances in our native country, to whom it is a terror or fearful thing that men should be handled so in Pennsylvania.

Virginia Slave Laws

Throughout the seventeenth century, indentured servants, who agreed to work for a stated number of years in return for their passage to the New World, were a convenient source of labor for the American colonies. Both Negroes and whites served under the system. White servants, after working out their period of indenture, often rose to respected positions in the community. However, Negroes, who numbered about 2,000 in Virginia in 1670, were seldom accorded the same treatment. By the middle of the century they were generally considered servants for life. In the late 1650s, laws referring to slaves began to appear in the Virginia statutes; the following sampling of Virginia Laws, passed between 1660 and 1669, clearly marks the distinction between white servants and Negro slaves. [*Source:* The Statutes at Large; Being a Collection of all Laws of Virginia, from . . . 1619, *William W. Hening, ed., Vol. II, New York, 1823, pp. 26, 170, 260, 266, 270.*]

I.

ON RUNNING AWAY WITH NEGROES (MARCH 1660)

Be it enacted that in case any English servant shall run away in company with any Negroes who are incapable of making satisfaction by addition of time . . . the English so running away in company with them shall serve for the time of the said Negroes' absence as they are to do for their own by a former act.

II.

ON THE NATIVITY CONDITIONS OF SLAVERY (DECEMBER 1662)

Whereas some doubts have arisen whether children got by any Englishman upon a Negro woman should be slave or free, *be it therefore enacted and declared by this present Grand Assembly,* that all children born in this country shall be held bond or free only according to the condition of the mother; and that if any Christian shall commit fornication with a Negro man or woman, he or she so offending shall pay double the fines imposed by the former act.

III.

ON BAPTISM AND BONDAGE (SEPTEMBER 1667)

Whereas some doubts have risen whether children that are slaves by birth, and by the charity and piety of their owners made partakers of the blessed sacrament of baptism, should by virtue of their baptism be made free, *it is enacted and declared by this Grand Assembly, and the authority thereof,* that the conferring of baptism does not alter the condition of the person as to his bondage or freedom; that diverse masters, freed from this doubt may more carefully endeavor the propagation of Christianity by permitting children, though slaves, or those of greater growth if capable, to be admitted to that sacrament.

IV.

ON CORPORAL PUNISHMENT
(SEPTEMBER 1668)

Whereas it has been questioned whether servants running away may be punished with corporal punishment by their master or magistrate, since the act already made gives the master satisfaction by prolonging their time by service, *it is declared and enacted by this Assembly* that moderate corporal punishment inflicted by master or magistrate upon a runaway servant shall not deprive the master of the satisfaction allowed by the law, the one being as necessary to reclaim them from persisting in that idle course as the other is just to repair the damages sustained by the master.

V.

ON THE KILLING OF
SLAVES (OCTOBER 1669)

Whereas the only law in force for the punishment of refractory servants resisting their master, mistress, or overseer cannot be inflicted upon Negroes, nor the obstinacy of many of them be suppressed by other than violent means, *be it enacted and declared by this Grand Assembly* if any slave resists his master (or other by his master's order correcting him) and by the extremity of the correction should chance to die, that his death shall not be accounted a felony, but the master (or that other person appointed by the master to punish him) be acquitted from molestation, since it cannot be presumed that premeditated malice (which alone makes murder a felony) should induce any man to destroy his own estate.

446

Adventures in the Slave Trade

Following Christopher Columbus' discovery and exploration of the West Indies, Europeans soon became aware of the potential commercial value of the new products of the region — and also of the profits in the slave trade that Columbus had established. Adventurous men such as the English admiral, John Hawkins, led trading ventures that often began with a stop on the coast of Guinea to capture Negro slaves. Hawkins embarked on his third voyage to the West Indies in 1567. Two different versions of some of the events of the voyage (which ended badly for Hawkins) are reprinted here. The first, by Hawkins himself, emphasizes the treachery of his Negro victims. The second, by one of Hawkins' gunners, emphasizes the peculiar habits of some strange and "monstrous" animals. It is hard to avoid the impression that neither man thought of Negroes as human beings. [Source: The Hawkins Voyage, London, Hakluyt Society, 1878, pp. 70-81. The Voyages of the English Nation to America, Edmund Goldsmid, ed., Vol. III, Edinburgh, 1890, pp. 226-230.]

SIR JOHN HAWKINS
Commercial Transactions

The ships departed from Plymouth on the 2nd day of October, Anno 1567, and had reasonable weather until the seventh day, at which time, forty leagues north of Cape Finisterre, there arose an extreme storm, which continued four days, in such sort that the fleet was dispersed and all our great boats lost, and the *Jesus* our chief ship in such case as [it was] not thought able to serve the voyage. . . .

But the eleventh day of the same month the wind changed with fair weather, whereby we were animated to follow our enterprise, and so did, directing our course with the islands of [the] Grand Canaries. There, according to an order before prescribed, all of our ships [that had] dispersed met in one of those islands, called Gomera, where we took water, and departed from thence the fourth day of November toward the coast of Guinea, and arrived at Cape Verde the eighteenth of November.

There we landed 150 men, hoping to obtain some Negroes, but

we got but few, and those with great hurt and damage to our men, which chiefly proceeded from their envenomed arrows; and although in the beginning they seemed to be but small hurts, yet there hardly escaped any, that had blood drawn of them, but [instead they] died in strange sort, with their mouths shut ten days before they died. I myself had one of the greatest wounds, yet thanks be to God, escaped.

From thence we passed the time upon the coast of Guinea, searching, with all diligence, the rivers from Rio Grande unto Sierra Leone, till the twelfth of January, in which time we had not gotten together 150 Negroes. Yet notwithstanding the sickness of our men and the late time of the year commanded us away, and thus having nothing wherewith to seek the coast of the West Indies, I was with the rest of our company in consultation to go to the coast of the Myne [Spanish Main?], hoping there to obtain some gold for our wares, and thereby to have defrayed our charge. But just at that instant, there came to us a Negro, sent from a king, oppressed by other kings his neighbors, desiring our aid, with the promise that as many Negroes as by these wares might be obtained, as well of his part as of ours, should be at our pleasure.

Whereupon we concluded to give aid and sent 120 of our men, who, on the fifteenth of January, assaulted a town of the Negroes of our allies' adversaries. [The town] had in it 8,000 inhabitants and [was] very strongly impaled and fenced, after their manner. But it was so well defended that our men prevailed not, but [instead] lost six men and 40 hurt, so that our men sent forthwith to me for more help. Whereupon considering that the good success of this enterprise might highly further the commodity of our voyage, I went myself, and with the help of the king of our side assaulted the town both by land and sea, and very hardly with fire (their houses being covered with dry palm leaves), and obtained the town and put the inhabitants to flight.

We took 250 persons, men, women, and children, and by our friend the king of our side there were taken 600 prisoners, whereof we hoped to have had our choice. But the Negro (in which nation is seldom or never found truth) meant nothing less; for that night he removed his camp and prisoners, so that we were fain to content us

448

with those few which we had gotten ourselves.

Now had we obtained between 400 and 500 Negroes, wherewith we thought it somewhat reasonable to seek the coast of the West Indies, where, for our Negroes and our other merchandise, we hoped to obtain [enough] to countervail our charges with some gains. Whereunto we proceeded with all diligence, furnished our watering, took fuel, and departed the coast of Guinea the third of February, continuing at sea with a passage more hard than before has been accustomed till the 27th day of March, [on] which day we had sight of an island called Dominica, upon the coast of the West Indies, in 14 degrees [North latitude]. From thence we coasted from place to place, making our traffic with the Spaniards, as we might, [but] somewhat hardly, because the King had straightly commanded all his governors in those parts by no means to suffer any trade to be made with us.

Notwithstanding, we had reasonable trade, and courteous entertainment, from the isle of Margarita unto Cartagena, without anything greatly worth the noting, saving at Capo de la Vela, in a town called Rio de la Hacha, from whence came all the pearls.

The treasurer who had the charge there would by no means agree to any trade or suffer us to take water. He had fortified his town with divers bulwarks in all places where it might be entered, and furnished himself with 100 harquebusiers, so that he thought by famine to have enforced us to have put on land our Negroes, of which purpose he had not greatly failed unless we had by force entered the town. This (after we could by no means obtain his favor) we were enforced to do, and so with 200 men broke in upon their bulwarks, and entered the town with the loss only of two men of our part, and no hurt done to the Spaniards because after they discharged their volley of shot they all fled.

Thus having the town, on account of some circumstances, partly by the Spaniards' desire for Negroes, and partly by friendship of the treasurer, we obtained a secret trade. Whereupon the Spaniards resorted to us by night and bought of us to the number of 200 Negroes. In all other places where we traded the Spanish inhabitants were glad of us and traded willingly.

JOB HORTOP
Negroes, Sea-Horses, and Crocodiles

It is not unknown unto many that I, Job Hortop, powdermaker, was born at Bourne, a town of Lincolnshire. From the age of twelve who was the Queen's Majesty's powdermaker. [Him] I served until I was pressed to go on the third voyage to the West Indies, with the right worshipful Sir John Hawkins, who appointed me to be one of the gunners in Her Majesty's ship called the *Jesus of Lubeck*, which set sail from Plymouth in the month of October 1567, [along with] another ship of Her Majesty's, called the *Minion*, and four ships of his own, namely the *Angel*, the *Swallow*, the *Judith*, and the *William and John*.

He directed his vice-admiral that if foul weather did separate them, to meet at the island of Teneriffe. After which by the space of seven days and seven nights, we had such storms at sea that we lost our long boats and a pinnace, with some men. Coming to the isle of Teneriffe, there our general heard that his vice-admiral with the *Swallow*, and the *William and John*, were at the island called Gomera, where finding his vice-admiral he anchored, took in fresh water, and set sail for Cape Blank, where in the way we took a Portuguese caravel, laden with fish called mullets. From thence we sailed to Cape Verde. . . .

There we anchored, took [to] our boats, and set soldiers on shore. Our general was the first that leapt on land, and with him Captain Dudley. There we took certain Negroes, but not without damage to ourselves, for our general, Captain Dudley, and eight others of our company were hurt with poisoned arrows. About nine days after, the eight that were wounded died. Our general was taught by a Negro to draw the poison out of his wound with a clove of garlic, whereby he was cured.

From thence we went to Sierra Leone, where be monstrous fishes called sharks, which will devour men. I amongst others was sent in the *Angel* with two pinnaces into the river called Calousa, to seek two caravels that were there trading with the Negroes. We took one of them with the Negroes, and brought them away.

In this river in the night time we had one of our pinnaces bulged

450

by a sea-horse [hippopotamus], so that our men swimming about the river were all taken into the other pinnaces, except two that took hold of one another, and were carried out by the sea-horse. This monster hath the just proportion of a horse, saving that his legs be short, his teeth very great, and a span in length. In the night he goes on land into the woods, seeking at unawares to devour the Negroes in their cabins, which they by their vigilance prevent, and kill them in this manner. The Negroes keep watch and diligently attend their coming, and when they are gone into the woods, they forthwith lay a great tree overthwart the way, so that at their return, for that their legs be so short, they cannot go over it. Then the Negroes set upon them with their bows, arrows, and darts, and so destroy them.

From thence we entered the river called the Casserroes, where there were other caravels trading with the Negroes, and them we took. In this island between the river and the main, trees grow with oysters upon them. There grow palmito trees, which be as high as a ship's main mast, and on their tops grow nuts, wine, and oil, which they call palmito wine and palmito oil. The plantain tree also grows in that country. The tree is as big as a man's thigh and as high as a fir pole, the leaves thereof be long and broad, and on the top grow the fruit, which are called plantains. They are crooked and a cubit long, and as big as a man's wrist; they grow in clusters. When they are ripe they be very good and dainty to eat. Sugar is not more delicate in taste than they be.

From thence . . . we sailed to Sierra Leone, where our general at that time was. He, with the captains and soldiers, went up into the river called Taggarin, to take a town of the Negroes, where he found three kings of that country with 50,000 Negroes besieging the same town, which they could not take in many years before when they had warred with it. Our general made a breach, entered, and valiantly took the town, wherein we found five Portuguese who yielded themselves to his mercy, and he saved their lives. We took and carried thence for traffic to the West Indies 500 Negroes. The three kings drove 7,000 Negroes into the sea at low water, at the point of the land, where they were all drowned . . ., for that they could not take [to] their canoes to save themselves. . . .

In that place there be many musk-cats, which breed in hollow

451

trees. The Negroes take them in a net and put them in a cage, and nourish them very daintily and take the musk from them with a spoon.

Now we directed our course from Guinea toward the West Indies. . . . In sailing toward the Indies, the first land that we escried was the island called Dominica, where . . . we anchored and took in fresh water and wood for our provision. . . .

From thence we sailed to Burboroata, which is in the mainland of the West Indies. There we came in, moored our ships, and tarried two months trimming and dressing our ships, and in the mean time traded with certain Spaniards of that country. There our general sent us unto a town called Placencia. . . . In our way up the hill to Placencia, we found a monstrous venomous worm with two heads. His body was as big as a man's arm, and a yard long. Our master Robert Barret did cut him in sunder with his sword, and it made it as black as if it were colored with ink.

Here be many tigers, monstrous and furious beasts, which by subtlety devour and destroy many men. They use the traded ways, and will show themselves twice or thrice to the travelers, and so depart secretly, lurking till they be past, then suddenly and at unawares they leap upon them and devour them. They had so used two of our company, had not one of them looked behind. . . .

[At Rio de Hacha we anchored before the town] till our general's coming, who anchored, landed his men, and valiantly took the town, with the loss of one man, whose name was Thomas Surgeon. We landed and planted on the shore, for our safety, our field ordnance. We drove the Spaniards up into the country about two leagues, whereby they were forced to trade with our general, to whom he sold [the] most part of his Negroes.

In this river we killed a monstrous lagarto or crocodile in this port at sunset. Seven of us went in the pinnace up into the river, carrying with us a dog, unto whom with ropeyarn we bound a great hook of steel, with a chain that had a swivel. This we put under the dog's belly, the point of the hook coming over his back fast bound. We put him overboard and veered out our rope by little and little, rowing away with our boat. The lagarto came and presently swallowed up the dog, then did we row hard, till we had choked him. He plunged

452

and made a wonderful stir in the water. We leapt on shore and haled him on land. He was 23 feet by the rule, headed like a hog, in body like a serpent, full of scales as broad as a saucer, his tail long and full of knots as big as a falcon shot. He hath four legs, his feet have long nails like unto a dragon. We opened him, took out his guts, flayed him, dried his skin, and stuffed it with straw, meaning to have brought it home, had not the ship been cast away. This monster will carry away and devour both men and horses.

453

Index of Authors

ADAMS, JOHN QUINCY (July 11, 1767-Feb. 23, 1848), diplomat and statesman. Sixth President of the United States (1825-29); U.S. senator from Massachusetts (1803-08); minister to St. Petersburg (1809-14); minister to Great Britain (1815); secretary of state under Monroe; U.S. representative (1831-48).

BAKER, RICHARD (1789-1871), jurist. Judge (c. 1836-71) of the Circuit Court of Virginia.

BIRNEY, JAMES G. (Feb. 4, 1792-Nov. 25, 1857), political leader and Abolitionist. Agent (1832-34) of the American Colonization Society; wrote a *Letter on Colonization* (1834), aligning himself with more vigorous antislavery movements; executive secretary (1837-45) of the American Anti-Slavery Society.

CALHOUN, JOHN C. (March 18, 1782-March 31, 1850), political philosopher, lawyer, and statesman. U.S. representative from South Carolina (1811-17); secretary of war under Monroe; Vice-President of the United States (1825-32) under J. Q. Adams and Jackson; U.S. senator (1833-43, 1845-50); secretary of state (1844-45) under Tyler.

CHILD, LYDIA M. (Feb. 11, 1802-Oct. 20, 1880), social reformer and author. Edited *Juvenile Miscellany*, the first children's periodical in U.S.; with her husband edited (1840-44) the *Anti-Slavery Standard*; wrote numerous books in behalf of the rights of women, slaves, freedmen, and Indians.

COFFIN, LEVI (Oct. 28, 1789-Sept. 16, 1877), financial sponsor and operational leader of the "Underground Railroad." His store at Newport, Ind., was a principal depot on the slaves' escape route (1826-46); founder (1864) of the English Freedmen's Aid Society; delegate to the International Anti-Slavery Conference at Paris (1867).

CORNISH, SAMUEL (fl. 1827), editor and Abolitionist spokesman. Cofounder and an editor (1827-29) of *Freedom's Journal*, the first Negro newspaper.

CUSHING, WILLIAM (March 1, 1732-Sept. 13, 1810), jurist. Chief justice of the Massachusetts Supreme Court; associate justice (1789-1810) of the U.S. Supreme Court; member of the first Massachusetts state constitutional convention (1779); member of the Massachusetts Ratifying Convention of 1788.

DEW, THOMAS R. (Dec. 5, 1802-Aug. 6, 1846), economist. Professor of political law and economy (1827-36) and president (1836-45) of the College of William and Mary; wrote numerous essays in defense of slavery.

DOUGLASS, FREDERICK (?Feb. 1817-Feb. 20, 1895), journalist, orator, and antislavery leader. Escaped from slavery (1838); agent (1841-45) of the Massachusetts Anti-Slavery Society; founded and edited (1847-60) the Abolitionist paper *North Star;* in Civil War, recruited Negro regiments and served as consultant to Lincoln; minister to Haiti (1889-91).

EMERSON, RALPH WALDO (May 25, 1803-April 27, 1882), poet, essayist, and philosopher. Wrote *Nature* (1836) and *Essays* (1841, 1844) on his transcendentalist philosophy, and for many years kept his *Journals;* edited (1842-44) the *Dial;* lectured in England and in the U.S. on a variety of subjects, such as self-reliance, individual freedom, and abolition of slavery.

FITZHUGH, GEORGE (Nov. 4, 1806-July 30, 1881), lawyer and sociologist. Wrote numerous works on the political economy of the South and the positive benefits of slavery, including *Sociology for the South; or the Failure of Free Society* (1854), *Cannibals All! or, Slaves without Masters* (1857).

FLOURNOY, J. J. (fl. 1838), letter writer.

FONTAINE, PETER (fl. 1757), clergyman in Virginia.

FORTEN, CHARLOTTE L. (1838-1914), author and teacher. Daughter of Robert Bridges Forten and granddaughter of James Forten, prominent Negro Abolitionists; taught school at Salem, Mass., and at Port Royal, N.C., in a post-Civil War government program to educate abandoned slaves; wrote for the *Atlantic Monthly* and for many years kept a *Journal,* published in 1953.

FOSTER, STEPHEN S. (Nov. 17, 1809-Sept. 8, 1881), Abolitionist and social reformer. Associated with William Lloyd Garrison in antislavery lectures and agitation; wrote *The Brotherhood of Thieves; or A True Picture of the American Church and Clergy* (1843).

FRANKLIN, BENJAMIN (Jan. 17, 1706-April 17, 1790), printer, author, philanthropist, inventor, scientist, diplomat, and statesman. Born Boston; published *Poor Richard's Almanac* (1732-57); signed the Declaration of Independence; in France, 1776-85; member of the Constitutional Convention (1787); author of *Autobiography.*

FURMAN, RICHARD (Oct. 9, 1755-Aug. 25, 1825), Baptist minister and educator. First president (1821) of the Baptist State Convention in South Carolina; founder (1825) of Furman University; president of the Baptist Triennial Convention.

GARRISON, WILLIAM LLOYD (Dec. 12, 1805-May 24, 1879), Abolitionist leader and journalist. Founded (1831) the *Liberator;* helped establish (1833) the American Anti-Slavery Society; its president (1843-65); advocate of immediate emancipation and of woman suffrage; opposed the American Colonization Society; wrote *Thoughts on African Colonization* (1832).

GIDDINGS, JOSHUA (Oct. 6, 1795-May 27, 1864), public official and diplomat. U.S. representative from Ohio (1838-59); censured by House (1842) for antislavery activities; minister to Canada (1861-64).

GRAYSON, WILLIAM J. (Nov. 2, 1788-Oct. 4, 1863), lawyer, author, and public official. U.S. representative from South Carolina (1833-37); customs collector at Charleston, S.C. (1841-53); author of *The Hireling and the Slave* (1854).

HAMILTON, ALEXANDER (?Jan. 11, 1755-July 12, 1804), soldier, lawyer, and statesman. Member (1782-83) of the Congress of the Confederation; New York delegate to the Constitutional Convention (1787); author with James Madison and John Jay of *The Federalist* (1787-88); secretary of the treasury (1789-95) under Washington and creator of the first Bank of the United States. Mortally wounded in a duel with Aaron Burr.

HARPER, WILLIAM (Jan. 17, 1790-Oct. 10, 1847), jurist and political writer. Wrote *Memoir on Slavery* (1837) as a refinement of the conservative Southern position on states' rights and slavery.

HAWKINS, SIR JOHN (1532-Nov. 12, 1595), English trader and admiral. First English slave trader; narrative of his 1564-65 expedition to Hispaniola introduced Englishmen to the potato and tobacco; as treasurer (1577) and comptroller (1589) of the Navy, he improved pay of seamen and rebuilt the fleet, adding more guns and faster ships; founded a hospital for sick and aged mariners (1592).

HOPKINS, SAMUEL (Sept. 17, 1721-Dec. 20, 1803), Congregational theologian, missionary, and philanthropist. Disciple of Jonathan Edwards; one of the earliest opponents of slavery.

HORTOP, JOB (fl. 1567), English powdermaker and seaman. Pressed into the Navy for Sir John Hawkins' third expedition to the West Indies (1567-68); marooned by Hawkins somewhere in the Gulf of Mexico (1568); eventually found his way back to England and recorded his adventures.

INGRAHAM, JOSEPH H. (Jan. 25-26, 1809-Dec. 18, 1860), clergyman and author. Protestant Episcopal missionary and priest in Mississippi, Alabama, and Tennessee (1852-60); wrote adventure novels and a collection of letters, *The Sunny South* (1860).

JAY, PETER (Jan. 24, 1776-Feb. 20, 1843), lawyer. Son of John Jay; member of the New York Assembly (1816-20); New York city recorder (1820); delegate to the New York state constitutional convention (1821).

JEFFERSON, THOMAS (April 13, 1743-July 4, 1826), lawyer, architect, agriculturalist, educator, political philosopher, diplomat, and statesman. Third President of the United States (1801-09); member (1775-76) of the Continental Congress; author of the Declaration of Independence; governor of Virginia (1779-81); minister to France (1785-89); secretary of state (1790–93) under Washington; Vice-President of the United States under John Adams; founder of the University of Virginia.

JOHNSON, WILLIAM (?-1851), Mississippi businessman; kept diary for 16 years.

KEMBLE, FRANCES ANNE (Nov. 27, 1809-Jan. 15, 1893), English actress and author. Wrote *Journal of a Residence in America* (1835), *Journal of a Residence on a Georgian Plantation* (1863).

KING, RUFUS (March 24, 1755-April 29, 1827), public official and diplomat. Member (1784-87) of the Congress of the Confederation and (1787) of the Constitutional Convention; U.S. senator from New York (1789-96, 1813-25); minister to Great Britain (1796-1803, 1825-26).

LYELL, CHARLES (Nov. 14, 1797-Feb. 22, 1875), English geologist and author. Traveled in America in 1841 and 1845; wrote *Travels in North America* (1845), *A Second Visit to the United States* (1849).

McDUFFIE, GEORGE (Aug. 10, 1790-

456

March 11, 1851), lawyer, orator, and public official. U.S. representative from South Carolina (1821-34); governor (1834-36); U.S. senator (1842-46).

MANN, HORACE (May 4, 1796-Aug. 2, 1859), educator. First secretary (1837-48) of the Massachusetts Board of Education; revolutionized public school organization and teaching methods; established (1839) the first state teachers college; U.S. representative (1848-53); president (1853-59) of Antioch College.

OLMSTED, FREDERICK LAW (April 27, 1822-Aug. 28, 1903), landscape architect. Designed Central Park, New York City; developed the grounds of the Capitol, Washington, D.C., the campus of Leland Stanford University, and the south Chicago lakefront; wrote *Journeys and Explorations in the Cotton Kingdom* (1861).

PHILLIPS, WENDELL (Nov. 29, 1811-Feb. 2, 1884), orator, Abolitionist, and social reformer. Disciple and colleague of William Lloyd Garrison; president (1865-70) of the American Anti-Slavery Society; advocate of prohibition, woman suffrage, penal reforms, and the organization of labor.

REMOND, CHARLES LENOX (Feb. 1, 1810-Dec. 22, 1873), Abolitionist and Negro leader. Agent (from 1838) of the Massachusetts Anti-Slavery Society; delegate to the World Anti-Slavery Conference in London (1841); recruiting officer for the 54th Massachusetts Infantry, the first Negro regiment in the Civil War.

RICE, THOMAS DARTMOUTH (May 20, 1808-Sept. 19, 1860), actor and founder of the minstrel show in America.

RUSSWURM, JOHN (Oct. 1, 1799-June 17, 1851), Abolitionist spokesman. First Negro graduate of Bowdoin College; cofounder and an editor (1827-29) of *Freedom's Journal*; superintendent of public schools (1829) in Liberia, Africa; governor of the Maryland Colony at Cape Palmas, Africa (1836-51).

SEWALL, SAMUEL (March 28, 1652-Jan. 1, 1730), jurist. Member (1684-86, 1689-1725) of the Massachusetts Bay Colony Governor's Council; presided over Salem witchcraft trials (1692); confessed error and guilt for his part in trials (1697); justice (1692-1718) and chief justice (1718-28) of the Massachusetts Superior Court.

STOWE, HARRIET BEECHER (June 14, 1811-July 1, 1896), Abolitionist and author. Daughter of Lyman Beecher, sister of Henry Ward Beecher; wrote *Uncle Tom's Cabin; or, Life Among the Lowly* (1851-52), which made slavery a moral issue and helped solidify Northern sentiment against it.

SUMNER, CHARLES (Jan. 6, 1811-March 11, 1874), Abolitionist and statesman. U.S. senator from Massachusetts (1851-74); leader of the anti-slavery faction in Congress and the first prominent official to urge emancipation (Oct. 1861); severely injured when attacked in the Senate (May 22, 1856) by Rep. Preston Brooks of South Carolina for his remarks on slavery.

TURNER, NAT (Oct. 2, 1800-Nov. 11, 1831), religious fanatic and the leader of a slave rebellion (1831) that spread terror throughout the South, and for which he was tried and hanged.

VASSA, GUSTAVUS (fl. 1758-94), slave and explorer. Born Olaudah Equiano in Benin (Nigeria), Africa; captured and sent to West Indies as a slave;

later freed and renamed for King Gustavus I of Sweden; traveled widely, even to the Arctic, and described his adventures in a journal.

WELD, THEODORE (Nov. 23, 1803-Feb. 3, 1895), social reformer. Toured the country (*c.* 1832) as a temperance preacher; agent (1834-38) of the American Anti-Slavery Society.

WHITTIER, JOHN GREENLEAF (Dec. 17, 1807-Sept. 7, 1892), poet, journalist, Abolitionist, and humanitarian. Editor (1830-32) of the *New England Weekly Review;* wrote *Justice and Expediency* and poems in behalf of the Abolitionist cause; also wrote religious works and poems of New England, including "Snow-Bound" (1866).

WOOLMAN, JOHN (Oct. 19, 1720-Oct. 7, 1772), Quaker leader, abolitionist, and author. His *Journal* (1756-72) is considered a classic record of religious experience.